ON JORDAN'S STORMY BANKS

RANDY J. SPARKS

ON JORDAN'S

STORMY BANKS

EVANGELICALISM IN MISSISSIPPI, 1773–1876

University of Georgia Press   *Athens & London*

© 1994 by the University of Georgia Press
Athens, Georgia 30602
All rights reserved
Designed by Barbara E. Williams
Set in Trump Mediaeval by Tseng Information Systems, Inc.
Printed and bound by Thomson-Shore, Inc.
The paper in this book meets the guidelines for permanence and
durability of the Committee on Production Guidelines for Book
Longevity of the Council on Library Resources.
Printed in the United States of America
98 97 96 95 94 C 5 4 3 2 1
Library of Congress Cataloging in Publication Data

Sparks, Randy J.
   On Jordan's stormy banks : Evangelicalism in Mississippi,
   1773–1876 / Randy J. Sparks.
      p. cm.
   Includes bibliographical references and index.
   ISBN 0-8203-1627-X
      1. Evangelicalism—Mississippi—History—18th century.
   2. Evangelicalism—Mississippi—History—19th century.
   3. Mississippi—Church history—18th century. 4. Mississippi—
   Church history—19th century. 5. Afro-Americans—Religion.
   6. Mississippi—Social conditions. I. Title.
   BR1642.U5S63 1994
   277.62'08—dc20   93-43020

British Library Cataloging in Publication Data available

CONTENTS

ACKNOWLEDGMENTS

THESE few lines are small payment to the many people who have contributed in large and small ways to the completion of this project, and though the recompense is insufficient, I nonetheless make it with gratitude. To listen to my colleagues in this profession, one might conclude that graduate programs were designed by the Marquis de Sade during a moment of intense inspiration and presided over by minions who studied at the master's feet. Such stories make me forever grateful that fortune gave me the opportunity to study with John B. Boles. His genuine warmth and good humor, combined with a love of teaching and an encyclopedic knowledge of southern history, made working with him a pleasure. His encouragement has continued since I left Rice University, and he has read and commented on several revisions of this work. Other friends from my graduate school days also deserve my thanks, especially Chris and Ken De Ville, Mary G. Winkler, Evelyn Thomas Nolen, Elizabeth Turner, Patricia Orr, Thomas Cockrell, Dean James, and Steven Strom. Once I entered the profession, my debts continued to mount, and I am happy to acknowledge W. Fitzhugh Brundage, Michele Gillespie, Katherine J. Haldane, Mart Stewart, and Amy Thompson McCandless, who have been especially generous with their time and offered careful criticisms of all or part of the manuscript. I would also like to thank the History Department and the Research and Development Committee at the College of Charleston for their generous funding.

My research has taken me to libraries and archives across the South, where staff members have been unfailing in their assistance. I would like to single out Anne Lipscomb at the Mississippi Department of Archives and History and Anne Wells, Lynn Mueller, Michael Ballard, and Leara Miles at Mississippi State University, who have gone above and beyond the call of duty.

My parents, through their emotional and financial support, contributed more than any others to my career. It is my chief regret that my father, John Russell Sparks, did not live to read this dedication, especially since he had begun to fear that I would be a career student. With love and respect, I dedicate this work to my mother, Mildred H. Sparks, and to the memory of my father.

ON JORDAN'S STORMY BANKS

INTRODUCTION

THIS book is a social history of southern evangelicalism from the late eighteenth century to the end of Reconstruction. Through an examination of the three largest evangelical denominations in Mississippi, the Baptists, Methodists, and Presbyterians, the book charts their rise on the southern frontier and their remarkable increase in numbers, wealth, and influence. As historian Donald Mathews pointed out, evangelicalism can best be understood as a *force*, a word that conveys something of the power behind the movement. The term *evangelical* is somewhat imprecise, though the evangelicals themselves seemed certain enough of their identity. In attempting to define them for the modern reader it is useful to use a definition given in a new religious periodical in 1818: "This term designates a peculiar class of sentiments, and system of doctrines derived from the holy scriptures. . . . Of this system, the principal articles are:—1. The total depravity of man. 2. The necessity of regeneration by the Holy Spirit. 3. Justification by faith alone. 4. The necessity of holiness as a qualification for happiness."[1]

Central to all evangelicals, overarching denominational differences, was a belief in the ultimate authority of Scripture. They searched the Bible to find support for church governance, rituals, and beliefs. Interpretation of Scripture was not limited to the ministers but open and available to all. Evangelicals saw man's nature as inherently sinful and believed that converts must experience a conversion, a regeneration by the Spirit. Once converted, they should share that experience with others. A commitment to evangelization was another hallmark common to the entire movement. Closely tied to the conversion experience was a conviction that salvation could be achieved only through faith. The dual emphasis on individual conversion and faith has contributed to the perception of evangelicals as focused on the individual, on personal rather than social responsibility, a dichotomy that created tensions within the movement. Concern for the social implications of evangelicalism found expression in vital social relationships such as those between masters and slaves, husbands and wives, and church and state. A holy life was, of course, the ultimate aim of every convert; this continuous, lifelong struggle shaped evangelical rituals and practices intended to shore up the faithful, a process that fostered the close, communal nature of the evangelical congregation.

Few fields in southern history have seen so rich an outpouring of scholarship over the last decade as religious history. Works by such scholars as Donald Mathews, John B. Boles, Albert Raboteau, Rhys Isaac, Samuel Hill, Eugene Genovese, and Elizabeth Fox-Genovese have raised the study of southern religion far above the denominational histories that first characterized the field and have brought a methodological and interpretive complexity to the subject. Because of the work of these scholars, historians have begun to appreciate the importance of southern religion for broader historical topics such as republicanism, slavery, intellectual history, and nationalism.

Evangelicalism began in the eighteenth-century South as a revolutionary movement of the plain folk, who consciously set themselves in opposition to the dominant culture of the gentry. In their egalitarian services and in their personal lives, these converts challenged the hierarchical structure of their society and welcomed slaves into their churches on terms approaching equality. The first evangelicals in Mississippi shared this revolutionary outlook and challenged first the Spanish Catholic government and later the planter elites. Fueled by the Great Revival, these sects expanded rapidly among the plain folk and slaves in the early nineteenth century.

In the biracial churches the evangelicals established, there occurred a remarkable and significant process of cultural exchange between blacks and whites. Taking a part in the broader process of democratization under way across the nation, evangelicals shaped a new culture that flouted elite rules of dress, behavior, and language. They also linked evangelicalism with the idea of republican virtue; the conversion of sinners would redeem not only the individual but communities and ultimately the entire nation. The evangelical relationship with slavery was complex and conflicted. They had largely abandoned any formal opposition to slavery before the movement came to Mississippi, though some antislavery sentiment emerged in the early period. Of greater significance was the position of blacks within the movement. Evangelical egalitarianism resonated powerfully within the slave community, and slaves came into the churches in large numbers. The typical church was a biracial one; the African-American influence on evangelical ritual and practice was significant and left an indelible imprint on southern religion.

The egalitarian nature of these early churches created unique opportunities for women as well as blacks. The success of the movement cannot be understood without appreciating the role of women, who made up a majority of church members. Women challenged their traditional subservient position in religious settings and carved out new liturgical roles for themselves in these churches. Though barred from the ordained ministry, women spoke in services, led in prayer and song, taught in Sunday schools, served as class leaders, and organized a wide variety of missionary and benevolent associations.

The 1830s marked an important transition in the history of evangelicalism. The Mississippi economy boomed; many of the plain folk moved up the economic ladder, and more wealthy converts came into the churches. Cultural revolt was replaced by complacency in the movement from sects to major denominations, a shift with momentous implications for ritual and practice within the churches and their relationship with the larger society. It was a controversial move that resulted in major splits within all three denominations as evangelical modernists and traditionalists squared off against one another. Evangelical ideology and strategy echoed in the democratic political revolution under way in the 1830s, when evangelicalism began to permeate southern culture. Evangelicals now sought to perfect the institution of slavery, not to abolish it, and they developed a biblical defense of the institution and a closely related mission movement to slaves. The years after 1830 saw a growing division between white and black evangelicals as the egalitarian biracial service was replaced in most churches by separate worship services, a shift that gave blacks more autonomy within the churches and laid the foundation for the dramatic rise of independent black churches after the Civil War.

The nature of the relationship between blacks and whites and men and women within the churches can also be explored by a study of the disciplinary process within these churches. "Order," "duty," and "discipline" were evangelical bywords, and the disciplinary process had important implications not only for the individual but for the creation of an orderly, virtuous society. The evangelical vision of that proper society—a patriarchal one organized around the household—becomes apparent through an examination of the church courts.

The orderly society evangelicals labored so hard to create quickly began to unravel with the outbreak of the Civil War. Through their impassioned defense of slavery and their division along sectional lines, evangelicals contributed to the conflict, though they did not usually lead in the secession movement. The evangelical vision of the virtuous republic was a potent one, which the Confederate government attempted to foster and capitalize on in the quest to create Confederate nationalism.

Evangelicals endorsed this nascent nationalism and preached that southerners were God's chosen people and that He would not abandon a just cause. Such a message proved to be a fatal trap, however, when optimism turned to gloomy pessimism and defeat loomed on the horizon. The only explanation for Confederate defeat was that the southern people were not virtuous enough, a view that contributed to a powerful revival during the war. Blacks, of course, had a far different vision of the war, and the prospect of Confederate defeat brought their enthusiastic participation in these revivals.

Defeat did not bring religious disaffection for most southerners. For whites, evangelicalism became entwined with the religion of the Lost Cause as they sought to understand their failure. For blacks, the Confederate defeat came as an answer to a prayer, and they began to carve out an autonomous religious life for themselves. The separation along racial lines following the war marks another major turning point in southern religious history. A century of biracial worship came to an end when blacks left the biracial churches to create their own, and the black churches soon became the largest institutions under black control and the bedrock of the black community.

What follows is an attempt to expand upon this brief overview of the religious history of the period, an effort to follow the multicolored strands that compose the fabric of southern evangelicalism.

CHAPTER 1

THE GROWTH OF A NIGHT
DISCOVERY AND EARLY SETTLEMENT

WHEN the Reverend Timothy Flint, a Presbyterian minister, returned to Mississippi in the early 1800s after an absence of several years, he marveled at the rapid expansion the territory had undergone. "A town in this region," he wrote, "is like Jonah's gourd, the growth of a night." In the late eighteenth and early nineteenth centuries Mississippi's population and economy boomed at a remarkable rate. The foundations of Mississippi society were laid during this period, as were the foundations of the evangelical movement. The future success of the movement could not have been predicted from its humble beginnings. Historian Rhys Isaac characterized the early movement in Virginia as an "evangelical revolt" that pitted the austere plain folk against the powerful gentry.[1] Although life on the frontier bore little resemblance to that in the more established states on the eastern seaboard, even on the frontier the evangelical movement had revolutionary potential, first against European colonial governments and ultimately against the frontier nabobs. Class lines on the frontier may not have been as clear-cut as in Virginia, but even in early Mississippi a socially and politically dominant elite emerged that would be challenged in religious terms.

Although the earliest explorers in the region—Hernando de Soto and his adventurers—were disappointed in their hope of finding quick wealth, later European colonists recognized the value of the rich, black earth and the potential of the many navigable rivers, none more important than the mighty Father of Waters that gave its name to the land. The Mississippi on the west with its many tributaries and the Tombigbee on the east provided a transportation network almost unmatched in the South. Except for the hills of the northeastern corner of the state and the pine barrens that reached up approximately two hundred miles from the Gulf Coast, the land was ideally suited to plantation agriculture. Of course, the Spanish and French explorers and settlers did not find the land unoccupied; tens of thousands of Native Americans of various tribes lived in the region. They ranged from smaller tribes such as the Biloxi, the Yazoo, and the ceremonial Natchez, to the larger Chickasaw and Choctaw nations. Many of the smaller tribes disappeared early; some relocated, others merged with larger tribes, some were decimated by European diseases, and still others, most notably the Natchez, were all but destroyed by the Europeans. Still, in the late eighteenth and early nineteenth centuries only a small portion of southern Mississippi was open for settlement; most of the territory remained in the hands of the Choctaws and Chickasaws.[2]

In the late seventeenth century the French established the first settlement in the region at Biloxi on the Gulf Coast. In 1716 they erected a fort on the future site of Natchez, but they concentrated their efforts around New Orleans, and their Mississippi settlements did not prosper. The French did not exert a major influence on the region, though they did introduce livestock, a variety of vegetables, and, more important, staple crops including tobacco, rice, indigo, and a hardy variety of upland cotton. They also introduced slave plantations modeled after their colonies in the West Indies.[3]

Large-scale settlement in the territory began only after Britain acquired the area from France in 1763. To encourage immigration, the British made land grants to former military personnel ranging in size from one hundred to tens of thousands of acres, the majority from five hundred to fifteen hundred acres. Many southern frontier settlements were isolated from markets, but Mississippi was integrated into the international economic system from an early period. New settlers quickly established plantations producing indigo, tobacco, and cotton for export, bought slaves directly from Africa or Jamaica, and soon held "considerable wealth in land, slaves, cattle and merchandise." British factors and merchants had offices in the territory; a nineteenth-century historian reported that "the wealthy inhabitants of the Natchez district sent their orders once a year, very often ordering their merchandise direct from the London house." Their orders ranged in cost from £300 to £1,000 and included such luxury goods as "a cask of London Particular madeira, a cask of sherry, a cask of porter, and a barrel of French cognac." Under the British, "the landholders were, for the most part, educated men; many of them had held commissions in the British and provincial army; others had held civil offices under the crown or the colonies. . . . The intelligent and cultivated class predominated, and gave tone to the community." The outbreak of the American Revolution in 1775 gave a major boost to the British colony of West Florida, which became an officially designated refuge for Loyalists, many of whom came from the propertied class.[4]

Some Loyalists later abandoned the colony, but the district's prosperity and the "predomination" of the "intelligent and cultivated class" continued after the Spanish acquired the territory from the British in 1779 in the wake of the Seven Years' War. The Spanish adopted a liberal policy toward the English-speaking settlers and encouraged immigration. Slavery increased rapidly; the number of slaves grew from 498 in 1784 to over 2,000 in 1796, when they made up 40 percent of the population. Planters turned to cotton production in the late 1700s; the first public gin opened in 1796, and by 1798 cotton production reached 1.2 million pounds. In 1797 Stephen Minor, a wealthy planter and government official, sold his crop for $51,200. Another nabob, John Bisland, owned nine plantations, placed huge orders for luxury goods in Liverpool and Scotland, and educated two of his sons in Scotland. When Dr. John Sibley, a Massachusetts native, traveled through the territory in 1802, he was struck by its fertility and wealth. Wherever he went he found planters "becoming Rich by the Cultivation of Cotton," and he described "a number of Handsome plantations" whose owners lived "in Handsome Stile."[5] The Natchez District never conformed to Frederick Jackson Turner's model of frontier society; even from the first settlement it was dominated by large landowners and tied to international markets.

Religious worship was apparently not a primary concern for the early British immigrants. There is no record of organized Protestant worship until 1773, when Richard and Samuel Swayze, planters from Morris County, New Jersey, settled near Natchez in an area that became known as the Jersey Settlement. Samuel Swayze was a Congregational minister who preached in the settlement, a practice that created problems when the territory passed to Spain in 1779. Under the Spanish, Catholicism became the established religion; Protestant religious books and Bibles were confiscated and burned. Swayze hid his Bible in a hollow sycamore tree and abandoned public services for secret ones. After his death in 1784, his son carried on the services for a few years, but when he died the church was not reorganized. Thus ended the first short-lived Protestant church in Mississippi.[6]

The next step in the planting of Protestantism came in 1780, when the family of Richard Curtis, Sr., and Phoebe Jones Curtis left South Carolina for the Spanish territory. The family included five sons and three daughters along with John Jones, Jr., Phoebe's son by a previous marriage, and his wife. Most immigrants to the territory during this period were

Loyalists, but according to family legend the Curtises and Joneses were ardent Patriots. Most of their neighbors in South Carolina were Tories. To escape their hostile surroundings, the family began the long trek to the Natchez country. After a dangerous journey through Indian territory, they arrived safely in Mississippi and settled about twenty miles above Natchez on Cole's Creek. They began the backbreaking labor necessary to carve a home out of the wilderness: building cabins, burning undergrowth in the Indian fashion, and planting corn. The Spanish government forbade Protestant worship so they met secretly in their homes for services, and their "meetings . . . soon attracted the attention of the American portion of the population."[7]

Richard Curtis, Jr., was a gifted Baptist preacher, and his followers increased in number. Problems developed when new converts, including a Spaniard, wanted to be baptized. Curtis was only a licentiate and not authorized to baptize; to resolve this dilemma Curtis wrote back to his church in South Carolina, which advised him to have his congregation elect a member to perform the rite. Naturally, Curtis was chosen and began to baptize converts. As the American presence grew, the Baptists became more bold: "Believing their cause was the cause of God . . . [they] bid their opponents defiance, and even went so far as to have their places of worship guarded by armed men, while they denounced in no very moderate terms the 'image worship' and other unscriptural dogmas and ceremonies of the Catholic Church." Despite their leniency, the Spaniards could hardly ignore such flagrant challenges. In a letter to don Manuel Gayoso de Lemos, the Spanish governor of the territory, Ebenezer Drayton, a Presbyterian, dismissed the Baptists as "weak men, of weak minds, and illiterate, and too ignorant to know how inconsistent they act and talk . . . too weak and undesigning to lay any treasonable plans." He informed the governor that the Baptists presented no real threat but warned, correctly, that "they would call any chastisement from Government for their disobedience, persecution, and suffering for Christ."[8]

Despite assurances that the Baptists were harmless, Gayoso took action against them in 1795. First, he wrote Curtis urging him to curb his activities. When Curtis refused, he was arrested and taken before the exasperated Gayoso, who threatened to deport him to work in Mexico's silver mines. Faced with that dire prospect, Curtis submitted to the governor's decrees. Gayoso issued an edict forbidding any assembly of more than nine persons for worship in any except Catholic services. For a time the Americans accepted the edict, but as their numbers grew, they became "more and more clamorous for religious, as well as civil, liberty." Their secret meetings resumed and quickly came to the governor's attention. Gayoso ordered the arrest of Curtis and two others, who decided to flee to South Carolina rather than risk almost certain death in a silver mine.[9]

The men hid in the woods waiting for supplies before beginning their long journey, but no man in the neighborhood would risk arrest by carrying goods to their hiding place. A determined woman, Chloe Holt, took the gamble; she issued a challenge: "If the men in the neighborhood are so faint-hearted that not one of them can be prevailed upon to take Dick Curtis and his companions . . . their promised supplies . . . if they will furnish me with a good horse . . . with a *man's saddle,* I will go in spite of the Spaniards, and they may catch me if they can." She dressed in men's clothing and made the delivery to save her fellow Baptists from "the clutches of these gospel-hating Catholics." Curtis and the others left for South Carolina, where Curtis was regularly ordained.[10]

Their flight did not end the Baptist challenge to Spanish authority. In 1795 Spain and the United States signed the Treaty of San Lorenzo, highly favorable to the United States, which transferred Natchez to the Americans. By 1797 the American presence in the territory had increased in anticipation of the Spanish evacuation, an event the Spanish continually delayed, much to the annoyance of the American population. Under the protection of American officials who were on the scene to survey the territory and carry out the transfer, evangelical ministers preached to what were described as "immense congregations" and railed against Catholicism. The most outspoken was Barton Hannon, an itinerant Baptist preacher who arrived in the territory in 1795. A native of Virginia, Hannon was a shoemaker who first emigrated to Alabama in 1791, where he raised livestock before moving to Natchez. He drew large crowds with his inflammatory anti-Catholic sermons and, "being a weak man, was extremely puffed up with the attention he received." Inspired by his success and perhaps "a little heightened by liquor," he unwisely "entered into a religious controversy in a disorderly part of town" inhabited by Irish Catholics, who "gave him a beating." The angry preacher called on Gayoso and demanded that the Irishmen be punished and threatened to do the job himself if the governor refused. Offended by his impertinence and threats to public order, Gayoso ordered Hannon placed in stocks inside the local fort.[11]

As armed guards escorted Hannon through the town toward the fort, he attempted to flee and loudly called on his fellow Americans for assistance. Immediately recaptured and placed in stocks, Hannon became a symbol of American opposition; at least three hundred armed settlers, including a group at Cole's Creek, roamed the countryside and threatened Gayoso. Violent rebellion appeared imminent. Gayoso's calm but firm response and the efforts of more levelheaded settlers prevented bloodshed, though the irate settlers at Cole's Creek were the last to lay down their weapons. Gayoso persuaded the people to obey Spanish law until the transition was completed the following year.[12]

Curtis and his friends returned from South Carolina once Natchez passed into American hands and found a church building already constructed. Their emotional homecoming was long remembered by the Baptists at Cole's Creek. Curtis officially organized the church in 1798; appropriately, after the years of turmoil and persecution, the Baptists called their church Salem, meaning "peace." These early Baptists were far from wealthy, as a 1792 Spanish census shows. Three charter members of Salem Baptist Church are listed on the census; two owned no land and very likely were squatters like many yeoman immigrants to the frontier. One owned four hundred acres of land but no slaves, hardly a princely estate. Only one, Margaret Stamply, whose home served as the Baptists' first meeting place, was a slave owner; she held one female slave but owned no land. There is no evidence that the other church members were any more affluent than these three.[13]

The strong communal nature of evangelical congregations led some groups to migrate to the territory, bound together by ties of Christian brotherhood. Richard Curtis, Sr., and his fellow Baptists were the first of such communal immigrations, but many other cases exist. In 1804, for example, a group of one hundred Baptists began the long and dangerous journey from the Beaufort district of South Carolina. They arrived in the territory in 1805, settled near the future town of Woodville, and built Bethel Baptist Church. In contrast to the plain folk who immigrated in groups, planters had the economic resources to visit the frontier before relocating; they acquired the best land and typically moved as individuals or in nuclear family units.[14]

The first Methodist society in the territory was organized by eight people in 1799 in Washington, the territorial capital. The Reverend Tobias Gibson, a South Carolina native, established this church shortly after his appointment as missionary to the territory. Gibson was unmarried, handsome, well educated, and had relatives in the Natchez region. He visited the Jersey Settlement and was warmly welcomed by the "shephardless flock, which although not of his denomination, yet from the Good seed already sown in their hearts . . . and their long . . . deprivation of religious instructions received him with joy and gladness . . . and soon resolved to erect a 'Meeting House or place of religious Worship.' " In the years following, the Methodists sent several other missionaries to the territory. Their task was difficult; when Gibson died in 1804, only 132 whites and 72 blacks had joined the Methodist churches in the territory.[15]

Launer Blackman, a Methodist missionary who arrived in the territory around the time of Gibson's death, described the obstacles facing evangelicals there. He wrote that many of the "Old Settlers" were "so rich they are above religion and religion is above them." The poor were "mostly very ignorant," and he found it "difficult to make impress on their minds about religion." He observed that blacks were numerous but "mostly very wicked." Only "a few of the old inhabitants that hold a mediocrity in life embrace religion." Blackman was encouraged when more settlers from the southern states arrived in the territory. Many of them were already converted, and they proved to be a means of reaching others by providing itinerants with food and shelter and by using their contacts with family, friends, and neighbors to assemble congregations.[16]

The Presbyterians were the last major evangelical sect to become established in the territory. In 1801 three missionaries sent by the Synod of Carolina arrived in southwestern Mississippi, where they labored for one year. They collected congregations, but, unlike the Methodist missionaries, they did not establish churches. In 1804 the Presbyterians organized their first church near Uniontown, in the Natchez region. One of the most prominent of the early Presbyterian ministers was the Reverend James Smylie, a North Carolinian of Highland Scots ancestry who arrived in the territory in 1805 as a missionary from the Synod of Carolina. He established several churches in the Amite and Adams County area and became one of the most influential ministers in the Old Southwest.[17]

Despite the missionaries' best efforts, evangelical churches attracted only a few hundred members before 1810. Natchez, with a population of about fifteen hundred, was the only town of any consequence in the territory, but neither the wealthy planters nor the riverboat men and gamblers were much interested in religion. In 1803 Lorenzo Dow reported that "there were not three Christians in the town, either white or black," and called it the center of "irreligion and every form of vice." When Jacob Young, a Methodist minister, arrived in the territory in 1807, he was shocked by what he found in Natchez: "I had often been among rough people," he wrote, "and had seen and heard a great deal of wickedness, but what I saw and heard there surpassed any thing I had ever seen or thought of." He was surprised to see "Americans, French, Spaniards, English, Irish, Dutch, negroes, and mulattoes—all mingling as 'fellows well met.' Many

Kentuckians were lying in their flat-boats, along the wharf, drinking, fighting, swearing, and acting like demons." The Methodists built a small church there in 1807, but for the first ten years it struggled along with little success. The Baptists did not establish a church until after the territory became a state in 1817. Visitors in 1815 reported that the Presbyterians had a new church but no preacher. A preacher who visited the town in 1812 found the people "very rich, very proud and very polite" but with "little humility, little religion and little piety." [18]

The evangelicals found their greatest strength outside Natchez among the farmers and plain folk who settled the fertile but unopened land. Amite County was a cradle of evangelicalism in these early years, [19] and an examination of its settlers can help identify the base of their support. Land claim records from the county indicate that these plain folk began life in the territory as subsistence farmers. Mark Cole, a Baptist, "began to get stuff for a house in February, 1803, and moved his family there early in March. His family consisted of a wife and six children and he made a crop of 2 or 3 acres the following season." John Courtney, another Baptist, "with his wife and seven children settled upon the land in November, 1802. . . . There was a camp in which he lived and he had about 5 acres cleared by the 3rd of March, 1803." An 1805 census shows that 882 people lived in the county, approximately one-quarter of whom were slaves. One-half of the heads of households owned slaves, but in contrast to the proud and wealthy planters of the Natchez area, these were small farmers; almost 95 percent of slaveholders owned fewer than ten slaves, and 78 percent owned fewer than five. Five years later the population had more than quadrupled, but the ratio of whites to slaves remained about the same, and 90 percent of slaveholders owned fewer than ten slaves. [20]

In such circumstances, master and slave lived in greater intimacy than on a large plantation; they labored together in the fields and shared much the same living conditions. The cramped living quarters contributed to intimate social relationships between blacks and whites and between men and women; according to sociologist Norbert Elias, such people had a lower "threshold of shame" and different ideas of privacy and individual autonomy than was typical in contemporary Western society. For master and slave alike, "cabbins were small and smokey [with] many inconveniences." John Hebron Moore, in an economic history of Mississippi, observed that before the 1830s and 1840s "most of the slaves . . . like their owners, were housed in the crudest sort of log cabins having dirt floors and chimneys made of sticks and mud." Rustic frontier conditions sometimes placed evangelicals of different races in intimate situations, and as Rhys Isaac observed for an earlier period, "Crowding people into a single room . . . made for a communal style of life." Methodist minister John Jones, for example, sometimes preached in a neighborhood made up mostly of free blacks. He dined with one interracial couple, a white man with a black wife, whom Jones described as "quite pious." He spent the night with a black man in his cabin, and though the thought was "somewhat repulsive to my feelings . . . I soon discovered that he was both the gentleman and the christian and I felt quite at home." These hardworking small farmers and slaves would make up the majority of the early evangelicals.[21] It should come as no surprise that such people developed a communal style of worship in which the elite rules of correct behavior did not apply.

Historian Bertram Wyatt-Brown has observed that crowded living conditions reduced individual privacy and changed relationships between men and women. Methodist itinerant William Winans described his experiences as he traveled his circuit: "Three nights, of five, I slept in rooms in which ladies slept; and, on occasion, my bed was sufficiently near to one in which two ladies slept for me to have put my hands upon them without raising or materially altering my position in bed." Winans observed that "classification, into . . . refined and rude . . . are much less common in newly-settled countries."[22]

Many of Winans's wealthier contemporaries, however, were quick to make such classifications. Joseph H. Ingraham, who visited Natchez in the 1830s, described the small farmers who brought their crops to market there; they "drive their own oxen," he wrote, "often conveying their whole crop on one waggon. These small farmers form a peculiar class, and include a majority of the inhabitants in the east part of the state." He found that "they are in general uneducated, and their apparel consists of a course linsey-woolsey . . . with broad-brimmed hats." Ingraham noted that "at home they live in log-houses on partially cleared lands, labour hard in their fields, sometimes owning a few slaves, but more generally with one or none."[23] His condescension toward and contempt for small farmers was shared by many of their social superiors in Natchez.

One young emigrant from Vermont, James Pearse, published an account of his residence in early Mississippi aimed at "men of ordinary life" who might consider a similar move. His description of his many travails was meant to discourage others, and perhaps he exaggerated his troubles, but his record of illness and misfortune has a ring of authenticity. Nothing in his New England farming background had prepared him for life in the Old Southwest; he described New England society as one based on equality

with "virtue being the only proper ornament of any station." Whereas
owning a small family farm was a source of pride in his home state, in
Mississippi he found that the planters held small farmers in contempt.
He described the "great distinction between the different classes" that
characterized Mississippi society:

> Few, who are raised to affluence, have any feelings for those below their
> rank. . . . The master is proud and overbearing on all below his imaginary
> greatness, whether white or black; often cruel, and pleased with a display
> of needless power. . . . Of course, there is nothing of that equality, which
> is to be found in the northern states. . . . I have heard it used almost as
> a proverb, that "a poor man is a mean man." Indeed, he is so in *public
> opinion.*"[24]

The self-styled nabobs of Natchez and the surrounding plantation region lived a far more luxurious life than Pearse and the plain folk; they
imported luxury goods from Europe and other parts of America, they
dined from silver plate, they commissioned portraits of themselves and
their families, and beginning about 1810 they built imposing mansions as
symbols of their wealth and social dominance. These homes were so impressive and stood out in such contrast to more humble dwellings that the
plain folk referred to their owners as the "pillared folk," a reference to the
mighty columns that dominate the facades of many of these residences.[25]

Mississippi society was more stratified than that in other frontier regions, and the plain folk and pillared folk were divided by wide social,
economic, and ideological gulfs. James Pearse's narrative bristles with the
democratic ideals of the Revolution. He articulated an emergent yeoman-
class ideology based on a vision of agrarian virtue and a belief that small,
independent farmers were the bedrock of the republic. The nabobs' aggressive acquisitiveness and ostentatious displays of wealth and luxury
had no place in a republican society. Agrarian republicanism was anticapi-
talistic and favored household independence and local exchange over the
commercial development pursued by the planters, who were increasingly
reliant on national and international markets. After 1815 the "market
revolution" created tensions even in rural areas like Mississippi, where
farmers were pulled between relative self-sufficiency and a full-fledged
commitment to the market.[26]

By the early decades of the 1800s the future contours of Mississippi
society had largely taken shape. Many of the elements that would dominate the region throughout the antebellum period were in place—plantation agriculture, slavery, and cotton, in particular. Though still very

much a frontier region, the territory was not a backwater; already there were rapidly expanding pockets of wealth tied to international markets. Although a wealthy elite dominated the territory economically and politically, more and more plain folk immigrated to the territory once the United States acquired it. Here, as in other parts of the South, this dynamic group challenged planter supremacy, and evangelical religion helped define this challenge.

CHAPTER 2

GENTLEMEN, IS THAT GRAMMAR?
PLAIN FOLK VERSUS PILLARED FOLK,
1805–1830

O NE early Methodist preacher in Mississippi encountered the following reaction from the gentlemen in his camp meeting audience:

> When a plain, unlettered man was preaching, the wicked portion of the audience had great merriment on account of his ignorance of correct language. At one time the grammar of this preacher was at fault, at another time his rhetoric, and then his logic, besides his gestures were awkward, etc. They did all they could to hedge up the poor man's way, and said he was not competent to preach. However, he was not to be intimidated by the laugh and sneer of his ungodly hearers. On one of his visits he took for his text the following: "Ye serpents, ye generations of vipers, how can ye escape the damnation of hell!" Then he said in tones of thunder, "Gentlemen, is that grammar?" He was divinely assisted in his sermon . . . he kept . . . pouring upon them passage after passage of divine denunciation of the wicked, frequently asking the annoying question, "Gentlemen, is that grammar?" So successful was that effort . . . his grammar never afterward was called in question.[1]

Such an incident might seem like an innocent case of a few gentlemen having a laugh at the expense of someone less educated than themselves, but the underlying situation was more complex. In this context, language represents power, and gestures indicate social status; by pointing out these "deficiencies," the gentlemen challenged the preacher's authority to be heard. Time and time again the plain folk faced opposition from the pillared folk; it became a struggle that defined their counterculture. The "evangelical revolt" was a part, and often the most dynamic part, of a broader process of democratization reflected in evangelical hostility to the traditional rituals of the more conservative churches, in new forms of

worship, in camp meetings, and even in language. The rise of evangelicalism in Mississippi in the early nineteenth century was far more than
a religious movement; it was a powerful movement of social change as
well. The religious revolt against elite culture received its impetus from
the Great Revival that blazed across Mississippi and brought thousands of
converts into the evangelical fold. Perry Miller saw the revival movement
as "a central mode of this culture's search for national identity." The dises-
tablishment of official churches after the American Revolution reflected
a recognition of the changed religious climate, but broader changes were
at work as well. Old patterns of deference gave way as the lower classes
challenged gentry domination and the hierarchical social structure that
supported it. Revivals and evangelicalism played an important role in
the contest between the gentry and the plain folk and helped establish a
foundation for the young republic.[2]

An examination of the evangelical movement in early Mississippi
shows this process at work. The early evangelicals in Mississippi were
powerless, at least in the usual meaning of the word; they were drawn primarily from the lower rungs of the social ladder, they lacked material resources, and they did not control the apparatus of the state. What they did
have, however, was an ideology that proved to be enormously attractive to
certain elements in society. Conversion was a dramatic event that completely changed the lives of many evangelicals; it was often an integrative
experience that brought a sense of empowerment. Emboldened by their
faith, the evangelicals fought a battle of ideas with the local elites; their
major weapons were words, primarily the spoken word. Words, songs,
and voices were imbued with new powers of social definition. The con-
tests between the evangelicals and the gentry took place in the emotional
evangelical services, especially in the camp meetings. Out of these con-
tests evangelicals created new identities for themselves, their region, and
ultimately the nation.

It seems appropriate that this synthesis emerged on the frontier. As
Bernard Bailyn noted, "The wilderness environment from the beginning
had threatened the maintenance of elaborate social distinctions." When to
that environment was added "epidemic evangelicalism," a volatile situation resulted. Anthropologist Mary Douglas, in a work historians have
found relevant, suggested that cultural forms, including religion, reflect
the distinctive social structure of every society. She wrote that in highly
structured societies where communal bonds are strong, the religion is
ritualist (which she defines as a belief in the efficacy of symbolic action),
but where structure is weak, ritualism declines. Antiritualism, which is

by definition revolutionary, emerges among those groups who experience "alienation from the current social values." Another important variable she calls "sparsity"; where the population is scattered, the level of social control declines and along with it the need for ritual forms.[3]

If Douglas is correct, the people of the South could hardly have continued to practice ritualistic religion tied to tight communal bonds on the European model. Those bonds were weak across most of the region, and certainly on the Mississippi frontier, where household economic autonomy rather than community interdependence was the norm. Settlement in Mississippi was sparse, even by southern standards, and, as Douglas suggests, that dispersed settlement pattern weakened social control. As a final ingredient in this volatile mix, the entire colonial social structure had been called into question by the American Revolution; a society based on hierarchy and deference gave way to one based on competition and individual autonomy. As Rhys Isaac wrote, "The reorganization of social action and social expectation can be discerned in the great movements of population that were taking place in the wake of the Revolution."[4] But these new cultural patterns did not emerge overnight or without opposition and conflict.

The pillared folk could hardly have been prepared for the challenge to their social and political domination that accompanied the camp meetings; Methodist bishop Francis Asbury described the camp meeting as "the battle ax and weapon of war." His military metaphor reflects the intensity of the struggle, and the meetings proved to be an effective weapon indeed. Methodist minister William Winans wrote that there was "an almost exclusive dependence on extraordinary meetings and extraordinary efforts" for conversion in early Mississippi; "insomuch, that it came . . . to be regarded as a strange thing if any person were converted under the ordinary ministry of the word." Camp meetings were, as their name implies, literally camps, clearings in the woods, usually removed from a village or town, where people isolated themselves from the world around them. The meeting ground was usually dominated by the preachers' "stand," a raised structure, sometimes roofed and partially walled, from which the sermons were delivered. The area in front of the stand was often heavily layered with straw in preparation for people to kneel or experience other "physical exercises." Services were held throughout the day and late into the night; the nighttime services could be especially moving, their effect enhanced by the darkness, broken only by the flickering of the torches and camp fires. Meetings were notoriously noisy affairs; the evangelicals either ignored or flouted their society's norms of "respectable" behavior in their revolt against elite culture. When the celebrated but eccentric Methodist evangelist Lorenzo Dow held the first camp meeting on Mississippi soil in 1805, the shocked residents who ignored his message asked, "Is God deaf, that they cannot worship him without such a noise?" The Methodists held the first camp meetings, but the Baptists and Presbyterians also employed them in these early years; often ministers from several denominations would preach at the same meeting. Jacob Young recalled a meeting at which "five or six Methodist preachers" and "five Calvinist preachers . . . some Presbyterians—some Baptists" hotly debated the merits of their faiths.[5]

The evangelicals' opponents frequently tried to disrupt their services. During the War of 1812 a group of "mounted and armed" cavalry volunteers attempted to break up a camp meeting by riding over the grounds, but the stubborn resistance of the men attending the meeting forced them to give up. At an 1823 meeting a "mob" caused a disturbance by cutting bridles and saddles and singing loudly. James Pearse found religion to be an ingredient in the class divisions he observed on the frontier; he wrote, "One day I heard some young gentlemen observe, that if there was not better order in the Methodist meeting-house, they would be willing to see a certain exhorter led out and whipped; and if any would assist, they would have it done." Indeed, such attempts were made; in 1829 the Reverend George Moore, a Presbyterian, was preaching in Vicksburg when "a group of drunken rowdies came into the building and noisily proclaimed that they had come to stop such silly doings as preaching." They ordered Moore to step out of the pulpit, and much to their surprise he did so. He pulled off his coat, marched down the aisle, and began "to pummel them right and left." The intruders fled, and Moore "went calmly back to the pulpit . . . put on his coat and began again to preach the glad gospel." Such confrontations clearly show that the evangelicals were perceived as a threat to the existing social order; they challenged a society based on deference and social hierarchy and posed instead a counterculture with different measures of worth and status.[6]

Camp meetings provided evangelicals with a means of spreading their message that was well suited to frontier conditions and to the needs of settlers of both races. They provided the perfect solution to the problem of a widely dispersed population and few ministers; as a Presbyterian wrote from Natchez in 1813, "The harvest in this country is great, but the laborers are few." The meetings often attracted huge crowds, at least in part because of the unusual sights to be seen and the rousing sermons to be heard. In 1823, for example, William Winans estimated that four to six thousand people attended a camp meeting, including a large number of blacks. The meetings provided a context for an important cultural exchange between blacks and whites that helped shape the evangelical movement. The early camp meetings were remarkably egalitarian, a characteristic that led a British visitor to describe them as "festivals of democracy." John G. Jones, whose family were yeoman farmers, recalled crowding into an ox cart with the few family slaves to attend camp meetings; he also recalled that blacks came from surrounding plantations to attend and camped around their own large fires built with pine knots. Revivals and other services revitalized Christians on the frontier and brought new settlers into the Christian community. They shaped the movement more than any other aspect of evangelicalism.[7]

Lorenzo Dow's 1805 meeting was a profitable and exciting one. Critical reports of the notorious evangelist in the Natchez newspapers aroused interest, and a large crowd attended the meeting. Dow brought his listeners to an emotional fever pitch; he wrote: "A panic seized the congregation, and a solemn awe ensued. We had a cry and a shout. It was a weeping, tender time." Dow reportedly encouraged the emotional outburst by paying black boys to climb trees and shout on cue. The meeting lasted four days, and fifty people converted. Momentum increased with the arrival of veterans of the revival movement in Kentucky. William Winans, a Pennsylvania native and Methodist minister, arrived in the territory in 1810 and became a leader in the revival. Winans's first ministerial appointment was in Kentucky, where he attended camp meetings and heard celebrated revivalists, including Dow. Winans was a man of humble origins who had received only two weeks of formal education, but his simple background was probably an advantage on the frontier, where he labored among men much like himself.[8]

Almost every contemporary description of Winans made much of his personal appearance. One writer described him as "a unique character, tall, thin, weatherworn, and looking the very image of a Green Mountain farmer." When he attended a meeting of the Methodist Conference in Cincinnati, Ohio, in 1836, a newspaper correspondent noted: "His appearance bespoke any thing, rather than a minister or an orator. With a rough manner, long shaggy hair, and a neck ignorant of a cravat, he seemed more like some lawless backwoodsman than the able and devoted minister." Winans often criticized people who took too worldly an interest in their personal appearance, but his lack of attention to personal grooming gave the impression of slovenliness; as one contemporary wrote, "His whole attire has the appearance of uniform neglect."[9]

Like almost every aspect of the camp meetings, the preachers' appearance had important symbolic implications. Mary Douglas noted the "distinctive appearance of prophets," who "tend to arise in peripheral areas of society, and . . . tend to be shaggy, unkempt individuals. They express in their bodies the independence of social norms which their peripheral origins inspire in them." Like Winans, Dow was known for "his bizarre appearance—long hair parted like a woman's, weather-beaten face, flashing eyes, harsh voice, crude gestures, and disheveled clothes." As Rhys Isaac and others have shown, clothing was an important symbol for early evangelicals, an outward form of identification, and a highly visible indication of status. The evangelicals' opponents often ridiculed their somber, outmoded style of dress. Winans described an incident when *"lewd fellows of the baser sort"* invaded a meetinghouse and "played many foolish pranks among which was the putting of a Tailor's sign into the pulpit." The tailor's sign must have been a hint that the ministers could use such services, but ministers were well aware of the symbolism behind their dress. Some young ministers hesitated to give up current fashions; Thomas Griffin "had a short but severe struggle about . . . donning the old-fashioned, round-breasted, colonial coat and vest, which were . . . adhered to with great tenacity by the Methodists of those days." The evangelicals clearly recognized the symbolism attached to clothing; they enforced a strict dress code among members, and ministers who wore fashionable clothes were ridiculed by their fellows.[10]

The symbolism associated with the body became perhaps the most notorious aspect of the camp meetings. Here, too, evangelicals cast aside traditional patterns of elite behavior. Sociologists and anthropologists have observed that each society sets its own limits of acceptable behavior and that the body is a "highly restricted medium of expression." Mary Douglas wrote that "the lack of strong social articulation" combined with weak social control led "people to seek, in the slackening of bodily control, appropriate forms of expression" for their newfound spiritual independence. Shouting was perhaps the most common form of expression among evangelical converts, but weeping was also common. Mourners, sorrowful would-be converts, were present at most meetings and were called forward toward the meeting's close. More dramatic "bodily exercises" frequently occurred and aroused intense criticism from opponents of the meetings. Some converts, feeling themselves overcome by the Holy Spirit, fell gently to the floor, and all their apparent bodily functions ceased for hours except a faint respiration. Their extremities and faces became cold to the touch, and their pulse rates decreased. Jones, who experienced this sensation, described it "as a rushing mighty wind" and called himself a "willing captive." He recalled: "It was unpleasant to be touched, or spoken to. . . . But O! the joy, the rapture, the dissolving and absorbing love felt in the 'inner man.'"[11]

Some of these "exercises" required physical strength and stamina. In the jumping exercise, "the subject would bound from the floor twenty or thirty times in quick succession, with a countenance beaming with holy joy . . . the feats performed in jumping over benches, and bounding from place to place without injury . . . were extraordinary." Women often experienced the dancing exercise in which they "would suddenly spring to their feet, and with countenances beaming with extatic joy, and their eyes turned upwards, they would gracefully jump up and down with a quickness, nimbleness, and apparent ease, not easily imitated." Critics of the revivals pointed to such behavior as evidence of nothing more than animal excitement, but those who experienced such outbursts described them as deeply moving expressions of spiritual independence.[12] The modes of expression also had symbolic importance; by flouting society's rules of acceptable behavior, evangelicals issued yet another challenge to their opponents.

In their discourse and in their preaching style, the evangelical ministers reacted against elite conceptions of language and authority. Kenneth Cmiel, in his study of popular language in the nineteenth century, wrote, "Attacking gentlemanly decorum meant that you did not necessarily have to be refined to have your words count. . . . Paradoxically, earlier ideas about social order were undermined by the spread of civil speech as much as by any new vulgarity." Camp meetings can be seen as theaters of discourse, as a structured space within which evangelicals attempted—ultimately with great success—to create an environment that worked to their advantage, a theater of their own design, where they wrote the play, produced it, and acted it out. Camp meetings served to broaden the field of discourse from the few to the many. Evangelical preachers cast aside elite rules of rhetoric and grammar (if they knew them at all) and spoke in the language of the plain folk, thereby validating that culture to the listeners who shared it. By creating a hierarchy of language, the gentry dismissed the language of the plain folk as "vulgar" and therefore without importance. Preachers recognized, and profited from, the hierarchy of language by turning it against those who first created it.[13]

Mary Douglas has further suggested that language and style are important antiritualist symbols; antiritualists were skeptical of external expression and valued instead inner conviction. They denigrated the value of polished, practiced speech and saw it as inherently artificial. They favored instead spontaneous speech that flowed from the heart and expressed true intentions. Members of movements of religious renewal are confident of their inner convictions and their direct access to God.[14] Douglas's theory helps explain the evangelicals' preference for the emotional, spontaneous, unpolished sermon and their distrust of a minister who prepared a written sermon rather than relying on divine guidance and inspiration.

Although preachers sometimes attacked the gentry's mode of speech directly, more often their attack was implied by their grammar and style. For example, a sermon by Thomas Griffin shows the use of language that was deliberately insulting; such abuse was often leveled at those considered to be "outsiders." The example also shows their playfulness, the delight some of them took in the language, and how they shaped their message to their rustic frontier audience. Such ministers clearly played to what Lawrence Levine has called "a seemingly inexhaustible appetite for the spoken word." When Griffin chose to elaborate upon the sins of the "debauchee," he referred to him as "the very frazzle-end of humanity; his debauched carcass would disgrace a wolf trap if put in it for bait. If he should die by the wayside a decent turkey-buzzard would consult the dignity of his beak before he would condescend to pick out his blood-shot eyes. If hell itself could be raked over it is doubtful whether a more deeply-fallen spirit could be found."[15]

In such sermons, not only the language but the mode of delivery was significant. These colorful sermons were usually extemporaneous; a Methodist bishop had to refuse a request to publish a sermon because he "never wrote a sermon before he preached it." Preachers were often impassioned performers; at one service James Pearse attended a Methodist preacher became "wild, disconnected, and furious." Bruce Rosenberg, in a study of the American folk preacher, referred to the unwritten sermons as "illiteratures" and compared their composition to the composition of epic verse. Like epics, the sermons were often metrical and delivered in a style similar to the epics. Sermons frequently became tests of endurance; one minister, for example, preached for three hours nonstop. Here, again, the comparison with the singers of oral epics is useful. Preachers frequently used the same biblical texts over and over, but obviously, in sermons of such length delivered without notes, no two performances would be the same. Probably, like the epic singers, the preachers employed "oral formulas," or phrases that could be manipulated and combined with spontaneous passages to produce a lengthy sermon. Preachers carefully manipulated their audiences. One listener recalled hearing Griffin and his brother-in-law

Miles Harper, both noted for their successful camp meeting technique. They often worked as a team:

> They were both men of . . . rough manners and severe aspect; often with a frown upon their brows; and full of pungent and sometimes very bitter satire . . . Mr. Griffin was rather harsh and sardonic. He would make the congregation quail, and shrink and hide their heads with fear and shame, and then Harper would solace and comfort them, and inspire them with hope and confidence; and between the two, whenever they preached, a revival was sure to follow.[16]

John G. Jones described the preaching style common in the early churches as the "heavenly tone," also called the "holy tone" or "holy whine." It was characterized by "assumed innotations of the voice, expressive of great earnestness, and . . . composed of the cadences of whining, mourning, lamentation and wailing . . . intended to arouse the sympathies of both preacher and auditors." Because of its rhythmic quality one hearer asked a preacher, "Brother . . . did you preach us a song or sing us a sermon?" Since so few of these early sermons were written and so much of their power was derived from the style of their delivery, this vital part of the evangelical service is particularly difficult to analyze. Fortunately, there is an extant oral tradition derived directly from this early preaching style; frequently referred to as "spiritual preaching," it survives among blacks—predominantly in the South but now scattered in black communities across America—and among whites in Appalachia and other rural areas. Combined with historical evidence, contemporary examples can enhance our understanding of preaching styles and the nature of these early worship services.[17]

The quotations in the preceding paragraph suggest that many camp meeting sermons had a musical quality, a style referred to as "chanting." The character of the chanted sermon is difficult to evoke through the printed word, but one recent observer gave the following description. The preacher

> begins his sermon in normal, though stately and carefully measured, prose. As he gets into his subject, he gradually raises the intensity of his delivery (though with well-timed ups and downs). About one third of the way into his sermon the prose has verged into a very rhythmical delivery, punctuated into periods (more or less regular) by a sharp utterance which I suppose might be called a vehement grunt. I haven't timed these periods, but I would guess that they fall about every three seconds, sometimes less.

Within the rhythmical framework, the rises and falls eventually build to a climax when he lapses into a sort of chant, still with the same punctuation, but with a recognizable tonic (tonal center). Some of the congregation (who respond *ad libitum* throughout) here lapse into humming along with him. After this climax he breaks off dramatically into normal prose, then builds back again, and finally tapers off into a subdued normal delivery at the end.

Like the camp meeting sermons, the modern version is extemporaneous, though certain formulas are often repeated. Just as the opponents of the early evangelicals were shocked by the weeping, clapping, and shouting that accompanied the sermon, strangers today are surprised to find the same emotional responses to the modern chanted sermon.[18]

Emotional intensity became a hallmark of such meetings across the South and in Mississippi. At a June 1812 meeting eight evangelists preached on a Saturday; by the nighttime services people were "on fire with exhortations." Winans reported with satisfaction that "we had a considerable disturbance." The following day, Lewis Hobbs, another Methodist minister, "set the people on fire or raised their passions to an incredible pitch." John G. Jones recalled that "it was a luxury not often otherwise enjoyed, to sit unobserved at night on a camp-meeting occasion . . . where one might laugh and weep alternately for an hour without restraint!"[19]

Such responses were an integral part of the service; the level of the congregation's response influences the preacher's timing, his performance, and the length of the sermon. Preachers encouraged such antiphonal responses, for only great fervor signified the presence of the Holy Spirit. A popular hymn from the period entitled "Holy Manna" expresses the cooperative nature of these services:

> Brethren, we have met to worship,
> And adore the Lord our God;
> Will you pray with all your power,
> While we try to preach the word?
> All is vain unless the Spirit
> Of the Holy One come down;
> Brethren, pray, and holy manna
> Will be shower'd all around.

Active congregational participation played a major role in early services, as it does in spiritual services today. These emotional services reflected the democratic nature of the early evangelical movement; one scholar's description of the congregation's role in modern services applies equally well to the early camp meeting congregations: "They are all a part of the sermon, and every bit as much as is the preacher."[20]

The camp meeting preaching style provides an example of the remarkable interaction between blacks and whites in the Great Revival. The origin of the chanted sermon is unclear, but elements within the style can be traced to both Africa and Europe; to argue for the primacy of one over the other is to miss the larger significance of the exchange. This process had been under way in the South since the evangelical revivals of the eighteenth century.[21]

Blacks and whites worshiped together in the Mississippi camp meetings, and black preachers were active in these early years as well (see chapter 4). Whites frequently reported hearing black preachers, and some whites converted under their ministry. For example, one former slave recalled: "I saw a preacher in Mississippi carry on a revival and he had persuaded the white man's son to go, and he professed and they would let him have meetings any time, 'cause that white man's son professed under him." A. C. Ramsey, a Methodist minister in southeastern Mississippi, recalled sharing the stand at camp meetings with a black preacher, "Uncle" Leaven McRae, in the 1820s. McRae was literate, "and being endowed with an investigative intellect and by strict application to reading the Bible and other books at his command, and above all having the grace of God in his heart . . . he became a good, sound, practical and doctrinal preacher, loved and admired by all who knew him." Pompey, a Methodist slave in north Mississippi in the 1830s, was among the first preachers in that part of the state and was popular with members of both races. One white Methodist who heard him at a camp meeting recalled the "power in his prayer" and described his impact on the audience: "The earth seemed to tremble under the weight of that power. . . . The whole audience seemed to sway to and fro. . . . Cries for mercy, groans of agony and shouts of praise were so numerous and loud that, strong and loud as his voice was, one could scarcely hear him, and he exclaimed, 'When de Lord preaches, Pompey stops,' and sat down." Clearly, both blacks and whites received the gift of the word and preached powerful sermons that transcended barriers of race and class. Timothy Flint, a Presbyterian minister who visited the state more than once in the early 1800s, observed: "Wherever the Methodists come in contact with them [slaves], their earnest and vehement address softens the obduracy of the blacks at once. They use a language that falls in their apprehensions."[22]

The same blending of cultures that produced the chanted sermon wrought a revolution in American music. The chanted sermon evolved along with the spiritual, and the two are so closely related that a common origin seems clear. The sermons and spirituals show the same repetitious structure, and indeed the modern sermons often borrow lines directly from the spirituals. The sermons are often chanted in the pentatonic scale, which is common in revival hymns, and the rhythms of both are the same. Perhaps a more significant relationship is the antiphonal performance of both; like the chanted sermon, camp meeting songs encouraged an active response from the congregation. Services opened with prayer and singing, blended into a sermon in which musical influence remained strong, then closed with singing. This pattern of blending speech and song is related to "the common use in Africa of recitative styles of singing, and the frequent transitions between a speaking and singing delivery." The songs were as important as the sermons in arousing the congregations. As one Methodist journalist wrote: "In revivals, it is well known that singing is an essential and powerful agent in awakening devotional feelings. Not dull and formal, but lively and energetic singing." William Winans described the closing scene at an 1823 camp meeting: "Bro. Harper offered up the concluding prayer; after which farewell songs were sung accompanied by much feeling and much noise and, indeed, the former is never known here without the latter." The rousing camp meeting spirituals encouraged such emotional responses; for example, one hymn entitled "Shouting Song" went:

> Jesus, grant us all a blessing,
> Shouting, singing, send it down;
> Lord, above may we go praying,
> And rejoicing in thy love.
> Shout, O glory! sing glory, hallelujah! [23]

Winans's observation that singing was accompanied by "much feeling and much noise" is significant; the evolution of gospel music was a part of the larger democratization of religion. In the period from 1780 to 1830 evangelicals broke with traditional church music and developed "indigenous folk alternatives." Evangelicals believed that worship in song need not be limited to biblical texts and psalms; they agreed with Isaac Watts, whose hymns were popular among them, that the purpose of singing was to "speak to our own experience of divine things." In Mississippi as in other parts of the country, preachers and converts composed gospel songs suited to their own needs and derived from their experiences. Singing was one of many gifts—like the gifts of preaching and prayer—that God bestowed on the faithful, and many early ministers were talented singers and songwriters. Thomas Owens, Jr., was one of these early songsters. Born in Charleston, South Carolina, in 1787, he moved with his parents to Mississippi in 1803. He became a popular camp meeting preacher and a talented emotional singer: "When singing 'with the spirit' he came as near singing all over, soul and body, as any man we ever saw. The people caught his tunes and learned his songs and choruses, so that in a short time the community was alive with his revival songs and tunes." Thomas Mercer, a prominent Baptist preacher in early Mississippi, published a collection of hymns, at least some of which he composed. Hymnals were scarce, and so great was the difficulty in acquiring them from outside Mississippi that in 1816 the Methodist Mississippi Conference printed a pamphlet of the most popular songs for distribution. Samuel Sellers, a Methodist itinerant, assembled the collection and noted in 1815 that he was "employed in making a selection of Hymns & spiritual songs by the request of Conference." These pocket "songsters" usually contained only the texts of the songs and were frequently sold at the camp meetings.[24]

Even without an adequate supply of hymnals, the stirring spirituals spread quickly among the evangelicals. As the example of Thomas Owens suggests, many people learned the songs by heart. Probably a majority of these plain folk were illiterate, as were most slaves, and members "learned the tunes, and memorized many of the most commonly used hymns, so that they soon became proficient." No doubt many of the tunes were already familiar because composers frequently borrowed popular secular tunes. The practice of "lining out" the songs also compensated for illiteracy and the shortage of hymnals; a song leader sang the first line and the congregation followed. The practice of lining out has European roots and may date back to the dissolution of choirs in the wake of the Reformation; it certainly existed in England and Scotland by the seventeenth century. It also embodied the call-and-response structure of African music. That the style resonated in both cultures may help explain its popularity, and, as one scholar observed, its origins are "so mixed and complex as to render the question meaningless." One result of lining out was slower singing, "which led to improvised embellishments to fill up the gaps or long notes." In camp meeting spirituals singers typically repeated lines, added refrains, or inserted tag lines; other spirituals used the call-and-response pattern. A visitor from Massachusetts who attended a Baptist meeting in Mississippi in 1816 saw this cultural blending at work; he wrote, "They sung in ancient style, lining the Psalm, and uniting in every part of the house, both white and black, frequently making discordant sounds, grating to an ear accustomed to correct music."[25]

Who sang was as important as what they sang; congregational singing emphasized the equality of all believers and encouraged wide participation. Blacks joined with whites in singing. Women, too, participated enthusiastically; indeed, one scholar noted that congregational involvement had "democratized" singing and "brought women their first significant liturgical role." Women not only sang but often led the song service as well. One Mississippi evangelical recalled: "My mother was a fine singer. She often had to lead the music in our little church when the men's hearts failed them. I can almost hear her voice as it rose above the volume of song as she sang the 'top line' of old Pisgah or New Brittain." John Jones's wife was a talented singer who often led blacks in singing when her husband preached to them in separate services. Congregational singing provides further evidence of the centrality of the laity in services and the lack of distinction between the laity and the preachers.[26]

Many preachers operated singing schools where they taught gospel music to young people. They often employed a form of notation called "shape notes" in which the shape of the note head corresponds to notes on a scale. The method originated early in the nineteenth century and flourished in the South. This system, crafted for untrained singers, enabled people to read music on sight. It was especially popular among the Baptists (and later the Primitive Baptists, who continue the practice today). Baptist services usually opened with song; in fact, some churches' rules of decorum stipulated that services open with prayer and song. In shape-note singing, the performers stood in a hollow square facing the center with each of four parts on one side; singers often swapped sides and rotated as song leader. As one writer commented, "Their meetings are models of musical democracy." Singing was a popular and potent force in the spread of evangelicalism; it was another way that evangelicals rejected tradition and shaped their worship anew. Singing became a part of the fabric of their lives; Henry J. Harris recalled that it was common for "friends to meet at each others houses and spend evenings . . . in social singing and prayer." In doing so, they wrought a revolution in American music. "Popular gospel music became a pervasive reality in Jacksonian culture because people wrested singing from churchly control," wrote historian Nathan O. Hatch. "The music created a spontaneous, moving medium, capable of capturing the identity of plain people."[27]

Church membership and the establishment of new churches reflected the revival's strength among both blacks and whites. Methodist congregations grew from 132 white and 72 black members in 1805 to 1,551 white and 410 black members in 1816—a dramatic 1,075 percent increase in white membership and 469 percent increase in black membership, a rate considerably higher than the rate of population growth. In 1807 the five Baptist churches in the territory organized the Mississippi Baptist Association; by 1818 the association had forty member churches. Membership grew from 196 in 1807 to 1,072 in 1818. Although total evangelical membership is difficult to tabulate with any certainty, one historian estimated that by 1817 one person in twenty was a church member.[28]

The revival movement brought hundreds of converts into the churches, where the regular worship services continued the simple and emotional style of outdoor worship. John Jones described a regular worship service characterized by the same emotional intensity as the camp meeting; he "preached with freedom—until I was compelled to stop by the loud shouts of the children of Zion—We had class meeting—and a precious time it was—Both preacher and members shouted outright." Services might be held on any day because itinerant ministers, common in the Methodist and Baptist churches, met with worshipers throughout the week. In 1811 and 1812, for example, William Winans served on the Wilkinson Circuit, which covered the territory from the Amite to the Mississippi rivers. It required four weeks for him to make a round of his circuit; he preached at twenty-four meeting places, most of them private homes, to 118 members. In 1827 John G. Jones served on the Warren Circuit, which included Vicksburg; there was no church in that town and only one log church among his fifteen stations. Irregular or infrequent visits from ordained ministers encouraged lay participation. One evangelical, Lorenzo Dow Langford, recalled that he and a few other converts built a log church and "agreed to meet every other Sunday one of us would read a chapter in the Testament sing and Pray after which sing & call on another we would have about 3 prayers some . . . conversation and all go home." He noted: "It was not an uncommon thing for souls to be converted in night meetings in private houses."[29]

Rhys Isaac observed that evangelicals in eighteenth-century Virginia did not "compartmentalize" their religion. Instead, they broke with the convention that confined religious worship to a Sabbath church service and diffused religion throughout their daily lives. Their services were not limited to the Sabbath, they were not confined to the church, and many of them took place without a minister present. Strong personal bonds grew up among members of such congregations. Norvelle Robertson, Sr., who led his Baptist congregation from Georgia to Mississippi, recalled that when he first attended a Baptist service he felt "that love, of which I had never before had the most distant idea. And to me it proved contagious. Fortunately I felt my affections run out to that people, and from that time

I felt an anxious desire to become as they were, and to have a name and a place among them."[30]

Evangelical services contributed to the close communion among church members and encouraged lay participation. Methodist class meetings and love feasts were intimate gatherings of spiritual renewal. John Wesley began both practices; he stipulated "that it may be more easily discerned whether the members of our societies are working out their salvation, they are divided into little companies called classes." The classes, often segregated by gender, met weekly, and a lay leader took each member through a series of questions intended to reveal "how every soul of his class prospers: not only how each person observes the outward rules, but how he grows in the knowledge and love of God." Class meetings opened with hymns and prayer, after which the leader might give a short exhortation before examining the members. Each member rose and discussed his or her trials and tribulations, doubts and fears, or confidence of salvation, often causing the meetings to become very emotional. John G. Jones described such a class meeting: "A precious time it was—Both preacher and members shouted outright." Class meetings were often seen as a training ground for ministers because many young converts first spoke publicly in this setting and served as class leaders. Attendance was recorded, and failure to attend could result in dismission.[31]

Love feasts often accompanied Methodist quarterly conference meetings. These sacramental meetings began with songs and prayers interspersed with testimonials from members who felt moved to speak. Love feasts could also be very emotional, and shouts and tears were common. William Winans described an 1821 love feast at which "many spoke to the purpose particularly old Sister Hampton. She spoke with an eloquence wholly irresistible for she spoke from the heart in the strong language of feeling." In separate love feasts Winans conducted for black Methodists, the same emotional responses occurred. Love feasts were open only to church members in good standing, and the Methodist *Discipline* specified that members must have tickets for admission. Although this rule was not always enforced, especially in later years, Mississippi churches sometimes required tickets. A. C. Ramsey recalled an 1813 quarterly conference and love feast:

> More rigid care was exacted then than now, in admitting persons to this prudential means of grace. Tickets were issued to all who wished to partake, and against whom no objections were interposed. A sentinel was placed at the door, to guard against unacceptable persons, and receive tick-

ets. . . . Love feasts, Class meetings, and communion service were in those days and for a long time afterwards seasons of refreshing, of joy, of spiritual strength to the church and often produced convictions among the people of the world. People . . . regarded it a privilege, yea, a great privilege to testify to the truth of our holy christianity.[32]

Although the Presbyterians' services were much less emotionally demonstrative, their biannual communion season had some of the characteristics of the class meeting and love feast. As Ramsey suggests, the maintenance of discipline was important in such intimate meetings; as Rhys Isaac wrote, "Their strict code of conduct symbolized order, and the close groups for the sharing and confirmation of religious experience functioned as effective popular agencies for discipline." The maintenance of order among church members was a part of the Presbyterian communion. Communion season lasted from three to five days and included a day of fasting and prayer followed by preparatory sermons and examination of members. The following description of communion season at Bethany Presbyterian Church illustrates this aspect of the service:

> There was a custom in this old church, which prevailed in all the older Presbyterian churches—that of using the communion tokens—but it passed out of use in the forties. Many a time have I heard my grandmother tell of her interest, as the communion season drew near, and her father, then an officer in the Union Church—made ready for the molding of the tokens. These were of pewter or lead, and were molded by an elder. At each prepatory service the entire membership was gone over, and if any brother had been guilty of taking a wee drop too much, or a sister had said too much of another, in a slanderous way, that member was denied a "token" when he or she applied for it. On the Sabbath, as the members gathered at the long narrow tables, each one either held his token up or laid it beside him, and unless the serving elder saw the token he was not allowed to serve the elements to that brother or that sister, a most dread thing for the poor transgressor.

Though not usually as openly emotional as Baptist or Methodist services, the communion season was a time of soul-searching for Presbyterians, and it was an opportunity for the churches to acquire new members. Before Presbyterians abandoned camp meetings and revivals, such events were held during communion season.[33]

The Baptists' most intimate ceremony, common in the early decades of the nineteenth century, was the "washing of the saints' feet." In 1810 the Mississippi Baptist Association declared that ritual to be a "christian duty." In 1814 a skeptical Methodist minister recorded that a local Baptist church had recently conducted such a ceremony and added: "Indeed of late this practice appears to revive among this People which I do not think was . . . intended by our Lord." References to the practice appear frequently in the church records; for example, the records of Salem Baptist Church in 1819 reveal that "after due deliberation—Resolved that washing of feet be done at our Next Augt meeting in course and that it be adopted as a rule . . . Bro. John Wells Purchase for the Church a Wash Pan, & 2 Towels." In some churches the ceremony was held annually; in others it was a biannual event.[34]

The church records do not disclose the emotional intensity that such services could unleash, but just as the chanted sermon continues among some present-day Baptists of both races, the foot-washing ceremony remains a vital part of worship for some black and white southerners. Howard Dorgan's description of a contemporary service in a white Appalachian Baptist church suggests what the service was like in the early nineteenth century. Today, the service begins with singing—these churches usually continue the practice of lining out hymns—followed by communion. Basins, pitchers of water, and white towels were then brought forward. In this church, as in early Mississippi churches, members were segregated by gender; in the foot-washing service those who washed each other's feet were always of the same gender. Members of the congregation who wished to wash a fellow member's feet went to the front of the church, filled a basin with water, tied a towel around their waists, then walked to the recipient. The individual then kneeled, removed the recipient's shoes, and gently dipped one foot at a time into the basin, pouring water over each foot. After the person performing the ceremony dried the feet with the free end of the towel, both parties stood, embraced, and usually wept. Dorgan found the ceremony "unhurried, gentle, and very loving, the essence of the event being a reverent humility demonstrated through service to a fellow communicant." He added: "Almost everyone seemed to be crying, shouting, or singing." The celebration continued with "dinner on the grounds."[35]

An account from the 1980s of a black Baptist foot-washing ceremony held biannually by members of the Sipsey River Association in western Alabama and northeastern Mississippi reveals striking similarities to the white service described by Dorgan. The ceremony began with lining hymns interspersed with prayer, a process that blended prayer and song with the same musical rhythm. The next phase demonstrates how African Americans altered worship practices to suit their own spiritual needs. In a ritual known as "fellowshipping," participants formed a loose circle, joined hands, and moved in time to the music. Fellowshipping seems to be "the only adult form of the ring dance in . . . northeast Mississippi." Several chanted sermons, singing, and communion followed. White towels and basins of water were then brought forward, and individuals who wished to perform foot washings would tie towels around their waists. Men and women were seated separately, and those gender lines were not crossed. The actual process was the same as in the white church; the person knelt in front of the recipient, washed one foot at a time, then the two stood and embraced.[36]

The observer of the black ceremony noted that "during the washing ceremony about half of the female participants go into possession trance," which they referred to as "groaning." It usually began with the oldest women, then spread through the group. It was characterized by "movements including holding both hands up in the air and shaking them in opposition with the torso . . . facial expressions range from tortured to ecstatic." Women overcome by such emotion also "repeat short phrases such as 'I'm dying,' 'I feel so good,' 'Thank you, sir,' [or] 'I'm as free as I can be.' " The phrases were followed by cries, and the person might finally collapse. The practice has much in common with "shouting and praising" among white women in Appalachian Baptist churches. A woman so moved rises to her feet, "arms thrown high above her head, hands bent sharply back at the wrists, palms thrust toward heaven. . . . The body sways with forceful jerks; the head is forced backward in a neck-straining, eyes-toward-heaven position. . . . 'Praising' is generally accompanied by the same set of physical behaviors, but now one or two exclamatory phrases replace the shouts: 'Oh what a sweet Jesus we have!' or 'Oh children, I'm going home!' "[37]

Such emotional and deeply personal services were vital in the creation of the evangelical community. They helped nurture the recent converts and guide them in the faith and enabled older converts to renew their faith by frequent testimony of their own experiences. In meetings such as these, Christian brotherhood and sisterhood were forged and maintained. In all these services, the emphasis was on a shared religious experience among the laity.

The close bonds among evangelicals carried beyond the church doors and were part of a socioreligious system that attempted to address the insecurity and disorder so prevalent on the frontier and exacerbated by the expansion of the market revolution. Church members sometimes responded to financial crises among their membership, as in 1815, when the members of Sarepta Baptist Church raised funds to enable Jonathan Scarborough, a church deacon, to save his land from his creditors and the members of Galilee Baptist Church collected "subscriptions" for the relief of needy brothers and sisters. The members of Jerusalem Baptist Church considered such assistance so important that their 1822 covenant required members to contribute "to the relief of the poor in the church." Norvelle Robertson, Sr., led a group of fifteen members of a Georgia Baptist church who relocated to Mississippi and organized a new congregation. Along with preaching, Robertson operated a mill, and when crops failed one season, poor members of his congregation faced a desperate situation. A "well-to-do" member of the church offered to pay cash for corn and was offended when the preacher refused to sell to him. Robertson said: " 'Brother—you have the money and can buy corn wherever you can find it. There are many poor people about here who have neither corn nor money. They can't buy elsewhere, for lack of money . . . I must let them have all the corn I can spare, to keep them from starving.' " Robertson offered his poor members more than just spiritual food even though they could not pay.[38]

The intensely emotional services and the intimate involvement in each others' lives contributed to the emergence of close-knit religious communities like Robertson's group. Although the great majority of frontier residents remained outside the churches, evangelicalism helped shape the character of communities dominated by the faithful. Henry J. Harris, who later became a Methodist preacher, was irreligious in his youth but wanted to open a school with a friend. He and his friend moved to a religious community in Smith County to pursue their goal, but his friend warned him that "the community to which we are going are all Methodists. You are guilty of vices they will not tolerate. They will not patronize you as a teacher of their children, nor even allow you to associate with their families if you persist in your habits." After boarding with a pious family, Harris was drawn into their fellowship and underwent a dramatic conversion.[39] Evangelicals attempted to create a communal unity unheardof on the frontier, to exert some control over the market, limit acquisitiveness and frivolous indulgence, and suppress individual aberration and self-assertion by focusing on the next world.

Poor men like Norvelle Robertson and Henry Harris were attracted by the close communion among evangelicals and saw in the movement an opportunity to acquire a "name and a place" not dependent on wealth, education, or social status. The evangelicals did make wealthy converts in these early years, but members of the elite were less interested in such services than the plain folk. Daniel de Vinne, a Methodist preacher, encountered this problem among his congregations: "Pride & love of the world take such a hold on some men," he wrote, "that they cannot serve the Lord. . . . There are a good many of what the world calls the better sort of people in society on this circuit. And oh how hardly shall they that are rich enter into the kingdom of heaven!" De Vinne did not consider the wealthy the "better class"; instead, he thought that "riches and worldly honours are so unfriendly to taking up the cross daily and following a lowly Savior." His wealthy members refused to participate in many religious activities: "In some of the wealthy societies I cannot get class leaders, I cannot get the members to pray in their families . . . love of gold! how many does it send to hell," he lamented. The strength of the evangelicals did not lie with the wealthy, but, as de Vinne wrote, "Bless the Lord, this [is] not the case [in] all the societies, nor a majority of them. . . . Among the moderately poor we can [get] class leaders, exhorters, and various helpers to carry on the work." Despite the occasional convert among the gentry, the real strength of the evangelicals continued to lie with the "moderately poor," as de Vinne described them, and the dangers of the things of the world continued to be a refrain among them. As one hymn assured evangelical converts, "Religion is a Fortune."[40]

The moderately poor were alienated from the prevailing social values, but through evangelicalism they defined a new popular culture. The wider implications inherent in this process of democratization are illustrated in an example provided by Jacob Young from 1807 or 1808. The first speaker to preach at a camp meeting he described was James Axley, who was considered very capable by his peers despite his humble origins. He was brought up in the wilderness and was an experienced hunter and woodsman. He had just returned to Mississippi after a missionary trip to the Louisiana frontier, where he had built a log church with his own hands. The hardships of the wilderness had taken their toll: "When he went to Louisiana he was a large, fine-looking man, but his flesh had since fallen off. . . . His clothes were worn out, and when he saw his brethren he could not talk for weeping." No doubt many of the people attending the meeting were hardworking frontier residents like Axley, but others were not. Young reported: "The congregation was unusually large for that country, and some of them splendidly dressed." Axley made luxury and finery the theme of his message and "declaimed earnestly against superfluous ornaments, and the passions, pride and vanity which occasion them." Some of his wealthy listeners were greatly offended: "There was a Madame Turnbull in the congregation with a gay daughter. Brother Axley perceived, by her movements with her servants, that she was offended, and about leaving the camp-ground." Axley attempted to persuade her not to leave. "He followed her to her carriage, made some apologies and invited her to come back the next day."[41] One wonders why Axley was so solicitous of Mrs. Turnbull. Did he hope to convert her? Did he fear to offend her? Or did she and her "gay daughter" provide a visible foil for his message?

His motives are intriguing because he continued the same message the following day. Once again, "the congregation was large, and made a splendid appearance." And "Madame Turnbull according to promise was there with her husband." They listened as Axley enlarged on "his favorite theme, the pride and vain-glory of the people of that territory." But "suddenly, Esq. Turnbull rose and told him to stop till he should speak a few words." Young, in an attempt to stop the esquire, "left the stand . . . and ordered him, in a commanding tone of voice, to take his seat, informing him that the meeting was not appointed for him to preach." The esquire "made a low bow and sat down, but before I reached my seat, was up again, hallooing at the top of his voice, 'Mr. Preacher, Mr. Preacher, stop and let me speak a few words.'" Young "went to him the second time, and pushing him off the seat, commanded him to be silent." But the esquire had succeeded in disrupting the meeting: "As I looked toward the stand I saw the preacher [Axley] was crying and the congregation in the utmost confusion. The Esquire was soon up again crying, 'Esquire Lewis, Esquire Lewis, assist here to take this man out of the pulpit—he is insulting the congregation.'" Lewis did not respond, but Axley "stepped back and sat down weeping."[42]

The meeting was saved from disaster by Lorenzo Dow, who was lying sick in a nearby tent but took the pulpit to quell the disturbance. It was a familiar role for Dow, who had "outwitted the rowdies on all occasions, so that they became afraid of him." Young believed that "many of them thought he was more than mortal." His actions were dramatic:

After standing and looking the people over a few moments, he ordered them, with authority, to hush and take their seats. In less than five minutes they were all quiet, and he began to talk about the American Revolution. This led him to take a summary view of the British colonies, in North America, their first settlements and their long prosperity. He then touched handsomely on the relation between the colonies and the mother country. This led him to explain what gave rise to the American Revolution. He then gave us a concise history of the war and its final termination showing at the same time, what we had gained by the Revolution, saying

> we were now the happiest people on the globe. Here he became animated, enlarging upon our civil and religious liberty. He proceeded to remark that when God confers great privileges on a nation, he holds her responsible for all she enjoys, and that where great privileges are abused sometimes they are turned into the heaviest curses. He stated many facts to show that we were abusing the Divine favor. . . . He described the prerogatives and duties of all officers, from the President down to the justice of the peace.

Here Dow must have been referring to Turnbull because "esquire" was a title traditionally given to justices.

> Turning to the Methodist Church, he showed what it had done for the United States. He showed the wonderful doings of Methodist preachers, their lives and sacrifices; that they were good citizens, always prompt to obey the laws of the land . . . and that any man who would interrupt a Methodist preacher while in the discharge of duty in his high office, was a mean, low-lived scoundrel, and that any Esquire that would do so was a perjured villain. He repeated the oath of office, and then referred to the circumstances that had just taken place before their eyes, and asked what was their prospect in the Mississippi territory, while they kept perjured villains in office. The angry Esquire did'nt say, "Mr. Preacher, stop;" but sat with his head down, took his family and left, saying, as he walked slowly along, "I always was a fool, and I would not, for five hundred dollars, have come to this place today." Suffice it to say the meeting closed well.[43]

This contest between evangelicals and a prominent esquire encapsulates many of the major themes of the conflict between the plain folk and the pillared folk. It was clearly a contest of power. Apparently, Turnbull was accustomed to giving orders and having them obeyed, and some evangelicals were not accustomed to questioning an esquire's authority.[44]

Winans and others did challenge their socially superior opponents; as the example from the camp meeting shows, evangelicals exercised authority in certain settings ("the meeting was not appointed for him [the esquire] to preach"). The evangelicals' response reveals the power they felt and the significance of speaking in that setting: "I . . . ordered him, in a commanding tone of voice," and again, "I . . . commanded him to be silent." Dow, too, "ordered them, with authority, to hush."

Once Dow restored order, he did not preach a typical sermon; indeed, he made no appeal to Scripture. Instead, he legitimized himself and his fellows and discredited the esquire by appealing to the patriotism of his listeners and by linking evangelicalism to the revolutionary quest for virtue. Others besides the evangelicals noted the link between the movement and democracy; the *Natchez Messenger* observed that both Christianity and democracy "acknowledge no distinction between men but that which arises from their virtues." Historian Jon Butler wrote, "Republican principles had enormous importance for American religion because, though they were often vague and elusive, they placed great authority in the . . . laypeople." The areas of greatest evangelical strength opposed the political domination of Natchez and the river counties. The split was obvious in the 1817 constitutional convention at which representatives of the dominant river counties enacted one of the least liberal constitutions in the region; it restricted the franchise to white males who paid taxes or served in the militia and required state legislators and the governor to own considerable property. Delegates from the eastern counties were able to block even more conservative measures, and these counties pressed for a new convention to liberalize the document. As the number of evangelicals increased, politicians sought their support. Winans noted that politicians courted ministers because of their "extensive influence among the people," and politicians often attended camp meetings to canvass voters, hoping to win the support of those evangelicals who were able to vote.[45]

Evangelicalism brought a sense of empowerment to a previously despised group—the plain folk who led the movement and made up the great majority of its members. As Donald Mathews has observed, evangelicalism can be thought of as a force, a term that conveys something of the energy of the movement. In the words of Joseph Campbell, "What we are discussing here is not what men have thought of others, but the force of their convictions based on experiences of their own; and this we may well call faith—in Ortega y Gasset's sense of the term, 'individual faith,' in contrast to 'collective': not faith in what one has been told to believe, or in what, for the earning of money, political office, or fame, it may be thought propitious to believe, but faith in one's own experience, whether of feeling, fact, reason, or vision."[46]

Evangelicalism gave many converts a sense of personal empowerment, a faith in their own convictions, and a mission. That mission could have political implications; men like Dow wedded evangelicalism to the idea of republican virtue—the conversion of sinners would redeem communities and ultimately the entire nation. Its social implications were equally important; evangelicals challenged traditional patterns of deference and called into question the very foundations of the social system. By bringing blacks into the fold, evangelicals created a sacred space within which a remarkable and lasting cultural exchange took place. For them, wealth, social position, education, and the trappings of an elite culture became symbols of all that was wrong with their society, stumbling blocks on the road to salvation. In the sight of God there was no respect of persons, and indeed the righteous poor were far more blessed than the unholy rich.

CHAPTER 3

A CHRISTIAN SISTERHOOD
WHITE WOMEN AND THE EVANGELICAL
EXPERIENCE

E VANGELICALS often attacked the traditional hierarchical structure of their society, but the weapon they chose—the doctrine of Christian equality—was in one sense a double-edged sword, for while it struck effectively at hierarchy, it implicitly undercut patriarchy as well. Evangelicals were unwilling to pursue the doctrine of the equality of all believers to its logical conclusions, but in the early years of the movement women played a vital and active role in the churches' work. Mary Douglas suggested that those groups removed from the locus of power and authority in their society—blacks and women in the Old South, for example—could be expected to express that marginality through religious worship. As feminist scholars have demonstrated, hierarchy and patriarchy have gone hand in hand and together have resulted "in a whole series of unequal power relations; God as father rules over the world, holy fathers rule over the church, clergy fathers over laity, males over females, husbands over wives and children, men over the created world."[1] Women responded enthusiastically to the evangelical message of equality and challenged, with some success, their traditional role in worship. The emotional temper of their religious worship was a direct outgrowth of the controls and repression they experienced in their daily lives.

Despite women's enthusiastic response to evangelicalism, their role in the churches, and their significant contributions to the movement's success, historians have not adequately examined the question of gender in southern churches. Elizabeth Fox-Genovese acknowledged the importance of religion in the lives of southern women, but because work on the topic "remains sparse," she largely ignored the role of religion, a decision with important consequences for her study. She argued, for example, that unlike northern women, southern women did not inhabit a separate sphere, and they lacked the rich associative life of northern women out of which the northern feminist movement grew. Her major point—that the South is not New England, and southern women did not have the same historical experiences—is well taken, and a careful consideration of southern women's religious life would not have led her to different conclusions. And yet women's religious associations were plentiful. That these affiliations did not lead southern women down the same path their northern sisters took is clear, but to ignore the rich and often separate religious sphere of southern women certainly reduces the argument and the grounds for comparison between southern women and their northern sisters. Donald Mathews has shown a greater appreciation of the importance of women in southern churches; indeed, he suggested that "women made southern Evangelicalism possible."[2]

Evangelicalism had special appeal for women; the antiritualism of the evangelical movement allowed them to assert themselves in new ways and to stake their claim in this newly created sacred space. Frontier conditions encouraged this challenge, and although the movement did not originate on the frontier, certainly the Great Revival that blazed forth from Kentucky in 1801–2 defined the movement. Mary Douglas has suggested that antiritualism is not a revolt against an overly structured society but rather a movement possible only in a society in flux, where institutions, hierarchical structures, and social controls are weak. She also theorized that emotionally demonstrative religious responses are likely to occur among "people who are peripheral to the central focus of power and authority." Women fit this category, she continued, because their social responsibilities are more confined, they are excluded from the central institutions of their society, and their social place is determined largely in relation to their husbands or fathers.[3] As seen in chapter 1, the youthful, dispersed, and highly mobile population of frontier Mississippi was engulfed in dramatic economic and social change, a perfect breeding ground for a movement such as Douglas described.

Women clearly viewed immigration to the Southwest differently than their husbands did. They expressed concerns about separation from family and health conditions on the frontier, whereas men were more likely to concentrate on economic opportunities. Life was difficult for everyone on the Mississippi frontier, and among the plain folk—the great majority of frontier settlers and the backbone of the evangelical movement—women labored alongside their husbands in the fields in addition to their many other duties. As Fox-Genovese emphasized, the South's staple agricultural economy centered in scattered households helped shape women's experience. When women complained, it was not of the hard work but of the

Table 1. Mississippi Population (in thousands) by Sex
and per Square Mile, 1800–1830

Year	Total	Per square mile	Female	Male
1830	137	2.1	65	72
1820	75	1.6	35	40
1810	31	0.4	13	10
1800	8	0.3	2	5

Source: U.S. Department of Commerce, Bureau of the Census,
Historical Statistics of the United States: Colonial Times to
1970 (Washington, D.C., 1975), 30.

loneliness and isolation, the separation from kin and connections, a separation that was reinforced by the economic structure and its concomitant settlement pattern. From its initial settlement until 1830, Mississippi remained one of the most rural states in the Old Southwest with a population widely dispersed even by southern standards (see Tables 1 and 2). As one young woman described her situation, "I am sad to night, sickness preys in my frame I am a lone & more than 150 miles from any near relatives in the wild woods of an indian nation, a stranger & unknown sitting in a low roofed cabbin by a little fire." Another young woman, Mary M. Perkins, wrote despairingly to her cousin, Elizabeth L. Winston (whom she addressed as "Dear sister Louisa"), "What are we to do? no matter how we were situated, if we were to be separated from our family we could not be happy . . . it appears to me, I am cut off from every enjoyment that I used to take delight in. Do you *ever* go to preaching? I have never heard a sermon since I left Columbus—Think of our class meetings and sometimes how reluctantly we used to attend them."[4]

Such women responded enthusiastically to the evangelical message; indeed, for many frontier women religious services were the only respite from their labors and isolation. Cut off from their blood relatives, women found succor and support from their brothers—and especially sisters— in Christ. Peggy Dow's experience mirrored that of many others; she moved with her famous husband, Lorenzo, to the Mississippi wilderness in the early 1800s. She called herself "a stranger, in a strange land," and found their tiny, isolated log cabin in the midst of a canebrake "such a lonely place." Her dynamic husband was frequently away, and only religious services broke her routine: "I seldom went out but to meeting— there I found most peace and consolation." Women's joyful acceptance of

Table 2. Residents (in thousands) per Square Mile in the
Old Southwest, 1800–1830

Year	Alabama	Louisiana	Tennessee
1830	6.0	4.8	16.4
1820	2.5	3.4	10.1
1810	–	2.2	6.3
1800	–	–	2.5

Source: U.S. Department of Commerce, Bureau of the Census,
*Historical Statistics of the United States: Colonial Times to
1970* (Washington, D.C., 1975), 24, 28, 35.

the evangelical message offered a prospect for wider social participation,
and the movement's antiritualism offered the possibility for new roles and
real power for them within evangelical churches.[5]

The women's response was so great that they composed a majority in
evangelical churches; the evangelical success cannot be understood without recognizing this basic fact. A few examples will illustrate the pattern
in Mississippi, which was much the same across the South. The record
book of the First Presbyterian Church of Natchez reveals that from 1817
to 1825 the church had 86 white members, 58 females and 28 males; from
1826 to 1836 the figures stood at 105 females and 45 males. Some churches
had a smaller female majority; for example, Bethany Baptist Church in
Lawrence County was organized in 1819 by 8 white men and 10 white
women; by 1843 there were 71 white men and 75 white women in the
church. One religious newspaper estimated that the number of women in
the churches was double or quadruple the number of men. But whether
in small or large numbers, women enjoyed a majority in the typical evangelical church. The female majority is even more significant because they
were a minority of the state's population (see Table 1).[6]

So great was the disparity in religious interest between the sexes that
occasionally only women attended religious services, and there are scattered examples of Mississippi churches organized entirely by women. The
Reverend Elijah Steele, an early Methodist itinerant, wrote in his journal: "I came, according to appointment, to Shiloh church, and found but
two hearers, (both sisters.) I read the 19th Psalm, and made some practical remarks, and felt that God's presence was not entirely confined to
great assemblies, but he condescends to meet with two or three." Steele
noted that the young Shiloh church had only three members, all women.

A. C. Ramsey, another Methodist itinerant in the Piney Woods section of southeastern Mississippi, described in his journal one weekday religious service in which "the congregation consisted of one white woman and one black woman." Ramsey was determined "to do the best I could for the white sister and the colored one." He preached from the text " 'Where two or three are gathered together in My name, there I will be in the midst.' " In 1832 nine women organized the Unity Presbyterian Church in Amite County and signed the church's charter. It is significant that although some of the women were married, all of them signed their own names and did not use their husbands' (for example, Margaret M. Crawford, not Mrs. Van Tramp Crawford). Nevertheless, the Presbyterian church's patriarchal structure required the Unity women to appoint a temporary male elder from a nearby church until men joined later in the year.[7]

The ideal of Christian equality did not extend to the ordination of women, and they were barred from the pulpit. Despite these restrictions, women publicly exercised a wide variety of "gifts." Many employed the gift of song and thereby acquired their first major liturgical role in worship services. The recollections of Sarah Knox Sager of Port Gibson demonstrate how female singers could find great satisfaction through their gift of song and how that gift could be employed as ministry: "I was always a favorite with ministers—probably because from the time I was *nine* years old I *sung* myself into their hearts. As far back almost as I can remember I was called upon to 'raise the tune' when ministers came round . . . it was always a great happiness to me—give the services of my voice in singing when desired—especially was it joy to comfort the sick and dying."[8]

Public prayer was another gift frequently employed by women. These long, emotionally charged prayers often had as much impact as a sermon. Hannah Swayze, the daughter of Samuel Swayze, the first Protestant minister in the territory, was noted for her religious zeal. After the death of her first husband, she wed Richard Curtis, Sr., another early minister. She joined the Methodist church under the influence of the preaching of Tobias Gibson in the 1770s. "She was a wise and safe counselor in religious matters, but her greatest excellence, perhaps, was in the eloquence and power of her public prayers . . . she seemed to have 'power with God and with men' in her approaches to the throne of grace." Her daughter Hannah Coleman Griffing "was also greatly gifted in extemporaneous prayer, and was often called on in the social meetings of the membership to exercise her gifts." Jane Oliphant Jones, wife of Methodist preacher John G. Jones, led in "extraordinary prayers of faith and power for which she was noted in revival meetings." Martha Thompson Hoover, also the wife of a Methodist preacher, was gifted in prayer, and it was said that "her prayers contain more theology than some preachers' sermons." As these examples suggest, through the exercise of such gifts women exerted considerable power and influence in services. One Methodist answered critics of such active involvement by women: "We see in this, as in other similar manifestations, that God's ways are not as our ways and that He . . . has chosen the weak things of the world to confound the mighty."[9]

The evangelical emphasis on the equality of believers and their view that any members could exercise whatever gifts God bestowed on them made it possible for women to take an active, forceful role in evangelical services. With their public speeches and prayers, women sometimes moved a camp meeting crowd when prominent male preachers could not. Elizabeth Hannah Osteen, the daughter of an early Baptist preacher in the territory, was well-known for her piety; "She was, in every true sense of the expression, one of the most influential and useful female members of the Church. . . . She often succeeded where others seemed to fail." At one camp meeting the preachers received a cold reception from the crowd until the presiding elder, Benjamin Drake, "proposed an open-air experience meeting." Even that failed to move the crowd until "Elizabeth Osteen arose and began to rehearse in glowing terms what wonderful things the Lord had done for her. She became inspired with the Spirit of God, and, turning to the congregation, gave a powerful impromptu exhortation, called for mourners, and soon had the altar crowded."[10] By addressing the crowd, Osteen adopted the role of preacher at the meeting (though under the guise of testifying and outside the preachers' stand) and did it with great success.

Although Hannah Swayze Curtis, Hannah Griffing, and Elizabeth Osteen successfully exercised their gifts in public, other women aroused controversy and opposition. One of the best-known religiously active women in early Mississippi was Hannah Miller, whose sister Peggy was the wife of Lorenzo Dow. Hannah's husband, Smith Miller, was an abusive alcoholic who was unable to support his family. The Millers moved from Massachusetts to New York, where they operated a tavern. Peggy lived with them, and there she met and married Dow. Hannah joined the Baptist church but left it because of her husband's opposition. She wanted to join the Methodist church in New York, but again he would not allow it. Hannah "was very industrious, and strove hard to live; but he [Miller] was negligent, and often spent more than he made." Miller lost the business and squandered whatever money came his way. Hannah supported them by sewing and other odd jobs. Perhaps her financial contribution gave her a feeling of independence, or perhaps Miller saw his new brother-in-law as a means of financial salvation and hoped to curry his favor, but in any event Hannah finally overcame her husband's opposition and joined the Methodist church in New York. Encouraged by favorable reports from Dow, the Millers moved to the Mississippi Territory and built a mill, an enterprise that put them in considerable debt.[11]

Hannah quickly became well-known among evangelicals. One Methodist minister wrote, "Such was the zeal[,] gifts & abilities of Millers wife that she attracted the attention of the people as much as any preacher in the Territory where she was known." Peggy Dow recalled, "My sister was very much respected by the people, both religious & irreligious. . . . She was possessed of good natural abilities, and considerable acquired knowledge." For about two years her fame spread in the territory.[12]

Unfortunately, Hannah's marital problems increased; her husband's drinking continued, and their business failed. After twenty years in an unhappy marriage, Hannah had an affair and fled with her lover to the "Spanish country." She was quickly condemned by her neighbors. Her frantic husband went for her, but she refused to return. One minister wrote that her flight "caused persecution to pour like a flood against the Methodist & greatly impeded the progress of religion." Male ministers were involved in similar sexual scandals, but there was no suggestion that they resulted in a general condemnation of the evangelicals.[13] Many people probably saw Hannah Miller's tragic case as evidence that women should not be allowed to step out of their traditional role.

Some women avoided criticism by working most closely with other women. William Winans described a camp meeting service in 1811 at which men and women were segregated and women conducted separate services:

We had a Camp-meeting, on Clark's Creek, near Dow's and Baker's Mill. I thought the preaching far better, and more calculated to do good, than is usual. Still, up to Sunday-night, it seemed as if little, if any, was accomplished. This excited much concern among both the preachers and lay-Christians on the ground. Moved by this concern, nearly every professing Christian of both sexes, retired, about sunset, into the adjoining forest, to wrestle with God in prayer for a blessing on the meeting. The struggle was long and generally earnest. At length, before it was quite dark, we, on the men's side of the encampment, heard a loud, and, as we thought, an alarmed outcry on the side of the encampment to which the ladies had retired. As we had, in the course of the meeting, been considerably annoyed by disorderly persons . . . our first impression was that some of these maruders had trespassed upon the ladies' retirement. We, consequently, sprang from our knees, and ran in the direction of the thrilling cries. . . . Our course lay immediately through the encampment. On entering this, we discovered our error. Instead of having been asailed by rowdies, the Sisters had received such an answer to their prayers, both for themselves and for others in whom they took special interest, that they shouted for joy; while their unconverted proteges, cut to the heart, were crying, in anguish of Spirit, for "the mercy of the Lord Jesus Christ. . . ." We met them as they entered the Campground, to "rejoice with those who did rejoice, and to weep with those that wept." The exercises of this extraordinary sort of meeting continued a great part of the night, during which twenty-five professed to be "justified by faith" and to "have peace with God." [14]

Again, the work of women led to a successful camp meeting. As Winans's account makes clear, women and men sometimes met separately at the meetings; indeed, they were quartered apart and came together only for meals and joint services. Gender segregation was common among the early evangelicals. In sharp contrast to the family pews of the colonial churches, where seating depended on social rank, evangelical men and women sat on different sides of the church (traditionally men sat on the right, women on the left). Many early churches had separate entrances for men and women. By breaking down the household unit within the church doors, evangelicals encouraged members to think of one another as brothers and sisters in Christ, and some churches in their rules of decorum even required members to call one another "Brother" and "Sister." [15] The idea of sisterhood, then, had an important meaning among evangelical women, and through seating arrangements, separate services, and terms of address, women occupied a separate sphere and were encouraged to think of themselves as a group.

Early preachers appreciated the vital role of women in the success of the evangelical movement. A. C. Ramsey recalled that in the 1820s and 1830s "the good sisters . . . were not only help mates, in these great religious efforts of moral and religious reform, but were in great measure the more active and successful agents in the accomplishment of the great good effected." He saw a part of their contribution in their accepted role as nurturers, mothers, nurses, and teachers but believed that their most important work was "in instructing, advising, encouraging and praying for the sin sick, and broken hearted; and by their many joyful shouts of praise to God . . . giving unmistakable evidence that they had been with Jesus." Although much of their work was done privately among friends and family, he also noted their public efforts, especially at the camp meetings, where they were responsible for many conversions. John G. Jones described the women of Kingston Methodist Church as "a happy Christian sisterhood" who "not unfrequently in their meetings for social worship . . . would indulge their rapturous emotions in loud and appropriate language." Evangelical hymns celebrated this active role for women; for example, the hymn "Holy Manna" contained the following verse:

Sisters, will you join and help us?
Moses' sisters aided him;
Will you help the trembling mourners,
Who are struggling hard with sin?
Tell them all about the Savior,
Tell them that he will be found;
Sisters, pray, and holy manna
Will be shower'd all around.[16]

Bodily symbolism was an important aspect of the emotional camp meetings. Mary Douglas wrote that because of their social experience, women were more likely to express their spiritual independence through an abandonment of control. John G. Jones described the "jerks," when converts' limbs jerked involuntarily and "their heads would . . . fly back and forward so quickly that the hair of females would be made to crack like a carriage whip." Next to exercises such as this, the more common shouting, weeping, and clapping seemed tame. One religious newspaper explained the greater emotionalism among women as a result of natural differences: "Women are naturally more warm hearted and enthusiastic than men, more easily excited, and give way to their feelings with less restraint." But such displays represented more than simple emotion; through these exercises women symbolically attacked the social system that attempted to keep them in check.[17]

The revolutionary potential of the concept of Christian equality and women's claim to a public role in worship sometimes led husbands to oppose their wives' conversion, as Hannah Miller's husband did. Husbands understood what Carroll Smith-Rosenberg has expressed in more sophisticated terms: "The denigration of hierarchical structure, the assertion of individual autonomy against the primacy of community and familial norms mirrored their particularly female experience of suppression under patriarchy. . . . A vision of new power and autonomy danced before them, held out and authorized, if only momentarily, by their male spiritual leaders." Hannah Miller may have struck out against community and familial norms, but other women retreated under pressure from their families. A Mr. Joor, a candidate for political office, attended a camp meeting with his wife and children hoping to gain evangelical support. "But, when his wife and children joined the Church, he obtained from the meeting more than he bargained for." William Winans, who preached at the meeting, recalled that Joor "requested me promptly not to recognize his children as members, and never rested till he induced his wife to withdraw her application for membership." In a similar vein, Samuel Sellers described a family riven by religious differences; after a young girl joined the Methodists, her father "treated her very cooly which rendered her situation disagreeable." "The Family," he continued, "at least the Female part of it is very Friendly disposed toward religion." He concluded, "I am truely sorry for some girls[;] I believe they wish to be Religious but are violently opposed by their Relatives." The most extreme example of violent opposition occurred in Vicksburg when an angry husband shot and killed the Reverend P. E. Green, the minister who converted his wife.[18]

Some families were clearly disturbed by the rebellious nature of the early evangelicals and the shocking bodily exercises common to female converts. Sarah Humphreys, the daughter of wealthy parents, joined the Methodist church in 1821, when she was nineteen years old. Her parents had exposed her to religion "as part of her education, and as one means of introducing her into society . . . but it was by no means the wish of her father's household that she should enter the Church." When young Sarah entered the fellowship, she chose to follow the strict evangelical code of behavior and dress, which was alien to her affluent family and friends. She gave up "worldly amusements" and "gewgaws of dress." Her friends and family viewed her decision as "an unexplained mystery."[19] For many women the decision was a deeply personal one, a statment of autonomy, and, for some, an act of rebellion.

As more and more women made that decision, their growing numbers gave them power within the churches. Although the churches did not ordain women or allow them to hold offices, many did allow women to vote in church conferences. This process can be followed most closely in the Baptist churches, though evidence suggests that women probably voted in some Methodist churches as well. In the Presbyterian churches, however, such authority was vested in the all-male presbytery. Most Baptist churches included in their rules of order a statement such as the following: "The government [of the church] is with the body of the church and is equally the right and privilege of each member thereof." Some church records suggest that attendance at the monthly conference meetings where business was conducted was more important for male than for female members. East Fork Baptist Church rules specified, for example, that men who missed one conference would be called upon to explain that absence, but women could miss three conferences before an explanation was required. Many women took their responsibility seriously. Mary Carter, who joined the Baptist church in 1825, remained a faithful member until her death in 1860 at the age of eighty-four. Her obituary in the church records (unusual in itself and a mark of her standing in the church) noted that "she was remarkable for her constant attention to all her church privileges & duties always filling her seat in Conference, Church and prayer meeting."[20]

Women could not take these rights for granted and sometimes had to struggle to protect them. The Sarepta Baptist Church covenant of 1810 clearly stated, "The Sisters shall be entitled to all the privileges of the male members in the church." But five years later the following amendment was enacted: "The subject of the sisters duty in the church considered we consider it their duty to learn of the Apostle [Paul] not to speak in the church nor usurp authority." Unfortunately, the sparse, matter-of-fact records do not reveal what provoked the change or the women's immediate response to it, but in 1834 the amendment was revoked: "Resolved that the rule making it the duty of sisters not to speak in the church be reversed and read thus 'They shall be entitled to all the privileges of the male members in the church.'"[21]

Women's struggles to join the churches and to retain their rights and privileges reinforced the idea of sisterhood and created an awareness that led naturally to separate women's religious organizations. Although some scholars have suggested that the associative movement was weak among southern women, in Mississippi they had a rich associative life that began early in the state's history. In 1816 a group of ninety well-connected Protestant women in Natchez organized the Female Charitable Society to support a charity school and maintain needy orphans and widows. Here the Natchez women followed the same pattern as other southern town women; Suzanne Lebsock found that Virginia women organized societies to care for orphans at about the same time. The women raised several hundred dollars annually to operate a school and care for needy orphans and also invested funds in bank stocks. They decided to build an orphanage, and to maintain "complete control" over it, they sought and received incorporation from the state legislature in 1819. In 1821 they opened the orphanage and successfully maintained it by contributions from all Protestant groups in the city.[22]

The women engaged in an almost constant effort to keep the orphanage on a firm financial footing. In 1820 they wrote, "While we continue then to ask the boon of charity, let none be weary of our solicitation." In 1825 they appealed to the state for financial assistance; their petition read in part: "For nearly nine years they have struggled with various difficulties & distress—they have begged & borrowed—bought & sold, & their sole object has been . . . to protect, sustain, & instruct the helpless & homeless orphan." Indeed, they had worked diligently to care for forty-nine orphans, and though the legislature approved an annuity of $500, apparently it was never paid. The asylum received occasional grants from the state and later the proceeds of a tax on billiard tables, but most revenue came from private sources. By the 1850s the women had raised almost $20,000 to construct a new orphanage, and they continued to operate the institution until after the Civil War. Women lost control of some benevolent enterprises in other parts of the South in the 1850s, but the Natchez women did not. As one minister noted in 1855: "The most interesting fact connected with the Institution, is that, it was originally established and has always been conducted by the ladies of Natchez. It is strictly and emphatically their enterprise. . . . The Orphan Asylum has been handed down from mother to daughter through three generations of the females of Natchez."[23]

In these early years Natchez was the state's most populous, most cosmopolitan, and wealthiest town, but women's religious groups also appeared in smaller towns and hamlets across the state. In 1820 a women's prayer meeting began in the nearby town of Washington. The Methodist minister there exulted, "We have a female prayer meeting established in Washington—may Zion travail [prevail?]." William Winans mentioned similar Methodist organizations in the 1820s, and they were well established by the 1830s. Women's societies were among the largest donors to the state Methodist Conference. To cite one typical example, the Female Sewing Society of Natchez and Washington "sent, as usual, a box of clothing, with eighty-one dollars in money, to be distributed among the most necessitous preachers. The presiding elders were the committee of distribution, and returned warmest thanks to the kind donors." A poem called "The Sewing Society" praised such efforts:

> Come, sisters, come, as we sit and sew,
> Let us try how fast our needles can go;

Not a single moment of time we'll waste;
Then onward sisters, haste ye, haste,
A blessing is with our work.[24]

Apparently the earliest women's groups among the Baptists were missionary societies. In 1816 the Baptist Board of Foreign Missions sent a missionary, James A. Ranaldson of Massachusetts, to the Mississippi Territory; Luther Rice, the board's founder, stressed the importance of women's groups, and female mission societies soon appeared. In 1822 Baptist women organized the Ladies Charitable Mission Society, an auxiliary to the Mississippi Baptist Missionary and Education Society. The society's constitution stated, "The Gospel . . . has laid our sex under a peculiar tribute of praise and gratitude." Membership was open to "any female who wishes to do good . . . by subscribing to the constitution, and paying annually in advance, in money, or in articles of clothing, or even in superfluous ornaments, to any amount within the compass of her circumstances, as the suitable expression of her degree of charity." Local groups sprang up across the state and actively raised funds. When the second Mississippi Baptist State Convention met in 1824, "the Ladies' Mission Society of Woodville . . . was respectfully acknowledged as auxilliary of the Convention." The treasurer's report showed a donation of $35.56 from this group and a $30.00 donation from the Ladies Society of Feliciana; these were the two largest donations made to the convention. Later reports from the convention noted donations from groups such as the Females of Palestine Church, the Baptist Missionary Society of Brandon, and societies in the many female denominational colleges. Their fund-raising events became a regular part of the activities in towns and hamlets across the state. For example, the women of the Jackson Baptist Church held a fair at the city hall to raise funds to repair the church, an event that brought in an impressive $590. Such organizations played a vital role in church life. In 1832 a Baptist church was organized in Columbus; the minister and his wife, John and Pamelia Armstrong, "organized a Female Society almost immediately and it became one of the most vital and vigorous forces in that great historic church." By the late 1830s the religious women of Columbus "maintained three Sunday Schools, three ladies' sewing societies, a Bible society, a foreign mission society, and a temperance society."[25]

Presbyterian women were also active; they were important in the Natchez Female Charitable Society, and in 1829 Presbyterians in Port Gibson organized the Ladies Benevolent Society. Such organizations were common in Presbyterian churches throughout the antebellum period.[26]

The Natchez Charitable Society, with its school and orphanage, was perhaps the most ambitious, but other groups from all denominations helped furnish local churches, contributed sizable amounts of money to their churches and missionary societies, and bought or built parsonages.

An example from Port Gibson shows how important the women's contributions could be to the church. Women there proposed to secure a parsonage; they "closed a bargain with Dr. Martin giving him $2500.00 for his residence." They paid the doctor over $1,000 in cash and expected to raise several hundred more "by their own exertions (by sewing & suppers) . . . they will have to borrow the balance $1,000.00 and mortgage the property for its security." The women's past success at fund-raising endangered their efforts by creating competition: "The ladies have averaged more than that for two years past, but seeing how successful they had been the ladies of the other chs [churches] organized, and have been dividing the patronage of the public with us, wh. [which] will greatly lessen our receipts." The women of the Yazoo City Methodist Church also purchased a parsonage before the Civil War, and one minister wrote that the women "manage the finances of the church." In churches across Mississippi women banded together in a variety of organizations. These organizations and their contributions are often ignored in the local church records, but they played a vital role both in the churches and in the lives of southern women. As Mathews wrote, "These organizations would become, with the churches, the focal point of social activities for women in the South."[27]

The extent to which emerging bourgeois ideals of a proper women's sphere influenced the lives of southern women has been the subject of scholarly debate. Elizabeth Fox-Genovese argued that the southern household economy differed so radically from the capitalist economy of the Northeast that "bourgeois social relations did not reign and did not dominate southern thought and feeling." And yet "Southerners participated in the unfolding bourgeois culture, including the ideologies of spheres, motherhood, and domesticity, but they interpreted and applied those ideologies according to their own social and gender relations." As a part of the concept of separate spheres women were denied access to gainful employment; men were expected to be the wage earners and providers while women were supposed to care for the home and family.[28] Religion, and particularly religious education of children, fell within the female sphere. Within these confines, women asserted themselves to the fullest in southern churches and acquired a measure of power by implementing that role in a way men probably had not envisioned.

The religious press proved to be a powerful means of spreading ideas among evangelicals, and articles for and about women were a regular feature in religious newspapers. Whether or not the South was bourgeois in an economic sense, the press held up a model of bourgeois family relations for southern women that extolled the so-called Cult of True Womanhood in terms familiar to their northern sisters. A typical article titled "The Good Wife" suggested that "the power of a wife, for good or evil, is altogether irresistible. Home must be the seat of happiness. . . . Man is strong, but his heart is not adamant. . . . He expends his whole moral force in the conflicts of the world. . . . To recover his equanimity and composure, home must be to him a place of repose, of peace, of cheerfulness, of comfort." Another article advised women to "endeavor to make your husband's habitation alluring and delightful to him. Let it be to him a sanctuary . . . make it a repose from his cares, a shelter from the world. . . . Let home be your empire—your world."[29]

With its emphasis on domestic virtues, the Cult of True Womanhood denied women access to formal higher education; but Mississippi evangelicals challenged that prescribed role. Just as the idea of republican motherhood could be used to strengthen the case for female education, so could the idea of evangelical motherhood. As one newspaper put it, "In no relation does woman exercise so deep an influence . . . as in that of mother." Another article, translated from the French, "Civilization of the Human Family by Women or The Education of the Mothers of Families," advised, "Let us then follow the laws of Nature; she does not consign us at our birth to the care of a pedagogue, nor the keeping of a philosopher: It is to the love and caresses of a young mother that she entrusts us." The same writer warned, "Here is then a law of eternal justice, man cannot debase women without partaking of their degradation."[30]

Fashionable accomplishments, then, were not sufficient; evangelicals became active supporters of higher education for women to help prepare them for their role as evangelical mothers. In 1818 the Methodist Conference established the Elizabeth Female Academy in Washington, Mississippi, but a group of local Methodist women were responsible for its creation. Although its claim to be the nation's first chartered institution for higher education of women may be exaggerated, it predates Emma Hart Willard's Troy Female Seminary in New York (established in 1821), which is generally recognized as the first school in the country to offer a secondary education to women. The buildings and grounds were donated by Elizabeth Greenfield, a member of the Methodist church, whose first husband left her a considerable fortune. Mrs. Greenfield was known for her "very penurious habits," but a group of "five or six ladies, members of the Church, undertook to obtain the necessary funds . . . to the surprise of every body, by their address and assiduity," they prevailed on her to donate a large mansion and its grounds. Following this success, "they then constituted themselves into a committee, and drove from house to house, and from plantation to plantation, until the funds were raised to repair the building and purchase furniture, books, and apparatus." The academy had a male superintendent, but a female governess took charge of the institution and taught the students. The governess was required by the by-laws to be "pious, learned, and of grave and dignified deportment." The by-laws also called for three "respectable Matrons" to serve as patronesses; they were to visit and inspect the school and report any problems to the all-male board of trustees. The school's ambitious curriculum included chemistry, natural philosophy, botany, Latin, intellectual philosophy, mythology, and history.[31]

Because of its religious affiliation, moral teachings were also important. Religious services were held regularly, and a strict moral code was enforced. Students could not receive visitors, and they were required to dress plainly without "beads, jewelry, artificial flowers, curls, feathers, or any superfluous decoration." As one religious newspaper warned, "Woman is not placed in this world to eat the bread of idleness, and to receive the flatteries of others." In keeping with the evangelical hostility to worldly amusements, the young women were prohibited from attending "balls, dancing parties, theatrical performances, or festive entertainments." As Mathews has pointed out, for women the evangelical ideal was a part of their challenge to the society around them: "Evangelicals distinguished between themselves and the world by focusing on the differences between worldly and converted women," he wrote. "They viewed the former as frivolous, flighty, and careless, mere ornaments to their men . . . invidious distinctions between Evangelical women and others were usually directed upward, against women of superior social position rather than against those of the same or lower class." Such a concern is clearly evidenced in the academy's prohibitions against finery and worldly amusements.[32]

The academy's sponsors drew upon the evolving vision of the republican wife in their creation of the school. The antipatriarchalism of the revolutionary era carried important changes for the status of women in the early national period. This republican ideology emphasized marriage as the most important familial relationship and showed more interest in the bond between husband and wife than between parent and child. In a construct that placed greater emphasis on the relationship between conjugal equals, women played a more central role not only in the family but in the larger society. Women would serve as the guardians of male virtue, and through their influence within the family, women would reform the morals of the entire society. Indeed, the very concept of virtue, so central to republican ideology, was increasingly feminized. It is in this sense that the founders of the academy expressed their belief that the institution would confer "so much benefit upon the state" by educating young women in the "principles of Liberty, Free government and obligations of patriotism."[33]

Although the enrollment was not large, scores of young women passed through the academy's halls. A Methodist preacher wrote in 1826 that "the school is full to overflowing."[34] The academy gave young women an opportunity to live away from their homes in an environment that encouraged the formation of close nonkin relationships that often persisted throughout their adult lives. The academy operated for over twenty-five years until the transfer of the state capital to Jackson led to the rapid decline of the town of Washington. The evangelical commitment to women's education continued, however, and by that time other denominational schools for women were available.

Evangelicals took pride in their support of female education. A speaker at the 1829 commencement at the Elizabeth Academy said, "Nothing reflects more honor upon the present age than the liberality displayed in the education of females." But women were not so content. Without directly challenging the idea of separate spheres, Mississippi women attempted to make the most of the sphere allotted to them and insisted on a greater commitment to women's education. As the republican synthesis faded in the 1820s, the ideal of the republican wife gave way to the ideal of the Christian mother, a vision that received greater and greater attention after 1830. For example, in 1836 a religious newspaper reprinted an article by northern reformer Sarah J. Hale criticizing the lack of educational opportunity for her sex:

Men have been busying themselves these six thousand years to improve society . . . and after all the mass of mankind are very ignorant and very wicked. Wherefore is it so? Because the mother, whom God has constituted the first teacher of every human being, has been degraded from her high office, or what is the same thing, been denied those privileges which only can enable her to discharge it with discretion and effect. God created woman as a helpmate for man, and . . . man, in his pride, rejects her assistance in his intellectual and moral career. . . . If half the effort had been directed to improve the minds of females, which have been lavished on the other sex, we should now have a very different state of society.[35]

Although women might have been confined to a separate sphere, women like Sarah Hale used that situation to demand a greater respect for the female role and to criticize male domination. Increasing education and literacy for women had a liberating effect; women joined the literate culture, and their importance within the churches gave them access to the expanding religious press where views like those above could find their way into print.

Many evangelicals agreed with Hale that the role of the Christian mother was central. The Baptists, in an 1835 circular letter titled "Duties of Heads of Families," observed that "the husband and wife, while both are living, must be considered as a joint head of the family," but lest that statement be misconstrued they added that "love is the chief duty of a man, and submission the chief duty of a woman." The Baptists did not attempt to explain why women should be both joint head of the family and submissive to their husbands; perhaps they could not. The status of women was clearly in flux, and contradictory images arose on every hand. An article in the evangelical press criticized husbands who refused to help care for their children; the writer noted that many mothers were unable to attend church "in consequence of her husband not taking his share of parental duty. Many fathers will suffer their wives to be kept from the sanctuary for weeks together, rather than take charge of their children."[36]

Many male evangelicals were uneasy with these new demands and with the women who played such an important role in their churches. In contrast to the view of women extolled by the Cult of True Womanhood was an older view of women as wicked temptresses, the troublesome daughters of Eve. William Winans recalled that a girl once became angry when he refused to dance with her; he concluded that he "was not the first to feel the force of female influence in solicitations to wrong-doing." He described women in the towns along the Mississippi River as "obscene Harpies . . . awaiting their opportunity to pounce upon and gobble up the prey which came within the reach of their infernal talons." Lewis Hobbs, another Methodist itinerant, made revealing comments about women, comments made more revealing by a Freudian slip; he remarked that "too great a familiarity is disgusting especially from the fear [fair] Sex." Another minister, John G. Jones, wrote, "As a means of self preservation, and to keep the devil from tempting, both myself and others, I kept at a great distance from females, especially young females." Recognizing these dangers, the Methodist *Discipline* warned ministers to " 'Converse sparingly, and conduct yourself prudently with women.' " Women protested against the idea that they were tainted by Eve's sin; one female newspaper writer mentioned famous women from the Bible, observed that women played an important role in Jesus' ministry, and asked, "Is it too much to say, that in this manner hath it seemed meet to God . . . to indemnify the sex for its original subjection, and to remove, in some degree at least, the reproach of the fall?"[37]

Evangelicals of both sexes struggled with contradictory views of women's role in church and society. On one hand, the notion of separate spheres was confining; Jean E. Friedman considers it as the sense of living in an "enclosed garden." But on the other hand, it provided a sense of newfound power and independence. The deritualization in evangelical churches and the emphasis on Christian equality enabled women to expand their role in churches, an opportunity they exploited to the fullest. The female majority in the typical church suggests that evangelical religion met important needs for these frontier women, and regardless of what some critics might have said, religion for them was more than simply emotionalism; it was for many a call to greater intellectual activity and self-control.[38]

Women assumed new, influential roles in churches by exercising a wide variety of gifts, including public speaking and prayer. Such roles could be controversial, however, and women faced less opposition when they worked among other women. Many evangelical practices, including separate seating for men and women, separate services, and the use of familial terms of address, encouraged the concept of sisterhood, a concept that fostered a rich associative life among women. Religious conversion and involvement went beyond conformity to a separate sphere; it could also be an assertion of moral strength, and it gave women an opportunity for active engagement in the most important institutions in the region. Women could use their seeming conformity as a force for change, as their demand for improved education illustrates. The period up to the 1830s was one of flux and change in which the boundaries for women were less rigid than they would later become.

CHAPTER 4

HEIRS TO THE PROMISE

MISSISSIPPI BLACKS, SLAVERY, AND THE
EVANGELICAL MOVEMENT, 1799–1840

ANTEBELLUM southern society was based on inequality and domination; although evangelicals challenged some aspects of their society, ultimately they did not attempt to alter the asymmetrical relations of power either between masters and slaves or between men and women. Elements in their ideology could be revolutionary if interpreted in certain ways, and blacks and women sometimes found a meaning in their faith that white men never intended. The evangelicals had largely abandoned any real attempt to abolish slavery before the movement came to Mississippi, but in these early years their partnership with the institution continued to be an uneasy one. The evangelicals wrestled with the contradictions between their militant egalitarianism and the demands of a slave society. During this period, however, evangelicalism brought changes to the lives of slaves, and, at the same time, slaves brought changes to evangelicalism. As W. E. B. Du Bois observed, "The religious growth of millions of men, even though they be slaves, cannot be without potent influence upon their contemporaries."[1] Evangelicals preached equality in Christ and offered advancement to blacks and women, though always under the guidance of white males. Still, evangelicalism before 1830 differed from its later form. The early years were a period of dynamic growth, change, and flux, of remarkable evolution in the aspirations and goals of the evangelicals, and of active participation by slaves and women in religious life. At the same time, evangelicals began to move away from the egalitarianism that made such broad participation possible.

The evangelicals, especially the Methodists and Baptists, continued to draw their strength from the plain folk and had difficulties with the wealthy pillared folk. One of Methodist minister Daniel de Vinne's many complaints against wealthy converts was that he could not "get them to feel rich enough to let their poor servants come to preaching." He often preached to a dozen slaves, he complained, "when the sound of the horn might summon 250 and 300 to meeting. . . . These poor creatures I never see & some never hear the gospel." As de Vinne suggested, large numbers of slaves were part of the early migration into Mississippi. The percentage of slaves in frontier Mississippi was high compared to that in other southern states, which helps explain the growing number of black evangelicals. James Davis estimated that in 1800, 10.4 percent of southern pioneers were slaves, in 1820, 27.1 percent, and in 1830, 30 percent. In Mississippi the black population increased from 39.4 percent of the total in 1800 to 46.4 percent in 1810, and from 43.5 percent in 1820 to 48.1 percent in 1830. De Vinne believed that many of these blacks were eager to hear the Word, and he was certainly eager to preach it to them, but suspicious or indifferent masters stood in the way.[2]

Despite opposition from some masters, evangelicals attracted a growing number of black converts. Black society was perhaps more in need of religious revitalization than white society. Although slaves retained a great deal from their African heritage, "the specifics of African religions . . . could not be transported intact to the American South." Slaves drawn from various African cultures shared many basic beliefs, but these beliefs lacked coherence. Blacks had to find some means of reconciling themselves to slavery and its demands. As Mechal Sobel wrote: "The African/American was thus uniquely ready for the Great Awakenings. First, coming from a living mystery faith in Africa, he was prepared to participate in the Christian mystery. Second, because of his noncoherent world view, he deeply yearned for new coherence and a new sense of unity and purpose." Blacks enthusiastically joined the first evangelical services in the Mississippi Territory; for example, a black man and his wife were two of the eight people who organized the first Methodist church in the territory in 1799. The vital role blacks played in the camp meetings and their impact on forms of worship were discussed in chapter 1. By the 1820s, as the number of interested blacks increased, evangelical ministers held separate services for them. Blacks who wished to join and be baptized were expected to have certificates from their masters, though ministers sometimes baptized slaves without them.[3]

As more and more blacks converted, they organized their own independent "African" churches, and occasionally whites assisted blacks in their efforts toward religious independence. In 1818, for example, the members of Bogue Chitto Baptist Church considered "the Request of the Black Brethren to be constituted into a church . . . the same is hearby granted. . . . The Constitution of the Black Brethren to be on the first

Lords Day in January next." Although the paucity of records from these early years makes it impossible to know how many independent black churches existed, the scattered references suggest that they were not uncommon. In 1820 the Pearl River Baptist Association had twenty-three member churches, including an African church that sent delegates to the association's meetings. In 1825 the largest church in the Union Baptist Association was an African church with 115 members; the twenty-two member churches together had only 635 members. At least one African church belonged to the Mississippi Baptist Association from 1810 to 1820. Jon Butler interprets the emergence of these African churches as evidence of a maturing African-American Christianity; their formation suggests that Christianity was spreading rapidly among the slave population.[4]

Independent worship was not limited to the Baptists; William Winans's journal shows that separate services for blacks were common among Methodists before 1830. In 1821 Winans "met the black Society" in Washington, Mississippi, "and baptized three of their children." Later the same year at Washington he "met the blacks in love feast order" and observed that "many spoke well." Sometimes whites attended such services and joined their black brethren in worship. In 1823 "we met the Blacks at the M[eeting] House" in Woodville "and held love feast. This was quite a refreshing season. Many of these poor people appeared happier than kings (unless the kings new the love of Jesus) and some whites that were present were very happy also."[5] Obviously, blacks and whites found the same message edifying and responded with the same emotional intensity. Even the services aimed particularly at blacks carried a greater message than simply "slaves obey your masters"; such a sermon would not have created a "refreshing season" among either blacks or whites.

In the Mississippi territorial days and during early statehood these independent African churches attracted more black members than did the biracial churches. Of the fourteen members of Jerusalem Baptist Church in 1822, only one was black. In 1824 Galilee Baptist Church had 109 white members, but only 10 blacks. In 1823 only 2 of Bethany Presbyterian Church's 40 members were black. In 1804 only 72 blacks belonged to the Methodist churches in the territory.[6] Of course, membership is not an accurate reflection of attendance, and more blacks may have attended the biracial services than these figures suggest, but the large membership figures available for independent black churches imply that blacks preferred to worship separately.

Slaves in the African-American and biracial evangelical churches gained powerful symbols of humanity and spiritual equality; they were ushered into a new community and given a social existence away from their masters. In a wide variety of ways, white evangelicals recognized blacks as their spiritual brothers and sisters with souls equal to their own, a recognition that shook the foundations of the slave system.

Although the ideology of slavery had not fully developed by the early 1800s, slavery had been justified by the slaves' heathenism, by a presumed racial inferiority, and even by a denial that blacks had souls. Evangelicals, however, ministered to blacks; admitted them to their congregations in the same ways as whites; listened as blacks recounted their conversion experiences; baptized them in the same waters; extended to them the right hand of fellowship, a symbolic rite welcoming new members into the spiritual community; often called them "Brother" or "Sister"; performed marriage ceremonies; and perhaps most dramatic, licensed blacks to preach. Blacks and whites worshiped together in the outdoor services, in the small log churches, and in private homes opened for services. Perhaps seated separately but still in close proximity, blacks and whites interacted and together shaped the character of worship services.

Blacks often joined whites in organizing churches on the frontier and were treated much the same as white members. Both blacks and whites were received into the churches in one of two ways, either by letter or by experience. People who joined by letter moved their membership from another church, while those who joined by experience were new converts who related their conversion experience before the entire congregation. In Baptist churches prospective members related their conversion experiences publicly, and members then voted whether to receive the individual based on the experience and on the convert's understanding of the faith. Presbyterian churches also held conferences or sessions where prospective members publicly related their experiences and their knowledge was tested. Methodists did not require a public recitation of the conversion experience, but the experience was a crucial part of Methodist love feasts and class meetings.

Many blacks joined by letter, which meant that they were already church members; this process was the vehicle through which newly arrived evangelicals of both races formed a Christian community. The Mars Hill Baptist Church records show that "Sisselea, a member of *coulour*," joined the church by letter and along with twenty other members subscribed to the church's "covenant articles of faith & Rules of *Deseplin*." Churches examined blacks' letters of dismission with the same care they gave to those of whites. When a slave named James asked to join Salem Baptist Church, he told the conference that "he belonged to the African

Church Lexican [Lexington] Kentucky but had no letter—was advised to remain as he is at present—Clerk ordered to write to . . . Lexington to ascertain the facts and procure a letter."[7]

New converts related their conversion experience and then received the ordinance of baptism. In 1813 "Sister Lizie, a woman of color," joined Jerusalem Baptist Church by relating her experience. The members of Clear Creek Baptist Church "heard the Christian experience of Virgin a Coloured boy belonging to Mr. Howell who was unanimously received & baptized." Blacks and whites were sometimes baptized together; in 1812 the members of Zion Hill Baptist Church met "at the water side" and baptized two white women and "Jacob a man of color."[8]

If congregations were not satisfied with a prospective member's conversion or understanding of the fundamentals of the faith, membership might be delayed. For example, "Bob a servant of Mr. Waddell & Ben a Servant of Mr. Harris, who were taken under the care of Session at the last communion again presented themselves" to the members of Montrose Presbyterian Church. The blacks had "a full & free conversation with the Session," and "it was thought prudent to admit them into full membership." Bob and Ben were willing to undergo such examinations until their membership was granted.[9] Their experience illustrates that white evangelicals often saw slaves as individuals, important additions to the religious community, whose full understanding of membership was vital, especially considering the high moral expectations evangelicals placed on all new members. When new converts gave their witness before other Christians, their experience was validated, and the common conversion experience united evangelicals of both races.

The conception of the biracial religious community as a family of God is reflected in the use of familial nomenclature. Ideally, secular distinctions disappeared once members were ushered into the fellowship; in the words of St. Paul, "There is neither Jew nor Greek, there is neither bond nor free, there is neither male nor female: for ye are all one in Christ Jesus" (Gal. 3:28). The apostle, of course, expressed an ideal seldom if ever achieved in any Christian community, but an egalitarian spirit clearly existed in the frontier biracial churches. Bethlehem Baptist Church, like many others, demanded that "the appellation of brother shall be used in the church by members in their address to each other." As many examples demonstrate, blacks and whites were often (but not always) called "Brother" and "Sister" in evangelical churches.[10]

Although the use of familial nomenclature does not imply complete equality, it does suggest that white evangelicals recognized that blacks had souls equal before God despite the badge of color and the bonds of servitude. The use of such terms of address may seem like a small thing, but in a hierarchical society forms of address were laden with meaning. Susan Dabney Smedes, daughter of a prominent planter, observed that slaves "called each other 'brer' and 'sis.' This referred not to the natural relationship, but to their relationship in the church." The young girl wondered aloud to her nurse, Maria, why blacks used such terms or the more formal "Mr." and "Mrs." among themselves. The indignant Maria replied, "Do you think 'cause we are black that we cyarn't [can't] have no names?" Nonevangelical whites typically used only first names when speaking to blacks; it was a code that both races clearly understood. In such a context the use of "Brother" and "Sister" in biracial churches carried special significance and recognized a changed status.[11]

Another ritual, extending the right hand of fellowship, followed baptism in the Baptist churches. When a person joined the church, the members filed past, shook the new member's hand, and welcomed him or her into the Christian fellowship. The act was an important symbol of acceptance, a public declaration that this individual now belonged to the religious community. When "Adam a black brother" joined the Louisville Baptist Church, he "came forward and related to the church what the Lord had done for him, the church being satisfied, unanimously received him a member and extended to him the right hand of fellowship." A comparison of his reception with that of a white woman shows that blacks received equal treatment: "Sister Susanah Bary came forward and related to the church what the Lord had done for her, the church being satisfied gave her the right hand of fellowship." In many churches, the right hand of fellowship was extended to both blacks and whites throughout the antebellum period.[12]

Of course, racial distinctions existed even in the early churches. Blacks and whites attended the same services, but blacks generally sat in the rear of the church or to one side. William Winans's journal reveals that biracial services were common in the early Methodist church. At an emotional biracial class meeting held in 1821, two whites and three blacks offered themselves for membership. In 1823 Meredith Renneau delivered a sermon to a biracial congregation, "followed by singing, prayer and some noise."[13] In such services, characterized by singing, shouting, and emotional intensity, the exchange took place between blacks and whites; the process of exchange may have begun in the emotional camp meetings, but it continued within many congregations.

Not only did blacks listen to sermons from white ministers, but whites heard sermons from black preachers; indeed, Eugene Genovese suggested that whites in the Old Southwest accepted black preachers more readily than did those in the eastern states. These black preachers had a considerable impact on evangelicalism, and evidence from Mississippi supports Donald Mathews's observation that "whites as well as blacks recalled the power and authority of black preachers." Joseph Willis, a free black and a licensed Baptist preacher, began his ministry in the Natchez region in 1798. He moved to Louisiana in 1804, organized the first Baptist church in the state, and served as the first moderator of the Louisiana Baptist Association. "Brother Willis" continued to attend the meetings of the Mississippi Baptist Association; in 1811, for example, the minutes record that "Bro. Willis from the Opelousas, was invited to a seat with us." The passage of Poindexter's code in 1822 temporarily interfered with the activities of black preachers because it required that services be conducted by a white minister. In 1822, for example, the members of Zion Hill Baptist Church considered licensing Smart, a slave, to "exercise his gift" to preach but delayed their decision "in consequence of an Act passed in the Legislature." A revision of the code permitted blacks to preach, and in 1826 Zion Hill allowed Smart to "exercise his gift within the bounds of the church as far as the Lord may direct him." A year later, he was allowed to exercise his gift outside the church.[14]

The story of Pompey, "a celebrated negro preacher" in early Mississippi, shows the impact of conversion on a slave and the interaction between the races. Pompey belonged to a family of nonbelievers, but he converted to Methodism. A white man once asked him why he became so excited about religion. Pompey replied that "it makes my soul so happy." The white man scoffed at him and said, "You simpleton, a negro has no soul." Although Pompey could not openly contradict the white man, he answered, "Then, master, it makes my body happy, for I know I am happy." Evangelical religion had given Pompey a shield against such attempts at dehumanization. The Methodists licensed the black man to preach, and he ministered with great success to both blacks and whites. Pompey was "a very impulsive and noisy Christian," and an exhortation, a sermon, or a song produced some vocal response from him. His master threatened to punish him for these outbursts but never carried out that threat because he saw that "religion made him [Pompey] a humble, obedient, and faithful servant."[15]

The effect black preachers had on the slave community is, unfortunately, almost impossible to document in these early years, but seeing one of their number elevated to a position of high visibility and prestige must have impressed other slaves. Certainly black preachers were at least partly responsible for the growing number of black converts. Slaves must have been deeply affected at seeing a fellow slave treated not only with a degree of equality but even occasionally as a superior, at least in the spiritual realm. Many whites must have shared the experience of one Baptist minister who was guided in religion by "a pious colored man."[16]

Their interactions in religious settings gave both blacks and whites new insights on each other. William Winans remembered that although he had seen few blacks as a child, he had somehow learned "to consider them as an inferior race of human beings." His opinion changed dramatically when he attended a love feast at which a black man recounted his religious experience. The black man's "deep and ardent piety" greatly affected Winans, who saw his faith as "the highest attainment to which man can aspire." Winans wrote: "Many, very many instances have, since that time, assured me that . . . 'God's no respecter of persons,' colors, or conditions. Among the most deeply pious Christians who I have known, have been many black people who, ignorant in other matters, degraded in conditions—many of them *slaves*, were children of God by Faith, and heirs to the promise of life eternal through Christ Jesus." Many slaves undoubtedly recognized and appreciated Winans's egalitarian sentiments. In a touching tribute to Winans, Limerick and Sukey Higdon, slaves who purchased their freedom in the 1820s, named their son Orville Winans.[17]

Such sentiments about slaves' religiosity were widespread among early evangelicals in Mississippi and led many of them to condemn slavery. John G. Jones, a native Mississippian who later became a Methodist minister, confessed that "previous to my embracing religion, I . . . thought it was right for us to have as many of them [slaves] as we could get, and took a pleasure in the government of them, even when I had to use some violence to keep them in subjection." After his conversion, however, Jones "began to look on slavery as a great moral evil." Many evangelicals apparently agreed with Jones; he wrote that before the late 1820s and 1830s "few professors of Christianity, either among the laity or clergy, thought of attempting the justification of African slavery . . . from Holy Scripture." Most people, according to Jones, assumed that slavery "was a great social, political, and moral evil, which, while it had to be endured for the present, ought as soon as possible to be removed." He suggests that most Methodists in the opening decades of the nineteenth century favored gradual emancipation. Alexander Talley, another Methodist minister, asked prophetically, "Has Heaven no blessing in store for this class of her creatures. Are we doomed to pass on until the secret thunder burst[?]"[18]

The issue of slavery plagued the Methodists in their state conference and the Baptists in their association meetings. Jacob Young, Methodist minister and presiding elder, recalled that slavery caused friction in an 1808 church conference. He wrote, "Our troubles began on the fourth day—slavery—we were sitting in a slave state—Slavery had given the church much trouble previous to this time; it has been giving trouble from that day to this & will continue to give us trouble while there is a slaveholder in the Church."[19] Unfortunately, Young gave no details of the stormy discussions at the conference, but clearly many ministers, including Young, opposed slavery and realized that the issue would not disappear.

The first query printed in the Mississippi Baptist Association's 1808 minutes was, "What steps would be most desirable to take with members of our society whose treatment of their slaves is unscriptural?" The association recommended that the churches "take notice of any improper treatment of their members toward their slaves and deal with them in brotherly love according to the rules of doctrine." One historian referred to this reply as "mild and ambiguous," but it was actually a clear directive. A master charged with cruelty would be treated the same as any other offender. A committee would be appointed to investigate the charges; if they were valid, disciplinary action would be taken. In 1827 the members of Pisgah Presbyterian Church called William Thompson before the church conference after he "cruelly whipped a slave." The 1810 covenant of the Sarepta Baptist Church included the statement: "We promise to treat our servants with humanity and not impose on them any thing cruel or unmerciful."[20]

Eleven years later the Mississippi Baptist Association published a lengthy address to masters and slaves outlining the obligations of both parties. A dutiful slave should "be industrious, honest, faithful, submissive and humble." The Baptists did not defend slavery as a positive good, nor did they offer a biblical defense of the institution. They did state, however, that "under the dispensations of God you have been brought into a state of bondage, however dark, mysterious and unpleasant those dispensations may appear to you we have no doubt that they are founded in wisdom and goodness." The Baptists enjoined masters to care for slaves' bodies and souls. They acknowledged that slaves had few pleasures in life, but their "drudgeries and toil . . . ought to excite sympathy and compassion in the hearts of those who enjoy the fruits of their labor." They warned masters to "let not Avarice . . . induce you to oppress your servant lest his groans, his sweat, and his blood ascent up to God as a witness against you."[21]

Oppression of and cruelty toward slaves in early Mississippi apparently were widespread. In James Pearse's unfavorable account of Mississippi, he wrote, "The master is proud and overbearing on all below his imaginary greatness . . . and pleased with a display of needless power. . . . *Cruelty* is another trait in their character.—They often inflict needless punishment on their slaves." Evangelicals sometimes defended slaves from brutal masters. Winans often chastised masters who mistreated their bondsmen. One master attempted to stop theft among his slaves by threatening to punish all of them unless they identified the culprit. Winans, outraged by this injustice, "remonstrated with him so warmly and . . . forcibly that I believe he abandoned his intention."[22]

Sometimes, however, even the most faithful and respected evangelicals inflicted terrible pain and suffering on their slaves. In 1821 Winans wrote, "This morning Bro. Foster gave a cruel whipping to a boy about ten years of age, leaving his clothes bloody in every part." Winans did not specify the boy's misdeed but noted that Foster inflicted the lashes "for no other offence than what is common to boys of any colour at his age." Winans "hesitated long whether I should denounce his conduct in severe terms of reprobation or only insinuate my disapprobation so as to make myself be understood."[23]

The minister faced a dilemma that troubled evangelicals as they sought to find their way through the thorny issues surrounding slavery. Winans acted forcibly in the earlier incident described above, but with Foster he hesitated. Foster was a wealthy planter, a founding member of the first Methodist church organized in Mississippi, a liberal donor, a hospitable host, and, paradoxically, an opponent of slavery. Perhaps such thoughts ran through Winans's mind as he studied his alternatives, and perhaps these considerations outweighed his concern about a child's suffering, the injustices committed by the strong against the weak, and the ordeal of parents and loved ones who stood by, impotent to prevent a man's abuse of a child. After a long hesitation, Winans chose to "insinuate" his disapproval,[24] a decision that foreshadowed the future evangelical compromise with slavery. It would be unfair to suggest that Winans sold his soul for thirty pieces of silver, but evangelicals needed money to pay preachers, to build churches, and to support their many benevolent activities; in Mississippi such funds could come only from slaveholders.

Evangelicals did not, however, completely abandon their black brethren. They publicly defended slaves' religious rights when in 1822 a new law code placed prohibitions on black worship. George Poindexter, the state's popular second governor, suggested a general revision of the state's laws, and the General Assembly assigned him the task. A Virginia native and son of a Baptist minister, Poindexter enjoyed a successful but scandal-ridden career in Mississippi. His popularity was considerable; in the 1819 governor's race he defeated his opponent by a two-to-one majority. State historian J. F. H. Claiborne referred to Poindexter as "the idol of the people."[25]

Winans wrote that Poindexter's code met with "general satisfaction" except for the restrictions it placed on slaves' right to worship among themselves and its requirement that services for blacks be conducted by a white minister. Winans wrote that "such a wanton curtailment of the religious privileges of the Slaves . . . aroused very general and strong feelings of opposition in all Christian Communities in the State; and it was deemed proper that this opposition should be such as to bear in a manner most forcible with politicians."[26]

Winans led the evangelical attack on the code and on Poindexter, who was a candidate for Congress in 1822. Winans was "conspicuous" in his opposition, and he "determined to render that opposition as effectual . . . as possible." He used the popular camp meetings as a platform to denounce the code. Many Baptists also opposed the code; both the Pearl River and Mississippi Baptist associations appointed committees to work for its repeal. Poindexter lost the election and blamed his defeat on Winans and the evangelicals. The state legislature heeded the message sent by the voters and revised the code along lines suggested by Winans. The new law no longer prohibited black preachers or black meetings, but it required that services either "be conducted by a regularly ordained or licensed white minister, or attended by at least two discreet and respectable white persons, appointed by some regular church or religious society."[27] The law made it necessary for African churches to have some affiliation with a white organization.

The controversy over the code was a pivotal event; it demonstrated the growing influence and numbers of the evangelicals. Initially, the odds against their winning a political victory against an established and popular politician looked slim indeed, but their stunning success gave notice that they could not be ignored. Poindexter expressed his "surprise" and "mortification" that an uneducated and politically naive preacher like Winans could rally the evangelicals and bring down the people's idol. More significantly, perhaps, the battle over the code foreshadowed the future of independent black worship. Evangelicals had preserved limited religious freedom for blacks, but the revised code was a forerunner of further legal restrictions in the wake of Nat Turner's 1831 revolt, which demonstrated the revolutionary potential of independent black worship and a dynamic black religious leader.[28]

The restrictions on independent black worship brought more blacks into biracial churches. In a circular letter written in 1829, the Mississippi Baptist Association decried the lack of religious instruction for slaves; "there is a criminal neglect among us," the Baptists wrote. They gave no biblical defense of slavery and reaffirmed the slaves' humanity: "An all wise God, in order to execute some of his unfathomable designs, has thought proper to permit a portion of the human family to be reduced to servitude." According to the Baptists, the slaves' condition was not an act of God: "Among us, those who are reduced to servitude are, also, *by the laws of the land,* made slaves." They hesitated to recognize the institution of slavery and wrote that despite the law "we shall only regard them in the light of servants." The Baptists condemned masters who abused slaves and described "men even in this, our own country, who look upon slaves with no more respect than upon a dumb beast." Holding firm to their egalitarian traditions, they wrote, "For, however sable their hue, and however degraded their condition in this life, they possess rational and immortal souls."[29]

The Baptists clearly and eloquently reaffirmed the spiritual equality of all people, but also in 1829 churches began to provide separate accommodations for black worshipers rather than seating them in the rear of the sanctuary as had been common practice. In that year the Salem Baptist Church attached a shed to the side of the church building for blacks. A high partition divided the races, but the raised pulpit allowed them to see the preacher. Other churches also explored ways to seat blacks separately.[30]

Even as they began to segregate black worshipers, evangelicals were moved by the radical vision that motivated their early opposition to slavery. In the late 1820s they began to support the efforts of the American Colonization Society. Initially the society's purpose was the transportation of free blacks to Africa, a course supported by many Mississippians. Not until ten years after its founding did the society attempt to organize in Mississippi, although it had received earlier notice in the state press. In 1827 the Reverend William Winans received a letter from the society asking if an agent would be successful in the state; Winans answered in the affirmative and successfully solicited funds on behalf of the society.

In the same year, the Methodist annual conference, acting upon a resolution introduced by Winans's close friend Benjamin M. Drake, endorsed the organization's efforts and asked preachers to take an offering for the society around July 4. The Methodists passed a similar resolution the following year and published their position in the *African Repository* and New York's *Christian Advocate and Journal*. By 1829 almost $1,000 had been collected, much of it from or by evangelicals. Efforts to organize a state society in the fall of 1828 failed because slaves heard rumors about the society and believed that its purpose was to gain their emancipation, a misconception that frightened slave owners.[31]

After the false start in 1828, the Mississippi Colonization Society was organized in June 1831 in Natchez. The society's organizers were predominantly from two groups—the planter elite and the evangelicals. For many years the two had eyed each other with suspicion, but the conversion of wealthy planters, the growing wealth of many evangelicals, and the influence exerted by prominent ministers had narrowed the gap. Among the society's elite members was Stephen Duncan, who served as president. He was a successful planter and physician, president of the Bank of Mississippi, and one of the state's wealthiest men. Gerard C. Brandon, the state's governor, and Cowles Mead, former secretary of the Mississippi Territory, were also officers, as was Isaac R. Nicholson, Natchez lawyer, speaker of the state House of Representatives, and later member of the state supreme court.[32]

Several evangelicals served as officers of the society, and one-fifth of its officers were ministers, including the Reverend John C. Burruss, Methodist minister and president of the Elizabeth Female Academy. He was described as "an elegant gentleman, a finished scholar, and an elegant preacher." Benjamin Drake, also an officer, was a prominent Methodist minister who succeeded Burruss as president of the academy. William Winans became one of the society's most tireless members. Edward McGehee of Wilkinson County, an active lay leader in the Methodist church, owned approximately one thousand slaves, making him one of the state's largest slaveholders. At least three of the officers were Presbyterian ministers: Zebulon Butler, who pastored at Port Gibson; Jeremiah Chamberlain, who served as president of Oakland College; and Benjamin Chase. Several members of the Mississippi Colonization Society also served as officers of the American Colonization Society; among them were Duncan, Winans, and McGehee.[33]

Although the stated purpose of the society was the transportation of free blacks out of the state to be colonized in Africa, the society soon turned its attention to freeing and transporting slaves. From its organization until around 1840 the society enjoyed some success. During that period Mississippians donated approximately $100,000 to the colonization movement. The Methodist conference appointed Winans to raise funds for the society in Mississippi and Alabama; he became one of its most visible and valuable supporters in the Southwest. No doubt Winans and the other evangelicals helped turn the society's attention toward freeing slaves in keeping with their long-held belief in gradual emancipation. At least four local auxiliary societies were organized in the southwestern part of the state. Agents from the national society visited the state frequently, raised considerable sums of money, and assisted in organizing local societies. Evangelical churches allowed these representatives to deliver their addresses in the churches, and they also allowed the state and local societies to meet in their buildings. Agents from the national society often opposed slavery, but their abolitionist views did not interfere with their efforts in the state during the 1830s. James G. Birney, an Alabama lawyer and slaveholder turned abolitionist, made successful visits to the state, spoke in churches, and received favorable notice in the press.

Birney praised the officers of the Mississippi society whom he found to be "remarkable for their intelligence, and for their liberality." In Natchez he spoke in both the Presbyterian and Methodist churches and wrote, "The *first* was well attended—the last still more numerously." He collected approximately $2,000 during this brief visit. He noted with satisfaction that "the subject of colonization is now open here,—talked about without concealment or privacy, and not necessarily connected with abolition or insurrection." He warned, however, that heated rhetoric or praise for abolition from northern members of the society could destroy the movement in the South.[34]

By the mid-1830s the state society was so successful that its leaders decided to establish a separate colony in Liberia for Mississippi blacks called Mississippi in Africa. Approximately 570 blacks, the majority of whom were freed slaves, settled in the colony. Many of these slaves were freed by evangelicals. William Foster, who died in 1834, freed twenty-one of his slaves to be transported to Liberia. Edward B. Randolph of Columbus, Mississippi, freed his slaves shortly after his conversion in 1834 and paid for their transportation to Africa. Randolph, a member of the prominent Virginia family, settled in the Columbus area in the 1820s and became a successful planter. He had reservations about the Methodists because of "class meetings, Love feasts & not least that enquiry in the discipline 'what shall be done to . . . Slavery?' " After his conversion, however, he became convinced "that Slavery is a great evil" and followed his conscience by freeing his slaves.[35]

Great hardships and suffering often accompanied the freed slaves in their move to Liberia. Elisa Thilman, one of Randolph's former slaves who settled in Mississippi in Africa, described his feelings to his former master in an 1844 letter. "I desire very much to hear from my mother and all my people," he wrote, "please to tell them they must Write to me." He told of his sister's death in Liberia and asked if his sisters in Mississippi were religious. Elisa's faith helped him bear his hardships: "I am yet on the lords Side and hope to continue so if it be his Wishes." He asked Randolph to tell his mother "that my head is much bowed down but looking up to Christ he is able to raise it up again." Mississippi evangelicals did not forget black Christians like Elisa in Liberia. Oakland College's missionary society planned to sponsor a white missionary there, and the Presbyterian Synod of Mississippi and Alabama purchased a black slave preacher, Harrison Ellis, and his family to serve as missionaries in Liberia.[36]

Despite its early success, the Mississippi Colonization Society faced many difficulties in the late 1830s. Most of its troubles related to the growing debate between northern abolitionists and southern slaveholders. Robert J. Walker, United States senator from Mississippi, told his colleagues that "among the unfortunate consequences which had been produced in Mississippi, owing to the . . . Abolitionists was the unpopularity of the Colonization Society, which previously . . . had been extremely popular." Members of the slaveholding elite abandoned the society, and evangelicals who remained friendly to the society found themselves branded as abolitionists. In the 1840s Winans faced such charges after he delivered a speech favoring colonization. Winans defended himself by embracing slavery, a lifesaving tactic that many other evangelicals must also have taken.[37]

Evangelicals and other southern supporters of colonization and gradual emancipation felt betrayed by northerners who abandoned more conservative positions in favor of immediate abolition. In an 1838 letter Winans criticized Gerrit Smith for leaving the colonization movement for abolitionism. Winans pointed out that the movement had freed hundreds of slaves and showed promise of even greater success until abolitionist agitation destroyed it. Abolitionism perpetuated slavery "by disgusting the white man against every measure which tends, no matter how remotely, to the accomplishment of . . . emancipation." When an agent for the colonization society visited the once liberal Natchez region in the 1840s, he could not collect enough money to cover his expenses. The Mississippi Colonization Society collapsed about 1840.[38]

Of the South in the postrevolutionary years, Eugene Genovese wrote, "One generation might be able to oppose slavery and favor everything it made possible, but the next had to choose sides."[39] His words are applicable to the first generation of Mississippi evangelicals. In the early years of the movement, the evangelicals remained ambivalent toward slavery, and some even advocated abolition. Their hostility toward the institution and their advocacy of egalitarianism encouraged black conversion; more and more slaves joined the churches, organized their own independent congregations, and entered the biracial churches when independent worship was no longer possible.

The fluid nature of worship encouraged interaction between the races and left an indelible imprint on southern religion. As the decade of the 1820s drew to a close, evangelicals continued to espouse egalitarianism and spiritual equality among all men, and many maintained their opposition to slavery, or at least wrestled with its larger implications, but in the late 1820s the seeds of compromise with slavery and racial separation, with its implicit inequality, were sown. Support of the American Colonization Society marked the final attempt by white evangelicals to end slavery.

CHAPTER 5

NO TAMENESS, NO SATIETY

FLUSH TIMES, 1830–1860

T HE period from the 1830s to the Civil War saw dramatic and far-reaching changes in Mississippi. As one resident recalled, "From the year 1828 to 1855, life in Mississippi, was full and rich, and varied with much incident and many strong passions. In a new country, teeming with wealth and full of adventurous spirits, there is no tameness, no satiety." Despite periods of economic uncertainty, the antebellum era was largely one of such remarkable growth and expansion that contemporaries called it the "Flush Times." The state's population more than doubled from 1830 to 1840 and nearly doubled again from 1840 to 1850 before slowing down in the final decade of the antebellum period. By 1840 blacks were a majority of the population, and slaves outnumbered whites throughout the remainder of the antebellum period (see Table 3). The growth in the slave population paralleled the expansion of the plantation system and increased output of cotton. Cotton production in the state soared from approximately 317,000 bales in 1837–38 to more than 1,200,000 bales in 1859–60; by the end of the 1830s Mississippi was the leading cotton producer in the South.[1]

The removal of the Choctaws and Chickasaws from the northern two-thirds of the state in the 1830s and the appropriation of their vast tribal lands sparked this expansion. The sordid and tragic history of their removal lies beyond the scope of this work, but by 1832 the process was complete.[2] The opening of millions of acres of fertile land led to a land rush reminiscent of the California Gold Rush; as one contemporary put it, "A new El Dorado had been discovered." The immigrants who rushed in to settle the cession lands were largely small farmers and planters from the piedmont regions of Virginia, Georgia, and the Carolinas. Although the state boasted some of the wealthiest of King Cotton's retainers, the majority of the agricultural population either owned no slaves or owned fewer than twenty. Estimates suggest that the planter class—those who owned twenty or more slaves—made up about 20 percent of the white farm population, though the proportion of planters in the population varied widely and was concentrated in the plantation regions.[3]

This newly acquired territory had all the attributes of a frontier as well as the accompanying problems and opportunities. Some evangelicals were shocked by the mad scramble for riches, and a writer in one religious periodical hoped that "Mississippi will not much longer deposit her religion in Cotton Bales." A Baptist group wrote: "The tide of emigration, setting in with such rapidity upon our State, from almost every direction, calls loudly upon us to increase our efforts. . . . A population as heterogeneous and unsettled as is generally found in every new country, possesses . . . the elements of civil discord and destruction." Edward Fontaine, a native of Virginia, arrived in Pontotoc, Mississippi, in 1836 in the midst of the land boom. He recorded his impressions of the scene:

Pontotoc is a flourishing embryo town in the centre of the Chickasaw Nation. . . . The first house was built here in June, 1835. Now there are 27 stores and near 1500 inhabitants. Its present prosperity is entirely ephemeral. The extensive mercantile establishments, and expensive taverns are supported almost exclusively by the crowd of speculators and adventurers who attend the land sales, and the Indians who have sold their reservations and received their value. . . . As soon as the land sales are over . . . the glory of Pontotock will fade, and its wild novelty vanish, and it will appear but as the other respectable inland towns of our country.[4]

In many respects Fontaine was an accurate prophet. The period of wild land speculation was short-lived—the financial panic of 1837 brought it to an abrupt halt—and Pontotoc did become another "respectable inland town." But that transformation to "respectability" depended largely on the efforts of the evangelicals, who moved quickly to confront the challenges of Christianizing a new frontier. Another contemporary, James G. Baldwin, complained: "Men dropped down into their places as from the clouds. . . . Nobody knew who or what they were, except as they claimed, or as a surface view of their character indicated." Evangelical religion offered one way to ascertain character and quickly establish the personal ties so valued by the plain folk. Although some charlatans passed themselves off as dedicated evangelicals and even as preachers, the close, personal nature of the services and the intimate descriptions of conversion and faith required in the communal services made such deception difficult, and imposters were exposed as soon as they were discovered.[5]

Table 3. *Population of Mississippi, 1830–1860 (in thousands)*

Year	White	Black	Total	Percent increase
1830	70	66	137	
1840	179	197	376	174.5
1850	296	311	607	61.4
1860	354	437	791	30.3

Source: U.S. Department of Commerce, Bureau of the Census, *Historical Statistics of the United States: Colonial Times to 1970* (Washington, D.C., 1975), 30.

Evangelical bodies moved quickly to send missionaries into the cession lands, and emigrants organized churches without outside agents. As early as 1821 the Carolina Conference of the Methodist church sent two preachers as missionaries to north Mississippi, and in 1832 the Mississippi Conference began making appointments in the cession lands. Many new settlers were evangelicals who yearned to belong to a religious community, seeking through evangelicalism a greater sense of stability and a means of forging personal ties in a newly settled land. Josiah Hinds, who settled in Itawamba County in 1839, described his new home: "We are among strangers now in a strange land, and in a wild[e]rness. . . . We are almost in the woods—one cabbin onley to shelter us and our little ones, and . . . a few neighbors who are kind but ignorant, [and] no Churches erected for the worship of God." The community-building function of religion was important to settlers like Hinds; he soon established class meetings, assisted in organizing a Methodist church, and formed a temperance society.[6]

Such informal gatherings of like-minded religious folk were common on the frontier and greatly facilitated the organization of churches. When George Shaeffer, a Methodist itinerant, began his rounds in north Mississippi in 1839, he "found a small class lead by Col. Joseph B. Fields, a zealous and devoted Christian who was always ready to cooperate with the preacher in promoting the work of Christ." Shaeffer encouraged the members of the class to build a log church, and "as soon as it was finished we had a protracted meeting there, which resulted gloriously, about fifty persons were converted, some of whom had been remarkably irreligious." Within a very short time the class meeting attended by a couple of families had grown into a thriving church with the help of a revival, a pattern that was repeated time and again.[7]

Across north Mississippi churches provided the nucleus of community organization. In 1834 a Presbyterian minister held services under a large oak tree in the Columbus area, and even though the "Presbyterians were few in number, widely separated, and . . . their residence here had generally been short," the event was well attended. The service sparked the organization of Bethel Presbyterian Church: "All those who subsequently united in the organization had located here since the previous first of January . . . they were, for the most part, strangers to one another. On this occasion, however, they were brought together as brethren, and they determined to satisfy the longings of their hearts, by securing the organization of a Church and the establishment of regular worship."[8]

Revivals and camp meetings fueled religious expansion in the cession lands. The camp meeting movement had subsided in southern Mississippi, but the conditions that had fed the movement two decades earlier were present on this new frontier. Again, thousands of immigrants poured into a wilderness environment where social structure was weak, communal bonds were almost nonexistent, and settlement was sparse. And once again scoffers were shocked by the emotional intensity of the services and the bizarre physical effects they produced. One minister recorded that his hearers "listened, gazed, wept, rose to their feet, pressed forward toward the speaker—were electrified. Sobs, tears, and shouts filled the air, and the whole encampment seemed to be overwhelmed with the divine presence." One convert was "literally struck to the ground under conviction, and for two whole days and nights neither ate nor slept, crying for mercy." Hundreds attended an 1845 camp meeting in Calhoun County, and at an emotional nighttime service the altar was crowded with over a hundred mourners. "A wild shout was soon heard . . . the spirit seemed to catch like wild-fire, and they all rose up at once . . . shouting and praising God; grasping hands and shouting. . . . The meeting, the shouting and singing kept up until long after midnight, many fell at the altar . . . some had the jerks; old Christians and new converts clasped one another. . . . All was confusion, all was happy."[9]

The organization of churches proceeded quickly in north Mississippi because many immigrants were already church members, and the evangelical denominations sent ministers into the cession lands shortly after their acquisition. Nonetheless, the growth rate was impressive. In 1830 there was not a single Baptist church in Choctaw County; by 1834 the Choctaw Baptist Association had thirty-four member churches, eighteen ministers, and a thousand members. Once established, Missionary Baptist associations routinely employed a "domestic missionary" to work within the bounds of the association. A. W. Elledge, the missionary employed by the Aberdeen Baptist Association in 1845, reported that he "rode 3560 miles; preached 238 sermons; delivered more than 180 exhortations; assisted in the Constitution of 3 churches . . . Assisted in the ordination of nine Deacons, and Baptised 51 persons."[10]

As the rapid organization of churches and associations suggests, north Mississippi quickly became the most populous portion of the state. Throughout the antebellum period (and beyond) the state was riven by sectional animosities drawn in large part along economic and geographic lines. As late as 1830 the counties of the old Natchez District contained only 34 percent of the white population but were home to 65 percent of the slaves, paid 69 percent of the taxes, and had 78 percent of the assessed property value of the entire state. The poorer, nonslaveholding Piney Woods counties and the farmers and small planters of the cession lands had little in common with the residents of the Natchez District, and they waged heated political battles over such issues as internal improvements, the interstate slave trade, Indian removal, the location of the state capital, and a revision of the conservative Constitution of 1817. The sectional divisions changed somewhat with the opening of the vast cession lands in north Mississippi and the expansion of the plantation system. By 1840 half of the white population of the state resided in these new lands, and political power shifted accordingly. As the plantation system expanded to the north along the Mississippi, Yazoo, Pearl, and Tombigbee rivers, the planters of the Natchez District found new political allies.[11]

Perhaps the most important political development of this period was the passage of the Constitution of 1832. Calls for a new constitutional convention began almost immediately after the enactment of the conservative 1817 Constitution, but the Natchez District blocked a new convention until the opening of the cession lands. At that point the voters of the district decided to accept the inevitable and support a convention before their political strength was further diluted. The convention was plagued by fighting among the political factions, but the document that emerged was the most democratic in the South, a symbol of the triumph of Jacksonian democracy. All property, tax, and militia requirements for voters and officeholders were removed, residence requirements for voters were liberalized, virtually all state officers, including judges, were to be popularly elected, and ministers were no longer excluded from office.[12]

The implementation of a democratic constitution led to a new political style. As elected officials searched for the means to reach and persuade mass audiences, they turned naturally to the evangelical example. One of the most successful of the new politicians in Mississippi was Franklin E.

Plummer, a native of Massachusetts, who moved to the Piney Woods section of Mississippi in the 1820s. The virtually penniless young man opened a school, began to practice law, and quickly rose to prominence in Copiah County. When the county was divided, he was elected to the state General Assembly from the newly created Simpson County. He became the champion of the Piney Woods counties in opposition to the Natchez District. His mastery of parliamentary procedure enabled him to "embarrass the House or disentangle it, at his pleasure," and he soon wielded "more power than men of higher grade and culture, or than all of them combined."[13]

Plummer entered the race for a United States congressional seat in 1830, one of several candidates. The apparent front-runner was Colonel James C. Wilkins, the aristocratic choice of the Natchez District faction. In stump speeches at backwoods political rallies (which had much in common with camp meetings) Plummer directed a withering fire at his opponent in terms that resonated with the evangelical revolt against the gentry. Evangelicals such as Lorenzo Dow and the other early revival preachers had paved the way for Plummer's attacks against wealth and privilege and his contention that virtue was the proper measure of worth. In one circular he said, "I base my prospect of success not on wealth, for riches I have none . . . but on the character I have formed during a residence of many years among you." "We are taught," he said, "that the highway to office, distinction and honor, is as free to the *meritorious poor* man, as to the *rich;* to the man who has risen from obscurity by his own individual exertions, as to him who has inherited a high and elevated standing in society, founded on the patrimony of his ancestors." His opponents were appalled at his attempts to divide the voters "into artificial and invidious orders, of rich and poor," but the voters had a different reaction. Plummer won an impressive victory although he received hardly a vote from the Natchez District.[14]

Not surprisingly, Plummer was a loyal Jacksonian in Congress and easily won a second term. He supported President Andrew Jackson on most major issues, though his opposition to the Force Bill cost him the favor of some Jacksonians. He portrayed himself as the workingmen's candidate, a group he defined as those "who stand opposed to the aristocracy, whether composed of birth, of wealth, of office, of learning, or of talents." In 1835 Plummer entered the race for the United States Senate, a decision that brought about his political downfall. The Jacksonian political organization in the state did not support him, and he turned instead to the Whig leaders, who provided much needed financial support. It was a Faustian bargain; as one contemporary recalled, "Previous to this, he had no connection with intriguors, cliques, banks, or combinations. . . . But now he had become one of a ring; in alliance with capitalists and men of aristocratic habits." He could no longer criticize the aristocrats and bankers who now paid his bills, and he lost the election. Although only in his thirties, Plummer vanished from the political scene and died in obscurity in 1852.[15] Plummer's meteoric career demonstrated the political possibilities inherent in the evangelical language of revolt, in the link evangelicals forged in the popular mind between religion, virtue, and democracy, and in the power of rallies and oratory to sway popular opinion.

A political campaign event described by Reuben Davis, a prominent lawyer and politician of Aberdeen, illustrates the many-layered connections between religious and political life in the period. Davis was the son of a poor Primitive Baptist preacher but not religious himself. During a campaign for circuit judge, he visited the town of Ripley, where he knew no one and had little hope of success; his only connection was a letter of introduction to a local minister. After introducing himself to the minister he told him that he was

> the son of a godly Baptist preacher, and my wife a most devoted Methodist. I did not know to which church he belonged, but felt sure it was either Baptist or Methodist. He at once became friendly, and told me he was a minister of the Methodist church. . . . The next morning there was a large crowd at his tavern, most of them members of his church. He introduced me to them, dwelling upon the fact that I had married an enthusiastic Methodist.

Following the introductions, the crowd moved to the grounds to hear the political addresses. The area closely resembled the layout of a camp meeting: "A stand had been erected in a grove near by, and there was a considerable crowd around it." After Davis spoke,

> an aged gentleman . . . stood up, and requested me to say whether I was not the son of a Baptist minister, named John Davis . . . I answered that I was. He then said he had known my father well, had stayed at his house and preached from the same pulpit, and that a better or more honorable man never lived. He added that he and his sons and sons-in-law would all go for me, and the members of his church, so far as he had influence.

Davis carried the district, a victory he attributed to his religious connections.[16]

If camp meetings were "festivals of democracy," perhaps it should come as no surprise that the form was so easily adapted to political festivals. Not only did the camp meeting and political rally or "barbecue" use the same physical setting, but their purposes were similar. Both were means of effecting conversion. Evangelicals found that a meeting at which preachers from different denominations hotly debated the tenets of their faith aroused interest, and political rivals spoke in succession at large rallies along the campaign trail. Camp meetings were edifying; evangelicals and would-be converts heard emotional harangues, but they also heard debates over such complex theological issues as predestination and Arminianism. Reuben Davis believed that political debates served a similar function and helped make the American population politically aware and fit for self-government.

A heated political campaign took on the attributes of a sweeping revival. Reuben Davis described the excitement surrounding the election of 1840: "There were speeches everywhere. Great barbeques succeeded each other, and were attended by multitudes" of both races. Just as camp meetings brought an outpouring of creative folk music, elections sparked "an outbreak of popular campaign ditties, containing a cheerful medley of patriotic fervor and wild plantation melody . . . from every field the mellow voices of the negroes softened the most rollicking ditty into the pathetic cadences peculiar to the African vocalist." The carnival-like atmosphere surrounding the political barbecues, where food, drink, and fun were plentiful, was not unknown at camp meetings, as critics often pointed out. Davis described a camp meeting where "men smoked and laughed and amused themselves on the outskirts of the crowd . . . and the young women coquetted with their beaux, and jested with each other as freely as if they were attending a picnic or barbeque." Evangelicals also attacked traditional forms of campaigning inherited from the colonial period. In 1838, for example, the Columbus Methodist Quarterly Conference disciplined a male member who placed a wager on the outcome of an election and "treated to a Barrel of Cider during the late electioneering."[17]

The great political orators of the day followed in the steps of the camp meeting revivalists. A description of a speech by Seargent S. Prentiss, acknowledged by friend and foe as one of the greatest orators of the day, illustrates the links between political and religious oratory. The following description was written by a member of the crowd at an 1844 rally in Rodney:

At the beginning of his speech the audience, a large one, composed of both ladies and men, was much scattered on the hill-side, but within the sound of his voice. As he warmed up in his masterly discussion of the political topics of the day . . . the audience began to move in the direction of the stand. I was myself a good way off, but moved up with the others, *insensibly* (so absorbed was I in his great thoughts,) until within a few feet of the speaker, and stood entranced, with the rest of the crowd, then hanging about the stand . . . shouting and weeping by turns; and when at the close, I gradually began to realize my individuality, I turned in the fullness of my heart to say something to whomsoever might be nearest me, when I found right at my side a devout and pious Methodist lady, wife of a leading *Democrat* of the town, whose first utterance, as my eyes met hers, then streaming with tears, was with uplifted hands, "Oh that he were a preacher."[18]

On a more practical political level, Davis's experience in Ripley showed the value of religious connections, a lesson that was not lost on other politicians. Evangelicals had succeeded in forging a link between religion and democratic virtue in the popular mind, which politicians exploited. Just as Lorenzo Dow could deliver a "sermon" on the link between evangelicalism and democracy, a politician like Seargent S. Prentiss could make campaign speeches that "related not so much to mere questions of public policy, as to those great ethical and social principles, which are at once the foundation and the informing soul of a Christian Republic." As one religious newspaper put it, "The Spirit of the gospel is republican. The government of the Church of Christ, as taught us in the New Testament, is purely Republican."[19]

Men like Davis and Prentiss, though not religious themselves, found that they ignored religion at their political peril. Davis said that to be successful, politicians had to demonstrate an "outward conformity with the popular ideal." As evangelicalism permeated southern culture, it became a part of that ideal and influenced conventions regarding gender. Its impact on the Cult of True Womanhood has already been noted, and it wrought a similar transmutation in the ideal of the southern gentleman. As Bertram Wyatt-Brown observed, "By the 1830s . . . religious precept, somewhat democratic in character, transformed the ideal of gentility." As Davis described it, the "popular ideal" was straightforward: "Their creed was generally simple. A man ought to fear God, and mind his business. He should be respectful and courteous to all women; he should love his friends and hate his enemies. He should eat when hungry, drink when thirsty, dance when he was merry, vote for the candidate he liked best, and knock down any man who questioned his right to these privileges."[20] Elements of this creed conflicted with evangelicalism, but the disciplinary actions of the churches demonstrate that Davis accurately described the behavior of many men, even members of the churches.

Although many southern men continued to fight, dance, drink, and engage in other vices once considered acceptable according to the southern code of honor, Christian gentility gradually arose to challenge the more common code of honor that Davis described. Even some planters who were not evangelical converts supported the evangelical cause and embodied the code of Christian gentility. They were men such as Thomas Dabney, the owner of five hundred slaves and a four-thousand-acre cotton plantation, who assisted the Methodists and Baptists in his neighborhood and gave liberally to Sunday schools, church construction, and other benevolent causes. His daughter recalled that he was "always a strong believer in the doctrines of Christianity, and had great reverence for religion. But he was not a religious man."[21]

A variety of behaviors once accepted as part of the code of honor came under attack from the evangelicals and were, to some extent at least, discredited. Since the colonial period southern gentlemen had employed gambling and horse racing in their quest for honor and distinction. High stakes and expensive thoroughbreds symbolized a gentleman's independence and assertiveness. Churches disciplined members who engaged in these activities, and ministers railed against them in sermons and in the press. The popularity and reputation of racing declined across the South in the 1830s and 1840s, though some gentlemen in Natchez, New Orleans, and Charleston, which had never been evangelical strongholds, continued to patronize the sport. The gambling associated with the race was a major factor in evangelical opposition to it; indeed, towns like Natchez and Vicksburg were notorious gaming centers, and all forms of gambling came under attack. An Anti-Gambling Society operated in Vicksburg, and laws were enacted and enforced against gaming in Natchez. A famous riot in Vicksburg in 1835 resulted in the hanging of several gamblers and drove the rest out of town.[22] Increasingly, the attributes of Christian gentility won out over the traditional pastimes associated with the sporting gentleman.

Perhaps no aspect of the southern code of honor received more criticism from evangelicals than dueling. Churches expelled members for even threatening to fight a duel, and as early as 1828 ministers and laymen organized an Anti-Duelling Society in Natchez. Evangelical ministers were vocal critics of dueling; as early as 1814 Launer Blackman condemned the practice as "a violation of the Law of GOD" and urged his fellow ministers to "exert themselves to stop this worse than savage practice . . . no murderer hath Eternal life." After a duel in Columbus in the 1850s, the Reverend James Lyon preached that dueling was murder. He refused to "recognize the binding authority of the so called 'code of honor'—but on the contrary regard it as a violation of the laws of God." Lyon personally interfered to prevent a duel between two prominent residents of Columbus who were prepared to attack each other with rifles and bowie knives. An article in the religious press referred to dueling as "that dark side of chivalry" that "lifted self will—the wicked will, above law." Again, evangelical criticism helped redefine southern honor. A writer in the secular press declared that people had begun to see dueling "as unchristian, barbarous and below the standard of civilization."[23]

The religious aspect of the code of gentility became a part of the advice parents gave their sons. For religious parents, admonitions to lead a godly life took precedence over other aspects of the code. One father, for example, gave his son a list of nine guidelines to follow throughout life; six directly involved religious matters. He advised his son to "commit your life to God" and *"to Keep holy the Lord's day."* For other fathers, religion remained within the female sphere, and it was considered the wife's duty to inculcate religious beliefs in children. Bazil Kiger asked his wife to have their son say nightly prayers and added: "I have much I have to be thankful for and still I throw myself upon my bed at night without one word of thankfulness to a Divine Providence. You my dear wife must remember all this in your devotions and our little boy (God bless him) learn him to be like yourself, do not let him neglect his little Prayers any evening . . . but this subject makes a woman of me and I will not indulge in it."[24]

Evangelicalism was affected by the political, social, and economic currents of the antebellum period and affected them in turn. The population explosion and the opening of new land gave evangelicals a new field of labor that they quickly moved to exploit, and churches often formed the nucleus of new communities. The diffusion of evangelical attitudes throughout southern culture can be seen in the democratic revolution of the 1830s as politicians adopted many evangelical strategies and echoed evangelical ideology. Evangelicalism also wrought subtle changes in the southern code of honor, though the tensions between evangelical ethics and the more violent aspects of the code of honor continued throughout the antebellum period and beyond. The Flush Times proved to be a turning point for evangelicals. Many of them benefited from the rapid economic growth and found the prosperity they sought on the frontier. The newfound wealth and the growing dependence on slavery that accompanied it would lead to dramatic changes in evangelical churches.

CHAPTER 6

APPLES OF GOLD IN PICTURES OF SILVER

FROM SECTS TO DENOMINATIONS, 1830–1860

As a hymn writer in the 1860s looked back over the changes in evangelicalism during the preceding decades, he wrote the following lament:

> Well may thy servants mourn, my God,
> The church's desolation;
> The state of Zion calls aloud
> For grief and lamentation.
> Once she was all alive to thee, . . .
> But now a sad reverse we see,
> Her glory is departed.[1]

What the hymn writer mourned was the move from sects to denominations, a major shift in the history of southern evangelicalism characteristic of revolutionary religious movements. By the 1830s the evangelical revolt had ended; anthropologist Mary Douglas suggested that in revolutionary religious movements the "protest stage" typically lasts no more than two or three generations until the movement's success creates a need for greater organization and coherence. Religious historian H. Richard Niebuhr described this process as a seemingly inevitable "institutionalization and secularization of the kingdom" characteristic of new religious movements throughout the history of Christianity. In Niebuhr's view, the change was well under way in American evangelicalism by the 1840s and was accompanied by a loss of vitality: "The Awakening and the revivals, poured white-hot convictions into the souls of men, only to have these cool off into crystallized codes, solidified institutions, petrified creeds."[2]

By any objective standard, all evangelicals should have looked on these decades as a time of triumph, a time when their membership, wealth, and influence were growing at a remarkable rate. Such a mournful lamentation as the one quoted above is surprising in light of the impressive national expansion of evangelicalism. In 1780 there were 6 Baptist associations in the entire country; by 1860 there were more than 500. In 1783 the Methodists had 1 conference; by 1843, they had 32. In 1776 the Presbyterians had 9 regional presbyteries; by 1855 the Old School Presbyterians had 148 presbyteries and the New School had 108. The number of congregations expanded similarly: Methodists had about 50 congregations in 1783 and about 20,000 in 1860; Baptist congregations numbered about 400 in 1780 and over 12,000 in 1860; and the number of Presbyterian congregations grew from about 500 in 1780 to 6,400 in 1860.[3]

Mississippi mirrored this dramatic national expansion. In 1818 the Methodist church in the state had 2,235 members; by 1860 the number had increased to 61,000. The Baptist churches grew from about 5,000 members in 1835 to 41,482 by 1860. The Presbyterian church, by far the smallest of the three, had only 634 members in 1830, a number that increased to 7,136 by 1861. But that growth and expansion came at a cost and brought changes to the churches that many evangelicals refused to accept. Though doctrinal disputes and even divisions were not new to the evangelical movement—the Great Revival had spawned its share of controversy and divisions—the move from sects to denominations brought a new round of conflict and divisions. As Jon Butler noted, the rise of denominational institutions was accompanied by a rise in authority from the top down, a change that clashed with the concept of the equality of all believers. The change marked a new stage in evangelical development; evangelicals would no longer be a people set apart, a despised sect challenging societal values. But secularization and institutionalization were not accomplished without considerable resistance and controversy.[4]

Institutional organization among Mississippi Baptists began in 1822 with the formation of a state convention, but tensions quickly emerged between Missionary and Anti-Missionary Baptists (also referred to as Hardshell or Primitive Baptists). The convention also faced a major challenge from the followers of Alexander Campbell, still nominally Baptist, who waged a bitter struggle against missionary societies and hierarchical ecclesiastical organizations. The Primitive Baptists and Campbellites viewed missionary societies as nonscriptural organizations, part of a scheme by northern and eastern ministers to spread their influence throughout the nation. Their criticism was aimed at men such as James A. Ranaldson of Massachusetts, who was sent to Mississippi as a missionary from the Baptist Board of Foreign Missions. He quickly began organizing mission societies and was a prominent leader in the state convention. He was also a member of the Mississippi Baptist Association and led efforts to support ministerial education by organizing the Mississippi Baptist Education Society. He was one of the authors of "Address on Ministerial Education," which read in part:

> Although we do not consider a classical education *absolutely* essential to the qualifications of an evangelical preacher, yet "he shall not be a novice." . . . They should be apt to communicate their ideas with sound speech, that cannot be condemned. The words of the wise should be delivered with the tongue of the learned: that being fitly spoken, they may shine as apples of gold in pictures of silver.

The rough-hewn camp meeting preachers had consciously disavowed this very mode of speech, and calls for an educated ministry became one of the most hotly debated and divisive issues of the period.[5]

The challenge posed by the Campbellites and other reform groups, the split over missions, and the debate over an educated ministry combined to destroy the Mississippi State Convention in 1829, but it was reorganized in 1836, again on missionary principles, and once again it led to divisions within the church. The Missionary Baptists found their strength in the towns and more prosperous regions of the state. They saw themselves as progressive, modern Christians whose means were suited to the times. Antimissionary churches and associations were generally located in rural areas outside the plantation regions; they believed that all authority should be lodged in the local congregation, and they held fast to their Calvinist heritage. They protested the convention's pro-missionary stance and its support of clerical education, and many of them joined a new denomination—the Primitive Baptists. A protest from New Bethel Church in 1837 illustrates not only opposition to missions but how a call for sermons delivered in the "tongue of the learned" could alienate a less educated congregation: "We . . . protest against all money mishionary supportion as they tend greatly to brake the peace of the church in general and is with out a president in the word of god and will not suffer them preach it in our meting days." By 1839 enough churches had broken away to form the Primitive Baptist Association.[6]

In their first circular letter the Primitive Baptists blasted their Missionary Baptist brethren; they expressed their opposition to the doctrine of general atonement; they protested against missionary, tract, Sunday school, and temperance societies because they found no foundation for them in Scripture; and they derided theological schools and calls for an educated ministry. They aimed their most bitter criticism at the educated ministry:

> All power is in the hands of God. If he wants a learned Moses, or a Saul of Tarsus, He will have them qualified before he calls them to his work. . . . Were it possible to see the apostles of our Lord in company with some of our modern Baptists—who call themselves the successors of the Apostles—what a contrast would appear! The one you would see going afoot with a pair of sandals on his feet; the other mounted on a fine steed, with fine boots on his feet—the one with his fisher's coat on; the other the finest broadcloth—the one with rough hands, all exposed by reason of hard labor; the other with fair hands covered with gloves. . . . The one saying, silver and gold I have none—and at another time, thy money perish with thee; the other saying three or four thousand dollars more will be of great benefit in advancing the Redeemer's kingdom.

Although exact figures are unavailable, there were at least six Primitive Baptist associations in the state by the 1850s, but in membership they lagged behind the Missionary Baptists.[7]

Even after the departure of the Primitive Baptists many of the issues that drove them from the fold continued to plague the Missionary Baptists. The Landmark Movement, which arose in the 1850s, aroused another storm of controversy among Baptists over the fundamental tenets of the faith. A central theme of the Landmark Movement, and one that links it closely with the Primitive Baptists, was the insistence that true churches were "isolated and independent" and, like the original churches described in the New Testament, were "independent of all other bodies, civil or religious, and the highest and only source of ecclesiastical authority on earth. . . . This church acknowledges no body of men on earth, council, conference or assembly as its head, but Christ alone." The Landmarkers were also hostile to ministers' claims to supreme authority within the churches. James Robinson Graves, publisher of the *Tennessee Baptist* and the primary leader of the movement, railed against the idea that ministers had any administrative authority in Baptist churches. In a characteristic statement of this position he wrote, "Such a power delegated to ministers, would tend to foster their pride, and inflate them with the idea of their superiority to their brethren."[8]

Their extreme hostility to cooperation with other denominations and their insistence on local church autonomy won Graves and his associates, including Amos Cooper Dayton, who resided in Mississippi from about

1839 to 1852, many followers in the state. In language that resonated with the ideals of republicanism so popular in the early days of the evangelical revolt, Graves warned that denominations with hierarchical structures were antirepublican:

> Where has the Hierarchy prevailed, that civil liberty has not been overthrown and the people denegrated and enslaved. . . . Let me write it then, as with a diamond point upon your hearts, just so long as parity and universal suffrage is triumphant in the churches of Christ, so long will it be in the state and NO LONGER! Then does not your duty to God, to yourself, and to your loved country, make it your imperative duty to give all your influence personally and religiously, to that denomination of Christians in this land, that is organized upon democratic principles, and thus is aiding by all the influence of religion, in the maintenance of our republican government? . . . How can he whom God has made free, bow before the throne of a bishop in the church of Christ, who would indignantly scorn to bow before the throne of a monarch in his state.[9]

Unlike the Primitive Baptists, the Landmarkers were not opposed to Baptist associations so long as they did not interfere with local church government, and they preferred that Sunday schools and theological seminaries be under their own control. Thus it was possible for Baptists to favor Landmark reforms without leading to the sort of schism that divided the Primitive and Missionary Baptists. That flexibility helps explain the broad support Landmarkers gained from organizations such as the Mississippi Baptist Association, which endorsed the Landmark cause throughout the 1850s and 1860s.[10]

The Methodist Episcopal church began as a hierarchical institution, though it was affected by many of the debates that shook the Baptist church. Mississippi was originally included in the Western Conference, a vast expanse of territory that included almost the entire Mississippi Valley. In 1813 the Mississippi Conference was organized, though for many years it included Alabama and Louisiana. Because of the expanse of wilderness and Native American territory that separated the Old Southwest from more settled regions, visits from bishops were rare. The church became involved in denominational and cross-denominational organizations, and by the late 1850s, the Mississippi Conference supported eight colleges and a successful Book and Tract Society in Vicksburg.[11]

The Methodists faced a challenge from the Methodist Protestant church similar to the one the Baptists faced from the Primitive Baptists; here, too, the underlying issues were hierarchical church structure, the role of the laity, and the status of the clergy. The movement began at the 1827 Annual Conference held in Baltimore, Maryland, when several disaffected preachers and twenty-two laymen were expelled from the conference. These reformers wanted to decentralize the church and allow laymen a greater voice in its governance. Three years after their expulsion, they founded the Methodist Protestant church.[12]

In Mississippi the Methodist Protestant church was strongest in the southeastern Piney Woods counties and the counties recently carved from the cession lands. The first church was organized in Jasper County in 1829, and the first annual conference met in 1841. At the time of this conference, the church reported seven circuits with 504 white members and 75 blacks. The church expanded in the Piney Woods and cession lands at the same time Franklin Plummer railed against aristocracy and praised complete democracy. Henry J. Harris served as a Methodist itinerant on a circuit in the Piney Woods in the 1840s; he wrote that the Methodist Protestant preachers denounced the episcopal organization "as tyrannical beyond endurance and *we* her ministers were regarded as mere tools or vassals of the Bishops, over whom they had absolute control and membership in our church was in the esteem of many a kind of religious serfdom." The Methodist Protestant preachers attempted to capitalize on the link between evangelicalism and republicanism forged earlier by preachers such as Lorenzo Dow and exploited by politicians like Plummer, and they cleverly used it against the Methodists, whose organization ran counter to the ideals of Jacksonian democracy. Harris recalled, "Our people were jeered and taunted for their submission to such authority, and appeals were constantly made to their manhood . . . to induce them to turn away from us."[13]

Such efforts met with only limited success, however, probably because men like Harris, a plain man from a humble background, made no claim to superiority over the people on their circuits. Bishops, after all, were far away and did not intrude on the day-to-day activities of the local churches. The conflict over the role of the laity, the status of the clergy, and the importance of an educated ministry continued to rock the Methodist Episcopal church, despite the failure of the Methodist Protestant church.[14]

Presbyterian ecclesiastical organization in the state took shape in 1814, when the Reverend James Smylie made the long and dangerous journey from Natchez to Tennessee, where the Presbytery of West Tennessee met in session. Smylie persuaded that body to petition the Synod of Kentucky to create a separate presbytery for the Southwest—the Synod of Mississippi and South Alabama—which met for the first time in 1815. The

Synod of Mississippi was created in 1835. The Presbyterians actively promoted education in the state; ministers like Smylie operated schools, and the presbytery supported institutions of higher learning, most notably Oakland College. As a whole, the Presbyterians were the wealthiest and most socially prominent of the evangelicals; they were a more homogeneous body, apparently content with their church's structure. The only controversy surrounded the division on the national level between the conservative Old School and the more liberal New School Presbyterians. The theological debates between the two intensified in the 1830s, and support for abolitionism also grew in the New School ranks. The dispute culminated in the church schism of 1837, a separation that most southern synods endorsed unanimously or with few dissenting votes. The Synod of Mississippi and South Alabama, however, approved the acts of 1837 by a vote of only twenty-two to fourteen. The dissenters bristled at the centralization of power in the General Assembly, criticized that body for "the assumption of powers not delegated," and warned that such a course would "end in ecclesiastical despotism and in 'driving the plowshare of ruin through the bosoms' of all our esslesiastical rights." The dissenters certainly did not support the New School's theological positions or abolitionism; rather, their protest hints at dissatisfaction among some church members over the church's centralized authority.[15]

Debates over ministerial education, the role of the laity, and church structure were nothing new to Presbyterians; they had fought these battles earlier in the wake of the Great Revival. The Cumberland Presbyterian Church broke away in 1810 over just these issues and became the fourth largest denomination in the state. The Presbyterian church remained strong in the southern part of the state, particularly in towns and plantation areas, but the Cumberland Presbyterians were more numerous in the northern part of the state, in rural and less prosperous areas.[16]

Although differences existed in the constitution and powers of these respective denominational bodies, they exercised many of the same broad functions. They brought ministers (and sometimes lay delegates) together on a regular basis. Ministers looked forward to these meetings as refreshing seasons of spiritual renewal. James Smylie expressed such sentiments when he was prevented by illness from attending the 1836 meeting of the Mississippi Synod:

> It would be exceedingly gratifying to be able to attend the session. Besides the pleasure of meeting & cooperating with my brothers in the ministry & with the Elders that may represent the different churches, I would also

enjoy the additional pleasure . . . of meeting where, during the Session,
you will, by night as well as by day, unite with each other in singing, praying, preaching, & transacting the business . . . of the Church unmolested
& I hope with one heart.

Ministers shared experiences and advice, welcomed new ministers into
the fold, mourned the loss of departed brethren, jostled for appointments,
debated the future direction of the church, disciplined or expelled errant
ministers or congregations, and conducted the finances of the church.
They received letters, reports, and other communications from distant
bodies and welcomed visitors or church representatives from afar, thus be-
coming part of a vast religious communication network stretching across
the nation.[17]

As part of their effort to civilize the frontier and further the cause
of religion, evangelicals created an array of cross-denominational religious, reform, and educational organizations. In 1815 a group of ministers
organized the Amite and Florida Bible Society; Ezra Courtney, its first
president, was a prominent Baptist minister, and James Smylie served
as one of its vice-presidents. For over twenty years this society distributed Bibles to poor residents of southwestern Mississippi, an effort that
was continued by a Natchez branch of the American Bible Society organized by a Presbyterian minister in 1830. Smylie was also a founder of
the Amite Literary Society, and William Winans was a founding member of the Franklin Debating and Literary Society. Evangelicals supported
the American Colonization Society. They actively joined in the formation
of temperance societies. The Synod of Mississippi and South Alabama,
for example, considered "the present efforts in favor of total abstinence
from ardent spirits as among the happiest signs of our times" and ordered
ministers to establish branches of the society in their churches.[18]

Education was an important part of the modernist evangelicals' program of social betterment. They were concerned not only with ministerial
education and the establishment of colleges; they also attempted to fight
illiteracy and bring educational opportunities to their members and to
the larger society. Modernists perceived a link between education, religion, and republicanism. In an address delivered at Oakland College, S. G.
Winchester, pastor of the Natchez Presbyterian Church, explained that
"religion and knowledge constitute the key-stone of our political arch,
the one base of which rests upon the unalienable rights of man, and the
other upon equal laws and a written constitution." Republican virtue,
he contended, was central to the nation's survival: "Righteousness exalt-

eth a nation, but the nation and kingdom that will not serve God, shall perish." "Unless sound and wholesome moral principles pervade and control the community," he continued, "the nation must inevitably work its own ruin." In a similar vein, an article in a Baptist newspaper stated that the "*uneducated mind is uneducated vice* . . . the safety of our republic depends upon the intelligence, and moral principle, and patriotism, and property of the nation." The benevolent empire alone was not sufficient unto the task; the government, too, had to assist in spreading these moral principles through legislation and public education.[19]

Evangelical support for education was not a new concept; many ministers operated private academies to supplement their meager salaries, but their efforts expanded after the 1830s. Modernists' support of the Sunday school movement is a case in point. The Presbyterians noted in 1831 that "there is an increasing attention to the education of the rising generation. The Great Head of the church has sealed his approbation of Sabbath School efforts." Although the movement got off to a slow start, the Presbyterians observed in 1838 that Sunday schools were prospering throughout the synod. Often these were cross-denominational efforts; several Protestant denominations in Jackson organized a Union School that met regularly in the basement of the Baptist church. Methodists and Presbyterians conducted a joint "free" Sunday school in Port Gibson as early as the late 1820s. The Sunday schools multiplied rapidly, and by the 1850s they were well established throughout the state. In 1837 the Sunday school in the First Methodist Church in Columbus, for example, had a superintendent, 8 male teachers, 7 female teachers, 64 male scholars, 61 females, and 105 volumes in its library; by 1851 the school had grown to include a superintendent, an assistant superintendent, a secretary, a librarian, a treasurer, 13 male teachers, 18 female teachers, 78 male scholars, 88 females, and a library of 1,000 volumes. In 1847 the Panola Baptist Association reported six Sunday schools in the district; four operated under the American Sunday School Union, though one Baptist school and one Cumberland Presbyterian school did not. Together the six schools had 40 teachers and 160 scholars. Another district reported nine schools with 45 teachers and 325 students. Sunday school celebrations became major events in towns across the state; the state's governor attended a celebration in Vicksburg in 1856 that included a steamboat excursion, and a similar celebration was held at the Jackson Fair Grounds in 1859 attended by 2,000 teachers and 2,000 students from towns across central Mississippi.[20]

Some evangelicals advocated Sunday schools for slaves, and though it is difficult to ascertain how many were actually established, apparently a few existed. A Baptist newspaper advised masters to bring slaves to Sabbath schools, using the familiar argument that "our servants would be better, more faithful and obedient." By 1846 Columbus Methodists operated a "Coloured Sabbath School," which was "in a most prosperous state and could Sufficient attention be paid them, much good would be done." Before the 1830s, blacks in some parts of the South learned to read and write in Sunday schools, but the primary means of instruction for Mississippi slaves was undoubtedly oral by the 1830s. State law prohibited teaching slaves to read and write, and suspicious masters vehemently opposed such instruction.[21]

Through Sunday schools and private academies evangelicals came to dominate education in the South. In the private academies they often taught planters' sons, and the Sunday schools gave them access to the children of the plain folk. By these means, evangelicals further spread their beliefs through southern society. As Eugene Genovese and Elizabeth Fox-Genovese observed, "This quasi-monopoly of education assured them the ability to instill the rudiments of a Christian sensibilty among broad segments of the population."[22]

In a further effort to spread literacy and religion, a group of evangelical ministers established a branch of the American Tract Society in Natchez, and still others supported their denominational tract societies. These societies distributed large numbers of free or inexpensive pamphlets in the decades before 1830; their efforts encouraged reading and virtually created mass media in America. Ministers and denominational associations also encouraged members to support the burgeoning number of religious newspapers and magazines. By participating in these activities, ministers helped diffuse religion through their culture and left their imprint on American society.[23]

This religious press was largely in the hands of modernist ministers who favored a departure from the old ways. The case of Ashley Vaughn, a Baptist minister and native of New York, illustrates this pattern. Vaughn arrived in Mississippi in 1834, and in 1836 he established the *South-Western Religious Luminary* at Natchez, the state's first religious newspaper. He used the paper as a platform to push for changes within the church. He championed the creation of the Mississippi Baptist Convention and served as its president. His newspaper became the official organ of the convention. Through articles in his newspaper, Vaughn called for a more educated ministry, encouraged Baptists to shift their interest from rural areas to towns, and urged them to minister to the rich as well as the poor. In an 1837 article he wrote that it was easy to preach to a poor man in a "mud-walled cottage," but he called on his readers "to ascend the steps of the royal palace, and enter the princely mansion."[24]

A growing number of laypeople looked on the changing aspirations of ministers with dismay. The hymn writer quoted at the beginning of the chapter described the new ministry:

> Her pastors love to live at ease,
> They covet wealth and honour;
> And while they seek such things as these,
> They bring reproach upon her [the church].
> Such worthless objects they pursue
> Warmly and undiverted;
> The church they lead and ruin too—
> Her glory is departed.

As the evangelicals moved from sect to denomination, many ministers sought a higher status—more recognition as professionals—an ambition that necessitated separating themselves from the laity and elevating their position within the churches and society. The desire for professional status was especially strong among the graduates of the new seminaries who saw a rapidly expanding professional society emerging all around them.[25] The issue was not simply one of greater respect for ministers or the maintenance of order and decorum in church services, but rather a fundamentally new definition of the ministry and the role of the laity in worship.

The changes that began in the 1830s had a dramatic impact on forms of worship within congregations, a change that accounts for the sometimes hysterical response from opponents to change. In the early church as described in the New Testament no distinction existed between the minister and the laity. The gift of evangelism was only one of many bestowed upon Christians, and all played a part in the church's ministry. All Christians received a call and gifts from Christ; Paul described to the Ephesians the various gifts Christ gave all believers; some should be prophets, some evangelists, others pastors and teachers, and all engaged in the work of the ministry. Paul described the church as a body in which each church member made a necessary contribution to the working of the whole (Eph. 4:7–16). The early evangelical churches, especially the Baptist and Methodist, functioned in just this way. Preachers were men much like the members themselves except that God chose preachers to exercise their gifts in public. Other members—including women and blacks—had equally important gifts, and the entire laity functioned as ministers of the church in this broad, New Testament definition of the word. For purposes of discussion, churches that emphasize such active involvement on the part of their members in worship services can be said to have a congregational ministry.

Keeping this definition of the ministry of all believers in mind, the following detailed description of a nighttime evangelical service (whether Methodist or Baptist is unclear in the records) in rural north Mississippi is notable. The writer was a young Presbyterian minister:

> The congregation was large the house being full. Stubbs got up and read a hymn which was sung standing, then he offered a prayer, the congregation kneeling. Another hymn was sung sitting, and then he read Lev. 7:17 ["But the remainder of the flesh of the sacrifice on the third day shall be burnt with fire."] as his text and preached a discourse. In my judgement the sermon was a very ordinary affair. In his manner or matter there was nothing indicative of special excellence. His object was to arouse the people. After sermon he came down and called for mourners while a small cluster were singing different hymns. His call was successful for a good many mourners went up. . . . They knelt around the "alter." The preachers and the members commenced talking to them, singing was kept up all the time . . . prayer was offered twice during this scene. One of the Miss Hoskins all at once commenced squalling and acting very foolishly. Presently she . . . ceased her noice [noise]. Just before the congregation was dismissed an old lady dressed in black . . . commenced a scene. Her voice was harsh, and while she was addressing with much gesticulation the group around her I could not but think of Paul's command "Let your women keep silence in the Churches" (1 Cor. 14:34) . . . of the meeting tonight the only objectional features to me was the hymn singing and the scenes above referred to. I do not think that such things are right. Confusion should not prevail in the house of God.[26]

A great deal of activity was going on, but was it as confused as the young Presbyterian suggested? The preacher led in singing and in prayer, then delivered a message. The young man may have been accurate when he wrote that the preacher showed no "special excellence." He was chosen from the laity to lead them in their ministry, but he was not chosen because of his education. The Presbyterian's observation that the preacher's chief object was to "arouse the people" was a criticism often leveled at evangelical preachers of both races. The criticism was legitimate as far as it went; the preacher did not aim to educate or instruct but to arouse, to act as a catalyst to bring the people to God. If the preacher, acting as the instrument of God, succeeded, as this one did, his role was over. He then called up mourners, those seeking salvation, and allowed the members of the congregation to exercise their gifts.

In this description we see members of the laity exercising gifts in song, prayer, teaching, pastorship, and prophecy. At first, the entire congregation sang the hymns, but later, after mourners came up, only a "small cluster" sang, those specially gifted in song. The preacher led the first prayer, but later prayers apparently were initiated by the congregation. Another group of laypeople joined the preacher at the altar, where they attempted to guide lost ones to Christ by teaching the tenets of the faith to nonbelievers. They must also have acted as pastors for those with particular griefs or problems. Two women in the congregation demonstrated what evangelicals recognized as the gift of prophecy, not in the sense of predicting future events but in sharing a divinely inspired revelation or utterance. Even shouting was a form of prophecy because the shout resulted from a perception of God's presence. In many respects, the most important part of such a service was not the preacher's message but the laypeople's exercise of their ministerial gifts. The work of the salvation of souls involved the entire church.

Many evangelicals attempted to hold fast to this traditional form of worship as debate began between older, more rural, and poorer evangelicals and a younger, more affluent group who wanted to abandon the old ways. The growing wealth of the church and many of its members often conflicted with its egalitarianism. The following incident, though perhaps apocryphal, is indicative of a polarization that increased in the 1840s and 1850s. Amanda Salome Guice Armstrong, known as "Aunt Mandy" to her friends, was a leader in her Methodist church and in the circuit's Female Financial Association. She was

an earnest and fervent Christian, gifted . . . in the art of prayer. She was also accustomed to shout aloud as her feelings prompted. On one occasion she was in Fayette during a revival meeting. Her yonger relatives had suggested to her that folks in town, even Methodist folks, no longer shouted, and that it was considered the proper thing to restrain one's emotions, especially in a town church. Aunt Mandy was impressed but not thoroughly convinced. . . . The pastor, knowing Aunt Mandy's reputation for being "powerful in prayer," asked her to lead the closing prayer, which she did. Under the stimulus of her own prayer she rose higher and higher, and at the close she rose to her feet and exclaimed "Fayette or no Fayette, hallelujah!"[27]

Whether or not this particular story was true, it expressed the growing divergence between town and rural evangelicals.

Many town churches became fashionable places. In 1837 a Methodist minister complained that the Presbyterians were completing "a fine church . . . and when it's done they will be likely to take some of our hearers—as a great many like fine things." Nancy M. Robinson of Port Gibson wrote that many people went to church "their dress to show." In 1855 William Winans, who had once expelled women from the church for dressing in finery, gave up the battle but continued to criticize; he wrote, "I found Georgiana Carter, who had, I believe, but six rings on her fingers besides considerable other jewelry. Such are many modern Methodists!" In 1848 one Baptist newspaper warned, "It is folly for persons to inveigh against dress and its seductions." Modernists were not suspicious of luxury. In many towns, the simple, unadorned meetinghouses were replaced by more elaborate and expensive structures. The Presbyterian church in Port Gibson, for example, cost $40,000. The pulpit alone in the Natchez Methodist Church reportedly cost $400. Town ministers expected to live in a style befitting their station; the Presbyterian manse in Natchez cost $16,000 in 1838, and the Methodist minister resided in an elaborate home called the Parsonage, a gift from a Natchez millionaire who resided in one of the city's finest mansions, Rosalie. These costly town buildings stood in stark contrast to the simple, unadorned log or frame country churches; for example, when the members of Academy Baptist Church in rural Tippah County decided to build a new church in 1844, they erected a frame building fifty feet long and thirty feet wide at a cost of $150. This structure was fairly typical of rural churches.[28]

Modern evangelicals who could afford fine things looked down upon poorer, more traditional church members. Augusta H. Rice, who spent part of the year on an Oktibbeha County plantation and the rest in Mobile, Alabama, wrote of a neighbor, "They live very plainly & made me feel rather uncomfortable talking about it all the while, as if it were a matter of vital importance & essential to worth." Perhaps she visited with the same attitude and equipage she took to the local Baptist church. She wrote a city friend, "You would have called me country, Oktibbeha, & everything else could you have seen me starting off on Sunday with the baby & nurse on the front seat, an extra attendant on the driver's box & a big champagne basket tied on behind." Clearly, if anyone called Mrs. Rice "country" it would be in jest. "I did not do as some of the neighbors did," she wrote disapprovingly, "namely to have the baby lugged in to nurse during service, which they did with the utmost complacency imaginable."

After two long sermons, common in many rural churches where preachers did not visit every Sabbath, she was so exhausted that she contemplated walking out when the meeting adjourned for lunch, which was followed by yet another sermon.[29]

The Baptist preachers did not impress Mrs. Rice, who lived in the city and attended a Presbyterian church there; in her opinion, "the preachers are rather sorry, to use a country expression." Many evangelicals, especially those in towns, agreed with her that the clergy should be educated, genteel men. A Methodist newspaper reported, "There is a growing tendency in the Methodist literature to accommodate the spirit of the age, by acknowledging that its ministry, is not exactly the thing for modern society . . . the intelligence of the people has outgrown the intelligence of the pulpit." The Presbyterians, of course, had always placed a high value on an educated clergy, but in the 1830s the Methodists and Baptists also debated the issue and their conferences and associations generally favored more strenuous qualifications for clergymen. In 1831 Benjamin Drake chaired a committee at the Methodist Annual Conference that recommended higher examination standards for ministers. Mississippi Methodists contributed to the support of several seminaries. The Baptists also praised education and established the Judson Institute in 1836 to educate ministers. One Baptist minister stated "that no man unless a Hebrew scholar, was qualified to occupy a pulpit!"[30]

The growing number of educated ministers in the state, concentrated in the towns, and a growing economic, social, and intellectual stratification among the clergy and the laity were part of a general southern and, indeed, a national pattern. Churchgoers in town demanded a different sort of preacher than rural congregations. In 1840 John G. Jones was disappointed by his reception in Natchez: "I was well received by the larger part of the church in Natchez especially the older members," he wrote, "but there was a later generation that did not like my plain and direct way of preaching. It might be well enough for the country but it did not suit the style of city people." Henry H. Bridges, a Methodist minister, attempted to comfort his friend and fellow minister Elijah Steele after the latter's appointment to Port Gibson, a wealthy cotton town. Bridges expressed his preference for the "poor, rich in faith and heirs to the kingdom." He wrote that "in our rich little towns, much wealth does not imply great or extensive knowledge in divine things." Bridges warned that town ministers were often tempted "to turn from 'the Old Way', and . . . tickle the ear rather than wound the heart. Others again who *can* relish plain food will not receive it unless it be served up in a 'lordly dish.' "[31]

Evangelicals had some difficulty finding ministers to fill town stations; Winans described the importance of churches in towns like Natchez and Vicksburg, but the Methodists had "comparatively few suitable men to fill them." In a similar vein, a Baptist newspaper writer wrote: "There is no great want of preachers to fill stations of ordinary usefulness. But when an individual is needed to man an important post . . . we look every where." The number of suitable—that is, educated and sophisticated—men increased, however. There were men like John Armstrong, a Baptist minister in Columbus, Mississippi, who graduated from Columbian College in Washington, D.C., and studied in France and Germany for two years. The Reverend Dr. Haden Leavel, a Methodist minister and physician who held appointments in Jackson and Vicksburg in the 1840s, was a Kentucky native, "blessed with a liberal education" and known for "his suavity of manners."[32]

Many of the town ministers became quite wealthy; indeed, as a group town ministers across the South were surprisingly prosperous. E. Brooks Holifield in a survey of southern town ministers found that their average wealth was approximately four times that of the average American; he noted that "this relative affluence distinguished these southern urban clergy not only from most other Americans but also from their counterparts" in northern cities. By the late 1840s many Mississippi ministers "had acquired for themselves plantations," often by marrying into the planter elite, a phenomenon that was common enough to arouse criticism. One Mississippi newspaper reported the marriage of a Methodist minister and a "young lady of fortune" with the comment that "there seems to exist a powerful attraction between divines of note and females of this class." Another minister encountered the same attitude from a group of women who speculated on why men entered the ministry; one said, "They want to marry! In proof of this, sir! they will preach around till they marry some rich man's daughter." The best example of a minister who married well was Charles K. Marshall, the Methodist minister in Vicksburg, who married the daughter of Newitt Vick, the founder of the city. His wife inherited a valuable tract of land on the riverfront and brought her husband an estate valued at $102,000. However controversial, such connections made these ministers even more acceptable to wealthy congregations in cotton towns like Natchez, Port Gibson, Columbus, and Vicksburg. In Natchez, for example, the Presbyterian minister, Perry Chase, had an estate valued at $65,000 in 1860 and W. G. Millsaps, a Methodist, held property valued at $45,000.[33] Perhaps their country brothers envied their material success, their social prominence, and their superior educations; certainly a backlash against them developed.

The country preachers questioned the value of an educated clergy. William Winans, who had only two weeks of formal schooling, understandably championed their cause. Though he was self-taught, no one questioned his intellectual abilities; a fellow minister called him "one of the greatest minds on the continent. . . . He was an intellectual giant." After his friend Benjamin Drake chaired the committee that recommended higher qualification standards, Winans challenged Drake's conclusions: "Much as we need polish, it seems to me we need *Stamina* more. I mean we need more of the spirit, the zeal, the industry, the devotion of the ministerial character more than we need intellectual culture." The town ministers "tauntingly asked 'Are you then in favor of having an ignorant ministry?'" To which Winans replied, "'By no means.' Nor will it result that such will be the character of a ministry from the fact that unlearned and ignorant men are admitted into it." Winans heaped scorn on the educated ministers:

They have other refined and elevated tastes that must be accommodated. The churches where they condescend to hear the gospel must, if possible, be magnificent piles of Gothic architecture. The seats must be *pews*, to keep apart the elite and the vulgar, and must be carpeted and cushioned. The music must be the scientific performance of a well-trained choir, accompanied by the deep, solemn, awe-inspiring tones of the organ. Nothing less than all this can match the pretensions of such excelsior, Methodist-taught graduates.

Drake came to accept Winans's view and believed that educational requirements for ministers posed the "greatest danger to our Church now." The country ministers maintained that God's call, not education, should determine who would preach the Gospel. The country preachers called for a return to evangelical roots. A Methodist reminded his readers that early Methodist preachers "turned the world upside down. They may not be learned, but they have done a work which learning with less piety has failed to do." He harked back to the church's egalitarian tradition and proclaimed: "We are sent to no particular class. . . . The poor man and his family must not be shut out."[34]

Some traditionalists did not limit their criticism of education to the clergy but questioned the value of formal education in general. As one

Methodist newspaper reported, "A human being may know how to read, and yet be a very stupid fellow; another may be ignorant of that art, yet become very intelligent, by an intimate acquaintance with man and with nature. Reading and writing are not magic arts; of themselves, they are of little value. The mere circumstance of being able to read and write, does not make the person thus endowed more intelligent than another."[35]

The same debate over the value of education occurred in Baptist churches, where the very idea of a professional, educated clergy ran counter to their tradition. When N. L. Clark, pastor of the New Chapel Baptist Church in the village of Pulaski, joined the Mississippi Baptist Association the church refused to let him preach any longer, citing the following reasons:

> Because you hold that every person rich or poor young or old black or white are indebted to you for your preaching and are not honest if they don't pay it . . . and you carried the hat around and dunned us all acordingly whilst the haughty gentleman Barnes [B. L. Barnes, another Baptist preacher] said we would spurn to take it as a deed of charity but want you to come up and pay us what you justly owe us. We are a poor people and not willing to get any more in debt until we pay what we allready owe.

Similarly, in 1849 the Fellowship Baptist Church in Lauderdale County split over the role of the ministry. One faction held the traditional view of a congregational ministry; they believed that God used only the direct agency of the Holy Spirit to convert sinners, a view that denigrated the minister's role and favored the active participation of the laity. A smaller faction thought the minister had a more active role to play in salvation, a view popular with many educated clergymen involved in the attempt to elevate their status and the importance of the ministerial gift and limit the laity to the role of spectators in the worship service. These modern clergymen were changing basic aspects of evangelical worship and creating what can be called a clerical ministry as opposed to a congregational one. The faction favoring a clerical ministry withdrew from the church. In 1853 Roland Wilkinson, a Baptist preacher, withdrew from Zion Hill Baptist Church after he became "convinced that the Baptist church or churches of that denomination as they are properly known are not . . . what they formerly were, but have widely departed from the simplicity of the gospel of Christ." The call for an educated ministry angered this country preacher; he charged that "ministers who have not enjoyed superior monetary advantages or literary qualifications but who have nevertheless been greatly blessed of God in the work of the ministry are now generally but lightly esteemed & crowded aside to make room for those who have not been called to God but have merely received the literary honors of a college or a diploma of a theological seminary." After his withdrawal, Wilkinson led in the organization of the Amite Primitive Baptist Association.[36]

The debate between the two groups did not stop with education; they disagreed over issues ranging from proper preaching style to the place of singing and music in worship. In broader terms, the argument was between those who favored a congregational ministry and those who favored a clerical ministry. Town ministers and country preachers criticized one another's preaching styles, and town and country congregations expressed their preferences. The town ministers favored a "smooth and harmonious" style free of "affectation" and "flourishes." The "heavenly tone," so popular with early evangelicals, fell out of favor. One young Port Gibson woman expressed her disappointment in a preacher who "labored so hard to get his discourse out, his distorted features & troubled body distressed me." If this preacher was trying to arouse his listeners, he had chosen the wrong congregation. By contrast, a member of a country church "heard the Rev. Capers *read* an essay of his on *Reason* & Religion" during which "a great many took short *naps*, & Some took tolerably long ones." Obviously, the Reverend Capers made no attempt to act as a catalyst to bring his hearers to God. He did not expect or even want lay involvement in the ministerial effort. A Presbyterian minister described a country preacher's sermon: "His manner of preaching was *Methodistical*, clapping . . . his hands stamping with his feet, and occasionally throwing in such expressions as 'God bless your soul' 'God love you' & c. characterized his discourse." Town ministers wanted to escape the association of this preaching style with all Methodists and Baptists. The country preachers called on their critics to remember their roots and put excitement back in their discourse.[37]

A cappella congregational singing played a vital role in early evangelical services. As part of the reduction in lay participation in services, many urban churches in the 1830s organized choirs rather than allow congregational singing, and the role of song in the church became a heated issue. In 1838 an article in an evangelical newspaper criticized the use of choirs and musical instruments. According to the writer, "It is well known that singing is an essential and powerful agent in awakening devotional feelings. Not dull and formal, but lively and energetic singing." John G. Jones wrote, "In many of the fashionable churches of the present day, all that the congregation hear during 'the service of song' is the mingled din of instrumental music and the screaming of human voices." The introduction of choirs and instruments had a far-reaching impact on the traditional evangelical folk music; lining out hymns and shape-note singing, for example, were impossible with choirs and musical accompaniment. Walter Edwin Tynes, later a Baptist preacher, recalled that as a young man he attended a singing school "taught by an old Methodist minister named William Townsend, vocal music exclusively, introducing the seven syllable note system instead of the four note system previously used. . . . Instrumental music was not tolerated in religious worship. The first organ introduced in church in this immediate section was denounced by one of the old preachers as a 'fiddle box', and thus related to the demoralizing dance."[38]

Again and again, country preachers called on evangelicals to remember the old ways and not follow the current fashion. Jones lamented that "large numbers of Methodist preachers, somehow, have lost the power of song." Jones clearly recognized that singing was an important gift and a powerful instrument of conversion. He wrote:

> It was no uncommon occurrence for hearts to be reached by the song that had remained unmoved by the sermon. We have known persons awakened, converted, sanctified, and otherwise abundantly comforted and edified under these concluding songs. But, alas for the spirituality of the Church, and, we may sorrowfully add, for the salvation of souls, this gushing, stirring, melting, and enrapturing method of singing . . . has been superseded by a new style, which . . . has but little—often none—of the spirit and power of our former "service of song."[39]

In 1838 the state Methodist Conference passed the following resolution: "It is the sense of this Conference that the introduction of instrumental music into public worship . . . and the conducting of the music in our churches by choirs . . . is injurious to the spirituality of singing, and is inconsistent with the directions of our Discipline." The Methodist *Discipline* devoted over half its directions to singing in worship, reflecting the importance attached to this form of ministry in the early church. The debate over choirs and instrumental music disrupted the annual conferences throughout the antebellum period and beyond.[40]

The issue also disrupted some local churches. In 1865 a male churchgoer recorded in his diary that his church (probably Methodist) "had the vote taken whether there should be a Melodion in the Church I voted for it. . . . Some of the Sisters got very hot indeed & jumped up & run out of the Church." The diarist did not suggest why the women felt so strongly about this vote, but many women were known for their gift of song. For example, "Mother" Sarah Epps, a South Carolina native who was converted by Francis Asbury before her move west in 1820, "took great interest in the . . . poetry of our excellent hymn books, and the singing of revival songs."[41] Singing gave women their first important liturgical role in the churches, and they opposed the trend away from lay participation, which often included choirs and instrumental music. A decrease in lay participation had a disproportionate effect on women because they were barred from filling church offices, and that may have motivated their attempt to keep traditional forms of worship intact.

New organizations such as Sunday schools and missionary societies, however, opened up fresh opportunities for women to expand their role. Women were active as teachers in Sunday schools, a position that many filled with dedication and pride. When Jane McGinnis died in 1899, the records of the First Presbyterian Church in Port Gibson noted, "For 50 years a S.S. [Sunday school] teacher Great loss to church & community." Sophia Hays, a young widow in Kosciuszko, taught Sunday school in the 1850s and found it a rewarding experience. She wrote, "Most of my class are interesting girls who are attentive & thoughtful—a circumstance which has quite encouraged me in the hope of being the means of benefitting them." When she contemplated leaving the town, she felt torn: "One of my greatest regrets in leaving is on account of my Sabbath School. I have learned to love them almost as my own family." Clearly, Sunday schools provided some women and girls with the opportunity to meet together and to create bonds of intimacy and affection without direct male supervision. Most schools were probably segregated by sex, but not all were; Robert Alexander noted in his diary, "I went to Sunday School heard a tolerably good Lesson from 4 or 5 girls in my class."[42] Whether the move from lay ministry to clerical ministry benefited or further restricted women is difficult if not impossible to measure, though the change may have encouraged greater segregation by gender in the expanding number of auxiliary religious organizations.

Many Methodist, Baptist, and Presbyterian churches moved away from the intimate, lay-oriented services that played such a vital role in the earlier decades of the century. Methodists began to abandon class meetings and love feasts, two traditional services in which lay participation and leadership were crucial and emotionally demonstrative worship was common. The love feast recognized "the preciousness and individuality of every Christian's experience; and by confidence and sympathy would draw it forth, for God's glory and the Church's edification." The ceremonies had been an important part of early Methodist worship, but by the

1830s some ministers refused to hold love feasts and class meetings. When John G. Jones took over a new appointment in the 1830s, he found that the previous minister had not enforced the *Discipline;* he promptly reinstituted class meetings, held them regularly after preaching, and noted that the participants sometimes "had a shout." He held similar services for his black congregations. Jones and others blamed reform-minded modernist ministers for not holding class meetings and love feasts. One Methodist called on the annual conference to enforce the *Discipline* and "do all you can to *revive* class meetings, for is it not the wheel within the wheel." Many Methodists recorded their moving experiences at these services and considered them an important part of their religious life. The Methodist Quarterly Meeting on the Carthage Circuit suspended Stephen Henry, a minister, for failing to attend class meetings. Rather than enforcing the *Discipline* and encouraging or requiring ministers to hold such services, the General Conference in 1866 recognized the new situation and changed the rule making attendance at class meetings a test of membership. In a similar vein, Missionary Baptist churches abandoned the intimate foot-washing ceremonies, and the modernist Baptist press declared that the ceremony was not an ordinance of the church. By the 1840s the festal Presbyterian communion season was also largely a memory.[43]

Some ministers and evangelicals also criticized revivals and camp meetings, both of which had played a major role in the early expansion of the church. Criticism of revivals was nothing new; many early evangelicals questioned their effectiveness, but beginning in the 1830s that issue became a part of the debate between the modernists and traditionalists. Faultfinders deplored these "religious pic-nics" and charged that revivals were nothing more than "school boy and girl excitement." Where critics saw excitement, proponents saw wonderful visitations of the Holy Spirit. At an 1855 revival in Homochito, Mississippi, "the convictions were powerful, sometimes prostrating the individual and depriving him of the use of his limbs, as in the times of Wesley, Whitefield, and Dow." At a revival held in Starkville in 1852, "there was an extraordinary display of the power of the Almighty, and an outpouring of His spirit." Hundreds and even thousands of people attended these services. Occasionally, Methodists and Baptists held joint meetings. Blacks often attended the services, and, like the whites, were powerfully moved. At one such meeting, 106 whites converted, "but there was no calculating those among the colored." Occasionally separate services were held for blacks.[44]

Proponents of revivals charged that many of their critics had been converted at revivals and camp meetings: "If they forget the rock whence

they were hewn, we must not." Revivalists had no patience with evangelicals who tried to raise their status. One revivalist asked "the Lord [to]
multiply revivals after the old style, and in great mercy to the earth keep a
people always upon it not too learned, or well-bred, or decent, to re-enact
the scenes of Pentecost."[45]

As the above illustrations indicate, emotionally demonstrative responses were common to both blacks and white plain folk. The association of shouting and "physical exercises" with these groups led to
criticism from modernists who considered themselves above such displays. John G. Jones described his wealthy congregation in the affluent
Natchez region as "quite respectful to religion." These people were cultivated and made pleasant company, "but there was a great want of New
Testament spirituality." Isham R. Howze, a Baptist planter in Marshall
County, wrote: "I do not think these seasons of excitement are favorable
to the proper instruction of Sinners.... Warmth, in religion, is ... pleasing
in the sight of God. Yet prudence should govern every man.... There is
such a thing as religious intemperance; an excess in animal feelings." The
Reverend Charles K. Marshall, a prominent Methodist minister, wanted
services to be free of "getting happy," shouting, and other emotional expressions. During the 1840 state conference many of those attending a
service, including ministers, shouted and clapped their hands during the
service. Marshall, outraged at his fellow preachers, criticized them the
following day; his remarks offended many traditionalists, and a motion
was made to remove him from the itinerancy and locate him permanently
without his consent. The motion was lost after a heated debate, but the
young and popular Marshall represented the wave of the future.[46]

The class antagonisms that appeared in the conflict between the modernists and traditionalists had implications beyond the religious sphere.
After the 1830s, as church membership increased and religious beliefs
and assumptions became more widely diffused through southern culture,
these religious conflicts carried over into the political sphere. In 1843,
Josiah Hinds, a prominent member of the Methodist church in north Mississippi, unsuccessfully ran for a seat in the state legislature. An important
plank in his platform was his support for the incorporation of Centenary
College, located in Brandon Springs, Mississippi, which was established
by the Methodist church in 1841. Hinds reported that the voters elected instead "as pure a delegation of anties as ever went from aney county in this
Itawamba county, and the anties have succe[e]ded no doubt throughout the
state. In this county our delegation is anti-bond, anti-temperance, anti-
missionary, anti-education, anti-everything like morral improvement—

one a Hardshell Baptist, one the son of a Hardshell, one a Baptist sinner, and one Protestant Methodist preacher."[47]

Hinds's political analysis is revealing in his suggestion of a strong connection between religious traditionalists such as the Primitive (Hardshell) Baptists and Protestant Methodists and opposition to moral reform movements. His analysis not only suggests how religious beliefs influenced political affiliation but also that Mississippi's religious and political culture was part of the national contest between Whigs and Democrats, which was heavily influenced by religion. The religious conflict coincided with the heated political debates between Democrats and Whigs and influenced party politics and affiliation in the state. Religious traditionalists were more likely to be Democrats, and modernists were more likely to be Whigs. Whigs looked favorably on the emerging competitive capitalist system and the market economy. Generally successful themselves, they were optimistic about the new individualistic social order but aware of the need for change in personal character—the need for personal control, discipline, and drive to meet its demands. To this end, they favored the creation of large organizations such as benevolent societies and corporations to replace the more personal relationships and ties characteristic of organic communities which had been dissolved by social and economic mobility. They also favored government regulation of ethics, morals, and beliefs. Democrats wanted less restraint on individuals and idealized a society that was localistic and egalitarian. They saw the emerging capitalist economy as a threat to their economic independence and political liberty and rejected the Whigs' "integrative approach" to morality, religion, culture, and politics.[48]

Often the opponents of religious modernization couched their rhetoric in language that reflected their uneasiness with the market economy. Primitive Baptists in Leake County, for example, criticized Missionary Baptists for "buying life membership in societies under the pretension of spreading the gospel, therefore placing the gospel side by side with common merchandise, and placing the poor brother on an unequal footing with the rich hypocrite." An association of Primitive Baptists in Monroe County charged that their opponents "are running greedily after the things of this world," condemned "fairs whare toys and merchandise of various kinds are vended," and found "many unfair means . . . for the purpose of getting money." Harking back to the early church, they reported that "no where do we hear of Paul or any other apostle Hiring himself out to preach the gospel for wages—for money." A writer in a Methodist newspaper blasted the love of filthy lucre: "One answer, and one alone, comes up to almost all the ills and desolations of human existance. . . . It rumbles out in the ruinous voice of the earthquake—in storm—in terror—in despair—the 'almighty dollar,' the 'dollar almighty.' "[49]

As the South was drawn ever deeper into the market economy, the yeomen's traditional aversion to the market with its inherent threat to self-sufficiency and community carried over into other aspects of their lives. The tendency to couch protests to religious modernization in terms of the marketplace and material culture can be traced back to the revolutionary period, when commercial goods took on great symbolic power in the colonial struggle with Great Britain. The challenge to British imported goods had given American patriots a ready tool to spread their ideology, a shorthand by which they communicated perceptions of status and political allegiance. In this sense, the early evangelicals' hostility to luxury goods, women's finery, or gambling and the hostility Primitive Baptists and other religious traditionalists expressed to the market, wages for ministers, expensive church edifices, or church fairs in the 1830s and beyond take on a deeper symbolic meaning. Although the choice of personal clothing and the acquisition of luxury goods were private consumer decisions, they reflected social status within a community or household. Revolutionary patriots had used the popularity of British imports to launch a powerful moral critique of colonial society; in the same vein, evangelical traditionalists used the language of goods to attack religious modernists. The language of goods provided a ready and obvious link between ideology and local, and even household, experience.[50]

Religion, then, helped shape an individual's sense of self and influenced basic assumptions about the nature of society, economic structure, and government, all of which had important implications for political behavior. The fusion of politics and religion is readily discernible regarding several issues that emerged in the 1830s and 1840s. One of these issues was temperance, a favorite cause among reform-minded evangelicals. The creation of temperance societies was encouraged by modernist ministers. Speaking for the modernists, the Baptist State Convention in 1839 urged "every friend to his country, every patriotic citizen, every one who is fond of good order in society" to support the temperance cause. Traditionalists, however, condemned such organizations, believing that they were unscriptural schemes to serve the ambitions of individuals. The temperance movement became politicized in the 1830s. In 1834 a state temperance convention was held in Jackson, and reformers began to push for legislation to curb alcohol consumption. In 1839 the legislature, controlled by the Whigs—"the party of temperance"—and their allies, enacted "An Act for the Suppression of Tippling-Houses, and to Discourage and Prevent the Odious Vice of Drunkenness." As Hinds's quote suggests, religious modernists favored the bill, while traditionalists opposed it. It proved to be unenforceable and was a divisive political issue until its repeal in 1842. Modernists, however, continued to agitate for temperance legislation as a part of their campaign to create an ordered society.[51]

Religious modernists saw education as a central part of their program to inculcate discipline and virtue in the people and led them to support denominational colleges and Sunday schools, both of which were viewed with suspicion and outright hostility by traditionalists. As Hinds suggested, education, too, became a heated political issue with religious overtones. In 1842 the Methodist church sought state incorporation for Centenary College. An act of incorporation passed both the House and Senate by a comfortable margin, but Governor Tilghman M. Tucker, a Jacksonian Democrat, vetoed the measure. Jacksonians saw incorporation of sectarian colleges as a violation of the separation of church and state and viewed such colleges as antirepublican institutions favorable to a particular group or class, a stand applauded by religious traditionalists who doubted the value of an educated ministry.[52]

Overarching these specific and relatively minor issues was a more important and complex connection between religion and politics. The traditionalist evangelicals' suspicion of wealth and hierarchy, their emphasis on egalitarianism and lay control, their opposition to national benevolent societies, their doubts about the value of education, and their intense localism affected their political outlook and contributed to their support of Jacksonian democracy. The modernists, with their more ecumenical outlook, their participation in the benevolent empire, and their support of education and professionalization likewise had a worldview more compatible with the Whigs' vision of society. This is not to say that religion determined party affiliation; the situation was considerably more complex. To cite one example, William Winans, the champion of the traditionalists' battle against educational requirements for the ministry, was a leader in benevolent associations and a committed Whig. As Ronald P. Formisano wrote, "Religion as a group experience and source of values profoundly influenced political behavior in nineteenth-century America. . . . not in terms of formal creeds coinciding with party ideologies but rather from religion shaping basic orientations to self, society, and government. . . . Religion joined with cultural background, socioeconomic conditions, and many other causes to influence party choice."[53]

During the period from 1830 to 1860, the debate between tradition-alists and modernists shaped the evangelical experience. Evangelicalism was transformed from small sects made up predominantly of white plain folk and blacks to large, wealthy, more inclusive denominations. In some respects, evangelicals became more influential and powerful as they at-tracted more wealthy members and became more affluent themselves, but they came to incorporate not only the elite but their attitudes and opin-ions as well. Splinter groups siphoned off from the three major denomi-nations many of the plain folk and those dissatisfied with the changes in the ministry and in worship services.

The debate between modernists and traditionalists had elements of class and social divisions. Modernists were centered in the towns and plantation districts among wealthier congregations, while traditionalists found their main support among poorer congregations in rural areas, the Piney Woods, and the northern part of the state. The lines were not always clear-cut, and not all traditionalists lived in obscure poverty; for example, Hiram Runnels, a Primitive Baptist from Lawrence County, became one of the state's most prominent Democratic politicians and was elected gov-ernor. As Bertram Wyatt-Brown wrote in his study of the divisions among southern Baptists, "The controversy exhibited deep-seated class antago-nisms within the South itself . . . antimissionism was one expression of a confused internal cleavage between the folkways of the poor and their social betters, a conflict that belies the notion of a monolithic southern cultural unity."[54]

As town ministers led the churches in the quest for status and prestige, they sought to gain a higher professional status for themselves. Increas-ingly, ministers set themselves above the laity; they elevated the impor-tance of the ministerial gift while depreciating gifts traditionally exer-cised by the laity. In more and more churches, the laity became spectators, and the enthusiastic services so common in the early churches were re-placed by a more sedate, less emotional service. This is not to suggest a grand conspiracy on the part of modernist clergymen, who saw them-selves as the leaders of a movement that would strengthen the churches through an expanded membership and an ever-growing network of aux-iliary organizations. Obviously, many members approved of the changes in the churches; certainly the burdens of membership grew lighter as the shift to a clerical ministry put fewer demands on the laity. Churches often sought to assume a dominant posture in their communities; belonging to the largest or wealthiest church could be a source of great satisfaction for many members. A formal service appealed to more refined church-goers, and others might be moved by a splendid interior and a practiced choir. The yearning for status, wealth, and influence impelled modernist evangelicals toward the acceptance of slavery and led them away from the egalitarianism of the early churches.

CHAPTER 7

THE LASHES OF A GUILTY CONSCIENCE

EVANGELICAL PROSLAVERY AND

SLAVE MISSIONS

I N 1836 the Reverend James Smylie published the first biblical defense of slavery by a Mississippian; his introduction, written in the third person, reads in part:

> From his intercourse with religious societies of all denominations, in Mississippi and Louisiana, he was aware that the abolition maxim, viz: *that slavery is in itself sinful*, had gained on, and entwined itself among the religious and conscientious scruples of many in the community, so far as not only to render them unhappy, but to draw off the attention from the great and important duty of a householder to his household. . . . Many a slaveholder, whose conscience is guided, not by the word of God, but by the doctrines of men, is often suffering the lashes of a guilty conscience, even when he renders to his slave "that which is just and equal," according to the scriptures, simply because he does not emancipate his slave.[1]

It is ironic that when Smylie searched for a metaphor to describe southern slaveholders' feelings on the subject of slavery he chose the graphic image of the lash, one so closely identified with the institution's brutality, as if every wound inflicted by the whip reverberated in the masters' minds and hearts. Slaveholders' guilt over the institution of slavery has been the subject of scholarly debate since the idea was introduced over half a century ago. Many historians have rightly questioned the prevalence of such attitudes among southern slaveholders. Southern slaveholding evangelicals were trapped in a moral dilemma as they confronted the obvious contradictions between their faith and the peculiar institution. Beginning in the 1830s, however, modernist evangelicals, led by Smylie, found a means of reconciling the faith with slavery to the satisfaction of most evangelicals and other slaveholders.

Just as modernists advocated a more hierarchical church structure, they envisioned a hierarchical family and society and repudiated individualism. The proslavery argument was a part of the headlong southern rush away from the bourgeois individualism associated with the emergence of capitalism in the urban Northeast. Thus the tendency among historians to view southern evangelicalism as focused solely on the individual is misleading.[2] By the 1830s evangelical modernists shifted their emphasis from the individual, as evidenced by their move away from a congregational ministry; criticism of the camp meetings and the emotional individual conversion experience; the abandonment of class meeting, foot-washing ceremonies, and communion seasons; the shift from gender-segregated seating to family pews; and the restricted role of laypeople in services.

The period from 1830 to 1860 saw a major shift in evangelical theology as modernists abandoned the traditional evangelical emphasis on the equality of believers for a more hierarchical, corporate view of the religious community, a change with tremendous implications for blacks and women. These clergymen and their supporters sought to expand evangelical influence not simply through individual conversion but through corporate bodies such as the various religious societies, schools, and colleges and through their vision of the household, perhaps their most frequently employed trope.

Important theological changes followed. Although a few evangelicals continued their antislavery efforts, another current developed within their ranks, and they would be forced to choose sides on the slavery question. Many evangelicals remained ambivalent about slavery and criticized it openly until the mid-1830s, but after that time criticism of the institution was not welcomed or well received as events outside the state, particularly the abolitionist movement, affected Mississippi churches. Along with increased abolitionist attacks on the institution of slavery came southern religious defenses of their peculiar institution.

Few Mississippi evangelicals could be described as rabid abolitionists even before 1830, but as Methodist John G. Jones observed, most believed that slavery "was a great social, political, and moral evil, which, while it had to be endured for the present, ought as soon as possible to be removed." Timothy Flint, a Presbyterian minister who lived in Louisiana and traveled extensively in the Southwest, reported the view typical of planters in the region: "I have never yet heard one, who does not admit that slavery is an injustice and an evil." But though planters acknowledged slavery as an evil, Flint continued, they did not favor immediate emancipation; instead, they believed that "the evil must go off as it came on, by a slow and gradual method." The belief that slavery was unjust represented a broad American consensus that grew out of the noblest ideals of the revolutionary era. Those sentiments echoed in an 1818 ruling from the Mississippi Supreme Court that stated, "Slavery is condemned by reason and the laws of nature." Abraham Lincoln referred to this consensus in his famous 1858 debates with Stephen Douglas; when reviewing the history of the republic, Lincoln observed that it had endured because "the great mass of the nation have rested in the belief that slavery was in course of ultimate extinction," a belief supported by the ideology of the Revolution and the policies of the Early National period.[3]

The key phrase, of course, was "ultimate extinction." Most southerners, including the majority of evangelicals, were content to decry slavery as an evil, wring their hands in despair over ever finding the proper time or method of abolishing it, and continue to buy, sell, and own slaves. George Poindexter, the popular politician and son of a Baptist preacher, expressed the prevailing sentiment in an 1830 speech: "It is not with us . . . a matter of choice whether we will have slaves among us or not; we found them here, and we are obliged to maintain and employ them. It would be a blessing could we get rid of them; but the wisest and best men among us have not been able to devise a plan for doing it."[4] Problems arose only when the abolitionists shifted from proposing gradual or voluntary plans for emancipation, which many southerners supported, to more radical schemes of immediate abolition. The debate was a religious one before it became political; it was fueled largely by religious leaders on both sides of the Mason-Dixon Line,[5] and it was no coincidence that religious institutions were torn asunder long before political institutions suffered the same fate.

John G. Jones's change of heart on the slavery issue illustrates the complexities many evangelicals faced. Jones grew up in a slaveholding family of yeoman farmers and, until his conversion, had no qualms about slavery. After his conversion, however, he became an opponent of slavery, and his journal from the 1830s contains many antislavery passages. He advised friends against buying slaves, distributed "Mr. Wesley's thoughts on the Slave Trade," and offered to free his slaves though they chose instead to be sold to a kindly master. He wrote of "the curse of negro slavery" and described it as "a great evil." His attitude changed dramatically, however, after the publication of Smylie's pamphlet with which he was familiar. In 1840, he added this postscript to an earlier antislavery passage in his journal: "More mature experience and a more thorough examination of the whole subject has greatly modified my views of 'negro slavery.'"[6]

He was not alone; between 1830 and 1840 most southerners modified their views and adopted a proslavery ideology. Mississippians took an early lead in elaborating upon the biblical defense of slavery, and many evangelicals like Jones were swayed by proslavery arguments based on Scripture. In the late 1820s Smylie, one of the first Presbyterian ministers to settle in Mississippi, began to defend slavery on biblical grounds. In his background and career, Smylie had much in common with his contemporary proslavery authors. He was born in Richmond County, North Carolina, in 1780 to James and Jane W. Smylie; his father had immigrated to America from Scotland in 1776. Little is known of his early life before he became a student at the Reverend David Caldwell's famous "Log College" in Guilford County, North Carolina, the alma mater of many if not most southern Presbyterian ministers in the late eighteenth and early nineteenth centuries. After his ordination in 1806, Smylie settled in Washington, the capital of the Mississippi Territory, along with other family members. In 1809 the entire clan relocated to the newly created Amite County, and Smylie purchased over a thousand acres of land, the core of his plantation called Myrtle Heath, where he lived in high style. His property in slaves reflected his increasing wealth; he owned thirteen slaves in 1830, increasing that number to thirty in 1840, so he was one of the largest slaveholders in the county and a member of the South's planter aristocracy.[7]

Smylie became one of the best-known clerics in southwestern Mississippi. He organized several churches, was responsible for convincing the Synod of Kentucky to create the Presbytery of Mississippi and South Alabama, and served as its clerk for many years. His stature was considerable; one biographer wrote, "From his weight of character and familiarity with ecclesiastical law and usage, his influence in that Presbytery, throughout his life, was almost magisterial." He was also well-known outside the church; he operated a classical boarding school that attracted the sons of the Natchez gentry, he helped organize the Amite Literary Society and the Amite and Florida Bible Society, and prominent Whig politicians in the state courted his favor.[8]

Like other proslavery advocates, Smylie was not an obscure country parson but held a prominent position within his church and society. His Presbyterianism also put him in the mainstream, for more proslavery writers came from that denomination than any other. No doubt the high educational requirements for Presbyterian ministers helps explain their preponderance, as does their theology, because Calvinism was free of the Arminian doctrines of equality. His background as an educator and slaveholder was also common among such authors. Perhaps the most important link uniting these proslavery ministers was their stance as religious modernists; as historian Larry Tise described them, "In every sense they were leaders, not followers; innovators, not imitators; thinkers, not mirror reflections of pat models."[9]

It was no coincidence that the defense of slavery in the state began with a wealthy slave owner who ministered to the most affluent denomination. Scholars have described authors of proslavery tracts as frustrated and unhappy men unable to rise to positions of prominence in the South or as neglected intellectuals who used the defense of slavery to carve out a respected place for themselves in southern society. Smylie, however, was a successful planter, a member of the state's slave-owning elite. He was "superior in literary attainments and pulpit abilities" to his fellow ministers and was "one of the leading ministers of his denomination."[10]

Smylie hardly expected or needed proslavery writings to raise his status. Indeed, his biblical defense of slavery initially set him apart from his fellow evangelicals, most of whom found his view at variance with evangelical tradition. John G. Jones, in his history of Mississippi religion, wrote that "while others were discussing various schemes for gradual emancipation, colonization, etc., Mr. Smylie sat down to a quiet, honest and critical examination of the Holy Bible," which convinced him "that the enslavement of the Hamitic race had been recognized as justifiable under every dispensation of the Church . . . that the holiest men . . . in the Bible had been connected with it, without censure, and that the relative duties of masters and servants were clearly defined in the New Testament Scriptures, which was demonstrative evidence that the relation was . . . compatible with Christianity." In the late 1820s, Smylie composed a sermon on the subject that he chose to deliver not in one of the rural churches he pastored in his area but at the Presbyterian church in Port Gibson, a prominent pulpit in a wealthy cotton town. He must have been shocked by the response from this slaveholding congregation and his fellow ministers; his sermon "gave great offense, not only to the church but also to his brethren in the ministry, who seriously advised him to preach that sermon no more."[11]

It is unclear whether Smylie delivered the sermon again, but he was a notoriously strong-willed man, convinced of the correctness of his opinions. In 1836 the Presbytery of Chillicothe, Ohio, a hotbed of abolitionism, sent an antislavery petition to the Presbytery of Mississippi. Smylie wrote a long response based on his sermon, but the Mississippi Presbytery was too disturbed by his radical ideas to accept it. Despite continued warnings from his colleagues, Smylie published the response as a pamphlet, but no publisher would accept it and he was forced to have it printed privately.[12]

The hostile reaction to Smylie's sermon and the presbytery's refusal to accept his response led him to anticipate that his pamphlet would provoke considerable controversy. He wrote: "My sentiments were at variance with the decisions of the General Assembly of the Presbyterian Church—with the Discipline of the Methodist Church—and with the Bishops of the Episcopal Church—They were also at variance with the commentators of the scriptures, on that subject of all societies . . . so that I felt doubtful whether the pamphlet with its author would not be kicked out of the synagogue of Presbyterian, Methodists, Baptists & episcopalians, so soon as it would make its appearance." No doubt the controversial nature of the pamphlet provoked interest in it, and it "circulated generally through the country, and was the first . . . ever published in the Southwest on that side of the question." His work won increased recognition because it was attacked by abolitionists; indeed, he "was covered with odium, and honored with a large amount of abuse from the abolitionists," a reaction he provoked by sending copies to them. He and New York abolitionist Gerrit Smith, for example, engaged in a fierce pamphlet war. Merchants in Mississippi and Louisiana sold copies of the tract at fifty cents per copy, and Smylie received letters from across the South requesting copies. The pamphlet circulated widely in the Southwest. Historian Walter Brownlow Posey believed that Smylie's work soon dominated religious thought on the question across the region. Despite the initially harsh reaction, the tide soon turned in Smylie's favor; he wrote with satisfaction, "Contrary to my fears, my Methodist, Presbyterian, Episcopalian & Baptist brethren, (so far as I have heard) cordially approve of the doctrines of the pamphlet." The modernist religious press responded enthusiastically. As one newspaper commented: "The pamphlet, mentioned in our paper week before last, seems to have an almost unbounded popularity wherever it is read. . . . The South can do no less than take up Mr. Smylie's present edition without any delay."[13]

The doctrines Smylie espoused were not entirely original to him; he was influenced by earlier proslavery writers, including David Reese. As Tise demonstrated, the basic outlines of the proslavery argument changed very little over time; indeed, a comparison of Smylie's tract with one written over a century before reveals striking similarities. The social, political, and religious climate had changed, and old arguments took on a surprising new force in the 1830s and after.[14]

What is perhaps most striking about Smylie's pamphlet is his emphasis on the household as the bedrock of southern society, the foundation on which all else rested. His concept of a hierarchical, patriarchal household was in a sense retrospective, a revival of a concept of the family that waned in the eighteenth century. Before the mid-eighteenth century white southerners held a traditional European view of the world that considered "the household responsible for, and the symbol of, the whole social system, which was thought to be based on the God-given principles of hierarchy, deference and obedience." It was a view deeply ingrained in Calvinists, who maintained that the father as head of the household was "to govern his subjects (here: wife, children, and servants) so that God would be honored among them." Republicanism, however, undermined this hierarchical "chain of governance," as did the evangelical emphasis on individualism and equality. By the early nineteenth century the tide once again turned to favor patriarchal, authoritarian families.[15]

For modernist clergymen like Smylie, the family was the first link in a chain of governance that kept individuals in check. The household, ruled by white males, was the foundation for a republican society also ruled by these free and equal heads of households. The Methodist Reverend Thomas C. Thornton of Mississippi, author of an 1841 proslavery tract, observed: "In our own families we possess both influence and authority . . . we shall be judged not only as individuals, but as the owners of a 'household.'" A Presbyterian minister in the state wrote, "The true Scriptural idea of slavery . . . is that of a patriarchal relation." The master, he continued, "is essentially the head of the household in all relations— the head of his wife—the head over his children—and the head over his servants."[16]

Abolitionism was only one of a series of threats to the order and stability of society. A threat to slavery was a threat to the household and to the authority of the head of that household; if slavery were tampered with, the entire edifice would tumble down with disastrous consequences. Smylie warned that abolition would lead to further erosions in the household and society: "The licentiousness of the female character in France," he wrote, "is a true test of the effects of the Rights of Women, written by [William] Godwin, one of the High Priests of the abolition of marriage." S. G. Winchester, another Presbyterian minister in the state, made the same analogy in an 1838 address at Oakland College: "We are all aware of the disorganizing and revolutionary tendency of the principles lately advocated by a demon in female form [Frances Wright]. . . . And domestic licenciousness invariably tends to political prostitution. We all know, too, the tendency to those fanatical movements which aim to disturb another of those relations which the Apostle Paul recognizes." These modernist ministers helped forge a new vision of southern society as a hierarchical one with its foundations based on the family and the church, a society that placed a heavy duty on the master/parent/husband and transformed patriarchy into paternalism.[17]

The proslavery vision of society subordinated women as surely as it did slaves. As long as the evangelicals focused their attention on individual conversion, denigrated a convert's ties to family while stressing only the individual's relationship with God, and preached the equality of all believers, it is hardly surprising that men so often opposed the conversion of their wives and children as forcefully as the conversion of slaves. Just as evangelicals assured masters that conversion would make better slaves, they assured husbands that conversion would make wives more content with their subordinate position. Any criticism of the subordinate relations within the family was intended not to threaten that subordination but to perfect it. In 1859 a writer in a Baptist newspaper advocated repeal of laws against teaching slaves to read. As he searched for a parallel to the slave experience he drew on the status of women; an educated slave posed no more danger than an educated wife, he argued. He admitted, however, that "there are *things* that some folks call men, who regard women no more than slaves, and would have them do more work than favorite negroes, or horses." Just as evangelicals argued that religion and even limited education would make better slaves, religion would also make better wives. Christianity and religious training prepared women for their proper station in the household, that of wives and mothers. Just as the education of slaves should be suited to their station, the education of women, too, had proper limits; as one writer warned, "Let us . . . follow the laws of Nature; she does not consign us at our birth to the care of a pedagogue, or the keeping of a philosopher."[18]

The proslavery ideology, then, marked a repudiation of the enlightened revolutionary ideals of individual rights, liberty, and equality and held up instead a vision of a hierarchical slave society based on mutual responsibilities and social cohesion. Proslavery writers and abolitionists engaged in a battle over the proper interpretation of the revolutionary heritage. Southerners questioned whether natural rights as expressed in the Declaration of Independence existed at all. As Thomas Thornton put it, "The phrases 'rights of man,' 'natural rights,' &c. have been well pronounced to be . . . very ambiguous terms, on which it is unsafe to bottom general reasonings." Rights, he argued, varied according to station and condition;

savages were clearly unfit for such responsibilities. William Winans denied that the rights Thomas Jefferson listed in the Declaration were inalienable, and in any event, he maintained that the enlightened author himself did not "consider the slaves of the United States as *parties* to her *political* Institutions, or *partakers* in her *political* rights."[19]

By repudiating the liberal legacy of the Revolution, the South cut itself off from the national mainstream and embraced a vision of society completely at odds with industrial capitalism and individualism. Proslavery ideology set the South on a course that led it ever further away from developments in the rest of the nation. Once again, Lincoln serves as a barometer to gauge how far the North and South diverged as they followed their separate paths. Lincoln cherished the Declaration of Independence and marveled at the willingness of southerners and their allies to destroy or mutilate it. Just as the nation had once stood united in its opposition to slavery, a national consensus had existed on the legacy of the Revolution; in an 1857 speech he said: "In those days, our Declaration of Independence was held sacred by all, and thought to include all; but now, to aid in making the bondage of the negro universal and eternal, it is assailed, and sneered at, and construed, and hawked at, and torn, till, if its framers could rise from their graves, they could not at all recognize it."[20] As the South adopted the proslavery argument, the nation became increasingly a house divided, the consequences of which Lincoln was quicker to recognize than most of his contemporaries. Abolitionists and proslavery clergymen waged a battle over the nation's history and the proper interpretation of its past, a battle with tremendous implications for the nation's future.

With an impressive display of exegesis, proslavery clergymen forged links between religion, family, slavery, and society in a way that maximized their influence. They became the chief defenders of the South's most cherished institution, but more than that, they became the arbiters of the entire paternal slave system. As one minister wrote to slaveholders, "They [slaves] are yours—wholly yours; and no one has, according to the teachings of Heaven, and the laws of men, any right to interfere, in the smallest degree, with you or them, except myself." As Smylie wrote, "The pulpit has, and must forever have, a prodigious influence. It is like the lever and the fulcrum, of the ancient Archemedes—it is competent to move a world."[21]

Proslavery ministers were unable to move the world, but they certainly moved their portion of it. Once linked in the popular mind with the defense of slavery and spread from prominent pulpits, through pamphlets and through the religious and secular press, their vision of southern society became the dominant one. Beginning in the early 1830s and accelerating throughout the antebellum period, more and more evangelicals adopted the biblical defense of slavery and defended the South against abolitionist attacks. The evangelical press helped spread the biblical defense of slavery, expressed opposition to the colonization movement, and debated reopening the African slave trade. In a typical statement, the Methodist Crystal Springs Circuit expressed its belief in the biblical defense of slavery and concluded "that slavery as it now *exists* in the South *is not a sin.*" In 1836 a statewide Baptist meeting criticized northern abolitionists "as *misguided* and *politic.*" In 1841 William Winans charged that abolitionists were "*incendiaries, cutthroats,* and . . . *hydra-headed monsters of inhumanity.*" The biblical defense also found adherents among politicians. A resolution introduced in the state legislature declared slavery to be "a blessing . . . the legitimate condition of the African race, as authorized . . . by the laws of God."[22]

Evangelicals who refused to join the proslavery chorus found themselves in an uncomfortable position. Some ministers who opposed slavery left for the North; for example, William Langarl preached to a Methodist congregation in Natchez, but because he favored the abolition of slavery he left the state in 1841 for Ohio. The Reverend George Potts, a Presbyterian minister active in the colonization movement in Natchez, moved to New York in 1835. Many Mississippians had earlier believed slavery to be a moral, political, and social evil, but proslavery quickly became the new orthodoxy. One newspaper in 1838 urged its readers to shun their neighbors who believed slavery to be "*morally, socially, and politically, wrong.*" Should such people be tolerated, the editors warned, the South might as well "lower our colours and capitulate to the Abolitionists at once. At this crisis we want no such men among us. The South should be purged of them."[23]

The local debate over the churches' position on slavery was tame, however, compared with the national debate. Southern clergymen proved entirely willing to sacrifice national religious organizations on the altar of slavery when it became clear that their defense of the institution would deprive them of leadership positions within these organizations. As early as 1820, heated disputes took place in the Methodist General Conference. Mississippi minister Thomas Griffin took the floor and in his usual colorful style defended southerners against northern ministers who were willing, he charged, to see southerners "damned and double-damned, rammed, crammed and jammed into a forty-six pounder and blown into the fiery vaults of a deep damnation for being connected with slavery!" The conflict came to a head in the 1844 conference, when the Methodist church was torn asunder. Mississippi Methodists debated the split; as John G. Jones reported, "Our church papers were filled with it, our ministers and members talked of little else, [and] our Churches and Quarterly Conferences debated the subject." Not all Methodists in the state supported the division, and Jones described the negative effect the split had on membership: "Instead of our usual increase we had a decrease of sixty white members."[24]

At least one Methodist minister in the state refused to support the division, and another wrote that the separation "was a sore trial to many members of our conference." Edward Randolph of Columbus, a prominent member of the town's Methodist church, wrote an open letter to "the Preacher in Charge and members of the M. E. Church in Columbus" in which he expressed his opposition to the division: "I do believe in opposition to a portion of the *ministers* and membership of the South That Slavery is a great evil as set forth in the book of discipline." He emphasized the role clergymen played in forging the new southern consensus on slavery. His stand was not popular; the following year he wrote that some members wanted him to leave the church, but he refused to do so without placing his case before a church conference. He did, however, resign his church offices.[25]

The division of the Methodist church attracted the most attention, but the Baptists and Presbyterians also divided along regional lines. Despite their fierce independence, Baptist congregations organized local and state associations and met in a national Triennial Convention. Sectional tensions became apparent in 1844, when the convention's Board of the Home Mission Society, which was dominated by northerners, refused to appoint a slaveholding preacher as a missionary. Southerners withdrew from the mission society and created their own Board of Domestic Missions. The split was completed the following year when delegates from eight southern states and the District of Columbia met in Georgia and established the Southern Baptist Convention, a move endorsed by the Mississippi Baptist Association.[26]

Technically, the Presbyterian church remained united until 1861, but its apparent national unity was possible only because of an 1838 division that took most abolitionists out of the church. The roots of the split can be traced back to an 1801 union between Congregationalists and Presbyterians, which led to a theological debate between the New School—liberal, dominated by New Englanders and supporters of abolition—and the Old School—conservative and strongest in the South. Although the two factions differed on many issues, slavery became the major bone of contention in the 1830s. In the 1837 General Assembly the Old School staged a coup, abrogated the 1801 Plan of Union, and ousted many of the New School supporters. Large numbers of New School supporters attended the 1838 General Assembly determined to undo the work of the previous assembly. The result was the creation of two general assemblies, one dominated by southerners and amenable to slavery. Other issues played a part in the split, but slavery was paramount in the minds of most southern Presbyterians. James Smylie was one of the authors of the statement issued by the Synod of Mississippi and South Alabama in support of the division. The statement read, in part, "The Synod has good reasons for believing, that an overwhelming majority of the seceding body, and of those of the North who adhere to it, are hostile to one at least of the domestic institutions of the South."[27] By 1845, then, the southern churches were firmly in the proslavery camp.

One Methodist newspaper wrote that the division of the church "left us of the Church, South, responsible for the salvation of the negro, to an extent difficult to realize and fearful to contemplate." Evangelicals had long maintained that meddling by northern evangelicals and abolitionists impeded their mission work to the slaves. Some masters were undoubtedly suspicious of evangelicals because of their early opposition to slavery, but by the 1840s their public support of slavery removed that obstacle. Evangelical interest in the salvation of slaves was not new, of course, but the organized mission to the slaves differed from earlier efforts and was based on a new set of suppositions. In part, the mission was a response to abolitionist attacks, but more important, it was a corollary of the biblical defense of slavery. Beginning with Smylie's tract, proslavery statements stressed not only the duties of slaves but also of masters. Most southern evangelicals came to accept the idea that slavery was not sinful when masters fulfilled their religious duties as defined by the clergy. Perhaps the master's most pressing responsibility was the religious instruction of his slaves. In return for their support of the institution, evangelicals expected masters' cooperation. Smylie, who spent his later years in slave missions and wrote a catechism for their instruction, often infuriated masters by criticizing their treatment of their slaves.[28]

In 1829 the Methodists took the lead in sending missionaries to slaves on plantations. In that year Thomas Clinton, who later served as a popular missionary to the slaves and helped prepare an oral catechism, introduced a resolution "to instruct our missionary committee to inquire into the expedience of sending missionaries to the people of color in our own country, which resolution prevailed." Using their itinerant system as a model, the Methodists proposed to send preachers to slaves isolated on plantations.[29]

The organized mission enterprise remained largely a Methodist phenomenon. One historian has found "a curious lack of enthusiasm" for missions among southwestern evangelicals, but a closer examination of slave missions in Mississippi shows a marked enthusiasm. The Methodists established thirteen colored missions from 1830 to 1840, nineteen from 1840 to 1850, twenty-three from 1850 to 1860, and sixteen from 1860 to 1867. Their efforts produced a substantial growth in black membership; from 1831 to 1845, for example, black membership in the Mississippi Conference increased 251.5 percent (from 2,645 to 9,302). White membership over the same period grew by 132 percent (6,380 to 14,834). In 1845, 38.5 percent of the members of the Mississippi Conference were slaves. By the 1840s and 1850s the majority of blacks in several districts worshiped in missions. In 1845, 58.5 percent of the blacks in the Natchez District were in missions. In 1852 the Vicksburg District had 63.2 percent of its 1,662 black members in missions while in the Aberdeen District the figure stood at 58.2 percent of 1,546 black members. In 1852 the Methodists had at least 5,000 black members in colored missions across the state.[30]

In their efforts to gain access to slaves, evangelicals appealed to masters' self-interest and flattered overseers. As one missionary wrote, "The intelligent planter has learned from experience as well as theory that religion inculcates honesty, sobriety, obedience, industry, and perseverance." Another missionary expressed sympathy with the overseers and their "ungrateful calling"; they often decided whether services would be allowed and whether slaves from other plantations could attend. An overseer responded that this minister exaggerated their influence. Certainly, some masters gave overseers detailed directives regarding the type of religious services to be allowed on plantations.[31]

Missionaries sometimes disagreed with owners over how the missions should be conducted. One debate between the owners and ministers arose over the question of allowing slaves from different plantations to meet together for religious services. One owner directed his overseer to allow "no assemblage of negroes from other plantations . . . on Sundays." Evangelicals, however, stressed the importance of drawing congregations from several plantations: "From the constitution of our nature, a *congregation* is . . . important as an occasion for the preaching of the Gospel." The evangelicals may have based their argument on the slaves' preference for interplantation meetings; certainly ministers knew that such meetings produced better results. Masters, however, were determined to keep a close eye on their slaves' religious instruction, and preaching on individual plantations became the norm for missionaries.[32]

Preaching on separate plantations was time-consuming and meant that missionaries reached fewer slaves than they could have otherwise. One hardworking missionary in the Mississippi Delta estimated that twenty thousand slaves lived within his three-county charge, but only about six thousand heard the Gospel on a regular basis. At least one planter recognized this weakness in the system; he wrote that the missionary preached at each plantation once in every three to six weeks, and even then it was "a hasty, hurried sermon, for the preacher has to preach four times that day." He observed that "the preacher becomes dull . . . and fruitless . . . preaching, as my cook said of one of the missionaries, 'as if there were no danger'—of eternal death."[33] Still, missionaries reached thousands of slaves who otherwise might not have had any opportunity for formal religious services. In many plantation areas, blacks had no other option; biracial churches were few because the white population was small.

The mission to the slaves differed in several respects from the traditional biracial services. Before the 1830s evangelicals proclaimed a Gospel open and available to everyone, easily understood by all ranks and classes in society, including slaves. In contrast to that egalitarian position, some supporters of missions argued that "the slave's mind is not capacitated to receive the same mode of instruction" as whites. Proslavery ministers did not emphasize the equality of all believers, but rather racial differences and black inferiority, sometimes in rabidly racist terms. Rather than bringing slaves into biracial churches, missionaries organized black congregations on plantations. Despite the brave pronouncements of some missionaries, the mission system gave slaveholders control over services, and they often chose the ministers. Some planters preferred to employ trusted local preachers rather than allow the Methodist Conference to appoint a missionary. Planters paid handsomely: "Some . . . colored charges, especially those in the valley between the Mississippi and Yazoo Rivers, became the best-paying circuits in the Conference."[34]

Not all ministers who labored with blacks received high salaries. From the third Sunday in February to the third Sunday in November 1856, one Methodist minister preached 80 times, visited 175 families, paid 440 visits, traveled 3,000 miles, sold $350 in books, and distributed $40 and 6,000 pages of tracts. He took in 2 whites and 160 blacks on probation and catechized 550 slaves. He "had chills and fever over half the year, and got

$80 salary."[35] Money did not motivate such men to serve as missionaries.

Among the most prominent ministers to enter the mission field was John G. Jones. In 1845 and 1846 he held an appointment at Cole's Creek Colored Mission, in 1860 and 1861 he served the Adams Colored Mission, and in 1863 he returned to Cole's Creek. He abandoned his opposition to slavery sometime before 1840. Evidently, his former position did not make masters suspect his intentions; he wrote that slave owners "generally let me take my own course with the religious concerns of their negroes," but nevertheless "planters were careful as to who they would employ to preach to their negroes." Masters often attended services, whether to check the content of the service or to join in Christian worship is unclear, although the former is more likely because few of them were Methodists. Jones's motives for undertaking a mission to slaves are uncertain, though he wrote that he "had long coveted an opportunity to give my time wholly to them." Many other missionaries to slaves across the South had once opposed the institution.[36]

Successful missionaries like Jones did not preach only sermons that entreated slaves to obey their masters; the idea that such a message could win thousands of slave converts is an insult to the intelligence of those black Christians. Missionaries found that they had to make accommodations in their preaching and services to attract slave members. As historian William Freehling observed, slaves "had some power over white preachers: precisely the power to sleep." Jones's success can be measured in part by membership figures; during his two-year stay at Cole's Creek, for example, membership in the mission rose from 179 to 303. Jones found that some slaves preferred to receive baptism by immersion rather than effusion, but after he "gave them a plain talk on the scriptural mode of baptism—they readily consented to receive the ordinance by effusion—since which time I have heard no more of any wishing to be immersed." A missionary to the slaves near Columbus, Mississippi, encountered the same problem; the slaves believed "that nothing but going *into* and *under* the water, will ever save them," he wrote. Slaves argued Scripture with him and apparently got the best of him. He reported that "the bare assertion that John baptized in Jordan, holds more weight with them than any argument that I can produce on the subject." The blacks' preference for immersion may have been part of their African heritage, as some scholars have suggested, but the missionary ascribed it to the influence of "old Baptist leaders" on the plantations.[37] Some slaves placed more faith in their own religious leaders than in the white missionary; they took from the mission services what they could use, wrought changes in the services where possible, and discarded whatever proslavery propaganda preachers might have employed.

Slave congregations demanded and often got an important role in services; like many plain folk who left the mainline denominations, they refused to give up their communal services. Jones and other missionaries found that slaves became very emotional and vocal during worship services. Jones wrote, "I often had to use all the ingenuity I could command to keep them from defeating my instructions by loud shouting." Jones understood, or at least thought he understood, the religious motivation behind their excitement, and "sometimes when . . . there was a very strong religious feeling among them, I would give place, and let them spin round, shaking hands, sing and shout for ten or twenty minutes." He observed, "It seemed to do them a great deal of good and they often appeared to be as truely happy as any christians I ever saw." Missionaries sometimes defended slaves' right to their own form of religious expression. One missionary explained to a doubting master that "the Bible says they shout like thunder in Heaven: but he has never seen any such passage (though a Missionary Baptist), and thinks religion is a quiet something. We read it to him from 19th of Revelations." Another missionary explained: "The excitement among the colored people which I have witnessed this year has not been an animal excitement. No, thank God, it has been a religious excitement; an excitement produced by the Holy Spirit upon the heart."[38] At a time when more and more biracial churches were moving away from the traditional emotional services based on the equality of all believers, the missions proved to be more responsive to the slaves' preference for just such services. That preference and the slaves' enthusiastic response to it helps explain why some traditionalist ministers like Jones were so attracted to mission work, even though the mission concept began with modernists.

The mission to the slaves was a complex affair. For modernists like Smylie the movement was an expression of evangelical power and prestige and a means of defending against abolitionist attacks. For men like Jones, once caught up in the evangelical hostility to slavery, missionary work was a means of rectifying the worst abuses of the system by emphasizing the duties of masters to their slaves, a way of reaching ever larger numbers of unchurched bondsmen, and perhaps a means of assuaging the feelings of guilt that Smylie described. Many masters were swayed by the evangelical assurance that Christianity made better slaves. As Donald Mathews aptly summarized, "Support for the Mission was a volatile compound of anxiety, shame, guilt, humane concern, rationalization, and self-interest."[39]

The theological, social, and racial assumptions underlying the mission to the slaves mark a major turning point for evangelicals in the Old South. Modernists abandoned the doctrine of the equality of all believers, that potent message that brought thousands of the plain folk, women, and blacks into the biracial churches on terms of relative equality; they could not possibly reconcile it with a biblical defense of slavery based on racial inequality and patriarchy. They abandoned, too, the legacy of the Revolution and its ideals of equality and individual rights. Proslavery was part and parcel of a much broader trend in southern evangelicalism, a trend marked also by the move from sects to denominations, by the growing wealth and higher social position of church members, by the restrictions placed on women in the churches, by an increased separation of the races in worship, and by the change from a congregational to a clerical ministry. The effects of the proslavery ideology went far beyond the churches, however. As much as any other group, these proslavery clergymen set the South at odds with the rest of the nation and thereby contributed substantially to the growth of southern sectionalism with all its tragic consequences.

CHAPTER 8

THE OUTSIDE ROW
THE BIRACIAL EVANGELICAL EXPERIENCE,
1830–1860

THE significance of the biracial church in the South and in Mississippi throughout the antebellum period merits examination. As John B. Boles wrote, "Historians have sufficiently recognized neither the role of the slave in the so-called white churches nor the role of those churches in the lives of the slaves."[1] Blacks joined Mississippi churches from their inception, and, until the 1830s, most churches were remarkably egalitarian when compared to the larger society. As white evangelicals embraced slavery and as more slaves joined the churches, physical and psychological barriers began to rise between the races. Often congregations separated entirely, perhaps sharing a minister and a building but not meeting together. The eventual division of the churches along racial lines after the Civil War was a logical outcome of this trend. The egalitarian current within the churches waned but survived in many churches and in the hearts of many evangelicals. The biracial religious experience was diverse throughout the antebellum period, but by the 1840s and 1850s the typical evangelical church was biracial.

When historians of slavery have considered the biracial churches, they have frequently characterized them as yet another control device exercised by masters over slaves, places where white ministers repeated their mantra, "Slaves obey your masters," to bored or dozing bondsmen. Throughout the antebellum period, however, both blacks and whites worshiped under the ministry of black preachers, a remarkable group of religious leaders that W. E. B. Du Bois characterized as "the most unique personality developed by the Negro on American soil."[2]

In the early decades of the evangelical movement, black preachers benefited from the ideal of the equality of all believers and exercised a wide ministry among both blacks and whites, and some blacks carried on successful ministries even after the 1830s. In August 1845, William Winans "walked to Midway, and heard Isaac, a Mulatto slave, deliver a very interesting discourse. I have heard Presiding Elders who could not equal his performance." Isaac preached to biracial congregations; Winans wrote of a later service: "Isaac . . . addressed the coloured people (of whom there was a great crowd) much to the gratification of many of the white people who heard him." Former slave Jim Allen attended a "neighborhood church" with a biracial congregation where "dere was a white preacher and sometimes a nigger preacher would sit in de pulpit wid him." A state Baptist newspaper praised Jack Hinton, a slave preacher, in an 1858 obituary. Hinton, a North Carolina native, came to Columbus in 1836 with his master. He was a member of the Baptist church there and "recognized as a preacher to the blacks." He was considered "earnest and effective," and the whites knew that "his influence with the negroes was almost incredible, while with the white people he was esteemed and highly respected."[3]

Some black ministers, like Hinton, managed to walk a fine line so they could carry on an open ministry, but the number of licensed black preachers apparently declined in the wake of what Donald Mathews calls the "white reaction" of the 1820s and 1830s. An 1860 article in the Methodist press stated:

> Negro preachers were formerly very common in the South, and many of them were very useful. We have listened with delight and profit to many a sermon from preachers as sable as ever came from Africa. Indeed, there are many of them yet, preaching more or less every sabbath. . . . Had there been no anti-slavery party, no free states, so called, no fanaticism, no abolition excitement, this state of things . . . would have increased and improved. But now it is on the decline. But few colored men are now allowed to preach. It cannot be otherwise, under the circumstances.

White discrimination prevented most blacks from preaching to biracial congregations after 1830 and encouraged the growth of the "invisible church" in the quarters, where black preachers continued to exert great influence.[4]

Slave preachers came under suspicion when whites began to show a greater interest in slaves' religious beliefs in the wake of the mission movement and Nat Turner's rebellion demonstrated the revolutionary potential of black religious leaders. After the late 1820s, black preachers increasingly suffered from discriminatory laws and harassment. In 1825 the Hopewell Baptist Church allowed "Br. John . . . to sing & pray and exhort among the people of his own color." Two years later the church imposed restrictions on John's ministry. In one instance he was charged with striking a fellow slave with a whip, and in 1829 the church ordered him to stop preaching because of "Sundry reports against" him. The Bogue Chitto Baptist Church allowed "Bro. Jessee" to preach. He became so popular that nearby Salem Baptist Church requested that he be allowed to preach there. In 1827 he was cleared of an adultery charge, but the next year he was dismissed from the church. In 1830 the New Hope Baptist Church resolved that the slave preacher Peter could "no longer exercise in publick, further than to sing, [and] pray amongst his own colour," and in 1832 he was charged with gambling. In 1832 the church allowed Cary to preach within the church, but two years later its white members questioned his gift and concluded that he was not called to the ministry. They allowed another slave, Jerry, to preach until 1839, when they determined that the state laws prohibited slaves from preaching "any where else but at home"; thereafter they allowed no slave member to preach. In 1853 the Magnolia Baptist Church charged that a black "by the name of Jeffrey (Styling himself a Baptist minister) has . . . been preaching to the colored population of Port Gibson and vicinity, teaching strange doctrine." Whether Jeffrey's "strange doctrine" was revolutionary is unclear, but whites were especially disturbed by slave preachers like Alfred Oates, who was charged for "holding Publick meetings and teaching the Collard People that it was not Right to obey there oners."[5]

Discrimination against black preachers was one aspect of changing attitudes toward blacks in the biracial churches. Many churches accepted blacks on relatively equal terms throughout the antebellum period; they worshiped together, were baptized together, received the right hand of fellowship from one another, and used familial terms in their address. In the majority of churches, however, barriers between the races arose in the late 1820s and 1830s. In a variety of ways black members were treated differently from whites, and separate services became common.

According to Patrick H. Thompson, a black church historian who published a history of black Baptists in the late nineteenth century, there were three types of churches for blacks in antebellum Mississippi: first, separate black churches under the supervision of a white church; second, churches where blacks used the same building as the whites but at different times; and finally, churches where slaves attended the same service as their masters but were segregated from whites. Thompson judged the third situation to be the most common. Beginning in the late 1820s, many churches provided separate accommodations for blacks partly as a result of growing black attendance. For example, in 1829 the Bethany Baptist

Church Conference "took under consideration the situation of the Black people who attend preaching at this church." A committee of five white men was appointed "to devise a plan of building an addition to our Meeting house for their accommodation." Their plan was not recorded, but it may have resembled that of Mountain Creek Baptist Church, which had "an enclosure the whole length of one side with an opening through which the slaves could see and listen to the services."[6] In such churches, blacks and whites heard the same sermon, but the physical separation of the races and the suggestion of black inferiority show a waning of the early churches' egalitarianism.

The overcrowding reported by churches throughout the state suggests that religious interest was on the rise among slaves. A committee appointed to consider "The Moral and Religious Improvement of Colored Population" in the Aberdeen Baptist Association reported in 1845 that "God is reviving his work among them; there is an increasing desire to hear the word preached; but it must be regretted that there is no provision for them at many of our churches. It is not uncommon to see them crowd about the doors, without seats or even shelter to shield them from the inclemency of the weather. Still on their part there is a manifest desire to hear the gospel." The committee members pleaded with their fellow Christians: "Dear Brethren, can we not do something? Will we not make some special effort to advance the Redeemer's kingdom among those who toil and labor for us? We should build additions to our churches, and give them better opportunities of hearing the gospel." Association records indicate that churches responded to this plea and black membership grew rapidly. The association records did not report black membership in 1845, but in 1848 only twelve of the thirty-three member churches reported any black members, and the total black membership was about 250. By 1861, however, twenty-two of the thirty-one churches reported black members with a total of 655 black and 1,354 white members. The pattern was similar in associations across the state; by the mid-1840s associations typically reported black membership separately and appointed special committees to consider the needs of blacks.[7]

In many churches, the building of a shed or gallery provided only a temporary solution. In 1839 the state Baptist Convention found that "some few of our Churches, and some of our Methodist friends, have adopted the plan of holding separate meetings for the blacks; and that such a course is generally attended with an increased interest among them."[8] Separate services for blacks resulted both from a desire on the part of whites to separate blacks physically and from a black preference for segregated services. No doubt blacks preferred a segregated service to a discriminatory biracial one.

Like many whites, blacks favored an emotional worship style and a congregational ministry; as more and more churches abandoned these traditional styles of worship, blacks chose segregated services over which they could exert more control. A frequent complaint from former slaves was that the formal, staid worship services typical of many evangelical churches by the late antebellum period did not appeal to them. Isom Weathersby reported: "Us went ter meetin' 'bout once a month to de white folks meetin' house, but us didn't jine in wid de services. The service wuz good but us liked our own whar us could git in de spirit an' pray an' shout."[9] Perhaps, too, slaves, who liked more emotionally demonstrative services, felt inhibited by the presence of whites and hence preferred separate worship.

The number of churches holding separate worship services for blacks increased throughout the antebellum period. Whites occasionally consulted blacks before holding segregated services; for example, the white members of Clear Creek Baptist Church "met . . . to confer with the Black Brothers and Sisters . . . to make some Raingment [arrangement] for them . . . William Whilden a greed to supley them as they had to look up to the church for there surport for preaching." Whilden, who also preached to whites at Clear Creek, had great success attracting black members. Blacks and whites often heard the same preacher, though occasionally a white lay speaker ministered to blacks. Typically, the white congregation met on Sunday morning, and the blacks gathered in the afternoon.[10]

The degree of control whites exercised over the separate black services varied. Liberty Baptist Church appointed a group of seven white men "to attend said meetings and act as police." At Concord Baptist Church, "Brethren be requested as many as can do so to be present during service to them." Probably few black meetings went unsupervised because state law required that whites be present at such services. At the Aberdeen Baptist Church slaves sat in the rear of the auditorium until their numbers grew too large. Blacks then had separate services and heard both black and white preachers. Supervision seems to have been light: "About once a month members of the white church were appointed to attend the negro church meetings." According to Dr. J. M. Heard of West Point, blacks there attended both the morning service and a later segregated service; he wrote that "the negroes all belonged to the same church with their owners, sitting in the rear of the church at 11 o'clock, and at 3 o'clock in the afternoon they had the whole church to themselves." At Mt. Helm Baptist Church in Jackson blacks worshiped in the basement; Prior Lee, a white lay preacher who worked among blacks, donated bricks to build a new church on the condition that blacks be allowed to use that part of the building. From 1835 to 1867 blacks used the building for a variety of services. According to Thompson, "Much of the early worship of this church was spent in prayer meetings. 'The Early Service Prayer Meeting' was one in which they spent their happiest moments, no white person being present to molest them or make them afraid."[11]

Church records and the slave narratives indicate that most slaves attended church with their masters. An 1851 membership list from Bethesda Baptist Church shows that of thirty-seven slave members, twenty-one belonged to white members of the same church. The growing black membership in the biracial churches resulted in part from the growing wealth of the white evangelicals; for example, Edgar and William Potts requested letters of dismission from Concord Baptist Church for themselves, their wives, and twenty-one slaves. Perhaps the wealthier evangelicals were more anxious to segregate themselves from their slaves than were their poorer brethren. Some affluent evangelicals attempted to separate themselves from their less fortunate brethren of both races by buying or renting pews. The Methodist Conference condemned the practice in 1838, but debate continued into the 1850s. When the Holly Springs Methodist Church opened its new building in 1837, the stewards voted to rent pews. The presiding elder, Robert B. Alexander, objected on the grounds that pew rental discriminated against the poor. When the stewards overruled him, he rented most of the choice pews himself and distributed them among the poor.[12] Like separate pews, separate services were another indication of the increasing stratification among evangelicals and the declining egalitarianism within the churches.

Quasi-independent black churches flourished in towns across the South, and in Mississippi towns, including Aberdeen, Natchez, and Vicksburg, they were among the largest congregations in the state. The black Baptist church in Aberdeen had 437 members in 1845, making it the largest church in north Mississippi. In 1847 the congregation built a church to seat 300 people. Black Baptists in Natchez technically belonged to the Wall Street Baptist Church, which in 1856 had 16 white members and 499 black members. The church reported in 1856: "White Church met but seldom; worship principally with other denominations. Colored Church worship together every Sabbath." Blacks worshiped in a separate building called Rose Hill Baptist Church built with contributions from whites and blacks and deeded to a free black man. Although a few whites attended services to ensure legality, blacks controlled their own affairs under the leadership of an unlicensed slave preacher named Randle Pollard.[13] An African Methodist Episcopal church also functioned in Vicksburg from 1846 to 1858. An Episcopal priest in Jackson, the Reverend James W. Hoskins, wrote: "I have . . . made several attempts to get a congregation of negroes, but have failed because they have a house of their own, where they go to make as much noise as they please. They do not believe in a religion that is not noisy."[14] These quasi-independent churches existed only in the towns and therefore did not reach most slaves, who lived in rural areas. As important and visible as these churches were, they affected only a few thousand blacks at most. The majority of blacks worshiped either in segregated or biracial services.

As the Episcopal priest suggests, slaves sought to control their worship services, and they held to the traditional ways of the early church. As more white evangelicals and ministers abandoned shouting, congregational singing, and active involvement by the laity in worship, blacks who attempted to exercise their gifts in the noisy traditional ways in biracial services were criticized. At an 1853 service attended by Winans, "there was a good deal of disorder, which I reproved severely." On another occasion Winans wrote, "When I was closing a negro man in the Gallery made a great noise, which occasioned much bustle among the whites." John G. Jones noted that a black woman who shouted during his sermon so disturbed the congregation that it "appeared to destroy or prevent all the good effect of my discourse." Partly because of the blacks' refusal to change their style of worship, many ministers were relieved to have them in separate congregations. Samuel A. Agnew, a Presbyterian minister in north Mississippi, wrote after a Sunday service, "My congregation was better than I have yet had, that is there was more whites though fewer negroes."[15]

As sectional rivalry and abolitionist attacks on southern religious institutions increased, Mississippians used the example of biracial services to deflect criticism of their churches and their peculiar institution. In 1858 the editor of a state Baptist newspaper visited Mound Bluff Baptist Church and recorded the following scene:

> One sight we saw, and it was not a new one there, nor peculiar to that Church, which we would that many of the deluded and fanatical of abolitiondom would behold. . . . We allude to the great number of servants that crowd the pews on Sabbath. The noble and chivalrous son of the

South . . . sat in close proximity to his well fed and well clothed servant, to listen to the word of life, and at the word both knelt in prayer at the same altar. . . . There sat ladies of refinement too, and on adjoining seats sat their household and farm servants, devoted in their attachments, and more proud of their owners than the pampered menials of Courtly halls ever dreamed of.[16]

The editor's description was highly romanticized. By 1858, blacks would have had a different view of these biracial services that clearly defined their position as "menials."

Even in churches where blacks and whites attended the same service, blacks were discriminated against. In early churches and in some later churches, the ritual of extending the right hand of fellowship included both blacks and whites. Other churches, however, followed the practice described in a query to a Baptist newspaper from members of a Baptist church: "Suppose a church, in which there are half a dozen colored members,—and suppose they never have any separate service . . . but unite with the white members in all their services. . . . Then suppose you were Pastor, and a white person should be received into the fellowship of the church, would you invite the colored members to extend the hand of fellowship? or would you pass them by?" The editor responded that the ritual was not a church ordinance and did not affect the validity of the reception. "As to the colored members," he wrote, "we would invite them as a body only when a colored member was to be received." He assumed that blacks would not perceive this as being overlooked, though blacks understood and resented the implications of such unequal treatment. Churches appointed committees or gave the pastor the responsibility of extending the hand of fellowship to blacks.[17]

In more egalitarian churches, all members heard the conversion experience of a member; the experience was central to the evangelical belief system and an important element in unifying a congregation. Special committees appointed to receive black members heard them relate their experiences, but the entire congregation did not. Whites continued to share their experiences before the congregation and receive the right hand of fellowship. In Magnolia Baptist Church, for example, "The com[mittee] on experience of colored persons reported that they had examined and received" a new black member.[18]

Unlike the right hand of fellowship, communion was a church ordinance. Methodists held separate communion services for blacks in the 1820s, and the Baptists and Presbyterians also segregated communicants by race. In 1849, for example, the church conference at the Louisville First Baptist Church decided that "it would be best to Administer the sacrement of the Lords Supper to the Coloured Church separately and apart from the white portion of the church." In an unusual move, Academy Baptist Church resolved that "Daniel, a colored brother, be appointed to wait on the blacks on Communion occasions." The church records offer no explanation for the separate communion services, although at Louisville the change was suggested by the white layperson who ministered to the blacks. Whether the suggestion came from the lay preacher or the black congregation is unclear.[19] Again, such separation struck at the heart of religious egalitarianism.

Churches also appointed special committees, usually composed of slaveholders, to regulate blacks' behavior, to receive black members, and to hear their testimony. The creation of such committees marked a dramatic departure from past practice; these committees set blacks apart and further illustrate the increasing racial barriers. The new committees had important implications for biracial worship. In 1854 Academy Baptist Church appointed a committee "to regulate the conduct of Blacks on Sabbath of our church meeting." A similar committee at New Providence Baptist Church was "to have an over sight of the blacks & have them disperse after preaching." A committee at Bethany Baptist Church ordered blacks to leave the church grounds immediately after services and warned that "if the said cullard people do not comply with the . . . Rules we do request that pateroles to . . . take them and chastise them according to law."[20] The threat by whites at Bethany to have "pateroles" discipline slaves was unusual, but the attempt to regulate black behavior at services was not. The social aspect of religious services was important for both blacks and whites, especially in Mississippi with its widely dispersed population. Sunday services provided slaves from different plantations with a rare opportunity to gather together, yet whites at least on some occasions attempted to deprive them of this opportunity, an act that inhibited the formation of a black community within the white-controlled churches.

An important corollary of separation and discrimination, one probably unanticipated by whites, was increased black autonomy within the churches. In 1845 the Concord Baptist Church decided that since blacks held separate services conducted by their white minister, they should also hold a separate church conference. They authorized their "pastor in connection with the white brethren present on such occasions, to hold conference, with the black members, for their special benefit, and that each couloured member be entitled to a vote in the reception, rejection & exclusion of those of their own coulour." Liberty Baptist Church appointed two slave men "as watchmen to report to this church any of our colored members who may become disorderly. Also to stimulate them to Christian duty." A Methodist circuit rider in the state observed that white supervision of separate black conferences was light. The white minister usually chaired the meeting, but the conference was conducted by the black secretary, who apparently wielded great influence. The secretary acted " 'as the presiding judge of their church trials' and was 'the umpire to whom is referred not only the minor difficulties of the church members, but of the colored people at large.' " Whether blacks in such positions were chosen by whites or elected by blacks is unclear, but the result—an increase in black autonomy—was the same in any case. By either allowing or forcing blacks into separate congregations and by giving them control over their members, whites unwittingly helped pave the way for the postbellum division of the churches along racial lines.[21]

Despite the increase in autonomy, many blacks resented the churches' abandonment of the egalitarian tradition and their unequal treatment. A white Methodist church member asked a "pious old negro man why he did not enter into the spirit of the services" at a revival meeting. The black man, drawing on his agricultural expertise, replied, "Ah master . . . there is not much in the outside row." As the white man explained, the elderly slave "had occupied the back seat in the church from necessity during the meeting, and finding himself after several days still unblessed . . . he compared his case to that [of] a reaper in the outside row, and very philosophically concluded that the back seats in the church resemble the outside row in the field," which produced a very low yield.[22]

The slave narratives show how deeply blacks resented segregated seating and preferred their own services in the quarters. Mattie Dillworth, a former slave from Lafayette County, recalled that "befor' de surrender I had to sit on a back seat, but dere cum a time sho Lord when I cu'd sit rite spang on de fron' seat." Jake Dawkins of Monroe County said, "The only time I 'member going to a meetin' was when de marster took all de slaves over to de white folks church at New Hope and had a white preacher to preach to us. But Lawd, he never did much preachin'. His text was, 'Obey your master and mistress', and he never told us a word about savin' our souls from hell fire and damnation." Another former slave, Jack Jones of Oktibbeha County, recalled that according to the white preacher, even heaven would be segregated: "He stated that the white preacher enjoined the Negro to be . . . good slaves. As a result they would go to the Negro

Heaven, or kitchen heaven. Uncle Jack laughed and said that anyway the slave thought, they would get plenty to eat."[23]

Many of the slaves who remembered attending biracial churches accompanied their masters to serve them at church. Vinie Busby, a former slave in Rankin County, said, "We went to Church at de white folks Church. We waited on de white folks a totin' water an' seein' bout de horses an buggies an' tendin' to de chillun." Frances Willis of Montgomery County recalled bitterly, "I'd go wid de white folks to church to brush dur shoes when dey got there, but they sho' didn't never read de Bible to me. Back in dem days us niggers was taught nothin 'bout a Savior for our souls. We was treated mo' like de work animals folks use today." Like Augusta H. Rice, who traveled to church in a carriage with a black driver and nurse, these masters and mistresses were concerned for their personal comfort, and perhaps interested in showing their wealth, but not in their slaves' salvation.[24]

Some churches expected blacks to continue in their role of servants by doing duties at church. In 1842, for example, Concord Baptist Church requested its deacons "to appoint some colourd member to attend to the sweeping of the meeting house."[25] No communal feeling was likely to develop among blacks and whites when blacks were not treated as individuals but continued in their prescribed roles.

A few slaves, however, recalled a positive experience in the biracial churches, additional evidence that the egalitarian tradition continued in some churches throughout the antebellum period, and the slave narratives suggest that slaves responded positively to traditional biracial worship. In a Webster County church, blacks "were allowed to go there and shout just like the white folks." Another former slave from Webster County said "we was allus welcome" at the local church. George Washington Miller described a Presbyterian church that had "pews for the white and for the black, and often the leading negro deacon 'Uncle Dick' sat in the pulpit. Everybody liked him. I remember preacher Reed, whom I thought almost was God hisself." Westly Little of Smith County vividly recalled his conversion at a biracial antebellum church service:

> We went to church at de white folks meetin' house. One Sunday when I wuz jes' a strip ob a boy de preacher preached on how man wuz made from de dust o' de earth an' would return to dust. I wuz converted at dat sermon. He open de do's [doors] ob de Church, but nobody went up, den he ask if any ob de darkies in de back part ob de Church wanted to jine. I wanted to so bad but didn't go. I worried all de way home. I wuz all tore

up an' went an' tole Miss Sally [his mistress]. She talked to me an' told me to pray an' jine de nex' time which I did.[26]

Slaves like Westly Little heard the same sermon whites did, and the message was clearly more than simply "slaves obey your masters." Henry Gibbs, a former slave in Clay County, recalled: "Our slaves all come to dis hard shell Baptist Church out dere at Church hill. In May, we'd have footwashins. De women would wash each others feet, and men would wash each others feet." When asked what he thought about religion, the former slave replied, "God Almighty gave every boy [body?] de same spirit—the Spirit of God."[27]

Despite the churches' wholesale adoption of the proslavery ideology, not all evangelicals, either black or white, accepted the idea that Christianity justified inequality, slavery, and racial discrimination. James Bond, a charter member of Palestine Baptist Church in Hinds County and a member of a pioneer Baptist family, asked in 1834 to be excluded from the church because "he was opposed to the views of the church with respect to church discipline among the blacks," which he considered discriminatory and severe. Isham Howze was only half convinced by the biblical defense of slavery. After he became angry and whipped a slave, Nathan, he wrote, "I have Sinned this morning in getting angry. May the Lord forgive me for all my transgressions . . . I do not consider the relationship, *per se*, sinful, yet I would be truely glad not to have any thing to do with it.— I feel, now, worse than Nathan." Howze did not own slaves, but he acted as a trustee for his sister and held the slaves for her.[28] He was, therefore, unable to dispose of them and was forced by family duty into a difficult and troubling relationship.

Other evangelicals shared Howze's sentiments. Patrick Sharkey, a Methodist planter near Vicksburg, owned two thousand acres of land and seventy-five slaves by 1860. Despite his holdings, he "never believed slavery was justified by reason or Christianity." His wife shared his sentiments, but state laws restricting the emancipation of slaves prevented Sharkey from taking that step. The Reverend Jeremiah Davis Mann, a Methodist minister in Aberdeen from 1837 to 1863, overcame the legal obstacles and freed his slaves a few years before the outbreak of war in 1861. Henry Gibbs remembered that "Parson Ellis," a Baptist preacher, also refused to own slaves. Gibbs said, "I don't know how come, but he got where he didn't want any slaves. He just concluded to turn em all over to Mr. Seth Pool, and he stayed with Mr. Pool until he died after the srender. Mr. Pool was a deacon in his church."[29]

The extent to which southern slaveholders felt guilty over their owner-
ship of slaves has been the subject of scholarly debate. David Donald is
probably correct in asserting that "it is impossible to demonstrate the
presence—or the absence—of widespread guilt feelings which, by definition, are unconscious." He is incorrect in assuming, however, that ambivalence over slavery disappeared after the 1830s. As the above examples
illustrate, some evangelicals were troubled by the institution up to the
eve of the Civil War. Perhaps evangelicals were more prone to feelings of
guilt than others because of the introspection and soul-searching that accompanied their religious life. But no doubt many evangelicals were like
Robert B. Alexander, owner of Happy Hill Plantation in north Mississippi.
A Methodist, he regularly attended worship services; for example, on one
Sunday in 1856 he attended a church service, a prayer meeting, and a class
meeting. He sometimes acted as class leader and recorded his moving experiences at such services. At one 1856 prayer meeting he "had a glorious
time," and on another occasion he reported that "we had a delightful love
feast one of the best I have seen for Many a day." He sometimes took a
few of his slaves to church with him (he owned more than twenty bondsmen), but he whipped his slaves without any apparent remorse. During
the cotton-picking season in 1854 he "paddled 9 or 10 of my hands they
improved very much."[30]

Many slave Christians continued to believe that slavery violated the
laws of God. Charlie Moses, a former slave who, significantly, was also
a preacher, said: "When I gets ta' thinkin' back on them days I feels like
risin' out o' this heah' bed an' tellin' everybody 'bout the harsh treatment
us colored folks was given. My Marster was mean an' cruel an' I hates
him, hates him. The God Almighty has condemned him to eternal fiah',
of that I is certain." Riley Moore, a former slave in Montgomery County,
believed that white ministers who preached the biblical defense of slavery
to slave congregations "ought to have been hung fo' preachin' false doctrin'. They was no such thing in the Bible."[31] A wide chasm divided many
slaves from the white evangelicals around them.

Evangelicalism, however, did sometimes bridge the gulf separating
black from white, master from slave. Egalitarianism was too much a part
of southern evangelical ideology to be completely erased by the proslavery
ideology, a weaker and more flawed concept. Perhaps many masters recon-
ciled Christianity with slaveholding, but as the above examples illustrate,
many others were unable to do so. Blacks and whites who worshiped in
biracial services sometimes looked beyond skin color or status. In 1836
the members of Clear Creek Baptist Church mourned the death of a fel-

low member: "Mary a Coloured Sister belonging to Mrs. Miner departed this life last March leaving behind the most cheering evidence both in her life & in her death that she has gone to the Socty [Society] of the Spirits of the just made perfect in heaven."[32] Clearly the white member who penned this tribute to Mary expected to meet her in that egalitarian society of the just, not in a separate "kitchen heaven."

Although the diversity of the biracial religious experience in antebellum Mississippi makes generalizations difficult, the broad pattern was a shift from relative egalitarianism to segregation and discrimination. This overarching trend should not obscure the fact that many churches held to the traditional evangelical style of worship and to the traditionalist theology emphasizing their belief that all are one in Christ. In these settings, blacks and whites continued to worship together, to be baptized together, to shout and sing together, and to meet on a common ground that temporarily transcended race. Even the discriminatory practices of many modernist churches held an unforeseen advantage for black Christians. For the first time since the early 1800s, blacks enjoyed the opportunity to worship with little or no white supervision. Blacks demanded and usually received a service in keeping with their theology. A few blacks were able to gain leadership positions in the biracial churches, especially in those that held segregated services. Despite legal obstacles and white harassment, black preachers continued to minister to members of both races. Separate services were a valuable training ground and helped prepare blacks for post-bellum religious independence. As John Boles observed, "In the churches black men and women found persuasive reason to live as morally responsible adults, discovered arenas for the practice of black leadership, and experienced a far greater degree of equality with the surrounding whites than anywhere else in southern society. No wonder the church was the dominant institutional force in the lives of so many black southerners throughout the antebellum period and into our own time."[33]

CHAPTER 9

A WHOLESOME GODLY DISCIPLINE
CHURCHES AS MORAL COURTS, 1806–1870

I N 1810 the members of East Fork Baptist Church eloquently stated the evangelical motivation behind the church disciplinary process:

> Our conduct and conversation both in the church and in the world ought to coreespond with the subline and holy systems of Devine Truth to . . . live soberly, Righteously, and Piously, in this world, endeavoring by all means to promote the peace and welfare of Society in general . . . we feel ourselves bound to walk in all humility and brotherly love, to watch over each other's conversations, to stir one another to love and to good works . . . to warn interest Rebuke, admonish in the spirit of meekness according to the rules of the gospel, at the same time we think ourselves obliged to sympathize with each other['s] weaknesses and other imperfections, we view it as absolutely necessary to our peace and prosperity and the honor of God to carefully maintain a strict gospel discipline all which duties together with those that respect the most peaceful conduct toward all who love our Lord Jesus Christ.

Like many records left by evangelicals in the early nineteenth century, this statement contains the sorts of grammatical errors that brought ridicule from their more educated opponents, but this simple affirmation reveals the beliefs that underlay one of their fundamental religious rites. The disciplinary process lay at the very heart of the evangelical experience. Its practice has a long history among Christians based on Jesus' directives to his disciples (Matt. 18:15–17). As one scholar of British church history wrote, "The underlying assumptions of Godly Discipline are an aspect of historic Christianity and not an eccentricity of particular churches." But, of course, not all Christians have practiced church discipline with equal intensity; for example, southern evangelicals continued a strict discipline long after New England Congregationalists abandoned the practice in the mid-eighteenth century.[1]

It may seem surprising that southern evangelicals vigorously maintained a rite that stalwart New England Puritans did not, but southern evangelicals throughout the antebellum period stressed its significance. As the Mississippi Baptist Association observed in 1810: "This is a subject of great importance. Much depends on a wholesome godly discipline." As the statement of the East Fork Baptist Church suggests, evangelicals attempted to conform to what they saw as God's sublime and holy system, an orderly and perfect plan that contrasted sharply with the disorder evidenced in their larger society. Evangelicals might live in the world with all its evils and temptations, but they would not be of the world; "every one who claims citizenship in this kingdom," one Baptist group stated, "should keep himself unspotted from the world . . . and 'walk with Christ in white.' " It was this denunciation of traditional society that made them such a radical force in the early years of the movement. On one level, they threatened to destroy hierarchical, deferential society, but on the other, they offered to replace it with a society based on new foundations.[2]

Evangelicals viewed the world as a battleground where the forces of Good engaged in a constant battle against the forces of Evil. Mississippi Methodist William Winans described the conflict in military terms: "In no situation are we a moment secure from his [Satan's] assaults . . . let us be ever on our gard. Let us never forget or neglect the orders of the Captain of our salvation. . . . Our enemy is artful, is malignant, is indefatigable." In a similar vein, Baptists wrote "that the church is in a militant state while on earth and constantly engaged in a warfare against her enemies which are the world, the flesh with its lusts, and Satan with his devices." The children of God battled Satan individually—within themselves—and also communally—in the world around them.[3]

Evangelicals were not expected to wage this battle against so great an enemy alone; the church was a redemptive community in which Christians grew in spirit and assisted one another to restrain their sinful natures. The individual conversion experience, a hallmark of evangelicalism, ushered the convert into this community of believers. The emphasis on the individual conversion experience has sometimes obscured the importance of the communal aspect of evangelicalism, though for the evangelicals themselves the two were interrelated and indivisible. The Mississippi Baptists believed that "the visible church . . . was never designed . . . to procure the eternal salvation of God's people; but seems to be designed for their salvation from error and delusion—false doctrine and false practice—to gather them together into one fold . . . where they are to be fed, and edified, and comforted. Here 'all things must be done decently and in order.' . . . We fellowship no disorder, which comes within the range of our knowledge." Evangelicals, then, sought to separate themselves from the world around them. They placed special emphasis on duty and order, especially important in a disorganized frontier society. The disciplinary process was not intended to be punitive, though for those who could not or would not conform it may have been. Rather, its aim was the recovery of the transgressor; its purpose was "the destruction . . . of the flesh, that the spirit may be saved."[4]

Donald Mathews has acknowledged the difficulty in ascertaining the primary focus of church discipline: was it on the individual or the larger society? As the Baptists at East Fork explained, evangelicals aimed to "promote the peace and welfare of Society in general," and in that sense discipline had implications beyond the individual or the congregation. Of course, church discipline in the South could not extend directly beyond the religious community as it had in Calvin's Geneva or in Puritan New England, where no separation between church and state existed, but that is not to say that discipline did not have a larger importance for the community and indeed for the entire nation. Evangelicals like Lorenzo Dow forged in the popular mind an "indestructible link" between the republic and religion, and only the latter could preserve the former. By joining the quest for individual discipline and the revolutionary belief that only virtue could preserve the republican experiment, evangelicals created a potent justification for their moral quest. Discipline was not simply a social control device, but rather an effort to foster self-control, a crucial attribute in a republican society.[5]

In the South's peculiar social system order and duty had a special resonance that helps account for the survival of the disciplinary process in southern churches. Southern religious modernists were comfortable with the expanding commercial society of the nineteenth century and agreed with their northern counterparts that individuals should internalize ethical standards to prepare them for this competitive social and economic system. Northern evangelicals moved away from attempting to impose order directly on individuals in favor of internalizing individual conscience. In the North this conviction helped fuel the remarkable expansion of the benevolent empire, which had a limited southern counterpart, but in the slaveholding South individualism had to take its place in a hierarchical slaveholding society made up not of individuals but of households governed by the master/father/husband whose rights and duties were firmly based on Scripture.[6]

Historians who question the influence of the churches on broader social norms point out that only a minority of southerners were church members in the antebellum period. Bertram Wyatt-Brown has developed the most sustained argument for the weakness of the churches in this regard. "The legal and community sanctions against deviancy were the chief regulators of conduct, not the church," he wrote. "The courthouse, not the clapboard church, the gossipers at the tavern or in the parlor, not the frowning deacons, exercised primary influence." It was the "circle of honor," not religion, that exerted the primary moral force in the community.[7]

The evangelical influence on morality and behavior was considerably greater than such arguments suggest. Although only one-fifth to one-third of southerners were church members in the antebellum period, membership is not an adequate measure of evangelical influence. Membership was not easily attained, and attendance at church services might be double or triple the number of members actually on the church rolls. A growing body of research indicates that at least in certain areas of the South evangelicalism spread into the majority of households. In addition, legal sanctions in the Old Southwest were notoriously weak, and "the criminal justice system remained imperfectly formed." Nor was the concept of southern honor completely antithetical to evangelical morality; as Wyatt-Brown acknowledged, evangelicalism wrought subtle changes on the code of honor as the nineteenth century progressed.[8]

Testimony from across the South emphasizes the importance of church discipline on community norms. One South Carolina Presbyterian evaluated the role of church discipline in his antebellum community. He wrote:

> The Session of Elders of Indiantown Presbyterian Church was the supreme court of all that section. In civil as well as religious matters, the people required no other tribunal than this ecclesiastical court. No Sanhedrin at Jerusalem nor College of Cardinals at Rome, in its time and place ever exercised more complete control. . . . It is very possible that no other community in this country has for so many years required so little interference by civil authority. The unwritten law is so high in conception and so strong in execution that hardly ever is it necessary for the State to use its authority.[9]

Likewise, historian Durwood Dunn, in a study of the Appalachian community of Cades Cove, found that the Baptist church acted as an "invisible government" and exerted a greater influence "over the community than either the civil authorities, political parties, or the prominent entrepreneurs." The church's influence did not arise out of sheer numbers, for in

Cades Cove as in the rest of the antebellum South the majority of residents were not members; rather, the church exerted its influence through what Dunn calls a "consensus mechanism." Open to anyone of whatever race or class, congregations could not easily be controlled by any single individual or group, and because decision-making authority was usually broadly based, such decisions reflected a congregational consensus. And even when churches or denominations came to be more representative of certain socioeconomic groups, they continued to share a basic outlook on fundamental questions of individual morality. Such highly motivated, well-organized bodies could exert considerable influence over the larger but disorganized society outside the church doors.[10]

In the Old South the Baptists, Methodists, and Presbyterians disciplined their members, though the process differed slightly among the three denominations. The Baptist churches dealt with such cases at their monthly conferences, usually held on a Saturday. Scarcely a conference took place without one or more disciplinary cases under discussion. Using Jesus' directives to his disciples as a guide, church rules required that members first attempt to settle disputes privately. If the attempt failed, the aggrieved person notified the church of the complaint. The conference then appointed a committee to investigate the matter and cite the other party in the dispute to appear at the next conference to explain his or her behavior. A second and equally important directive involved individual transgressions. Church members were expected to inform the conference of any offense—drunkenness, profanity, adultery, and the like—committed by another church member, and the offender was then cited to attend the next conference, though if the case were clear-cut a vote might be taken when the charge was made. Churches often required a unanimous vote to establish guilt or exclude a member. Some research suggests that poorer members were more likely to be disciplined than more wealthy members, and traditional evangelicals condemned modernist ministers, whose concern for numbers and money, they charged, led them to neglect discipline or to show favoritism to members of "influential family."[11]

But on the whole the process was remarkably democratic; no one—white or black, deacon or minister, male or female—was exempt from the process, and equal care was shown in investigating most cases. In the Presbyterian church such cases were handled in the monthly meetings of the presbytery. A small group of people, usually the male presbyters, decided guilt or innocence. The Methodists regulated their members' behavior in class meetings, and cases often came before meetings of the quarterly conferences as well.[12]

Throughout the period under discussion, discipline played a vital role in the churches and affected members of both races and genders, but important changes took place over time. The rate of discipline declined markedly after the 1820s (see Table 4) and largely disappeared by the end of the nineteenth century. Edmund S. Morgan, in his study of the early Puritans, demonstrated that strict discipline was essential to militant sects but less compatible with more inclusive denominations. "Historically the magnification of the minister's office has often gone hand-in-hand with a comprehensive policy of church membership," he wrote, "while a limited membership, emphasizing purity, has been associated with a restriction of clerical authority." Modernist clergymen in Mississippi did not enforce discipline as actively as the traditionalists or the early evangelicals. The decline in discipline accompanied the general move away from a congregational ministry. Modernists were less willing to see such authority vested in the hands of the congregation, a power that had frequently been used against the preachers themselves. Rowland Berthoff estimated that up to half the preachers in the early days of the Old Southwest faced disciplinary action. Modernists preferred to see such authority lodged with the state synods, conferences, or associations under their control. Traditionalists charged that modernists were too concerned with numbers, status, prestige, and worldly influence to pursue a strict discipline. In part, of course, they were correct; the decline in discipline reflected a different vision of the church and its mission.[13]

The practice might have disappeared from the modernist churches even earlier had it not been for the mission to the slaves and the rapid rise in black membership. Discipline was far more than simply a white device for control; it was a useful tool in the maintenance of a closer "watch-care" over a body of members considered to be by nature less capable of self-restraint, more prone to a loss of self-discipline. It is no coincidence that cases of discipline dropped dramatically after blacks left the biracial churches during the Reconstruction period.

A careful study of disciplinary actions by race and gender can reveal a wealth of information about the nature of religious life in the South. The following discussion is based on a study of thirty church and circuit records with a total of approximately twelve hundred disciplinary cases. Of the cases in this sample, the gender of the offender can be determined in 1,169 cases. These case records are often taken verbatim from such proceedings and reflect the life and concerns of evangelicals as few other sources can. They are also among the best surviving records of the southern plain folk, and their usefulness for the study of slavery has yet

Table 4. Exclusions in the Mississippi Baptist Association, 1807–1847

Year	Baptisms	Membership	Exclusions	Percent of total membership
1807	3	196	1	0.5
1808	2	236	9	3.8
1809	15	251	5	1.9
1810	9	277	9	3.2
1811	13	334	4	1.2
1812	91	494	2	0.4
1813	246	914	13	1.4
1814	106	1,071	29	2.7
1815	80	1,048	41	3.9
1816	23	695	32	4.6
1817	43	1,158	35	3.2
1818	44	1,072	48	4.5
1819	4	1,125	23	2.0
1820	61	863	21	2.4
1824	45	551	8	1.5
1826	57	612	8	1.3
1827	84	348	4	1.1
1828	88	833	19	2.3
1829	80	870	22	2.5
1830	110	734	14	1.9
1831	28	790	17	2.2
1832	27	670	10	1.5
1833	15	530	14	2.6
1834	8	416	5	1.2
1835	18	475	8	1.7
1836	111	581	8	1.4
1837	554	1,155	15	1.3
1838	101	1,227	24	1.9
1840	56	1,242	17	1.4
1841	465	1,661	23	1.4
1842	332	1,420	43	3.0
1843	89	1,360	30	2.2
1844	35	668	13	1.9
1845	57	816	11	1.3
1846	103	1,051	18	1.7
1847	73	1,103	11	1.0

to be widely appreciated. Any attempt to quantify the records runs the risk of losing the richness of language and social context that makes them so valuable; on the other hand, it is impossible to tell over a thousand individual stories. In an attempt to reach a compromise between these extremes, each section will open with the story of one case.

Discipline of White Men

In the 1820s the members of Salem Baptist Church, the oldest Baptist congregation in the state, faced a series of difficult disciplinary cases that threatened to destroy the church. The dispute centered around B. E. Chaney, an active member of the church who held the office of church clerk and whose extended family also played an active role in church affairs. In June 1821, Chaney confessed that he had been intoxicated, and the church forgave his transgression, as they often did when a member voluntarily confessed and expressed a determination to repent. In August 1822, he was charged again with the same offense, and this time he was suspended. In November 1822, he once again faced the same charge. According to the church records:

Br[other] B. E. Chaney charged with a repetition at Franklin Court of the sin of intoxication acknowledged the fact whereupon the pastor urged the duty of withdrawing fellowship from him for so scandalous a series of disorderly acts which was objected to by Br. Wm. Chaney on the ground of his profession of sorrow and a determination to drink no more Spiritous liquor he moreover brot [brought] forward Mat. 18th 21 and 22 verses to prove the duty of forgiving him Br. Wm. Erwin being present expressed an opinion favorable to the views of Br. Wm Chaney Br. Jacob Stampley agreed with the sentiments of the Pastor: that whereas Br. B. E. Chaney had been under censure . . . and had repeatedly been publicly guilty of the same offense and finally after making confession to the ch. so nearly satisfactory that it was expected he would have removed the obstacle to fellowship by a public confession on the Lords day—but alas instead of this about 10 days after had been again drunk at Franklin—Br. Stampley moved the exclusion of B E Chaney. Br. Erwin in the chair Br. McCall seconded the motion the question taken Brethren Stampley & McCall were for his exclusion Sister E. and P. Coleman & E Farror agreeing, but Br. Wm Chaney opposed the motion to him agreed sister Chaney, sister Cole and sister Wilds.

Chaney was excluded by a single vote, though the troubling case was far from over. In January 1823, Chaney was restored and given a letter of dismission. Those members who had voted to exclude him were apparently dissatisfied with the decision to restore Chaney, despite his decision to leave the church. Stampley and McCall, along with seventeen other members, applied for letters of dismission in March 1823. This mass exodus left only about a dozen active members in the congregation, and they lamented their "deplorable situation." The group struggled along until 1834, when the church dissolved, a sad ending for the oldest church in Mississippi.[14]

Over half the cases in this sample, 55.9 percent (654), involved white males, far higher than their percentage of the membership. In the hierarchical society of the Old South, white men shouldered heavy responsibilities not only for themselves but, more important, for the households that composed the organic southern community. The white men who largely controlled the disciplinary process watched their fellows carefully, for how could proper order be maintained if those most responsible for its exercise failed in their duty? As the Chaney case demonstrates, men could differ sharply in their views of what constituted a proper exercise of duty. In the view of the narrow majority at Salem, Chaney was guilty not only of disorder but of repeated public displays of disorder that discredited not only him but the entire congregation.[15]

The case from Salem is representative of charges against white men in that it involved intoxication, by far the most common charge leveled against them. A total of 593 charges against white men can be identified in the sample of church records; of these, 33.6 percent (199) involved alcohol abuse. In the early churches, either fewer evangelicals drank or the offense was taken more lightly; from 1806 to 1820 only five charges of intoxication came before the churches in this sample, 15.2 percent of the charges brought against white men. William Winans believed that the consumption of alcohol had increased so rapidly that by the early 1820s in "all classes from those who are lowest to those in high official stations, men are to be found who are not ashamed of being seen wallowing in the filth of this debauch in the very streets." Winans and other preachers denounced the sin of drunkenness from their pulpits, and congregations punished church members who drank or sold liquor. Evangelical opposition, combined with a highly successful temperance campaign, produced results; historians have found that alcohol consumption declined after 1830. The decline is reflected in the number of cases before the churches; for example, the percentage of intoxication charges in the total fell from 45.8 percent in the decade from 1820 to 1830 to 20.7 percent in the decade from 1860 to 1870.[16]

Evangelicals were concerned about alcohol abuse not only because of its effects on the individual but because it affected the family and the community as well. The Methodist preacher Thomas Griffin, known for his sharp tongue, denounced the drunkard as "a far worse character than the frantic suicide who would take a pistol and blow out his brains, thus ridding his family of a pest and leaving his property for their maintenance, whereas the drunkard, after cursing and disgracing his family . . . afflicting them with his drunken revels, wasting his property, breaking the heart of his wife, and hanging his poor, ragged, uneducated children on the horns of poverty, is in the end a self-murderer." Over and over again evangelicals encouraged fathers to shoulder the responsibilities of patriarchy. As one Methodist newspaper admonished, "Are you not the head of the family? Does not the government of the household devolve upon you?" Alcohol consumption not only affected the family's economic well-being, it could also lead to other actions threatening to the family. For example, in 1850 a member of Liberty Baptist Church was excluded for intoxication and adultery. A member of Galilee Baptist Church was excluded for intoxication, wife abuse, and adultery.[17]

Because intoxication was often linked with violent or aggressive behavior, alcohol abuse threatened the order and stability of the entire community. The link between alcohol consumption and aggression is not a causal one but varies from one culture to another. In some cultures there is no relationship between alcohol and violence, but significantly, in the late twentieth-century United States, "there seems to be more alcohol-related aggressiveness in the rural south than in the north." In this sample, there are twenty-four cases (12 percent of the alcohol cases) that specifically link alcohol and aggressive behavior. For example, a member of New Zion Baptist Church was excluded for drunkenness, profanity, and beating his slave. The most common aggressive behaviors associated with alcohol were fighting and profanity.[18] Profanity was the second most common charge made against white men (10.6 percent of the total or sixty-three cases); fighting ranked fourth (8.6 percent or fifty-one cases).

Dancing ranked third in the list of allegations made against white men, accounting for 9.1 percent (fifty-four) of the total number. Evangelicals considered dancing unholy, unprofitable, sensuous, senseless, barbaric, and devilish. Dancing was a popular amusement among elite Mississippians, who danced cotillions and reels, and among the plain folk, who enjoyed a variety of folk dances, but whether elite or popular, evangelicals condemned the practice. In 1844, H. W. Walter, a member of the Holly Springs Presbyterian Church, asked to be excluded because he and the church "differ widely as to the propriety . . . of many of the common gayities and amusements of life," especially dances. "The Church condemns, I approve them, and approving enjoy them." The church honored his request and excluded him.[19]

Taken together, the four most common charges—intoxication, profanity, dancing, and fighting (or quarreling)—account for 61 percent of the total. Almost 20 percent of the cases (19.1 percent) are general, nonspecific allegations, including disorder, misconduct, nonfellowship, and contempt. The remaining 20 percent may be grouped into general categories; of these, sex and family life and race relations are most significant for an understanding of the complex relationship between gender, race, churches, and households.

Twenty-eight of the miscellaneous charges involved sex or family life. Fifteen of these related to marriage; there were seven charges of adultery, six of bigamy, and two of desertion (2.5 percent of the total). Cases involving marital or family relations could be especially difficult for churches because of their belief in the responsibilities of the master/parent/husband for his household. When a male member of Bethlehem Baptist Church confessed that his wife's first husband was still living, the church called a council of sister churches to help decide the case. On occasion, members refused to answer charges involving their marriages and were therefore excluded, or they refused to accept the church's ruling and hence excluded themselves. In April 1850 the Bethesda Baptist Church Conference appointed a committee to investigate a report of wife abuse against John Kilcrease. He refused to answer the report or attend "court" and warned the church not to send another committee to discuss the subject. The conference excluded him in June. In July another man asked that Kilcrease be restored and that a letter of dismission be granted to his wife. In August the conference indefinitely postponed his restoration and refused to grant his wife a letter. Another member then charged Mrs. Kilcrease with unchristian conduct, and the conference excluded her in January 1851. In May 1851 John wrote the church asking for forgiveness for both him and his wife, a request the conference refused. He wrote again in August confessing his sin and asking for forgiveness and letters of dismission. After this contrite confession, the conference gave letters to the husband and wife.[20]

Men who abused their wives or children sometimes defended their action as "correction," an interpretation of abuse that evangelicals sometimes refused to accept. In 1816 the Salem Baptist Church conference excluded a man who claimed to have been correcting his wife by whipping her. Winans described a family of three sisters with terrible tempers. One of their husbands said, "You are a remarkable family of Sisters— three of you have been whipped by your husbands in as many months." Winans expressed no surprise or disapproval at this remark, nor did he comment on the tempers of men who whipped their wives. A male member of Bethlehem Baptist Church denied that his treatment of his children could be considered abuse, but testimony convinced the conference otherwise and he was excluded. As Winans's attitude suggests, evangelicals expected women to remain in certain roles; a Baptist circular letter of 1835 stated that "submission is the chief duty of a woman." When women stepped out of this role, as the sisters did, then male evangelicals saw nothing amiss in "correction." But the other examples demonstrate that evangelicals also outlined male duty in a way that condemned abuse by husbands. The same circular letter that required women to be submissive stated that "the husband and wife . . . must be considered as a joint head of the family" and noted that "love is the first duty of a man."[21]

Abused wives had little recourse in the law; only the churches brought such actions to light and condemned them. Evangelicals attempted to revise the ideal of patriarchal marriage to include companionship, love, and mutual respect. The evangelical emphasis on family life, the duty of spouses, nonviolence, and the education of women at least helped create a climate hostile to such abuses. The evangelical attack on "masculine" attributes resulted in a new appreciation of "feminine" characteristics. An 1859 obituary praised the Methodist William Fisk McGeehee for being "pure and modest as a woman . . . loyal, docile, loving to obey." Another Methodist, the Reverend Hamilton Watkins, was called "as gentle as a woman."[22]

The category of charges dealing with race relations is perhaps most significant for its small size; it contains only nine examples. Evangelicals were extremely reluctant to interfere in this sensitive area because the power of the master over his household was considered primary. Only two white men were charged for beating a slave; one case also involved intoxication. The second case occurred in Bethesda Baptist Church. The church conference in December 1858 alleged that J. T. Martin struck a black boy with a stick and then whipped him. The case might never have come before a church conference except that the slave belonged not to Martin but to J. H. Collins. Both men were leaders in the church. The conference also charged Collins for taking legal action against Martin before trying to reach a settlement in the conference. Both Martin and Collins were excluded, along with members of their families. When the White

Oak Baptist Church accepted the Martin family as members without letters of dismission, Bethesda sent a committee to White Oak to protest. White Oak refused to reconsider its action, and Bethesda requested that a council of churches consider the case; a council composed of representatives from three other churches and two associations heard the dispute. The case dragged on until November 1860, when Bethesda followed the council's recommendation, restored Martin and his family, and granted them letters of dismission, thereby allowing them to transfer their membership to White Oak. Obviously, the abuse of the slave youth was lost in the dispute between the white men over the treatment of a household member.[23]

More serious than beating slaves were cases involving the shooting of a slave and a slave's death. The first case, from Concord Baptist Church, reads simply, "Brother Wragg through Brother R. D. Brown laid his case before the church of shooting a negro which confession being satisfactory he was acquitted." It is impossible to tell whether the black person lived or died. The conference did not appoint a committee to review the case or examine the evidence, perhaps because Brown confessed. The case of a slave's death comes from Ebenezer Baptist Church in November 1858. Peter A. Green came before the conference and "stated he had a difficulty with a runaway negro in attempting to arrest him, which resulted in the death of the negro by Bro. Green." A motion was made that Green be excluded, but it was tabled until January 1859, when it was taken up and lost. Again the conference made no attempt to investigate the charge as it would have done in relatively minor cases involving only whites. Like the civil courts, the conferences handled such cases with kid gloves.[24]

Two other cases in the records involved masters' use of their slaves' labor in violation of religious commandments; such cases put Christian slaves in extremely difficult positions. In July 1832 the Bethany Baptist Church Conference charged a master with intoxication and sending his slaves to help clear a race track; he was excluded. In 1853 the Galilee Baptist Church Conference excluded a slave owner who forced his slaves to work on the Sabbath. Occasionally religious slaves risked punishment rather than violate their beliefs. In 1820 Winans found "Sister Bryant" "with a whip in her hand ready to castigate a servant because . . . the servant was not willing to work while other servants were keeping holy day." For most slaves a preacher probably did not appear at such an opportune moment. Slaves who were given orders that violated their religious beliefs held their masters responsible. Andrew Jackson Gill, a former slave in Lincoln County, said, "Dey [the master and mistress] was responsible fer us an' if dey tol' us to do somethin' it was on dey conscious if it was wrong, not our fault." White evangelicals agreed. Religion provided some slaves with psychological defenses against the dehumanization of slavery and gave them a sense of moral superiority over irreligious masters. As one former slave recalled: "There was an old man on the place that was a kind of a preacher. They whipped him one day but he wouldn't deny. He said that was his victory over hell, and if they whipped him to death, when they turned him loose, he was going on the same way."[25] The slave preacher had found a path to victory not only over the eternal hell but also over his hell on earth.

An examination of disciplinary actions against white men reveals a picture of their duties and responsibilities. As heads of households they were expected to protect the family—white and black—and guard the order of the larger society, a responsibility they could not carry out unless they controlled their own passions and vices. Evangelicals seldom questioned white males' authority within the household except in especially egregious cases.

Discipline of White Women

In August 1857 James B. Quinn, a trustee of Bogue Chitto Baptist Church and a frequent delegate to the Mississippi Baptist Association, charged Edda White and Elijah Cothran [or Cotterane] with fornication, and the conference appointed a committee to examine the charges. The following month the committee made its report:

> Sister Catherine Dunaway says in February or first of March last She a woke in the night say about midnight and heard some person snoring in the bed occupied by Mrs. E. White and further says that She is certain that it was Elijah Cotterane that She is well acquainted with the noice he makes when snoring and that he also coughed when he a woke by which she also recognized him . . . and that she got up to make a light and went to the fire place for the purpose & that she heard two persons get up and walk from the bed occupied by Mrs. E. White to the direction of the door & that Mrs. E. White opened the door and got a drink of water, then returned & came and kindled up the fire, but that she did not see the other individual she heard walking from the house it being dark & c and that she heard Mr. E. Cothrans dogs Bark about the time she thought he could get home.

Edda White made no defense to the charge and was promptly excluded. Cothran, however, denied being her partner, and the church considered his case until November, when he, too, was excluded.

These small personal dramas in southern communities have long been grist in the mill for southern novelists, but in the church courts they played themselves out month after month, year after year, though the sparse records never reveal as much information as a historian might want. A novelist might well speculate on Edda White's anxiety as she sat in the meeting listening to the charge against her and also on the effects such a case could have in the household Edda White shared with Catherine Dunaway, whose testimony was so damaging to her reputation. The novelists might ask, too, how the case came to the attention of the church. Did Catherine Dunaway spread the rumor abroad or did one of the partners discuss the encounter? Clearly such cases could put the church in the center of the sorts of conflicts and scandals that flowed below the surface of these communities.

An examination of females' trials indicates that women found it much easier to conform to evangelical expectations than did men. White women faced 150 identifiable charges in this sample, far less than the 593 against white men, even though women made up a majority in the typical evangelical church. In none of the churches surveyed here did the disciplinary actions against women approach their percentage of the membership. For example, Bethany Baptist Church had a majority of female members by 1843 (52.6 percent), yet cases against women accounted for only 15.3 percent, and even this figure is high compared to many other churches. In Academy Baptist Church white women made up 37.7 percent of the membership in 1860 but only 4.8 percent of the exclusions. Despite their majority in membership, women did not control the disciplinary process. In those Baptist churches where women voted (usually Primitive Baptist churches) they could influence the process and their votes could be decisive. Often in such churches women also served on committees appointed to visit other women who faced charges in the church courts. In most churches, however, white men oversaw the disciplinary process.

Men's control of the process, along with other evidence, led historian Jean E. Friedman to describe discipline as an "important factor that inhibited the development of female networks and reinforced traditional sex roles . . . by enforcing a double standard of discipline." Her research in church records from North Carolina and Georgia revealed that women were more often convicted of "serious" offenses than men, particularly sexual misconduct, and, once charged, they were more likely to be excluded than men.[26]

The issue is not simply one of a double standard, but rather of a different standard for women; they were responsible for the duties of mistress/wife/mother. The evidence from Mississippi and other southern states differs sharply from the sample Friedman found in the seaboard states. Most charges against Mississippi women were for relatively minor offenses. Dancing accounted for over one-third of the charges (40.7 percent) against white women, but only 9.1 percent of the charges against white men, though the raw numbers are very close (fifty-four charges for men versus sixty-one against women). Evangelicals feared that dancing would lead women into sin and temptation. In 1861, for example, the Presbyterian Synod of Mississippi condemned dancing and "all kindred amusements which are calculated to awaken thoughts and feelings inconsistent with the seventh commandment ["Neither shalt thou commit adultery," Deut. 5:16]." They considered the "practice of promiscuous social dancing by members . . . a mournful inconsistency."[27] Evangelicals believed women to be naturally more emotional and less capable of self-restraint than men. As one religious newspaper observed, "Women are naturally more warm hearted and enthusiastic than men, more easily excited, and give way to their feelings with less restraint."[28] Another 21.3 percent of the charges are general, unspecific allegations such as misconduct, disorder, nonfellowship, contempt, or immorality. Unfortunately, these cannot be identified with any certainty, though only the charge of immorality was usually applied to a serious offense, often of a sexual nature. The next most sizable group, twenty-six cases (17.3 percent), charged women with joining another denomination. The same charge occurred only seven times (1.2 percent) in the male group. This discrepancy likely results from women who wed husbands from another denomination.

Intoxication accounted for only five (3.3 percent) of the allegations against white women. Only two cases involved intoxication and aggressive behavior, and both women were also charged with profanity. Even today "aggression seems never to be an important component in the image of drunken comportment on the part of women." The small number of allegations reflects the norm against female drinking.[29]

The four categories of charges discussed above constitute 82.7 percent of the total. The remaining miscellaneous allegations may be divided into the same general categories used in discussing males: sex and family life and race relations. Sex and family life includes fornication, illegitimate births, leaving husbands, adultery, bigamy, and unscriptural marriage. These accounted for 8.7 percent of the total allegations against white women, compared to 4.7 percent of the allegations against white males. These percentages are far lower than those found by Friedman, who calculated that 44 percent of female offenders in her sample were accused of a sexual offense, while 6 percent of the males were so charged. The dramatic difference in these findings is difficult to explain. Friedman's sample of fifteen churches is smaller, but the number of cases against women in her sample is larger (235 versus 150).[30]

A reference to numbers rather than percentages in the Mississippi sample shows seven charges of adultery against men compared to two against women; six allegations of bigamy against men and one against a woman; three charges of fornication against men and three against women; two allegations against men for leaving their wives and three charges against women who left husbands. Of course, no man was charged with an illegitimate birth, while three women were. But by the same token, women were not charged with spouse or child abuse, attempted rape, or in family disputes, while nine such charges were made against men. As the opening case involving Edda White and Elijah Cothran demonstrates, evangelicals were as ready to exclude men as women for sexual offenses.

Perhaps a more thorough study of the disciplinary process across the South will be necessary before adequate explanations can be made, but in light of the Mississippi findings, conclusions concerning discrimination against white women in the process cannot be made. If the Mississippi sample is representative, it is difficult to argue that a double standard existed for men and women charged with sexual offenses; equal numbers of men and women faced charges of sexual misconduct.

Only two charges in the sample involve women and blacks. One woman was charged with the ambiguous offense of holding a "Negro Party" during the troubled Reconstruction period. In a more serious case, a white woman was charged with murdering a slave. In March 1858 the Ebenezer Baptist Church Conference appointed a committee to investigate rumors that in 1856 Sister Jane Roark murdered a slave girl belonging to Henry Marston of Clinton, Louisiana. The committee presented certificates from Marston and from Dr. P. O. Langworthy, the attending physician in the case. Marston wrote that he could not swear that the girl's death "was caused by the violence of Mrs. Roark"; likewise, Dr. Langworthy refused to accuse Mrs. Roark but wrote that death "was caused . . . either by an accidental or intentional injury." The testimony was ambiguous at best and hardly proved Mrs. Roark's innocence, yet the conference discharged the committee and dismissed the case.[31]

The sample of allegations against women demonstrates that the most common charge involved a relatively minor offense—dancing. In contrast to earlier studies, the sample does not show discrimination against women in church conferences. If discrimination was at work, it operated against men, who were disciplined and excluded at far higher rates than women. For example, an 1860 membership list from Academy Baptist Church also shows which members were excluded. The roll reveals that 6.7 percent of the white males were excluded, but only 1.2 percent of the white women were so severely punished. Viewed another way, 28.6 percent of the twenty-one cases involved white males, but only 4.8 percent involved white females.

Elizabeth Fox-Genovese has argued that slaveholding white women deeply internalized the evangelical ethic: "Religion lay at the core of slaveholding women's identity. It provided their most important standard for personal excellence and legitimated their sense of self in relation to the other members of their society." Certainly the low number of disciplinary cases against women lends credence to her suggestion; white church women were more successful in shouldering the burdens of evangelicalism than white men. The duties evangelicals imposed on white men sometimes conflicted with prevailing social norms, but the subordinate position of women in the churches reinforced their position in the larger society.[32]

Discipline of Black Men

In May 1849, Harden, a slave member of the Louisville Baptist Church, faced a charge of gross unchristian conduct, and the conference appointed a committee to investigate. Like many biracial churches with substantial numbers of black members, the Louisville blacks had separate services and held a separate conference at which they disciplined members. The investigative committee consisted of three other black men. Harden attended the next monthly meeting to answer the charge; he acknowledged "keeping out of the way of his master and refusing to be corrected by him, the charge of disobeying him in any other Respect he denies and wishes his mistress to be seen to know the certainty of the fact." The case was laid over while a white man was appointed to visit Harden's mistress as he requested. Her response is not given in the records, but the conference excluded Harden at its September meeting.[33]

Exclusions against white males and females accounted for 33.4 percent of the total at Academy Baptist Church; obviously, blacks made up the remainder. This example suggests that if there was any discrimination, it most affected blacks. Of the twenty-one exclusions there, 38.1 percent were against black males, who made up only 10.7 percent of the membership; 28.6 percent of the cases were against black females, who composed

10.2 percent of the membership. Of the black men on the 1860 roll, 34.8 percent were excluded; 9.1 percent of the black women faced exclusion. Of course, slaves had specific duties peculiar to their divinely ordained station, duties clearly prescribed in Scripture. The study will show that although the disciplinary process sometimes functioned as a white control device in that it lent support to the slave system, in the majority of cases, the churches disciplined blacks for the same transgressions that plagued whites. The study also demonstrates that in most cases, with a few important exceptions, blacks received fair hearings conducted in the same way as those involving whites.

The high rate of discipline of blacks resulted in large part from their different standards of morality. When blacks joined evangelical churches they pledged to abide by the strict moral code evangelicals demanded; like white men, many blacks found it a heavy burden. There were real contradictions between the evangelical code and the code of the black community, a difficulty not fully resolved until the postbellum separation of the churches.

Lawrence W. Levine wrote that slaves, out of necessity, sometimes lied, cheated, or committed theft because of need. Such actions, though technically violations of the Christian teachings accepted by many slaves, could be "neutralized." He wrote, "Thus it was possible for slaves to rationalize their need to lie . . . and steal without holding these actions up as models to be followed in all instances, without creating, that is, a countermorality." Riley Moore, a former slave in Montgomery County, recalled a white preacher who "would take a text tellin' us . . . Don't steal, be good to Marsa an' Missus an' don't run away. Dey ought to have been hung fo' preachin false doctrin'." Slaves recognized the hypocrisy of a system that denied them an adequate share of the product of their labor because, according to Scripture, "they shall not plant and another eat . . . mine elect shall long enjoy the work of their hands" (Isa. 65:23).[34]

A breakdown of cases against black males by decade shows that disciplinary actions against slaves increased steadily as black membership grew and as slavery became a more important concern in the churches. In Mississippi the number of cases against blacks increased dramatically after 1830 though a corresponding increase in black membership indicates that discipline did not become harsher.[35]

The two most frequent charges against black men were directly related to the slave system: running away and theft. The most common allegation against black men was running away (thirty-three charges or 17.3 percent of the total). Twenty-three of those charges were made against black men who joined Federal troops during the Civil War and are therefore not applicable to the antebellum period. Evangelicals attempted to prop up the institution of slavery and maintain order during the war, but many slaves escaped to freedom. Several churches appointed committees to determine the number of blacks who had fled and often excluded runaways at once.[36] The next most frequent charge, theft (twenty-three cases), made up 12.0 percent of the total. The charge appeared only six times against white males (1.0 percent of the total).

The next most frequent charge against black men was the most common against white men—intoxication—which accounts for 10.5 percent of the total. Six of the twenty-three cases linked alcohol and aggressive behavior (26.1 percent), twice as high as the percentage among white males. Psychologists have found that drinking enhances a "sense of personalized power."[37] No doubt many slaves vented their aggressive feelings through alcohol consumption and temporarily overcame feelings of powerlessness. It may be a testimony to the strength of the black community that alcohol consumption was not epidemic.

Alcohol was readily available to blacks who had money to spend. One black man was accused of selling liquor, but the charge was not sustained. In 1852 the Bethesda Baptist Church Conference excluded a black man for selling eggs and corn without his master's permission and using the proceeds to buy whiskey in Jackson. Another church excluded a white man for selling liquor to blacks and Indians on the Sabbath. Churches attempted to prevent selling and drinking of liquor at meetings. Bethany Baptist Church resolved to fine whites who sold liquor at church $30; blacks guilty of the same offense would be lashed. Bethany also resolved that a white man found guilty of drinking would pay $5 for each offense. A black man guilty of the same offense would get fourteen lashes for the first offense and double that number for subsequent offenses, "provided that the Punishment Prescribed . . . shall not be inflicted in view of the church."[38] Presumably if blacks had money to buy liquor, they could also have been fined rather than lashed.

The next most common charges were general allegations of misconduct, immorality, or disorder, which are, again, impossible to identify with certainty. These charges constitute 9.9 percent of the total.

The allegations against black males discussed above constitute half of all charges made against them. Again, the remaining charges will be divided into general categories: individual behavior, infractions of the slave code (other than those already discussed), and sex and family life.

The category of individual behavior includes profanity, lying, fighting or quarreling, nonattendance, and Sabbath-breaking. Allegations of profanity account for 7.3 percent of the total, slightly lower than the 10.6 percent against white males. The charge of lying constitutes 5.8 percent of the total, higher than the 2.0 percent against white males. The charge of lying was often linked with that of theft. Allegations of fighting or quarreling account for only 2.1 percent of the black charges but 8.6 percent of those against whites. Two blacks were cited for nonattendance, one for working on the Sabbath, and another for joining the Methodists.

Allegations involving sex or the family relationship include charges of adultery, fornication, desertion or bigamy, and wife abuse. The eleven charges of adultery compose 5.8 percent of the total, higher than the 1.2 percent (seven cases) against white males. Fornication allegations account for 2.6 percent (five cases) of black cases, but only 0.5 percent of whites (three cases). Another five black men were charged with either leaving their wives or having two wives; eight white men faced these charges (1.3 percent). Allegations of wife abuse account for 2.1 percent (four cases) against blacks and 0.67 percent (also four cases) against whites. Although the percentages are higher for black males in cases involving sex or family life, the actual numbers of white and black cases are remarkably similar.

Evangelicals attempted to support black family life, but here they confronted one of the most troubling and tragic consequences of slavery. In 1853 a slave man, Nathan, owned by Isham Howze of Tennessee, became engaged to a woman on a neighboring plantation. Nathan was compelled to break his engagement, however, when his master moved to Mississippi later that year. The forced separation troubled Howze, who wrote, "This evil of Slavery he [Nathan] will have to bear. . . . It is an evil—the family relation—and the greatest evil in the institution. The evil is in this— wives and husbands, parents and children & c. can be separated, according to the will of the master. If this could be avoided," he believed, "slavery would be a Small evil."[39]

Some evangelicals went to extraordinary lengths to keep slave families together. In 1835 John G. Jones purchased a slave woman. She and a slave belonging to his neighbor, J. W. Bryan, wished to marry, but Bryan refused to allow his slaves to marry off the plantation. Jones offered to sell Bryan the woman, but he refused to buy her and promised to keep the slaves apart. Jones later sold the woman to a fellow preacher, "but when he came this morning to take her home she bursted into a great flood of grief and said 'she could not and would not leave her *husband*—that she would rather die.'" Jones was "utterly astonished" and asked who her husband was. She replied that she and Bryan's man were married and had been living together for three months. Jones "began to cry mightily to God . . . for His direction in the affair." To his relief, "though not without some difficulty," he persuaded Bryan to buy the woman "and let her and the man she loves get married." Jones gave thanks to God "that I have gotten pretty safely through . . . this delicate matter—and think I will try more than ever to keep clear of the curse of negro slavery."[40]

Even late in the antebellum period few slaves were married by a minister. In that year a Baptist editorialized that the issue of slave marriages had received little attention in the state. He believed that marriages should be performed by a minister and that such unions should be binding. "Our civil laws are here seriously perverted," he wrote, "and still unheeded— our religious institutions outraged, and still not investigated." Samuel Agnew, a Presbyterian minister who lived on his father's plantation, did not marry slave couples; a slave, Big George, conducted the ceremonies. Only after the Civil War did Agnew perform marriages for former slaves. There is greater evidence of white ministers performing ceremonies after the war, though some did so in the antebellum period.[41]

In 1865 James Lyon, a Presbyterian minister in Columbus, Mississippi, prepared a report calling for reforms of the laws regarding slave marriage for his church. His letter to Governor Charles Clark brought a favorable response, and Lyon drew up a reform bill, which he sent to the state legislature, then meeting in Columbus. His bill died in committee. Lyon wrote, "It seems that there should be such reluctance to do any thing that would in the slightest mitigate the abhorrence that the world has of negro slavery."[42] Perhaps the legislators saw the futility of reforms in 1865, when the entire institution was crumbling around them.

Eighteen allegations in the sample (9.4 percent) refer to other infractions of the slave code; these include disobedience, hiding runaways, rebellion, threatening a white person, and possession of a weapon. The largest number (fourteen cases) involved slaves who disobeyed their masters. Frequently, the masters themselves brought charges before the conference. In 1858 John H. Oates, a member of Bethany Baptist Church, charged three of his slaves—Harrison, Pompey, and Minter—with disobedience and running away; all three were excluded without further investigation.[43] Four slaves in the sample were charged with hiding runaways. No doubt slaves saw this as an act of courage, loyalty, and friendship rather than a religious transgression.[44]

The charges of rebellion are vague but probably refer to slaves who ran away to join Federal troops. Other charges struck at the heart of the master-slave relationship. In 1823 a black male member of Bethany Baptist Church was excluded for threatening his mistress. In 1827 a male member of Zion Hill Baptist Church was found guilty of possessing a knife; whether he threatened someone with the weapon is unclear, but such charges show rare but significant examples of black resistance.[45]

Evidence demonstrates that blacks were disciplined at a rate higher than their percentage of the membership in some churches. The sample also shows how the disciplinary process sometimes worked as a control device. Still, less than half the charges (41.4 percent) were for offenses peculiar to or encouraged by the slave system, and in light of the length of time under consideration, the total number of cases was small.[46] Evangelical support of the black family represented a more positive aspect of the system but one that never received legal sanction and therefore could have had only limited impact.

Discipline of Black Women

In May 1849 a committee appointed by Bethany Presbyterian Church gave its report on Ursula, owned by J. Dixion, who was charged with criminal assault against a fellow slave. On the morning of March 10, Ursula and several other slaves were working in their master's field, supervised by a slave driver. Ursula urged two other slaves, Charlotte and Mary, to help her kill the driver with their hoes. They refused to do so, even though she prodded them throughout the day. That night "she encouraged the same persons to make assault upon the slave person with axes." Despite Ursula's obvious hatred for the driver, she was unable to convince others to help her, and she made no physical assault.[47]

In June, Ursula pleaded innocent to the charge of criminal assault. The conference examined several other witnesses, including Dixion and five slaves, before finding her guilty. Ursula "then acknowledged her guilt [in encouraging an attack] and said she was deeply sorry and had prayed and would pray for forgiveness." Despite the severity of the charge, her punishment was light; the session "admonished her of her sin" and warned her against similar conduct.[48]

As Ursula's case suggests, the church records can offer tantalizing glimpses into the workings of the slave community. Because of the convergence of race and gender, disciplinary actions against slave women had different dynamics from the discipline of white women or black men. In this sample, only 9.1 percent of the charges were brought against black females. An examination of these charges shows that the most common allegation was adultery, with eighteen examples (17.8 percent). The same charge accounted for only 1.3 percent of those against white women (two cases) and 5.8 percent (eleven cases) of those against black males. An additional 8.9 percent (nine cases) involved fornication while 7.9 percent (eight cases) concerned illegitimate births. An additional 2 percent (two cases) were against women who left their husbands. Taken together, these account for over one-quarter of all charges against black women. In part, the high number of such cases against black women resulted from the slave code, which denied the legitimacy of the marriage bond. Perhaps more important, blacks held different ethical standards for unmarried women than did whites. As Herbert Gutman wrote, "Many slaves distinguished between prenuptial intercourse and 'licentiousness' and believed prenuptial intercourse and pregnancy compatible with settled marriage." Gutman's conclusion that blacks found no contradiction between prenuptial intercourse and faithful marriage is supported by the small number of cases against black women who violated the marriage bond.[49]

The contradictions between the evangelical belief in the sanctity of marriage and the realities of the slave system troubled congregations who heard testimony from black women. In 1824 the Bethany Baptist Church Conference asked another church to send delegates "to assist them in a difficulty relative to the marriage of a black sister." Conferences called for such assistance only in especially difficult cases, and the request demonstrates the importance the church attached to the case.[50]

In 1849 the Bethlehem Baptist Church considered a case involving a slave woman belonging to James Woodson. She wished to join the church but had been excluded from another church because "she was ignorant at the time, that she was married to a man that had another wife." According to standard practice, she could not join another Baptist church without a letter of dismission, but the members of Bethlehem sympathized with her and agreed "that the cause for which she was excluded was such as this church could not see was founded on justice." She was admitted to membership.[51]

The second most common charge against black women was the same as that for black men—theft. No such allegation was made against a white female. There were fourteen such charges in the sample (13.9 percent). Because many husbands lived on different plantations, the black woman was responsible for providing for her family on a daily basis. Also, because of their jobs, black women may have had greater opportunity to take from the white folks.

The next most frequent allegations against black females were the general charges of disorder, misconduct, and immorality (seventeen cases, 16.8 percent).

Running away accounted for 11.9 percent (twelve cases) of the total charges against black women, a percentage only slightly lower than that for men (17.3 percent). A surprising number of females ran away from their masters. Genovese estimated that at least 20 percent of runaways were female, but in this sample, a higher percentage of runaways were female—28.3 percent. If we consider only those slaves who fled during the Civil War, when escape was easier and the chances of success were very high, the percentage rises to 30.3 percent.[52]

The charges already discussed account for approximately 80 percent of those made against black women. The remaining allegations will be divided into two categories: other violations of the slave code and individual behavior.

Only four of the remaining allegations (4.0 percent) are other violations of the slave code. One woman was charged with harboring a runaway, another with disobedience, another with possession of a weapon, and another with striking her mistress. The latter case occurred in November 1865 and illustrates the tensions prevailing at the war's end.[53] The case of the woman who slapped her mistress is one of many examples revealed here of slave women behaving in surprising and forceful ways; in addition, two black women were charged with assault.

There is one charge in the records against a black woman for fighting. It is the only example of one slave bringing charges against another. Significantly, it occurred in 1816, when blacks enjoyed relative equality in the biracial churches. In March of that year, Seleh, a member of Zion Hill Baptist Church, charged her fellow member Hetty with "*quarreling* with *her* for giving *her* abusive language." The conference excluded Hetty in May after a careful consideration of the case.[54] The final charge in this category is intoxication. Only one black woman was charged with drinking, the smallest number for any group.

Black women were disciplined at a higher rate than white women and were far more likely to be charged with sexual offenses. The sample shows black women in a variety of roles—attempting to assault a hated driver, striking a mistress, possessing a weapon, hiding a runaway, stealing food or other goods from whites—that show they were not simply passive victims.

Evidence suggests that black church members took the disciplinary process and their church membership seriously. When Sarah, a slave member of Fellowship Baptist Church, was charged with having an illegitimate child, she appeared before the conference and "stated that she knew She had done wrong that she hoped she had obtained forgiveness from the

Lord for her Transgression and Requested the church to forgive her." Her request was granted. In 1858 Stephen, a male slave charged with lying at Concord Baptist Church, "acknowledged his offence and begs the church to bear with him as he is very sorry for what he has done. The church agreed to bear with him."[55] Whites considered cases against blacks carefully and attempted to inculcate in blacks the self-control necessary to lead a Christian life. Both blacks and whites had duties to perform, duties mandated by God and necessary for the creation of an orderly community.

Significantly, conferences did not automatically accept a white person's word against that of a black member. For example, in 1842 and again in 1844 the Concord Baptist Church Conference found Carolina innocent of charges made against her by whites. When Lewis, a member of Academy Baptist Church, denied the charge against him, he was exonerated.[56] Again, these examples testify that the conferences attempted to treat blacks fairly, carefully considered their individual cases, and listened to their testimony with respect.

In some churches with large black memberships, slaves held separate services and met in separate conferences where they handled their own disciplinary cases under white supervision. Blacks at Concord held a separate conference beginning in 1845. In 1848 the white secretary made the following entry in the church records: "Held conference with the Black members. The case of Tony was taken up [charged with gross misconduct] and he excluded. . . . Jack servant of Bro. S T Potts was reported as guilty of swearing and other misconduct on the vote being taken he was excluded." Blacks at the First Baptist Church in Louisville were given a separate conference in 1848; when blacks were charged with transgressions, they appointed their own committees to investigate.[57]

Blacks may have felt more confident of a fair hearing from their peers, and some boldly stated their opposition to verdicts from white conferences. In 1852 the Antioch Baptist Church Conference charged Abram with adultery. He told the committee "that he believed, there was none of the male members of Antioch Church, but what was guilty of the same act . . . he was Said to be guilty." In 1832 New Hope Baptist Church granted a slave, Carey, the right to preach in public, but in 1834 it withdrew that right after concluding that he "was not called to the Ministration of the word. After words of insult offered to the church he was excluded from fellowship." In 1832 Peter, a member of the same church, was charged with gambling; he "did not deny gambling," but, more important, "he did not appear to impress any sorrow but said he did not intend to come to church, whereupon he was excluded."[58] Some slaves, at least, took an active part in the process and boldly expressed their opinions; others defended the validity of their gifts, even if whites denied them; and others withdrew from the biracial congregations rather than change their behavior. Slaves were not simply passive participants, nor did whites expect them to be.

The process was sometimes used as a white control device against slaves, as the large numbers of allegations for running away and disobedience attest. But it also gave religious blacks an arena for moral growth, supported black family life, and was sometimes under black control in segregated services. When evangelicals adopted the biblical defense of slavery, they agreed that certain duties were required of both slave and master. The low number of cases in the records against masters who violated these precepts may suggest that blacks were held more strictly accountable, but if conditions for slaves improved in the antebellum period, evangelicals must receive much of the credit.[59]

The large number of cases against blacks for violations of white concepts of proper sexual behavior cannot properly be considered discriminatory because large numbers of whites were also tried for the same offenses. When blacks chose to join the churches, they vowed to uphold its teachings. White evangelicals cannot be faulted for expecting them to do so or for refusing to accept black definitions of proper sexual behavior when these contradicted evangelical beliefs. Evangelicals of both races struggled to uphold the strict moral code; it is not surprising that so many failed, but that so many succeeded.

Church discipline remained an integral part of evangelical worship throughout the antebellum period and then declined sharply by the 1880s.[60] "Wholesome, godly discipline" provided evangelicals with a structured method of confronting disorder and bringing members a realization of their duty. Through discipline evangelicals reaffirmed their hierarchical vision of society; the system was profoundly influenced by their view of the orderly community as one composed of households whose members had specific biblical duties to perform. The public, confessional nature of the proceedings reflected the evangelicals' perception of their society as one of individuals caught up in a web of social dependencies, tied to the community in various personal ways. Church discipline reflected these ties and was not limited to the person charged but extended to his or her family, the congregation, and the community at large. Bishop Robert Paine of the Methodist Episcopal Church, South, left the following record of an 1818 case that illustrates the multilayered consequences of discipline:

> After preaching, and discussing the audience, I proceeded . . . to hold class-meeting, with closed doors, *as usual*. The leader suggested that a certain

brother present had been intoxicated, and a trial was needed. . . . A profound silence ensued, while every head was bowed in grief and sympathy. The accused was under middle age, an industrious and successful young planter, who . . . was popular and respected. His wife, with two children, was there. . . . Their parents, on both sides, and nearly all their kin, were present; for the family were Methodists. . . . The erring brother . . . pleaded guilty to the charge, and in subdued tones submitted his case. I read the law—drunkenness is "a crime expressly forbidden." I was in trouble—all were troubled. Must he be expelled? He was a young convert, and expulsion and degradation likely involved ruin. I began by asking him: "Why, my brother, have you brought yourself and us into this fix? Have you any explanation to give for your conduct? When, where, how did it happen?" Then . . . his wife's head sunk down as if she was crushed, and I broke down. Then he raised his head a little, and while great scalding tears were coursing down his . . . face, he said slowly . . . "I didn't *intend* it, brother. It wasn't in a *doggery*; my *merchant* said I needed something; it was so cold—brought it—now suppose it was raw whisky or brandy. . . . Never was drunk before. Can't help it now; it's over, and I am *ruined*." Here he broke down, and his poor wife brought a low, long wail. . . . We all broke down. "No, no, brother," I said; "can't you *quit*?" "Quit!" he replied. "I *have* quit. Suppose you must turn me out . . . I deserve it; but do as you may, I will never taste the thing again; never so help me God!" And then the wife shouted, and the elder child climbed into his father's lap. . . . The old members shook hands and blessed God. . . . In conclusion, I proposed that . . . we would forgive him, and say nothing more about a trial. . . . The members agreed to it, and this was the first temperance society I formed. I often heard of him afterward, and learned he had kept his vow. . . . The class-leader prayed, all left happy, and at a camp-meeting held there that summer more than one hundred and twenty professed religion and joined the Church. That trial did good.[61]

Individual, family, and community were saved as a result of church discipline. Such was the ideal vision of the purpose and nature of the process.

CHAPTER 10

THE DESOLATIONS OF ZION

EVANGELICALS IN THE CIVIL WAR AND

RECONSTRUCTION, 1861–1876

THE outbreak of war in 1861 brought drastic changes to the evangelical community. The orderly patriarchal society they had labored to create soon began to unravel under the strains of war. Evangelicals as a group did not lead the secession movement; in fact, they were surprisingly reticent on this vital issue. But by adopting the pro-slavery ideology, by dividing along regional lines, and by harshly criticizing northern abolitionists, they made their sympathies clear and thereby contributed to secession. Many evangelical ministers opposed secession and the war, but few made that opposition public, and their exact numbers can never be known. Many churches filled with women in mourning as thousands of Mississippians died on the battlefields. Federal raids and occupations disrupted many churches. Biracial churches lost many black members who fled to freedom during the conflict. Despite the horrors and disruptions of the war, or perhaps because of them, many other churches enjoyed periods of revival during which large numbers of new black and white converts joined the churches. The Confederate defeat and the abolition of slavery led to soul-searching among many white evangelicals who had accepted the biblical defense of slavery and believed that God favored the South in the struggle.

For blacks, however, the war was an answer to a prayer, which may explain the growth of the black membership in many biracial churches during the war. An important consequence of the Confederate defeat, one that marks the sharpest break between religious life in the antebellum and the postbellum South, was the division of the churches along racial lines. The roots of the division lay in the segregated services common in many biracial antebellum churches. The division did not occur immediately after General Robert E. Lee's surrender, however; blacks and whites continued to worship together until the 1870s. Only from the vantage point of the modern South can the revolutionary change in church life be appreciated. Commenting on the breaking of barriers between the races in the 1960s, 1970s, and 1980s, Mississippi author Willie Morris, a perceptive social critic, wrote, "The churches will be the last institutions to integrate, of course."[1] Perhaps Morris and many modern southern evangelicals would be surprised to learn that completely segregated churches appeared only after the Civil War.

Neither evangelical ministers nor the religious press openly advocated secession, but their defense of slavery and attacks on abolitionists increased sectional tensions and did nothing to soothe the troubled waters. A writer in a Methodist newspaper said, "Were it not for the attacks of Northern papers, the organs of our church would never agitate any question connected with Slavery." But agitate they did. The writer continued, "Abolitionists are responsible for *free negrodom*—a growing social and political, disease." A Baptist newspaper article criticized "the fanatics of the North" and defended slavery "because of our honest conviction that it is socially, politically and morally right." Ministers such as William Winans called abolitionists *"fanatics—lunatics"* and praised the South's "chivalric notions in regard to foreign interference in domestic concerns." Evangelical voices joined a growing chorus; one evangelical recalled the period before 1861 as one of "fierce and bitter political prejudices and fiery speeches of impassioned orators which had been multiplying and growing in heat for more than a generation, until the climax was reached in secession."[2]

When secession came, no doubt most evangelicals favored it; the secession movement was powerful in the state, "more powerful than in any other state except South Carolina." Even in Mississippi, however, the voter turnout in the election for delegates to the secession convention was low, and the convention refused to submit the ordinance of secession to a popular vote.[3]

Though the convention's reluctance to allow the citizens to vote on the ordinance may have been unfounded, evangelicals' support of secession was not unanimous. Thomas C. Teasdale, a prominent Baptist minister in Columbus, criticized "reckless, lawless filibusters," "daring political adventurers," "secular editors," and "a subsidized, profligate press" for their "open disregard of existing Statutes, both State and National." "If a law be unwise," he wrote, "let it be abrogated by the proper authority. But until it is repealed, let us submit to its behest." Teasdale and James A. Lyon, Presbyterian minister in Columbus, outraged the fire-eaters when they led a successful campaign to prevent the sale of a group of Africans illegally brought to the city in 1859. John A. Aughey, pastor of the French Camp Presbyterian Church, angered many in his congregation when he preached a sermon on the illegality of secession. He fled north after an attempt on his life.[4]

Like Lyon, Teasdale, and Aughey, John G. Jones believed that the laws of the land should be respected, and he thought that southerners should fight for their rights under the Constitution. In his autobiography he wrote: "I shall not have much to say about the war. I was utterly opposed to it . . . I was as much opposed to secession as I dared to be." He had faith in the Constitution, "which guaranteed the perpetuity of slavery. Not that I wished to perpetuate slavery one day beyond the will of God, but I wished to be let alone, so that we, or our descendants, might dispose of it in away not to ruin either master or slave."[5]

Bishop Robert Paine of the Methodist Church, South, was described as "a prudent Christian patriot." A resident of Aberdeen, Mississippi, a small but wealthy cotton town in north Mississippi, he traveled across the South on the eve of secession in connection with his office. He presided over the South Carolina Conference of his church in 1861, and when resolutions were introduced in favor of secession, he declared them out of order. He also labored to keep politics out of the Mississippi Conference. Paine did not oppose slavery—he was a slaveholder himself—but he realized that slavery "became a wedge in the hands of impassioned partisans and un-compromising fanatics to rend and nearly destroy the boasted fabric of our national Union." More clear-sighted than most, "he prepared himself for the defeat which he well knew was sure to come." In the early days of the war, when victory still seemed possible, "he visited Richmond . . . and sought to arouse the . . . President to a sense of the certain ruin that was soon to come to Mississippi, and then to all the South." President Jefferson Davis did not heed Paine's warning, of course. Paine spent the war years as quietly as possible, occasionally preaching to soldiers and fleeing Yankee raids. While some ministers may have encouraged war, Paine was proud of his opposition to it; he wrote, "The evils of it [the war] are inconceivable, and the responsibility for it must be decided by the only court of *supreme* jurisdiction. If I felt in any degree responsible for it, I think it would craze me. Thank God, I do not!"[6]

Most of the moderate ministers described above occupied prominent positions in slaveholding districts. At least two of them, Jones and Paine, owned slaves. Their determination to keep political questions out of the church prevented them from speaking out. The reluctance to engage in political debate was in large part a result of the slavery controversy. William

Winans had entered the political fray without hesitation in the early days of the church. These moderates agreed that a small group of southern radicals pushed the South to secession; they believed that a calmer consideration of the question would prevent bloodshed. Their opposition to secession grew out of the tenets of their faith. Though evangelicalism could produce social revolution, it was basically conservative. The 1810 covenant of Jerusalem Baptist Church read, "We will . . . conduct ourselves . . . in a peaceable and friendly manner towards mankind . . . and pay a conscientious regard to civil government." From the origins of evangelicalism in Mississippi, religious men and women labored to create a society based on order and duty. Many evangelicals had no desire to see their stable communities upset by war. Many no doubt agreed with Jones that the Constitution protected southern interests and war was therefore unnecessary. Years of sectional controversy had not destroyed the patriotism of men like Lyon, Jones, and Paine.[7]

Once war began, Jones and other evangelicals rallied to the Confederate cause, though often reluctantly. Jones considered it his Christian duty to submit to the new government, but he "never could pray in faith for the success of the Confederacy." A Baptist minister from Ocean Springs on the Mississippi Gulf Coast volunteered in 1861 "to fight in defense of my country. (Not in defense of slavery, for I was opposed to slavery.)" Walter Tynes, who lived in southeastern Mississippi, recalled, "My father and every man of his neighbors were unanimously against secession . . . but after we were plunged into war, our sympathies were naturally with our young men . . . our preachers all preached and prayed for the success of the Confederacy,—or were silent on the subject. Indeed it was a capital crime with a death penalty to do or be otherwise."[8]

As the Confederate government attempted to create and nurture a sense of nationalism, the support of the evangelical churches became vital. Religion could link the move for independence to a higher moral quest, the defense of the South's divinely ordained civilization. The Confederate government sought the blessings of religion by proclaiming public fast days, which churches observed. In June 1861 Robert B. Alexander, a slave owner in north Mississippi, "went to church [and] heard Rev. See preach or rather give a war Talk & a very good one at that." In 1862 he wrote, "To day we fasted, Negroes & all we went to Church heard Rev See deliver a fine lecture on the war." President Davis proclaimed nine fast days, and "Congress, state legislatures, and denominational bodies designated so many more that a strict compliance with all might have saved enough food to feed Lee's hungry army." Compliance was not always strict; one group of well-meaning Mississippi church women celebrated a fast day with a church fair and a supper. Many religious southerners recognized the hand of God in the Confederate victories at Manassas, the Seven Days, Chancellorsville, and Chickamauga, all of which followed fast days. A woman in Crawfordsville, Mississippi, expressed her faith in the good effect of the observations when she asked the state government to proclaim yet another fast day: "From a thorough search of God's word I find no denial of peace to nations that humble themselves before God. Another fast day is absolutely necessary for the good of the land." The observances served the Confederate government as propaganda that was especially powerful because of the high visibility of many preachers and the importance of church life for many southerners.[9]

The war also opened a new field of labor for southern women, who responded by organizing aid societies, producing articles for soldiers, and working in hospitals. Church women in Carthage, Mississippi, organized their Ladies' Soldiers Aid Society in February 1862. Its officers, all women, included a president, approximately twelve vice-presidents scattered across the county, a secretary, treasurer, and five managers. These women also worked in a local hospital, despite criticism from some men who "seemed vexed at them for their ministering to the wants of the soldiers." In 1862 James Lyon referred to Columbus as "one great hospital"; all public buildings, including churches, were used as hospitals. Lyon noted that women, including his wife, "took an unusual interest in the hospital." When wounded men poured into Holly Springs in 1862, five hospitals were set up. Cordelia Lewis Scales reported, "You cant cross a street or turn a corner, but what . . . you see wounded or sick soldiers." The Scales home served as a hospital, and Cordelia Scales labored to care for the needy. The pace was so hectic that "for five days I did not take my clothes off."[10]

Confederate women turned to the church for support in such trying times, and as more and more men left for war, the female majority in churches increased. Samuel Agnew, a Presbyterian minister in the northern part of the state, found the largest congregation he had seen at Mount Zion Church almost entirely female. In 1863 at Ebenezer Church he found another large congregation, "especially of ladies." Federal raids or occupations often made regular services impossible, much to the consternation of faithful women. Lettie Vick Downs, who lived near Vicksburg, lamented in 1863 that she had been unable to attend church during the past year because of the war, and she longed for the day when she could worship there once again. The records of Bethlehem Baptist Church for

June 1862 provide a typical example of the disruptive effects of the war: "Note: oweing to war there has not been much business during the past year. The pastor did not visit us for nearly six months. Only three or four conferences during the year and then no business of import could be handled there were so few members present." The Reverend Samuel Agnew left a vivid account of the difficulties he encountered during the period. On one Sunday in 1862 he found a small congregation at church. "The males were principally pickets," he wrote. "The pickets now occupy the Church and feed their horses in the Church-yard. They use some of the benches for troughs." The following year he traveled to hold church services, but "when I got to the Church I found only 2 persons. . . . There is too much excitement in the hills for people to go to Church."[11]

Excitement of a different kind swept the black community. Many believed the war came in answer to their prayers for freedom. As Dora Brewer, a former slave, recalled, "When de niggers got sense enuf to pray for freedom den de war come." Another former slave, Dora Franks, said: "I started prayin' for freedom and all de rest of de women did de same thing. De war started pretty soon after dat and all de men folks went off and left de plantation for de women and de niggers to run." With many men away at war and Federal troops moving through the state, many slaves found it relatively easy either to ignore their owners or to escape to freedom. The Reverend Samuel Agnew found the slaves belonging to his family openly hostile and unwilling to obey orders; he said of one slave, "She does not conceal her thoughts but plainly manifests her opinions." Many of the Agnew slaves escaped. Mrs. Alfred Ingraham encountered the same situation on her family's plantation near Vicksburg: "The men are far more respectful and obliging than the women; the latter refuse to come and work one and all." Because Federal troops were nearby, the Ingrahams could neither keep their slaves on the plantation nor exact obedience from those who chose to remain. Slavery disintegrated across the South; James L. Roark observed, "On some estates power shifted from the 'big house' to the slave cabins."[12] Disciplinary actions against slaves for running away rose dramatically during the war.

While many blacks rejoiced at the opportunity to escape to freedom, many whites lost their enthusiasm for the war as Confederate reversals mounted, especially after the defeat at Vicksburg. The Reverend Walter E. Tynes described "a great revolt in public sentiment" in 1863. He wrote:

New Orleans had fallen into the hands of the Federals the year before, and now with the fall of Vicksburg and Port Hudson, the Mississippi River was wholly in the control of the Federals from one end to the other, and then that most disastrous defeat of General Lee's splendid army at Gettysburg, all forced overwhelming conviction that the cause was a failure, and that further bloodshed was useless. Added to this was the passage of a law by the Confederate Government conscripting all men between certain ages, excepting only a few, but especially every man who owned as many as twenty Negroes. This law provoked much criticism and the charge that it was a "rich man's war and a poor man's fight." Many men both in the army and out lost all enthusiasm for the cause. Then it was also learned that President Davis and Vice-President Alexander H. Stephens had disagreed about the conduct of the war. . . . It was a time of general demoralization, beyond description.[13]

That demoralization became evident among evangelical ministers and congregations.

For many ministers the fast day sermons became a sore trial. In Columbus the Reverend Lyon delivered a fast day sermon only because the Baptist minister was away and the Methodist minister cleverly "plead indisposition." Lyon, never a supporter of secession, suffered from the general malaise. He wrote:

I had no comfort to give the people—no flattery for them or their rulers—their *sins*, their violations of God's law had brought the sword upon the land—and the only hope was in repentance. . . . Three gentlemen . . . left the house, in a way that showed that they were offended—but I could not change my tone. My text was the 1st verse of the 58 chapter of Isaiah ["Cry aloud, spare not, lift up thy voice like a trumpet, and shew my people their transgressions, and the house of Jacob their sins."]. . . . I will not be compelled to preach "smooth things."

The fast day sermons changed from the "war talks" Alexander described at the war's outset to jeremiads in which ministers castigated southerners for their transgressions and blamed Confederate defeats on a sinful people. Ever since the Early National period evangelicals had linked virtue with national success; this evangelical republicanism, so potent in times of peace and prosperity, offered little comfort in a time of defeat.[14]

Lyon's refusal to preach "smooth things" and his outspoken opposition to secession and war won him many enemies. In 1863 Lyon was accused of leading a "Reconciliation party" in Columbus. His son Theodore wrote a letter in response to that allegation in which he blamed "reckless politicians" and "demagogues" for the war. Leading politicians in the city who had led in the secession movement were understandably outraged and saw an opportunity to attack their old foe through his son. Theodore Lyon was arrested and barred from attending a public meeting on the issue. The Reverend Lyon spoke in his stead, and his speech was interrupted by cries of *"treason, treason, treason!!"* Theodore ran for the state legislature and received one-quarter of the vote despite threats against his supporters. Because of his words and actions, Theodore, who served in the Confederate army, was reduced in rank, separated from his regiment, sent to Virginia, and deprived of $700 in back pay. Lyon concluded, "There never was on the face of the earth a more absolute despotism, than that which now prevails in the land." Lyon and his family escaped lightly; a Unionist minister in Macon, Mississippi, the Reverend James Phelan, was murdered for his views.[15]

The malaise that swept the state in 1863 did not usually express itself in Unionism. Most evangelicals agreed with Lyon on one point: failure resulted from sin, and repentance offered the only hope. When the congregation of College Hill Presbyterian Church met in 1863, they issued the following eloquent statement of their sorrows:

Resolved that those present deem it their duty to place on record for the benefit and information of posterity some facts as history which will show the dealings of God with us as a church and congregation. . . . We would first note that a large number of members at the first call of our country enlisted in her cause for whose preservation, safety, and spiritual welfare many sincere and fervent prayers have been offered up to Almighty God. . . . Some of these loved ones have . . . fallen on the field of battle bravely standing up in the defense of their country. . . . A melancholy gloom overhangs our beloved community. . . . The hearts of many of our members as they weekly enter the sanctuary are bowed in sorrow. . . . But acknowledge the hand of a sovereign God in these sore afflictions and submissively kiss the chastening rod and say thy will be done, O Lord.

The community was spared the ravages of war until late in 1862, when thirty thousand Federal troops moved into the area. They occupied the church, took food, animals, and other goods, burned some homes, and encouraged slaves to leave their masters. The Presbyterians estimated the loss at $200,000.

Such is a mere outline of the heavy calamity which God in his providence has seen fit to inflict upon our community. To say that there were good reasons for this . . . is saying what the Bible and the providence of God in all past ages has taught the nations of the earth. . . . The sin for which punishment is inflicted in this life is brought to our knowledge by the penalty inflicted upon us. Thus our sin . . . is not honoring God to the full extent of our duty. . . . Then it is our duty . . . to humble ourselves, repent in the dust, plead for his mercy, his grace, and the light of his Holy Spirit to enable us henceforth to devote ourselves, our powers of body and faculties of mind, our callings and property to the service of the church and benefit of the world.[16]

Many evangelicals, like the Presbyterians at Church Hill, internalized the lessons of the jeremiads and bore a burden of guilt over Confederate losses and Federal incursions; clearly southerners had been tested and found wanting. Out of that sense of despair grew a conviction that greater faith was required to turn the tide once again. As one woman wrote in 1863, "We will come out of the furnace doubly purified for the good work & fight that God has given us to do For to the people of the Confederacy is given the sublime mission of maintaining the supremacy of our Father in Heaven."[17] Such sentiments helped fuel a widespread revival movement among Mississippi evangelicals.

In 1863 reports came from across the state of a series of revivals. The Mississippi Conference of the Methodist church showed impressive gains, especially in churches west of the Pearl River in central Mississippi. Membership in one charge rose from 6 to 115 in 1863. In September 1863, a woman in Scott County reported that she had attended revival meetings continuously for over three weeks. In the same year ministers from several denominations held successful revivals in Starkville, Mississippi, also lasting over three weeks. The Strong River Baptist Association rejoiced "that we have been blessed with a larger accession to our churches than in any previous year since our organization. The number added to our churches by baptism . . . being 320." That figure compared to 79 members added by baptism in 1861. An 1864 revival at Spring Hill Baptist Church in Choctaw County added 35 new converts. The Aberdeen Baptist Association in north Mississippi reported that "some of the churches of our Association have been blessed with precious revivals of religion . . . abroad we hear of extensive revivals, and from the army the revival news is glorious." Troops stationed in Mississippi towns sometimes participated in revivals. The Reverend George Shaeffer, a Methodist minister, wrote early in 1865: "We are holding a meeting for the soldiers in our church in Columbus every night. The soldiers appear interested . . . many of them evidence a desire for salvation." A religious newspaper observed that "the period of the war was remarkable for extensive revivals of religion throughout the armies and States of the South."[18]

Revivals and a deepening of individual religious faith helped many Mississippians at home withstand the difficulties of war. The strict evangelical moral code meshed well with the rigorous demands of wartime. By demanding order and duty from members of both races, churches attempted to maintain stability; as one historian wrote, during wartime only the church could "exercise a direct and guiding influence on the conduct of the individual citizen." Churches attempted to control some of the worst abuses resulting from the war. One Baptist association, for example, issued a warning against the evil of extortion in 1863: "It is denounced in God's word, and yet, with sorrow be it said, our country, in its present distressed condition, is thronged with those who Extort not only from the rich, but who wring from the indigent the means of subsistence to the last dollar. We cannot expect the favor of God in our struggle for independence as long as we indulge in known sin." Extortion was evidence of materialism and greed, sins that undercut republican virtue and endangered the entire war effort.[19]

The revival affected members of both races, though perhaps for different reasons. An 1864 revival in New Providence Church added 7 black and 15 white members. In 1861 this church had 29 slave members and 64 white members; by 1865 38 black and 81 white members belonged to the church, a 27 percent increase in white membership and a 31 percent increase among blacks. Following a revival in August 1864, the Zion Hill Baptist "church congregation met at the river," where 29 whites and 8 slaves were baptized. Black membership in the Aberdeen Conference increased from 655 in 1861 to 761 in 1864, while white membership declined over the same period. Black membership in the Mississippi Presbytery rose from 493 in 1859 to 728 in 1863. Agnew found in 1864 that "the negroes seem to manifest more interest in the meeting than the whites."[20] No doubt the traditional order and stability offered by the churches appealed to members of both races during the troubled times; many families, both black and white, were disrupted and uprooted; sickness and death knew no color. But unlike whites, blacks rejoiced to see their prayers for freedom and a Confederate defeat answered.

Biracial churches continued to hold services for blacks, but the war virtually destroyed the mission to the slaves. Henry P. Lewis, Methodist missionary to slaves at the Cayuga Colored Mission, wrote: "Slaveholders were afraid to have their slaves preached to. One good man . . . wanted me to remain on the work and preach to his negroes. But after consulting with my presiding elder and prominent men of the work it was thought best not to attempt to organize." No slave mission in the Mississippi Conference showed a gain in membership in 1863, and many were abandoned altogether.[21] The shortage of ministers, Federal occupation of the large mission areas along the Mississippi River, lack of funds, and the escape of many slaves from the plantations brought about the collapse of the missions.

When the war ended in 1865, many evangelicals must have shared the sentiments expressed by the Reverend Tynes and his neighbors: "We were all grieved and broken-hearted over the loss of so many thousands of our brave young men, yet there was a feeling of great relief that the cruel war was over." With that relief came a period of soul-searching for many white evangelicals. One evangelical wrote, "One is tempted to fear that we are a 'God-forsaken' people. . . . The religion of the country has been weighed in the balances, and found wanting." When the members of Unity Presbyterian Church assembled in July 1865, they acknowledged that "much of this church is in a cold & luke warm state forgetful alike of its duties to itself, the world & to God whom it professes to love & worship." They added, "Deeply deploring our past in gratitude in neglect of duty, [we] do turn from our backsliding, confess & repent of our sins & renew our engagement to our covenant."[22]

Some evangelicals believed that God had abandoned them as punishment for the evils of slavery. The Reverend James Lyon wrote that slave owners "vilely abused" slavery and used it "only for selfish and sordid purposes, regardless of the natural rights of the slave." He listed thirteen fallacies expressed by the demagogues he held responsible for the war, one of which was that "slavery is *right*—our cause is righteous and a righteous God is bound to guarantee our ultimate success, & c & c." When a Baptist Committee on the Colored Population met in 1866, it acknowledged that not "all has been done for their evangelization that ought to have been done." As the members reviewed their prewar efforts on behalf of the slaves they found grave deficiencies: "We mourn that our time, and talents, and wealth, (when we had it) had not been more sacredly devoted to the advancement of human happiness, and the promotion of the Redeemer's Kingdom" among slaves.[23]

In a similar vein, Edward Fontaine told his listeners in an 1865 sermon:

> We of the South have committed sins for which we are receiving the chastisement of this war; and for which we should humbly repent and pray for our pardon. Among these sins we may enumerate that avarice and

ostentation which pervaded all classes of the educated, & wealthy slaveholders. . . . But few plantations were adorned with churches for the slaves,
and furnished with salaried ministers to teach them their duty to God
and their masters. . . . If the same amount of money expended in paying
"severe overseers," in useless & ostentatious ornaments . . . had been devoted to building churches, paying missionaries, and providing pious and
talented teachers for our slaves, I do not think this war would have visited
the South with all it's unspeakable horrors.[24]

Ever since they embraced the biblical defense of slavery in the 1830s,
evangelicals had warned masters that divine sanction of the institution
depended upon a proper exercise of duty. Now they held slaveholders
responsible for the terrible destruction brought about by the war.

At the close of the war, the state of the churches appeared grim indeed, and some of the faithful wavered as they surveyed what one group
of Baptists described as "the desolations of Zion." Church buildings had
been burned and desecrated, thousands of members were dead, ministers
were few, congregations were scattered, and the association of evangelicals with a defeated cause sowed seeds of doubt in many minds. As Walter
Tynes wrote, "A fratricidal civil war, involving Christians and Christian
ministers on both sides in a bloodthirsty strife over political issues, and
the extremes of prejudice and hatred in the professed followers of the
Christ, led me to doubt . . . in all religion." An article in the religious press
described the dismal situation: "Many churches had been burned, and
in the principal cities . . . those that remained were occupied by Northern Methodist ministers." The Methodist General Conference of 1866 left
twenty-three charges without appointed ministers.[25]

Evangelicals looked to religion to provide "some stabilization out of the
chaos that was so prevalent after the close of hostilities." They saw instability within themselves, in their personal lives, and in the larger society,
just the sort of instability they had fought, with apparent success, in the
antebellum years. Myra Smith lived a comfortable life before the war, but
the end of the conflict "finds me a houseless, homeless widow with an
afflicted family. . . . The war that has desolated our land for over four years
has suddenly come to a close, bringing with it defeat, and bankruptcy to
very many, we among the number . . . I am brought very low in regard to
this world's goods, my wants are known only to God, from whom cometh
all my help." Like Smith, Walter Tynes turned to religion to overcome his
mental anguish. The solution was not to abandon religion but to renew
the covenant. Defeat did not mean that southerners were no longer God's

chosen people; instead, defeat laid the groundwork for a further expansion of evangelicalism in the postbellum South.[26]

Though the proslavery arguments promulgated by clergymen and the division of the churches along sectional lines contributed to the outbreak of the Civil War, most church leaders faced the prospect of violence and bloodshed with trepidation. A few clergymen expressed outright hostility to the war, but most others, like the majority of southerners, supported the effort once war came. Ever since the growing divergence between the northern and southern churches began in the 1830s, southern clergymen had argued that the South was God's chosen land. When war came, they continued to maintain that God would bless the Confederacy. When the tide turned against the Confederacy in 1863, a dismal pall fell over many evangelicals as ministers and laypeople alike cried that God had turned his back on them. Some historians have argued that this sense of despair fatally weakened the cause.

Rather than turning against religion, whites flocked to the churches as their world grew dark and turned in the postbellum period to the religion of the Lost Cause for solace. Ministers preached that the South would ultimately benefit from suffering, that it would be tried by fire, and they reassured their listeners that God worked from a master plan that was unfathomable but just. Blacks, who saw in the Confederate defeat an answer to their prayers, looked not to a Lost Cause but to a victorious one and demonstrated their gratitude to God by joining the churches in increasing numbers. For white churches not scattered or destroyed and for the emerging black churches the war years and postbellum period saw some dramatic increases in membership.

The Reconstruction period gave many southerners occasion to wonder if their trials were over, for many troubles still lay ahead. Of all the momentous changes of that remarkable period, none was more far-reaching for the evangelical churches than the separation of the churches along racial lines. That separation was part of a broader black movement for individual and community autonomy.[27] During Reconstruction the biracial worship that had characterized southern evangelicalism since the eighteenth century came to an end. For historians who argue over whether the Civil War marked a major watershed in southern history, evidence of a major break can be seen in what happened to the churches. Sometimes the change occurred quickly and with bitterness, but typically the separations came gradually and with surprising goodwill.

Historians have readily acknowledged the importance of the black church in the Reconstruction period and after. Along with the family and schools, the churches served as a bedrock of the black community. What has too often been overlooked is that these churches did not spring up as if by magic, but rather were the direct outgrowth of the antebellum biracial churches. In the biracial churches blacks had never been completely free of white supervision, and important elements of black Christianity as practiced in the invisible church in the quarters seldom intruded into these institutional settings. Once blacks began to form their own congregations, however, a dramatic and significant merger between the institutional church and the invisible church began, a process that many white evangelicals watched with dismay and that set black evangelical churches apart from white churches of the same denominations.

The most far-reaching social change in the postbellum South involved the status of the newly freed slaves, and tensions ran high. In one area of northern Mississippi, for instance, whites were so afraid of a black uprising that they searched freedmen's homes and took their weapons. A white man in Monroe County wrote, "I fear there will be a war between the negroes and white people." The Reverend Agnew described the "antipathy between the two races" in 1865.[28] But the bonds of mutual dependency were too strong for any wholesale racial war, despite the antipathy that sometimes flared into violence.

Such individual and societal tensions shaped evangelical activities in the postwar period. The Reverend James Lyon, perhaps more outspoken than most, challenged those whites who blamed blacks for postbellum problems, who considered blacks inferior, and who refused to treat blacks justly. He told his congregation that "the great sins of the South were connected, directly or indirectly, with slavery—[I] set forth the great fact that the negro, so recently our *slaves* were now 'God's poor' at our doors, and must be regarded & treated as such, if we would avoid still further chastisements." He challenged whites "to be . . . instrumental in elevating the black race . . . in the scale of christianity & civilization." The "radicals" in Columbus responded "by ridicule, brow-beating and scorn," but Lyon followed the dictates of his conscience. Agnew was also criticized for his efforts on behalf of blacks; he wrote, "Many people say *hard things* about me for preaching to the Blacks. It matters not what people say or think. Duty is duty and I am going to do my duty."[29] In view of the larger tensions in society and the hostility of many whites toward blacks, the evangelical efforts to maintain biracial churches, although clouded by paternalism and racism, carried a special significance.

The black desire for autonomy conflicted with a white desire to control blacks and particularly black labor. The planters' need for labor gave blacks bargaining power in the immediate postwar period, and churches were often a part of the bargain. Planters sometimes agreed to assist blacks in building churches (which often doubled as schools) in order to secure laborers. A. T. Morgan, a northerner who leased a plantation near Yazoo City in 1865, found that "the freed people had long been anxious to have a church of their own, but did not feel able to pay the cost of such a one as they desired." He helped construct a building for $1,200 to serve as a church and school in a successful effort to compete for labor. Such schools were virtual extensions of the black churches; Morgan wrote, "The pastor, a very light colored man, who had been a slave . . . and all officers of the church, were present either as scholars or teachers." Some planters attempted to control black worship on plantations by hiring the white or black preacher of their choice or by including provisions in their labor contracts limiting religious worship to particular times and places, but these efforts met with little success.[30]

Churches were the centers of the black community, and they served not only as schools but as meeting places for political gatherings and centers of black resistance to oppression. One black association required ministers to "instruct their congregations to get pass books, and keep their own accounts straight with all men; then when they come to settle their accounts with the merchants, they will know how much they owe." Another black association pledged that "we, as an association, will ever pray for the success of that great party known as the Republican Party, that gave us our freedom." According to A. T. Morgan, "The Sabbath-school on the hill, in the little church we helped to build, was to me a sanctuary, our Yankee stronghold, one of God's fortresses."[31]

Black preachers, often among the best educated and most respected men in their communities, played a central role in black politics. The most famous example of the preacher-politician in the state was Hiram Revels, the first black to serve in the United States Senate. Of sixteen blacks elected to the state's 1868 Constitutional Convention, six were ministers. Black preachers also made up over 40 percent of black Union League organizers in the state whose occupations can be identified. A Jackson newspaper charged: "Certain colored clergymen, residing in this city, are said to be agents of these Leagues, under pay, and thus while pretending to teach the gospel, they, in fact, get their flocks together under the pretense of religious service, and then administer to their deluded victims the unlawful, irreverent, irreligious and blasphemous oaths of the Loyal League." This political activism made the churches targets of violence. During a riot in the town of Meridian in 1871, for example, at least thirty blacks died and black churches were burned. The black Mount Olivet Baptist Association demanded that "it is the moral duty of the City of Meridian to replace that [Baptist] house."[32]

But despite attempts at intimidation, blacks refused to relinquish control of their religious life either to southern whites or to northern missionaries. Blacks knew that they lacked the advantages of higher education and recognized that they could profit from northern teachers, but the church was a different matter. Northern whites, like most southern whites, had little appreciation for the complexities of African-American religious beliefs and insisted that blacks desperately needed reform in their religious practices. Northern agencies such as the American Missionary Association (AMA) moved into Mississippi as early as 1863 and organized religious meetings and schools in the contraband camps. At first, the missionaries were favorably impressed with the freed people's deep religiosity; as one white missionary wrote from Natchez, "*most of them are a praying people*," and another had high praise for black preachers: "We find examples of talent, faith and zeal among some of their preachers that would edify any christian pulpit[.] Uncle Rufus would command respect of any audience in the land—although he can not read a word of the written page—But he has read the Book of Observation—made his own reflections and guided by his own good sense and the Spirit."[33]

The AMA often worked in black churches and depended on black religious leaders. The first AMA schools in Natchez were conducted in black churches, and many of the first native black teachers were ministers or religious leaders. Blacks willingly attended AMA Sunday schools and prayer meetings, but the attempts to establish Congregational churches among them were a dismal failure. One official recognized that such attempts were not likely to succeed "as the people now belong or the mass of them to the churches (Baptist & Methodist) already in existence." Southern whites greatly feared northern influence on black religious life. As one Baptist association warned, "We conceive that there is great danger of this work passing out of our hands into the hands of men and institutions antagonistic to the interests and welfare of our beloved South." But southern blacks had no intention of losing their religious autonomy; even efforts by northern black denominations such as the African Methodist Episcopal church met with only limited success because missionaries often demanded an educated ministry and had little respect for the emotional services southern blacks preferred.[34]

These emotionally charged services reflected blacks' newfound control over their religious life; religious practices formerly hidden in the invisible church became a vital part of postbellum institutional worship. Though some of these practices originated in the Great Revival, others clearly reflected African traditions. Among the beliefs and practices with African roots were reports of visionary conversion experiences or "travelin'." One missionary in Columbus reported:

> A "revival" is in progress in the colored M.E. Chh. and three of my scholars have "come thro" as they say, having been three days & nights in an unconscious state and after "coming thro" telling *wonderful tales* of *visions* & c. . . . There are two colored chhs. in this city One a large M.E. Chh. . . . This is terribly immoral. Their services are of the most frantic nature, the pastor often gets the "power" & jumps & throws himself (physically) in his pulpit.[35]

Maria Waterbury, an AMA teacher, recorded many such instances during her stay in the state. In 1872, for example, she attended a baptism service at which twenty-four blacks were immersed in the muddy waters of the Tombigbee River. She noted that a thousand people thronged the riverbanks, about one-third of them white. Before the baptism, converts participated in a service in the "African church," where they related their "experiences." She wrote:

> An old man said, "I started travelin', an' went on, an' on, 'til I cum to ole hell, an' I see de devil, an asked him ef I might plow dar. He said I might, an' I plowed tu furrows on de firey mane o' hell. Den I seed an ole woman wid her hair all burnt off. Den I seed a pair o' balances, an' was weighed in 'em an' was light as a feather. Ef I'de a knowed God wus sich a sweet God, I'de prayed my knees tu de bone."
>
> Another said, "I started travelin', an' went on, an' went on, 'til I cum to hebben, an' Peter opened de door an' let me in, an' he an John guv me sliced water-melon, an a golden server, an' I had on golden slippers, an' went a slippin' an' a sliden' up an' down de golden streets."

Over and over again the converts related similar visionary experiences until

> one poor man, only said, he came to Jesus, and he took his sins away; he could now pray for his enemies and believed the Lord saved his soul. This candidate was about to be rejected, because he had no wonders to tell, but a white friend came to the rescue, and said to the colored preacher . . . "You'll have to let him in, for he says he trusts in Jesus to the saving of his soul. What better can any one do?" "Well," said the grey-haired Afri-

can preacher, "we'll vote on his case," and he barely passed, but received a reprimand from the preacher, which ran thus, "You have been a believer for six months, and you ought by this time, to *have delivered yourself of an experience.*" Here the session of two hours came to an end . . . and all went to the river to attend the baptisms.[36]

Waterbury also recorded one of the few examples of the ring shout in the state:

It usually began when the preaching was nearly done. Aunt Chloe, or Dinah, would get blest, and seemed to be unable to contain the blessing, and would spring to her feet, and begin shaking hands with the nearest one to her, and in a moment the example would be contagious, and two-thirds of the congregation would rise to their feet, each shaking hands with some other, the men on one side of the church, women on the other; and soon all would swing into the center of the church, in front of the pulpit, and shouts of some would rend the air, while those who could sing, would sing as though their life depended on their making a noise, all the time swaying their bodies up and down and circling among each other, shaking hands, and moving feet as if keeping time to the music. The preacher would come down out of the pulpit, and stand ready for the hand shaking. All would seem either solemn, or joyous, and perhaps after twenty minutes of such exercise, the pastor would lift his hand, when instantly the noise would cease, while he pronounced the benediction, and the worshipers would pass out of the church. . . . One of the scholars, who had participated in the dance, . . . said "That's what is called the Heavenly Dance." The songs usual on the occasion were

> "I wonder Lord will I ever get to heaven
> To walk them golden streets."

or,

> "I'm just at the fountain, Lord,
> That never runs dry."[37]

These blacks were Baptists, and certain aspects of their services had much in common with the early evangelical services or those in Primitive Baptist churches, but other elements of their theology and ritual were fundamentally different from those of the white or biracial churches, which dismayed many white evangelicals. When in 1871 Bethany Baptist Church appointed a committee to visit black churches nearby, the committee reported that the black churches' rules and regulations were "wholly unknown to Regular Baptist Churches." In 1869 one Baptist association warned against "the danger of the colored people, if let alone, retrograding into superstition." And another association in 1867 condemned "their ignorance of the teachings of the Bible" and observed that some former slaves "are endeavoring to impose upon their fellows supposed revelations from God." Methodist preacher John G. Jones watched with anger and frustration as former slaves left his mission church; he wrote, "I am told that most of them have joined an independent negro Baptist church but whether they are christians or not is doubtful."[38]

The degree to which black evangelicals integrated the practices of the invisible church into their postbellum churches varied, and not all blacks looked favorably on the services. Within a few years of the war's end, black Baptists began organizing their own associations, patterned closely after the white associations. In 1868 blacks organized the Jackson Missionary Baptist Association and the First Baptist Antioch Association; by 1876 more than twenty-five black associations existed in the state.[39] Unfortunately, few records from these early black churches and associations are extant but those from the Mount Olivet Baptist Association, organized in Macon in 1869, demonstrate the process at work.

In July 1869 delegates from fourteen black Baptist churches across northeastern Mississippi assembled in Macon to organize the Mount Olivet Baptist Association. Delegates at this first meeting were assisted by two white ministers; they approved articles of faith and rules of decorum borrowed directly from white Baptist associations, and they appointed corresponding messengers "to the Choctaw and other Associations of white Missionary Baptists within our territorial limits." By 1871 the association included thirty-nine churches, and fifteen others applied for admission. The proper qualifications for ministers was an important issue before the association, and the delegates called for higher educational requirements. The association appointed a Committee on Education, which reported that "the subject of education is one of great moment, of intrinsic value, and indispensable to all branches of science and professions. . . . If the Gospel Minister would copy the example of his Savior, he must have . . . all other sciences of earth combined in himself, to be a workman, approved of God, well skilled in the work and one that need not be ashamed. . . . The Gospel Minister has need to be a living, walking library, nay more; a living, walking Encyclopedia." Similarly, the black First Saints Baptist Association resolved "never to ordain a minister who cannot read the Scriptures." Such calls for an educated ministry were a regular feature of black Baptist associations throughout the Reconstruction period.[40]

Such requirements prompted many black preachers to seek an education. Maria Waterbury recalled that she "taught young colored preachers, who had been preaching some time, but couldn't read a word, and their conferences had now voted they should learn to read." Westly Little, a former slave from Smith County, recalled that "I wuz called to preach but needed mo' learnin' so I went to school wid my chillun an' made a preacher."[41]

Along with higher educational requirements for ministers, the associations also urged their member churches to abandon the elements of African-American worship that differed from traditional biracial practices; in 1872 one black associational leader recommended "that our ministers discourage the practice of moaning, shouting, and jumping in churches. . . . We, then, as the true church, must fight against barbarism, superstitution, conjuration." Associations recommended that ministers not preach funeral sermons years after burial because "it is necessary for us to quit these old customs." Others condemned the practice of cohabitating without marriage as a holdover from slavery.[42]

Even though these associations accepted white assistance and condemned certain aspects of slave religion, they were not under white control, as their outspoken support of the Republican party illustrates. Many blacks found in their faith a sense of moral worth and saw in the end of slavery evidence that they were God's chosen people. One minister reviewed recent history in a sermon before a statewide black Baptist convention:

Had the Southern people been educated up to that high moral standard that should characterize the civilized world, all this war and devastation, and carnage would not have happened in our midst. But instead of that, they were educated to believe that they were the peculiar and favored work of God's hand, and that the poor African race was born to be their slaves. That made them believe that a negro had no rights that a white man was bound to respect. But we praise God . . . we find in the face of all that heathenish teaching, that slavery is dead; as such we all ought to be engaged together in building up the old waste places. . . . If one people will oppress the other, God, ere long, will throw confusion in their midst.

The Baptists were remarkably successful in their efforts, and by 1873 the statewide General Missionary Baptist Association of Mississippi included 327 churches with 29,524 members.[43]

The Missionary Baptists, along with other denominations, especially the Methodists, benefited from postbellum revivals. For whites, the revivals grew out of a profound sense of loss and disillusionment and the perception that their social, cultural, and economic lives had been overturned. Blacks, too, saw tremendous disruptions in their lives, confronted white hostility, and searched for order and stability in the changed society. Revivals continued throughout the troubled Reconstruction period.

From across the state came reports of great revivals at the war's end. No doubt many Mississippians shared the sentiments expressed by Allan Hargrove in an 1864 letter to his wife, Mary: "My humble prayer is that this cruel war may soon come to a close & we be permitted to return home to worship God under our own vine and fig tree." The revival tradition was well established; the end of the war and the return of weary troops accelerated a revival movement already under way. At Crystal Springs, Mississippi, "the whole community is in a blaze of religious fervor. The church has been crowded twice each day . . . a crowd of mourners knelt . . . some were praying aloud, some shouting, and many weeping bitterly." A "meeting of days" at Spring Hill Baptist Church in October 1865 added fifteen new members, half of whom were black. White membership in the Salem association rose from 836 in 1865 to 1,362 in 1872, an increase of 63.7 percent. White membership also rose dramatically in churches in the Aberdeen District; at Pontocola white membership rose 103 percent (35 to 71) from 1865 to 1868, while Shiloah showed a 93.1 percent increase (58 to 112) over the same period.[44]

Samuel Agnew's diary records the beginning of the 1865 revivals in his area and illustrates the general pattern. Almost immediately after the Confederate surrender, congregations attending local churches increased dramatically in size. Religious interest and expectations rose throughout the year until the revival season arrived in August. In that month Agnew noted revivals in progress at several area churches and wrote, "Protracted meetings seem to be the order of the day." Revivals ended in October, but large crowds of both races continued to attend regular worship services.[45]

In August 1866, revivals began again, and enthusiastic crowds were in attendance. In late August Agnew estimated that from four to five hundred people had converted. A visiting minister, Dr. R. Burrow, "created quite an interest in the Millenium, which he thinks just at hand." At a September meeting "there have been 43 professions and 29 of these joined the Baptist Church." The pattern repeated itself; meetings ended in the fall and began again the following summer. At an 1867 biracial meeting a black preacher joined the Baptist church and was ordained to preach. It was an emotional service: "Several mourners went up, and from their sobs I judge they were much exercised . . . after his reception by the church [the black preacher] indulged in a 'holy laugh.' It seemed to me to be unnatural, but mayhap I err."[46]

The same religious cycle continued through the following years. By 1869 blacks held their own revivals, though whites, including Agnew, often attended and joined in worship. Blacks organized separate churches, but biracial services and separate services in biracial churches continued as well. When members of Bethany Presbyterian Church organized a subscription drive to build a new church, black members enthusiastically joined the effort and pledged over $100. Agnew wrote, "Blacks are taking hold of the new church with the right spirit, I am glad to see such an interest taken in the church . . . the Blacks will give the church enterprise a better life than I hoped for." Later that year, after a heated discussion, the white building committee refused "to receive the negro subscription for the Church." Following that decision, blacks purchased a building site and even contemplated leaving the Presbyterian church for the Methodists. Blacks at Bethany, like former slaves across the South, tested their newfound freedom and sought a more equal footing in society, an attempt that many whites resented and angrily repulsed.[47]

Not surprisingly, black attendance at Bethany declined sharply after the whites refused to accept their subscription. Agnew wrote, "They are offended I suppose." In August 1874, Agnew and a black member "took the name of 12 [blacks] who adhere to the Church. The names of the balance will be erased from the roll. This is a sad duty . . . but no other alternative is left. . . . They have persistently neglected their duties for 18 months. . . . This action takes from our rolls the names of 44 persons . . . I cannot but think that a rooted antipathy of race is the source of this conduct of theirs."[48]

Variations of Bethany's experience occurred in churches across the state. Everywhere, the position of blacks became a central issue of concern. Some blacks apparently expected that political equality would translate into social equality. As Leon Litwack observed, "This was the appropriate time, some of them [blacks] thought, to give substance to their new status, even to challenge and revamp the traditional and seemingly inviolate code of racial etiquette." Charlie Davenport, a former slave in Adams County, remembered that "de shawl-strop folks (carpet-baggers) . . . tole us we had a right to go to all de balls, church meetings en entertainments de white folks give," but whites refused to attend with blacks who broke racial etiquette. At an 1866 Baptist revival in Corinth attended by Elizabeth Irions, "there was an old nigger woman who went all thro the congregation shaking hands. Before she got to us . . . I vowed I would'ent shake hands with her. . . . So we folded our arms and pretended not to see her. But the first thing we knew she was 'grabbing' at our hands, and Addie Myers just bursted right out laughing!"[49] Not all whites found black efforts to redraw racial boundaries amusing. The blacks at Bethany and the elderly black woman in Corinth attempted to meet whites on terms of equality. Certainly Bethany's black members showed a willingness and a desire to continue biracial worship, but only if a new relationship could be established.

Most whites, of course, had little interest in breaking down racial barriers either inside or outside the churches. Some whites hoped to use the biracial churches to exert control over the freedmen and to prevent blacks from joining the African Methodist Episcopal church, the Methodist Episcopal Church, North, or some other northern-based institution. An 1866 meeting of the Starkville District of the Methodist church discussed "the importance of immediate zealous action upon our part to save the negro from the clutches of those who, under pretext of laboring for his welfare, only enable them to . . . swallow . . . up the M.E. Church, South." Former slave owners attempted to use the church courts to shore up their weakened control over the freedmen. For example, in September 1865, three black members of Academy Baptist Church were excluded for disobeying their former masters.[50]

Whites were often puzzled, angry, and hurt by the blacks' desire for autonomy. William Venables, a native of England and an associate of Lorenzo Dow, settled in Mississippi in the early 1800s and became an active lay leader in the Methodist church. He was described as "a plain, unostentatious" man considered blessed by the Holy Spirit and gifted in prayer and exhortation. Perhaps these qualities account for his success among the slaves; he was licensed to preach and spent the last fifteen years of his life ministering to them. John G. Jones described Venables's experience after the war: "At the close of the late war he had in his vicinity two hundred colored members under his pastoral oversight. But a negro seems to be constitutionally incapable of what we call gratitude. As soon as they found themselves at liberty to do so, they all, with but few exceptions, turned their backs upon their faithful old pastor and went into some newly introduced colored organization. This was a grief to the old patriarch."[51] Jones's bitter attitude toward the former slaves can be explained by his own experience. He, too, spent many years preaching to slaves and considered himself a kind and honest master. His former slaves remained with him for two years but then left. He wrote, "I feel that my responsibility about those negroes was ended forever."[52] Not only did the blacks leave him, they also left the Methodist church, a double blow to Jones.

The revivals and the establishment of new churches also resulted in a revitalization movement that helped some blacks create a religious life peculiarly suited to their postbellum needs, one that combined elements from the invisible church. Although blacks often joined in the postwar biracial revival services, they also held separate revivals. In 1866 Agnew noted that "the whites crowd them out of the Church . . . the negroes prefer having their preaching to themselves." Agnew wrote that five hundred blacks attended an 1869 meeting in Guntown. Mollie Edmonds, a former slave from Coahoma County, recalled, "After surrender us held our meetings in big tents and had a preacher, what could tell us the word of God." Many former slaves recalled that Christianity spread rapidly among the freedmen. Mollie Edmonds said that before the Civil War "there wasn't much Christianity amongst us." A remarkable former slave in Grenada County, Cindy Mitchell, led a group of freedmen known as "Cindy's Band." A brief outline of her doctrine shows how well suited it was to the freedmen's new condition: "Among the things she taught her fellowmen were cleanliness in home and person, thrift, industry, self-respect, and unity among members of the Band." By the 1890s, at least one hundred families belonged to Cindy's Band. In a bit of irony, whites who attended her services occupied the back seats or sat outside by the windows.[53]

Although Cindy Mitchell's ministry is exceptional, black women enjoyed a prominent role in the new black churches. Unlike white or biracial churches, at least some black Baptist churches created the office of deaconess for female members, though unfortunately the duties of the office are unclear. Just as white women joined benevolent societies, black women in the postbellum period taught in schools, participated in community charitable organizations, and collected money for church causes. Black church women were especially active in raising money for educational activities. In 1878 the president of a black Baptist organization observed that "our new field of labor that we opened for the sisters, is doing very well for a new thing. . . . There are a great many good sisters in our churches, who have never had the opportunity to work for the education of their own sex. But we are organizing the 'Five Sisters' at Natchez."[54]

At the war's close blacks had the freedom to control their religious life. As the above examples illustrate, many left the biracial churches and organized independent, segregated churches. Others, however, chose to remain in the biracial churches for several years after the war. Whites were not always hostile to blacks who wanted to organize separate churches. The Methodists in the Starkville District agreed in 1866 that "where they desire it, and their numbers justify, to organize them into separate congregations." As Methodists in the Mississippi Conference acknowledged, "It must be evident to the most casual observer that the old plan of involuntary provision for them [blacks] will not answer. They feel that it is not of their own choice, and hence . . . they set up for themselves." The conference resolved to "encourage and help the colored people to build churches." The Methodist General Conference set up a separate Colored Conference in 1867.[55]

Often, however, blacks did not seek white approval or assistance; they simply left the churches. In 1866, for example, New Providence Baptist Church appointed a committee to visit the "colored brethren who have absented themselves from the church for mos. [months] past." In 1864 Jerusalem Baptist Church had sixty-five black members, but all of them were gone by 1866. As former slave and postbellum preacher Charles Moore recalled, "I didn't spec' nothin outten freedom septin' peace an' happiness an' the right to go my way as I please. An' that is the way the Almighty wants it."[56]

In other churches, biracial services continued after the war, though often blacks gained more autonomy than they had previously held. Blacks continued to be a part of Academy Baptist Church after the war, but they met separately and had a black preacher. In 1869 the church called a conference "for the purpose of organizing the colored people of Academy into a separate church by a unanimous request from them." Though organized as a separate church, the blacks used the Academy church building until the 1870s. In 1867 the members of Magnolia Baptist Church met and transacted the following business: "On motion before the white members present it was Resolved that all the colored members of this church have the privilege of formally withdrawing from this Church to unite with the church about to be constituted." Blacks used the church building until December 1871, when the whites withdrew that privilege. Whites in Liberty Baptist Church agreed to allow blacks to choose their own minister and use the meetinghouse one Sunday each month. In 1867 the church licensed Jerry Blow, a black preacher. Later that year, the old slave gallery was removed. Blacks were allowed to use the building until 1872.[57]

It should be stressed that blacks withdrew from—they were seldom pushed out of—the biracial churches, and generally the separations occurred amicably. In 1865 at Bethesda Baptist Church whites appointed a committee of seven white men, including former masters, to oversee black members. Whites allowed blacks to use the church once each month and selected a white preacher for them. In 1866 the committee suggested that a former slave, York Horton, who had joined the church in 1855, be licensed to preach to blacks. Undoubtedly, the white committee acted on requests from the blacks; the appointment of a black preacher was apparently the committee's last act and marked a new level of black autonomy within the church. In 1867 the church agreed to ordain Horton, and in 1868 blacks organized a separate church and agreed to pay $30 annually for use of the meetinghouse. Whites assisted blacks in organizing the church and included the following statement: "Be it resolved by the White portion of the church, that no objections is entertained or obstacle thrown in the way of a mutual and christian separation and having great sympathy and christian desire for the spiritual and temporal welfare for our colored brethren." Blacks continued to use the building until 1870.[58]

Gradual separation of the blacks and whites occurred throughout the state's biracial churches. The Salem Baptist Association in Jasper County met in 1870 and recommended that where black members "are of sufficient numbers as to form churches and can procure preaching, and wish to form churches of their own, that they should be dismissed in order and assisted in doing so, but where they wish to remain with us as heretofore and are orderly, we think they should be allowed to do so." In 1872 the association suggested that separate churches should be organized. Black membership in the Salem association's churches declined from 206 in 1865 to 122 in 1870. As late as 1872, 81 blacks continued to worship in biracial churches in the association. Blacks were mentioned in the records of Fellowship Baptist Church as late as 1876.[59]

The Civil War brought dramatic changes to the biracial churches and accelerated a trend toward separation that began in the antebellum period. The death of many members, the flight of slave members, the destruction of church buildings, and the dislocations caused by the conflict closed many churches. Others, however, experienced revivals and added both black and white members. The Confederate defeat and the resulting problems might have endangered evangelicalism, but white southerners turned to the churches to understand their wartime reversals and their defeat. A revitalized religion formed the bedrock of the postbellum white community and through the religion of the Lost Cause brought a sense of healing and comfort to those who had suffered defeat and loss.

During Reconstruction, blacks created their own religious institutions and forged an identity and religious life suited to their needs as free people. Among the most lasting and important achievements of the period, the churches were the first and by far the largest institutions under black control. Although biracial worship continued in many churches during the period, whites' refusal to recognize blacks as equals and blacks' desire for autonomy led to racial separation, an event that forever altered the southern religious landscape.

EPILOGUE

I N THE Old South a religion based on love, egalitarianism, and
selflessness confronted a socioeconomic system grounded in violence, inequality, and materialism. It is, perhaps, a sad commentary on the
human condition that in such confrontations between a people's noblest
ideals and their material success, the flesh generally triumphs over the
spirit. It is thus hardly surprising that religion in the Old South never fulfilled the promise of its egalitarian origins, but the seeming inevitability
of that compromise cannot lessen the tragic sense of loss surrounding the
evolution of evangelicalism.

More than most other members of southern society, evangelicals
wrestled with the moral implications of the region's peculiar institution.
In the early years of the movement they concluded that the institution
of slavery was incompatible with the teachings of a lowly Savior whose
sympathies lay with the poor and downtrodden, who often cast Himself
in the role of a suffering servant, and who above all else admonished His
followers to observe the golden rule. But as later historians have observed
and as the evangelicals themselves quickly discovered, such strong opposition to an institution that became increasingly central to the southern
way of life after 1790 would only destroy the movement, a disaster that
would benefit neither master nor slave.

White evangelicals understandably sought compromises; they continued to criticize slavery, many of them refused to own slaves, some
defended slaves from cruel masters, and still others supported plans for
gradual emancipation. Their hostility to slavery was one part of an ideology that resonated with the revolutionary ideals of equality, virtue, and
simplicity. Dedication to a democratic, localistic church structure mirrored the faith of many in the Jeffersonian vision of local, self-sufficient,
agrarian life.

Southern blacks found in evangelicalism an opportunity for spiritual renewal and collective spirituality. The egalitarian message of early evangelicals and their open attack on elite culture caused whites to welcome blacks into the churches, where poor whites and slaves worshiped together. Thousands of slaves came into the churches, and, indeed, the typical church was biracial. The remarkable cultural exchange that began in those churches and camp meetings shaped evangelicalism and left indelible imprints on white and black culture in the South.

As slaveholding and its ethos spread, as more white evangelicals moved higher in status as they aged, as more slaveholders joined the churches, and finally, and most dramatically, as northern abolitionists launched an impassioned attack on slavery as a moral evil, evangelicals were forced to choose sides on the issue of slavery. Halfhearted compromises would no longer suffice, and the great majority of evangelicals openly embraced slavery when southern clergymen articulated a persuasive biblical defense of the institution. Evangelical proslavery marked the final stage of the complex and tragic relationship between evangelicals and slavery in the Old South. The proslavery ideology had profound implications inside and outside the church doors. It was an ingenious and impressive ideology; it used a literal interpretation of Scripture to propose an ideal hierarchical social structure based on households headed by white men. That extremely localistic—almost atomistic—view appealed to many white men, even those who otherwise might have opposed the hierarchical, corporate society and church envisioned by the proslavery modernists. Inside the churches the proslavery ideology contributed to a greater reduction in the privileges enjoyed by both blacks and women, though ironically both groups found a greater degree of autonomy as a result of discrimination and exclusion.

A quest for a more hierarchical, centralized church ran counter to the localism and egalitarianism so basic to the early churches. After the 1830s evangelicalism moved from a movement of sects to formation of denominations, a move marked by a growing organization, stratification, and professionalization. All the major denominations experienced schisms growing out of the fundamental tensions between traditionalists and modernists within the movement. The fissures between traditionalists and modernists were tied to larger currents in southern society. Directly and indirectly religious issues carried over into the political arena and influenced political affiliation and the political battles between Whigs and Democrats. Indeed, the practice of politics and the language of political debate were shaped by evangelicalism. Southern churches also fostered the view that slavery lay at the bedrock of the southern way of life and sundered their own national religious institutions out of loyalty to slavery. When secession came, few evangelicals opposed it, and the majority embraced the vision of a God-fearing, decentralized slave republic as the logical culmination of a trend under way for several decades. The Confederate government attempted to use evangelicalism to foster a sense of nationalism, and southern churches linked the Confederate experiment with the idea of divine providence, a well of optimism in times of victory but a leaky vessel for southern hopes in times of defeat.

Of all the radical changes of the Civil War and Reconstruction, the greatest in religious terms was the division of southern churches along racial lines. With the end of the war, biracial churches became a house divided; newly freed blacks refused to continue in subservient positions, and racist whites refused to grant them equality. The obvious solution was black autonomy, and after a long period of biracial worship, blacks left the churches and organized their own institutions. The black churches quickly became the cornerstone of the black community and the largest institutions under black control.

Beginning in the eighteenth century, evangelicalism unleashed powerful currents in southern society, which continued to flow even after the Civil War reshaped southern life. The tensions between modernists and traditionalists reemerged in the postbellum period in the Holiness and Pentecostal movements, arguably the most dynamic religious outpourings since the Great Revival and, like that movement, egalitarian and biracial in origin. Like the antebellum traditionalists, the members of Holiness and Pentecostal sects emphasized charismatic experiences, gifts of the Spirit, and biblical primitivism and discounted material possessions. The antebellum fusion of politics and religion resurfaced in the Populist movement, when rallies took on the trappings of a camp meeting, and the republicanism, agrarianism, and hostility to the market economy so characteristic of the Populists can be traced back to the antebellum religious traditionalists.

Of all the important characteristics of antebellum evangelical worship, perhaps the biracial nature of that experience is the least appreciated today. Increasingly as the years passed, black and white evangelicals forgot their common history—so much so that the biracial worship that seemed natural to a southerner in the antebellum period became anathema to many southerners of the following century. While the history of biracial worship holds a special significance for southern churches, still the most segregated institutions in society, the stories of individual and collective struggles for personal growth and redemption within the confines of an oppressive, discriminatory society have much wider implications. The history of evangelicalism in Mississippi in the nineteenth century is complex, filled with contradictions, human failings, and occasional glimpses of Christianity's ability to bridge the gulf between master and slave.

NOTES

Introduction

1. *Virginia Evangelical and Literary Magazine*, January 1818, 2.

Chapter 1. *The Growth of a Night: Discovery and Early Settlement*

1. Timothy Flint, *Recollections of the Last Ten Years* . . . (Boston, 1826), 293; Rhys Isaac, *The Transformation of Virginia: Community, Religion, and Authority, 1740–1790* (Chapel Hill, 1982).

2. By far the best study of the early history of the region and the complex relationships among various ethnic groups is Daniel H. Usner, Jr., *Indians, Settlers, and Slaves in a Frontier Exchange Economy: The Lower Mississippi Valley Before 1783* (Chapel Hill, 1992). See also John Hebron Moore, *The Emergence of the Cotton Kingdom in the Old Southwest: Mississippi, 1770–1860* (Baton Rouge, 1988), 1–5; Richard A. McLemore, *A History of Mississippi*, 2 vols. (Hattiesburg, Miss., 1973), 1:117–27; D. Clayton James, *Antebellum Natchez* (Baton Rouge, 1968), 5–21; Thomas D. Clark and John D. W. Guice, *Frontiers in Conflict: The Old Southwest, 1795–1830* (Albuquerque, N.M.: 1989), 1–28; Ian W. Brown, "Natchez Indians and the Remains of a Proud Past," in Noel Polk, ed., *Natchez Before 1830* (Jackson, Miss., 1989), 8–28; J. F. H. Claiborne, *Mississippi, as a Province, Territory and State* . . . (1880; rpt. Baton Rouge, 1964), 1–101, 483–526.

3. Claiborne, *Mississippi*, 17–91; Moore, *Emergence of the Cotton Kingdom*, 1–2; James, *Antebellum Natchez*, 5–11.

4. Claiborne, *Mississippi*, 17–91; Allan Kulikoff, *The Agrarian Origins of American Capitalism* (Charlottesville, Va., 1992), 256–57.

5. James, *Antebellum Natchez*, 45–52; Kulikoff, *Agrarian Origins*, 256–58; Terry Alford, *Prince Among Slaves* (New York, 1977), 39–62; G. P. Whittington, ed., "Dr. John Sibley of Natchitoches, 1757–1837," *Louisiana Historical Quarterly* 10 (October 1927): 494–97; Usner, *Indians, Settlers, and Slaves*, 112–13.

6. John G. Jones, *A Concise History of the Introduction of Protestantism into Mississippi and the Southwest* (St. Louis, 1866), 20–21, 23–24, 27–47, 70–71;

Daniel S. Farrar, ed., "Alexander K. Farrar's Deed to Kingston Church, 1874," *JMH* 17 (January–October 1955): 135–41. The Spanish restrictions on private worship were quite lenient in practice. See Jack D. L. Holmes, "Spanish Religious Policy in West Florida: Enlightened or Expedient?" *Journal of Church and State* 15 (Spring 1973): 259–69; Claiborne, *Mississippi*, 106–7.

7. Jones, *Concise History*, 20–21, 23–24, 27–47, 70–71 (quotation on p. 31); Charles H. Otken, "Richard Curtis in the Country of the Natchez," *PMHS* 3 (1900): 147–53; Walter Brownlow Posey, *The Baptist Church in the Lower Mississippi Valley, 1776–1845* (Lexington, Ky., 1957), 5–7; Richard A. McLemore, *A History of Mississippi Baptists, 1780–1970* (Jackson, Miss., 1971), 6–7.

8. McLemore, *History of Mississippi Baptists*, 33; James, *Antebellum Natchez*, 39; Jack D. L. Holmes, "Barton Hannon in the Old Southwest," *JMH* 44 (February 1982): 69–79 (second quotation on p. 79); and Holmes, *Gayoso: The Life of a Spanish Governor in the Mississippi Valley, 1789–1799* (Baton Rouge, 1965).

9. Jones, *Concise History*, 33–35; Holmes, *Gayoso*, 82–83.

10. Jones, *Concise History*, 35–45.

11. Holmes, "Barton Hannon," 69–73; Holmes, *Gayoso*, 189–91.

12. Holmes, "Barton Hannon," 73–79; James, *Antebellum Natchez*, 70–72; Holmes, *Gayoso*, 191–99; Alford, *Prince Among Slaves*, 62. Hannon became an American citizen and landowner, though there is no evidence of further religious activity on his part.

13. Jones, *Concise History*, 48; McLemore, *History of Mississippi Baptists*, 13; Salem Baptist Church Records, Jefferson County, Miss., 1816, SBHC; Kulikoff, *Agrarian Origins*, 60–61, 87–88, 207.

14. R. W. Jones, "Some Facts Concerning the Settlement and Early History of Mississippi," *PMHS* 1 (1898): 86–89. Norvelle Robertson led a similar group from Georgia in 1817. See Robertson Autobiography, MDAH. For other examples see Kulikoff, *Agrarian Origins*, 215–16. The letters of Leonard Covington, a Maryland planter who emigrated to the Mississippi Territory in 1810, reveal the extensive preparations that wealthy slaveholders made before moving to the frontier. See B. L. C. Wailes, *Memoir of Leonard Covington by B. L. C. Wailes. Also Some of General Covington's Letters*, ed. Nellie Wailes Brandon and W. M. Drake (N.p., 1928), 49–64.

15. John G. Jones, *A Complete History of Methodism in the Mississippi Conference*, 2 vols. (Nashville, Tenn., 1908), 1:105; 2:230; Jones, *Concise History*, 99, 101–2, 116; Learner [Launer] Blackman Journal, 1, Cain Archives; Farrar, "Farrar's Deed," 137.

16. Blackman Journal, 5–6; Jones, *Complete History*, 1:362.

17. Samuel J. Mills and Daniel Smith, *Report of a Missionary Tour . . .* (Andover, Mass., 1815); Jones, *Concise History*, 225–30; T. L. Hamer, "Beginnings of Presbyterianism in Mississippi," *PMHS* 10 (1909): 213–14; Albert E. Casey, comp., *Amite County Mississippi, 1699–1865*, 2 vols. (Birmingham, Ala., 1948), 2:171–72; Frances Allen Cabiness and James Allen Cabiness, "Religion in Ante-Bellum Mississippi," *JMH* 6 (October 1944): 222; Randy J. Sparks, "Mississippi's Apostle

of Slavery: James Smylie and the Biblical Defense of Slavery," *JMH* 51 (May 1989): 89–106.

18. Jones, *Complete History*, 164; Jacob Young, *Autobiography of a Pioneer* . . . (Cincinnati, 1857), 222–23; Henry G. Hawkins, *Methodism in Natchez* (Jackson, Miss., 1937), 38; see also William Winans Autobiography, 56–57, Winans Papers, Cain Archives; Mills and Smith, *Report of a Missionary Tour*, 26; Flint, *Recollections*, 295; James, *Antebellum Natchez*; Estill Curtis Pennington, "The Aesthetics of Everyday Life in Old Natchez," in Polk, ed., *Natchez Before 1830*, 114–15.

19. See Randy J. Sparks, "Religion in Amite County, Mississippi, 1800–1861," in John B. Boles, ed., *Masters and Slaves in the House of the Lord: Race and Religion in the American South, 1740–1870* (Lexington, Ky., 1988), 58–80.

20. "Journal of the Board of Commissioners for Land Claims West of Pearl River . . . 1803," quoted in Casey, comp., *Amite County*, 1:496–99. For a description of living conditions among yeoman farmers in the territory see Alford, *Prince Among Slaves*, 43, and Usner, *Indians, Settlers, and Slaves*, 119–20.

21. Elias quoted in Bertram Wyatt-Brown, "God and Honor in the Old South," *Southern Review* 25 (April 1989): 287; Gaston Bachelard, *The Poetics of Space* (Boston, 1969), 29; Blackman Journal, 6; Winans Autobiography, 122; Moore, *Emergence of the Cotton Kingdom*, 89, 75, 87, 88, 94, 135, 144; Alford, *Prince Among Slaves*, 43; Isaac, *Transformation*, 72, 30–42, 70–80; John G. Jones Journal, March 21, 1835, MDAH; James Pearse described the primitive living conditions in early Mississippi in his *Narrative of the Life of James Pearse* (Rutland, Vt., 1825), 38, 51. Mechal Sobel noted the similarity of houses for blacks and whites in early Virginia and the implications for social interaction in *The World They Made Together: Black and White Values in Eighteenth-Century Virginia* (Princeton, 1987), 100–126.

22. Wyatt-Brown, "God and Honor," 287; Winans Autobiography, 163, 117.

23. Joseph H. Ingraham, *The South-West, by a Yankee*, 2 vols. (New York, 1968), 2:170–72; Moore, *Emergence of the Cotton Kingdom*, 94.

24. Pearse, *Narrative*, 9, 10, 51–57, 72.

25. In 1804 Colonel Ferdinand L. Claiborne compiled a "List of the Gentlemen Little Nabobs of the Mississippi Territory" (quoted in Alford, *Prince Among Slaves*, 76, see also p. 62). Morton Rothstein, " 'The Remotest Corner': Natchez on the American Frontier," in Polk, ed., *Natchez Before 1830*, 96; Samuel Wilson, Jr., "The Architecture of Natchez before 1830," in Polk, ed., *Natchez Before 1830*, 143–51; Pennington, "Aesthetics of Everyday Life," 115–21; Mark Swearingen, "Luxury at Natchez: A Ship's Manifest from the McDonough Papers," *JSH* 3 (May 1937): 188–90.

26. Kulikoff, *Agrarian Origins*, 16–17, 21–24, 29, 43–47, 69–77, 112–32, 142–51, 264; Michael Zuckerman, "Holy Wars, Civil Wars: Religion and Economics in Nineteenth-Century America," *Prospects* 16 (1992): 205–40; Charles G. Sellers, *The Market Revolution: Jacksonian America, 1815–1846* (New York, 1991), 3–33, 152–53; Joyce Appleby, *Capitalism and a New Social Order: The Republican Vision of the 1790s* (New York, 1984), 25–105; Harry L. Watson, *Liberty and Power: The Politics of Jacksonian America* (New York, 1990), 28, 34, 45–49; Gordon S.

Wood, *The Creation of the American Republic, 1776–1787* (Chapel Hill, 1969), 413–25; James Oakes, *Slavery and Freedom: An Interpretation of the Old South* (New York, 1990), 113–17.

Chapter 2.   *Gentlemen, Is That Grammar?: Plain Folk Versus Pillared Folk, 1805–1830*

1. James Bradley Finley, *Sketches of Western Methodism . . .* (Cincinnati, 1854), 219.

2. Perry Miller, *The Life of the Mind in America from the Revolution to the Civil War* (New York, 1965), 6; Isaac, *Transformation*, and "Evangelical Revolt: The Nature of the Baptists' Challenge to the Traditional Order of Virginia, 1765 to 1775," *William and Mary Quarterly* 3d ser., 31 (July 1974): 345–68; Donald G. Mathews, "The Second Great Awakening as an Organizing Process, 1780–1830: An Hypothesis," *American Quarterly* 21 (Spring 1969): 23–43; Nathan O. Hatch, *The Democratization of American Christianity* (New Haven, 1989); Jon Butler, *Awash in a Sea of Faith: Christianizing the American People* (Cambridge, Mass., 1990), 212–24; Sellers, *Market Revolution*, 30–31, 157–61; Zuckerman, "Holy Wars, Civil Wars," 205–40.

3. Bernard Bailyn, *The Ideological Origins of the American Revolution* (Cambridge, Mass., 1967), 273; Mary Douglas, *Natural Symbols: Explorations in Cosmology* (New York, 1973), chaps. 1, 5, 12, 16, passim (quotation on p. 40). Carroll Smith-Rosenberg employed Douglas's theory in *Disorderly Conduct: Visions of Gender in America* (New York, 1985).

4. Wood, *Creation of the American Republic*, esp. 593–615; Isaac, *Transformation*, 310–22.

5. Asbury quoted in Hatch, *Democratization*, 49; Winans Autobiography, 66; Lorenzo Dow, *History of the Cosmopolite; or the Writings of Rev. Lorenzo Dow . . .* (Cincinnati, 1857), 218; Young, *Autobiography*, 235–39. Samuel Sellers described encounters between Methodist, Baptist, and Presbyterian ministers. See, for example, Sellers Diary, June 17, 1815, July 19, 1822, Cain Archives.

6. Winans Autobiography, 94; Winans Journal, October 5, 1823; Sellers Diary, June 1, 1814; Pearse, *Narrative*, 70; Cabiness and Cabiness, "Religion in Ante-Bellum Mississippi," 202. Rhys Isaac describes many such encounters in Virginia and calls the evangelical movement a "counterculture." See, for example, *Transformation*, 161–77.

7. Winans Journal, June 6–8, 1812, May 12–13, 1815, October 5, 16–21, 1823; Winans Autobiography, 66–67; Jones, *Concise History*, 102, 110, 48; Jones Autobiography, 50; Ernest Trice Thompson, *Presbyterians in the South, 1607–1861*. 3 vols. (Richmond, Va., 1963), 1:142; Hatch, *Democratization*, 58. On black involvement in camp meetings across the South see Albert J. Raboteau, *Slave Religion: The "Invisible Institution" in the Antebellum South* (New York, 1978), 59–61, 131–34, 223–25; Sobel, *World They Made Together*, 53, 180, 204–5; Isaac, *Transformation*, 316–17; Dickson D. Bruce, *And They All Sang Hallelujah: Plain-Folk Camp-Meeting Religion, 1800–1845* (Knoxville, Tenn., 1974), 3, 73–75, 86, 89.

8. Dow, *History of the Cosmopolite*, 218; Jones Autobiography, 42; Jones, *Complete History*, 1:81–83, 122–24, 217; Winans Autobiography, 1, 33; James, *Antebellum Natchez*, 246. Evangelicals quickly learned the value of the press in arousing interest in their meetings. See Frank Lambert, "Pedlar in Divinity: George Whitefield and the Great Awakening, 1737–1745," *Journal of American History* 77 (December 1990): 812–37.

9. Clippings in Winans Scrapbook.

10. Douglas, *Natural Symbols*, 118; Hatch, *Democratization*, 37; Jones, *Concise History*, 175; Winans Journal, December 20, 1820, April 12, May 6, July 15, 16, 1821, July 22, 1823; *New Orleans Christian Advocate*, September 9, 30, 1854; Rev. Walter Edwin Tynes Diary, 5, MDAH; for an example of church rules against rich apparel see Salem Baptist Church Records, July 1820; Isaac, *Transformation*, 43–44, 106, 129, 164, 325; Leigh Eric Schmidt, " 'A Church-Going People Are a Dress-Loving People': Clothes, Communication, and Religious Culture in Early America," *Church History* 58 (March 1989): 36–51; Sellers, *Market Revolution*, 154–57.

11. Douglas, *Natural Symbols*, 15–18, 39, 74, 118–19 (first quotation on p. 93, second and third quotations on p. 114); Hatch, *Democratization*, 49–58; John B. Boles, *The Great Revival, 1787–1805: The Origins of the Southern Evangelical Mind* (Lexington, Ky., 1972), 67–68, 87–89, 90, 95–97; Isaac, *Transformation*, 168, 264–65, 316; Jones Autobiography, 131, 132, 136, 138; Winans Journal, May 19, 1812, May 28, 1815, May 13, 1821. Another Methodist minister, Samuel Sellers, described physical exercises, including shouting and the jerks, at camp meetings; see, for example, Sellers Diary, March 11, April 30, May 28, December 6, 1814.

12. Jones Autobiography, 135–37.

13. Kenneth Cmiel, *Democratic Eloquence: The Fight for Popular Speech in Nineteenth-Century America* (New York, 1990), 63–64; John B. Thompson, *Studies in the Theory of Ideology* (Berkeley, 1984), 49–52; Lawrence W. Levine, *Highbrow/Lowbrow: The Emergence of Cultural Hierarchy America* (Cambridge, Mass., 1988), 36. R. Laurence Moore has suggested that camp meetings and revivals might be characterized as "religious theater." See Moore, "Religion, Secularization, and the Shaping of the Culture Industry in Antebellum America," *American Quarterly* 41 (June 1989): 219, 228–32. Hatch, *Democratization*, 138–39.

14. Douglas, *Natural Symbols*, 74–75.

15. Jones, *Complete History*, 145, 178–83; Levine, *Highbrow/Lowbrow*, 36; Cmiel, *Democratic Eloquence*, 15, 63–64.

16. Jones, *Complete History*, 2:145; Pearse, *Narrative*, 70–71; Bruce Rosenberg, *The Art of the American Folk Preacher* (New York, 1970), 4–5; Raboteau, *Slave Religion*, 236–37; Anthony F. C. Wallace, *Religion: An Anthropological View* (New York, 1966), 240–41; Jones Autobiography, 42; Winans Autobiography, 93; *New Orleans Christian Advocate*, September 9, 1854.

17. Jones, *Concise History*, 48, 63, 55, 66, 71, 76, 209–10; Jones, *Complete History*, 1:61, 79, 145, 327, 334, 409, 447, 2:220, 159; L. S. Foster, *Mississippi Baptist Preachers* (St. Louis, 1895), 493, 495; *New Orleans Christian Advocate*, September 9, 1854; Winans Journal, May 28, 1815, July 27, May 13, 1821, June 14, July 22,

1823; Rosenberg, *American Folk Preacher*, 4, 5, 9–10; Gerald L. Davis, *I got the Word in me and I can sing it, you know: A Study of the Performed African-American Sermon* (Philadelphia, 1985), 8–9, 25; Posey, *Baptist Church*, 28–29.

18. Rosenberg, *American Folk Preacher*, 7, 9–11, 35–45 (quotation on p. 11); Raboteau, *Slave Religion*, 236–37.

19. Winans Journal, June 6, 7, 1812; Winans Autobiography, 81; Jones, *Concise History*, 183. After one sermon, Samuel Sellers wrote, "I succeeded better in making them Laugh than in making them cry" (Sellers Diary, April 30, 1814).

20. Rosenberg, *American Folk Preacher*, 7, 14, 35–36, 105 (quotation); Davis, *I got the Word in me*, 25, 27; Raboteau, *Slave Religion*, 236–37; *Sacred Harp* hymnal (1869), p. 59; E. B. Cobb, Jr., *The Sacred Harp: A Tradition and Its Music* (Athens, Ga., 1978), Appendix B.

21. Sobel, *World They Made Together*, 198–99, 202–3, 204–6; Davis, *I got the Word in me*, 10; Rosenberg, *American Folk Preacher*, 14–15.

22. Raboteau, *Slave Religion*, 233; A. C. Ramsey, *The Autobiography of A. C. Ramsey*, ed. Jean Strickland (N.p., n.d.), 86; Gene Ramsey Miller, *A History of North Mississippi Methodism, 1820–1900* (Nashville, Tenn., 1966), 43–44; Flint, *Recollections*, 343. Leaven McRae was not alone in his literacy; northern missionaries who visited the territory in 1815 found that although most blacks lacked Bibles, "there are many individuals among them that can read" (Mills and Smith, *Report of a Missionary Tour*, 27); see also Posey, *Baptist Church*, 89, 93.

23. Peter Van Der Merwe, *Origins of the Popular Style: The Antecedents of Twentieth-Century Popular Music* (Oxford, 1989), 34, 77–78, 139–40; Rosenberg, *American Folk Preacher*, 16–20; Jones, *Complete History*, 1:448; *South-Western Religious Luminary*, February 1838; Winans Journal, May 26, 1823; Sobel, *World They Made Together*, 205–6; "Shouting Song," *Sacred Harp* (1869), 80. For other examples of songs in the *Sacred Harp* encouraging shouting and emotional responses see pp. 35, 49, 62, 79, 85, 134, 277, 319, 344, 397, 406, 421. See also John G. McCurry, comp., *The Social Harp* (1855; rpt. Athens, Ga., 1973), 37, 42, 53, 81, 104, 106, 111, 137. On the importance of song in such services see Bruce, *And They All Sang Hallelujah*, 96–122; George Pullen Jackson, *White Spirituals in the Southern Uplands* (1933; rpt. Chapel Hill, 1965); Jackson, *Spiritual Folk-Songs of Early America* (New York, 1937); J. N. Sims, "The Hymnody of the Camp Meeting Tradition" (Ph.D. dissertation, Union Theological Seminary, 1960); J. C. Downey, "The Music of American Revivalism, 1740–1800" (Ph.D. dissertation, Tulane University, 1968); Boles, *Great Revival*, 76, 121–24; Mechal Sobel, *Trabelin' On: The Slave Journey to an Afro-Baptist Faith* (Westport, Conn., 1979), 153; Stephen A. Marini, "Rehearsal for Revival: Sacred Singing and the Great Awakening in America," in Joyce Irwin, ed., *Sacred Sound: Music in Religious Thought and Practice* (Chico, Calif., 1983), 71–91.

24. Hatch, *Democratization*, 146; Watts quoted in Marini, "Rehearsal for Revival," 80. Marini considers Watt "the most widely-published and read writer in eighteenth-century America." Jones, *Complete History*, 256; Casey, comp., *Amite County*, 2:565; Sellers Diary, January 12, 1815.

25. Van Der Merwe, *Origins of the Popular Style*, 77–79, 138–39; Pearse, *Nar-*

rative, 68; Jones, *Complete History*, 1:61, 327, 334, 409, 447–48; Michael Chibbet, "Sung Psalms in Scottish Worship," in David F. Wright, ed., *The Bible in Scottish Life and Literature* (Edinburgh, 1988), 145–47; Walter Pitts, "Keep the Fire Burnin': Language and Ritual in the Afro-Baptist Church," *Journal of the American Academy of Religion* 56 (Spring 1988): 381–83; Marini, "Rehearsal for Revival," 73–74. As late as the 1850s a missionary to the Piney Woods found that "there are but few reading people here," and a newspaper writer noted that lining the hymns was important for the many illiterate members of the church (*New Orleans Christian Advocate*, June 28, 1856, April 12, 1851).

26. Marini, "Rehearsal for Revival," 76; Augustus Harvey Mecklin Autobiography, 3, MDAH; Jones Autobiography, 91. The hymn "New Brittain" is the shape-note version of "Amazing Grace." See *Sacred Harp* (1869), 45. In a similar vein, Natalie Zemon Davis described the importance of singing for Protestant women in sixteenth-century France and observed: "For laymen and laywomen in the service the common voice in praise of the Lord expressed the lack of distance between pastor and congregation" ("City Women and Religious Change," in *Society and Culture in Early Modern France* [Stanford, 1975], 86).

27. In 1815, for example, Winans noted that he "rode early to the school house where Bro. Taber was, teaching vocal music. He sang till 12" (quoted in Casey, comp., *Amite County*, 2:510). Gordon A. Cotton, *Of Primitive Faith and Order: A History of the Mississippi Primitive Baptist Church, 1780–1974* (Raymond, Miss., 1974), 87; Rev. Henry J. Harris Autobiography, 20, MDAH; Hatch, *Democratization*, 153; Mecklin Autobiography, 3, 20, 22; Cobb, *Sacred Harp*; C. L. Ellington, "The Sacred Harp Tradition of the South: Its Origin and Evolution" (Ph.D. dissertation, Florida State University, 1969). For an example of church rules of decorum requiring singing, see Bethlehem Baptist Church Records, Choctaw County, MSU, and Casey, comp., *Amite County*, 2:54.

28. Jones, *Concise History*, 102, 110; "Comparative Statement of the Condition of the Churches Composing the Mississippi Baptist Association, from 1807 to 1847 inclusive," in Mississippi Baptist Association, *A Republication of the Minutes of the Mississippi Baptist Association, from Its Organization in 1806 to the Present Time* (New Orleans, 1849), 264; Mills and Smith, *Report of a Missionary Tour*, 26; John F. Schermerhorn and Samuel J. Mills, *A Correct View of That Part of the United States Which Lies West of the Allegheny Mountains, with Regard to Religion and Morals* (Hartford, Conn., 1814), 29; Margaret DesChamps Moore, "Religion in Mississippi in 1860," *JMH* 22 (October 1960): 224.

29. Though itinerancy is usually associated with Methodists, in 1813 the Baptists appointed fifteen itinerant preachers. See Mississippi Baptist Association, *Republication of the Minutes*, 35; Winans Autobiography, 76; Jones Autobiography, 128; Jones Journal, March 20, 1835; Lorenzo Dow Langford Autobiography, 14, 22, Cain Archives.

30. Isaac, *Transformation*, 263–64; Robertson Autobiography.

31. Osmon C. Baker, *Guide-Book in the Administration of the Discipline of the Methodist Episcopal Church* (New York, 1855), 54; Methodist Episcopal Church, South, *The Doctrines and Discipline of the Methodist Episcopal Church, South*

(Charleston, S.C., 1851), 72; Jones Journal, March 20, 1835; Jones Autobiography, 42; Walter Brownlow Posey, *The Development of Methodism in the Old Southwest, 1783–1824* (1933; rpt. Philadelphia, 1974), 117–18; ? to Elijah Steele, June 14, 1838, Elijah Steele Letters, MDAH; John Burruss to B. M. Drake, May 1, 1826, Benjamin M. Drake Papers, Cain Archives. For other descriptions of meetings see the *New Orleans Western Methodist*, November 8, 15, 29, December 13, 27, 1833, January 17, April 25, June 13, 1834.

32. Posey, *Methodism in the Old Southwest*, 116–17; Winans Journal, February 18, July 22, August 12, 1821, July 22, 1823; Benjamin M. Drake, *A Sketch of the Life of Rev. Elijah Steele* (Cincinnati, 1843), 16; Ramsey, *Autobiography*, 31; *New Orleans Western Methodist*, December 27, 1833.

33. Isaac, *Transformation*, 264; Kate M. Power, "Centennial Celebration of Old Bethany Church," in *Minutes of the Presbyterian Historical Society of the Synod of Mississippi* (N.p., 1908), 29; Thompson, *Presbyterians in the South*, 1:226–29. For a more complete discussion of communion season and its importance for revivalism see Leigh Eric Schmidt, *Holy Fairs: Scottish Communions and American Revivals in the Early Modern Period* (Princeton, 1989).

34. Mississippi Baptist Association, *Republication of the Minutes*, 20; Sellers Diary, July 11, 1814; Salem Baptist Church Records, June and July 1819. For other examples see Sarepta Baptist Church Records, 1810, MSU; Bethany Baptist Church Records, November 1822, January 1823, and March 1827, MDAH; "Minutes of Zion Baptist Church of Bucatunna, Wayne County, Mississippi," *Mississippi Genealogical Exchange* 19 (Winter 1973): 123.

35. Howard Dorgan, *Giving Glory to God in Appalachia: Worship Practices of Six Baptist Subdenominations* (Knoxville, Tenn., 1987), 119–22.

36. Joy Driskell Baklanoff, "The Celebration of a Feast: Music, Dance, and Possession Trance in the Black Primitive Baptist Footwashing Ritual," *Ethnomusicology* 31 (Fall 1987): 381–94.

37. Baklanoff, "Celebration of a Feast," 389–90; Dorgan, *Giving Glory to God*, 62–63.

38. Sarepta Baptist Church Records, September 1815; Galilee Baptist Church Records, December 17, 1825, January 7, 1826, and Jerusalem Baptist Church, cited in Casey, comp., *Amite County*, 1:59, 214; Robertson Autobiography, 8; Sellers, *Market Revolution*, 154–61.

39. Harris Autobiography, 8–20; *New Orleans Christian Advocate*, September 20, 1856.

40. E. Hearn to Benjamin Drake, June 6, 1823, De Vinne to Drake, August 22, 1823, Drake Papers, Cain Archives; "Religion Is a Fortune," in McCurry, *Social Harp*, 42. John G. Jones observed that few people joined evangelical churches "to gain position in society" (*Complete History*, 1:232). Another early convert recalled that "very few persons in those days had intended to be Methodists" (*New Orleans Christian Advocate*, November 5, 1853). Samuel Sellers wrote after an unsuccessful meeting, "This is a Barren hard place but little hopes of doing much good so true is that saying of Christ's how hardly shall they that have riches enter into the

Kingdom of God" (Sellers Diary, March 17, 1814). See also the hymn "Greenwich," in McCurry, *Social Harp*, 173.

41. Young, *Autobiography*, 241–42.

42. Ibid., 242–43.

43. Ibid., 243–45. For similar events involving Dow see Hatch, *Democratization*, 131–33. On the respect accorded justices in the colonial period see Sydnor, *American Revolutionaries*, 64–65. On the extensive power exerted by justices in early Mississippi see John Hebron Moore, "Local and State Governments of Antebellum Mississippi," *JMH* 44 (May 1982): 105–16.

44. Winans Autobiography, 154.

45. On the importance of virtue to the success of the republic see Wood, *Creation of the American Republic*, 65–70, and Wood, *The Radicalism of the American Revolution* (New York, 1992), 95–225. Perry Miller discusses the link between revivalism and national regeneration in *The Life of the Mind*, 10–35. *Natchez Messenger*, September 13, 1805; Butler, *Awash in a Sea of Faith*, 213; Edwin A. Miles, *Jacksonian Democracy in Mississippi* (New York, 1970), 31–34; Winans Autobiography, 86, 172.

46. Donald G. Mathews, *Religion in the Old South* (Chicago, 1977), 48; Joseph Campbell, *The Masks of God*, vol. 4, *Creative Mythology* (New York, 1968), 84.

Chapter 3. *A Christian Sisterhood: White Women and the Evangelical Experience*

1. Anne E. Carr, *Transforming Grace: Christian Tradition and Women's Experience* (San Francisco, 1988), 135–37; Susan Juster, "In a Different Voice: Male and Female Narratives of Religious Conversion in Post-Revolutionary America," *American Quarterly* 41 (March 1989): 34–40; Smith-Rosenberg, *Disorderly Conduct*, 129–44; Douglas, *Natural Symbols*, passim. On southern patriarchy see Bertram Wyatt-Brown, *Southern Honor: Ethics and Behavior in the Old South* (New York, 1982); Michael P. Johnson, "Planters and Patriarchy: Charleston, 1800–1860," *JSH* 46 (February 1980): 45–72; Allan Kulikoff, *Tobacco and Slaves: The Development of Southern Cultures in the Chesapeake, 1680–1800* (Chapel Hill, 1986); Catherine Clinton, *The Plantation Mistress: Women's World in the Old South* (New York, 1982). For a critique of the use of the term *patriarchy* for the Old South see Elizabeth Fox-Genovese, *Within the Plantation Household: Black and White Women of the Old South* (Chapel Hill, 1988), 63–64. This chapter focuses on the experience of white women. The religious experiences of white and black women were different enough to warrant separate analysis.

2. Fox-Genovese, *Within the Plantation Household*, 44–45, 402. For a more thorough critique of Fox-Genovese's work on these and other grounds see Suzanne Lebsock, "Complicity and Contention: Women in the Plantation South," *Georgia Historical Quarterly* 74 (Spring 1990): 59–83. Mathews, *Religion in the Old South*, 101–24 (quotation on p. 102). David T. Bailey recognized that in pioneer churches "religion was primarily the business of women," but the role of women in the

churches was not a major topic in his study (*Shadow on the Church: Southwestern Evangelical Religion and the Issue of Slavery, 1783–1860* [Ithaca, N.Y., 1985], 52).

3. Douglas, *Natural Symbols*, 114–18; Smith-Rosenberg, *Disorderly Conduct*, 140.

4. Nancy M. Robinson Diary, July 28, 1833, MDAH; Perkins to Winston, September 26, 1835, E. T. Winston and Family Papers, MDAH. James Pearse described the many hardships that confronted his wife on the Mississippi frontier in his *Narrative*. See also Moore, *Emergence of the Cotton Kingdom*, 143; Fox-Genovese, *Within the Plantation Household*, 37–99; Lillian Schlissell, *Women's Diaries of the Westward Journey* (New York, 1982), 27–31; Jane Turner Censer, "Southwestern Migration Among North Carolina Planter Families: 'The Disposition to Emigrate,' " *JSH* 57 (August 1991): 412; Joan Ellen Cashin, "Family, Kinship, and Migration in the Antebellum South" (Ph.D. dissertation, Harvard University, 1985), 90–100.

5. Peggy Dow, "Vicissitudes; or The Journey of a Life," in Dow, *History of the Cosmopolite*, 639–46.

6. First Presbyterian Church, Natchez, Record Book, 1816–1902, MDAH; Bethany Baptist Church Records, 1819, 1843; *New Orleans Christian Advocate*, March 17, 1855. I collected membership figures from approximately fifty churches over the period from 1845 to 1876. Women made up a majority of members in 82 percent of the churches in that sample. The average ratio of men to women was 62:38, a figure that supports Donald Mathews's estimated ratio of 65:35 (*Religion in the Old South*, 47–48, 102). For similar estimates see Suzanne Lebsock, *The Free Women of Petersburg: Status and Culture in a Southern Town, 1784–1860* (New York, 1984), 215. The preponderance of women among church members was a national phenomenon. See Butler, *Awash in a Sea of Faith*, 170. Fox-Genovese suggests that the proportion of women to men attending church may not have been as great as in the North and that the membership figures do not reflect actual attendance. Her supposition is based on limited evidence, and Mathews's estimate, I believe, is nearer the mark. See Fox-Genovese, *Within the Plantation Household*, 46, 403–4, n. 15. See also Elizabeth Fox-Genovese and Eugene D. Genovese, "The Divine Sanction of Social Order: Religious Foundations of the Southern Slaveholders' World View," *Journal of the American Academy of Religion* 55 (Summer 1987): 226–27.

7. Drake, *Sketch of the Life of Rev. Elijah Steele*, 54; Ramsey, *Autobiography*, 106; Unity records in Casey, comp., *Amite County*, 2:401–12. In 1852 one of the four churches in the Biloxi Baptist Association could not be represented at the association's annual meeting because it had only female members who were not eligible to serve as delegates. See Jesse Laney Boyd, *A Popular History of the Baptists in Mississippi* (Jackson, Miss., 1930), 145. Women met alone for services in other southern states as well; for an example from Georgia see Finley, *Sketches of Western Methodism*, 532–36. On signatures see Lebsock, *Free Women of Petersburg*, 198.

8. Sarah Knox Harris Sager Recollections, Sager Collection, MDAH.

9. Jones, *Complete History*, 2:205; Jean E. Friedman, *The Enclosed Garden:*

Women and Community in the Evangelical South, 1830–1900 (Chapel Hill, 1985), 4–5; Bruce, *And They All Sang Hallelujah*, 76, 79, 86–87; Jones Autobiography, 90; *Biographical and Historical Sketches of Mississippi*, 2 vols. (Spartanburg, S.C., 1978), 1:949; Finley, *Sketches of Western Methodism*, 536.

10. Jones, *Complete History*, 2:295; Bruce, *And They All Sang Hallelujah*, 86–87. On women preachers in other regions see Judith L. Weidman, ed., *Women Ministers* (San Francisco, 1981); Virginia Lieson Brereton and Christa Ressmeyer Klien, "American Women in Ministry: A History of Protestant Beginning Points," in Janet Wilson James, ed., *Women in American Religion* (Philadelphia, 1980), 171–90; Joan M. Jensen, *Loosening the Bonds: Mid-Atlantic Farm Women, 1750–1850* (New Haven, 1986), 145–66.

11. Dow, "Vicissitudes," 631–32.

12. Blackman Journal, 19; Dow, "Vicissitudes," 633.

13. Dow, "Vicissitudes," 634; Blackman Journal, 19–20; Winans Autobiography, January 1811.

14. Winans Autobiography, 72–73.

15. Isaac, *Transformation*, 64–65. For examples of churches requiring the use of familial forms of address see New Hope Baptist Church Records, Monroe County, Rules of Decorum, 1819, Evans Memorial Library, Aberdeen, Miss.; Bethlehem Baptist Church, Choctaw County, Rules of Decorum, 1835, MSU. Even when not required, the terms are standard in the overwhelming majority of church records examined here. Members were sometimes listed by gender in the membership rolls. See, for example, Jerusalem Baptist Church, Membership List, 1822, and Line Creek Baptist Church, Membership List, 1839, transcribed in Casey, comp., *Amite County*, 1:58,78.

16. Ramsey, *Autobiography*, 56–57; Jones, *Concise History*, 209; *Sacred Harp* (1869), 59; Cobb, *Sacred Harp*, Appendix B.

17. Douglas, *Natural Symbols*, 118; Jones Autobiography, 135–37; Boles, *Great Revival*, 68; Sellers Diary, May 28, 1814; *Mississippi Baptist*, September 1836.

18. Carroll Smith-Rosenberg, "Women and Religious Revivals: Emergence of the American Bourgeoisie," in Leonard I. Sweet, ed., *The Evangelical Tradition in America* (Macon, Ga., 1984), 215–16; Winans Autobiography, 172; Sellers Diary, May 4, July 9, 1814, October 1, 1816; *Mississippi Baptist*, October 28, 1858. See also Mathews, *Religion in the Old South*, 103–5.

19. Humphreys obituary in the *New Orleans Christian Advocate*, November 17, 1866.

20. Galilee Baptist Church, Amite County, in Casey, comp., *Amite County*, 2:211. For similar examples see Line Creek and East Fork Baptist churches, in Casey, comp., *Amite County*, 2:54,78. The 1839 Rules of Decorum for Enon Primitive Baptist Church stipulated that "all male & female members shall have privileges in church government" (Enon Baptist Church, Itawamba County, Records, MSU). Some churches put limits on women's voting rights; Concord Baptist Church, for example, allowed women to vote only on the choice of a pastor and the reception of members (Concord Baptist Church, Choctaw County, Records, MSU). Church records rarely give names when listing votes taken in conference,

but a few examples show women voting in church trials. See Salem Baptist Church Records, November 1822; Bogue Chitto Baptist Church Records, September 1860, MBHC. Jean Friedman does not believe that women exercised real authority in these sessions because they were conducted by men and the presence of male members determined a quorum (*Enclosed Garden,* 13).

21. Sarepta Baptist Church Records, 1810, August 1816, June 1834. For another example of a church denying women the right to vote, then reversing that decision, see Bethesda Baptist Church, Hinds County, Records, May 1846, September 1850, SBHC. At Bethesda in 1850 there were thirty white female and eighteen white male members.

22. Friedman, *Enclosed Garden,* 18–20; Fox-Genovese, *Within the Plantation Household,* 70, 80–82. On the important role of women's associations in the North see Carroll Smith-Rosenberg, "Beauty, the Beast, and the Militant Woman: A Case Study in Sex Roles and Social Stress in Jacksonian America," in Nancy F. Cott and Elizabeth H. Pleck, eds., *A Heritage of Her Own: Toward a New Social History of American Women* (New York, 1979); Smith-Rosenberg, "The Female World of Love and Ritual: Relations Between Women in Nineteenth-Century America," in Michael Gordon, ed., *The American Family in Social-Historical Perspective* (New York, 1978); Nancy F. Cott, *The Bonds of Womanhood: "Women's Sphere" in New England, 1780–1835* (New Haven, 1977); Mary Ryan, "The Power of Women's Networks: A Case Study of Female Moral Reform in Antebellum America," *Feminist Studies* 5 (Spring 1979): 66–85; Natchez Orphan Asylum, *Annual Report of the Managers and Officers of the Natchez Orphan Asylum . . .* (Natchez, Miss., 1855), 15; Lebsock, *Free Women of Petersburg,* 196–211; James, *Antebellum Natchez,* 219; Joseph B. Stratton, *Memorial of a Quarter-Century's Pastorate* (Philadelphia, 1869), 52–53; Myrtle Graham Hicks, "The Woman's Work in the Synod of Mississippi Presbyterian Church, U.S., 1822–1832," in Fred R. Graves, comp. and ed., *The Presbyterian Work in Mississippi* (Jackson, Miss., 1927), 5–6.

23. Natchez Orphan Asylum, *Annual Report,* 9–26; "An Act to Incorporate the Female Charitable Society of Natchez," Legislature, First and Second Sessions, 1816–19; Petitions and Memorials to the Legislature and Bills, 1823–26, Official Archives of the State of Mississippi, MDAH; Natchez Orphan Asylum Records, Natchez Trace Collection, Barker Center; Lebsock, *Free Women of Petersburg,* 228–29.

24. C. T. Stiles to W. Winans, March 11, 1820, Winans Correspondence; Winans Journal, November 1, 1823; First Methodist Church, Columbus, Records, Second Conference, 1837, MSU; Jones, *Complete History,* 2:388; *Tennessee Baptist,* June 12, 1847.

25. Baptist State Convention, *Second Annual Report . . . 1824* (Natchez, Miss., 1825), 3; *Proceedings of a Meeting to Consider the Propriety of Forming a Baptist State Convention Held . . . December, 1836* (Natchez, Miss., 1837), 21; Women's Missionary Union of Mississippi, *Hearts the Lord Opened: The History of Mississippi Women's Missionary Union* (Jackson, Miss., 1954), 13, 14–18, 21; Boyd, *Popular History,* 277–78; *Mississippi Baptist,* April 14, 28, November 3, 1859; Moore, *Emergence of the Cotton Kingdom,* 199–200. In the late 1830s Columbus had a population of about fifteen hundred.

26. "The Women's Auxiliary of the Synod of Mississippi," in Graves, comp. and ed., *Presbyterian Work*, 106–7; and Hicks, "Women's Work," 6.

27. J. [?] to "Dear Doctor," April 14, [n.d., 1840s?], Charles B. Dana Papers, MDAH; *New Orleans Christian Advocate*, September 22, 1866; Mathews, *Religion in the Old South*, 110. Suzanne Lebsock wrote that the predominance of women in the churches was a source of "chronic embarrassment" to churchmen, who "coped in public by inflating the importance of their own efforts and by minimizing those of the women. The most striking feature of the records left by the men of the white churches is their persistent failure to acknowledge women's collective contributions" (*Free Women of Petersburg*, 225–26).

28. Fox-Genovese, *Within the Plantation Household*, 55, 64. The historiographical debate over this issue is too voluminous to be cited here, but see Cott, *Bonds of Womanhood*; Barbara L. Epstein, *The Politics of Domesticity: Women, Evangelicalism, and Temperance in Nineteenth-Century America* (Middletown, Conn., 1981); Lebsock, *Free Women of Petersburg*; Mary P. Ryan, *Womanhood in America: From Colonial Times to the Present* (New York, 1979); Smith-Rosenberg, *Disorderly Conduct*; Barbara Welter, *Dimity Convictions: The American Woman in the Nineteenth Century* (Athens, Ohio, 1976).

29. *Tennessee Baptist*, May 8, 1847, April 27, 1848. Though published in Tennessee, this newspaper circulated widely in Mississippi, especially when the state did not have its own Baptist paper, and the Mississippi Baptist Association often recommended it to its members. See Mississippi Baptist Association, *Abstract History of the Mississippi Baptist Association for One Hundred Years . . .* (New Orleans, 1906), 76, 95, 111. For similar articles see *South-Western Religious Luminary*, March 1835; *Mississippi Baptist*, March 10, 1860.

30. *Tennessee Baptist*, July 13, November 16, 27, 1848. See also October 12, 1848. *Mississippi Baptist*, July 22, 1858.

31. Charles F. Deems, *Annals of Southern Methodism* (New York, 1856), 279–80; *Tennessee Baptist*, June 1, 1848; Charles B. Galloway, "Elizabeth Female Academy: The Mother of Female Colleges," *Publications of the Mississippi Historical Society* 2 (1899): 169–78; Winans Autobiography, 91–92; *Natchez Gazette*, March 11, 1826, typescript in Elizabeth Female Academy Subject File, MDAH; Clinton, *Plantation Mistress*, 129–30; Anne Firor Scott, "The Ever Widening Circle: The Diffusion of Feminist Values from the Troy Female Seminary, 1822–1872," *History of Education Quarterly* 19 (Spring 1979): 3.

32. Galloway, "Elizabeth Female Academy," 177; *Tennessee Baptist*, March 6, 1848; *New Orleans Christian Advocate*, April 2, 1853, December 22, 1866; Mathews, *Religion in the Old South*, 111.

33. Ruth H. Bloch, "The Gendered Meanings of Virtue in Revolutionary America," *Signs: Journal of Women in Culture and Society* 13 (Autumn 1987): 37–58; Jan Lewis, "The Republican Wife: Virtue and Seduction in the Early Republic," *William and Mary Quarterly* 3d ser., 44 (October 1987): 689–72; Clinton, *Plantation Mistress*, 130.

34. John Burruss to Benjamin Drake, May 1, 1826, Drake Papers, Cain Archives.

35. Galloway, "Elizabeth Female Academy," 177; *South-Western Religious Luminary*, September, October, December 1836; Lewis, "Republican Wife," 721;

Christian Advocate, March 1, June 21, 1851, May 29, 1852. A writer in the *New Orleans Christian Advocate,* February 6, 1860, said, "If we undertake to educate our women, let us follow them out into life . . . and see that they have a field for their energy."

36. Mississippi Baptist Association, *Republication of the Minutes,* 164; *South-Western Religious Luminary,* February 1837. In a similar vein, Lizzie Newton, author of a newspaper column for women, asked, "Should not fathers consider *their* responsibility, and do they not, to some degree, endeavor to avoid the duties which rest upon them, throwing into a mother's hands entirely the training of their children?" (*New Orleans Christian Advocate,* June 21, 1851). S. G. Winchester, pastor of the Natchez Presbyterian Church, agreed that submission was the chief duty of wives and warned that "domestic licenciousness invariably tends to political prostitution" (*The Religion of the Bible, the Only Preservation of Our Civil Institutions . . .* [Natchez, Miss., 1838], 23). Evangelicals developed their ideas of hierarchical family structure and its relation to the larger society more fully as time passed. See Fox-Genovese and Genovese, "Divine Sanction," 220–22.

37. Winans Autobiography, 7, 17; Lewis Hobbs to Winans, December 29, 1813, in Benjamin M. Drake and Family Papers, MDAH; Jones Autobiography, 105; Mathews, *Religion in the Old South,* 106; *New Orleans Christian Advocate,* December 25, 1852; *Mississippi Baptist,* June 24, 1858.

38. Friedman, *Enclosed Garden;* Davis, *Society and Culture in Early Modern France,* 80.

Chapter 4. *Heirs to the Promise: Mississippi Blacks, Slavery, and the Evangelical Movement, 1799–1840*

1. W. E. B. Du Bois, *The Souls of Black Folk: Essays and Sketches* (Greenwich, Conn., 1961), 142.

2. Daniel de Vinne to Benjamin Drake, August 22, 1823, Drake Papers, Cain Archives; James E. Davis, *Frontier America, 1800–1840: A Comparative Demographic Analysis of the Settlement Process* (Glendale, Calif., 1977), 128. Opposition from slaveholders to the conversion of slaves dated from the colonial period and plagued evangelicals in the early years of the movement. See, for example, Winthrop D. Jordan, *White Over Black: American Attitudes Toward the Negro, 1550–1812* (Chapel Hill, 1968), 180–93; Alan Gallay, "Planters and Slaves in the Great Awakening," in Boles, ed., *Masters and Slaves,* 20–36; Isaac, *Transformation,* 220, 280, 286; and Raboteau, *Slave Religion,* 98–103, 107–8.

3. John B. Boles, *Black Southerners, 1619–1869* (Lexington, Ky., 1984), 140–55; Sobel, *Trabelin' On,* 99–135; Raboteau, *Slave Religion,* 3–144; Mathews, *Religion in the Old South,* 188–98. In an argument reminiscent of Stanley Elkins, Jon Butler described "a holocaust that destroyed collective African religious practice in colonial America" (*Awash in a Sea of Faith,* 129–63, quotation on p. 157). Some African slaves in Mississippi and other parts of the South were Moslem and may not have found Christianity as foreign as did other native Africans, though their

numbers and their influence are difficult to measure. See, for example, Alford, *Prince Among Slaves*; Jones, *Complete History*, 1:105.

4. Bogue Chitto Baptist Church Records, November, December 1818; Winans Journal, February 11, April 1, 22, July 22, August 12, 1821, July 22, 1823; Z. T. Leavell and T. J. Bailey, *A Complete History of Mississippi Baptists: From the Earliest Times*, 2 vols. (Jackson, Miss., 1904), 1:75, 129; Mississippi Baptist Association, *Republication of the Minutes*, 21, 41–42, 50, 57, 60, 70, 72, 87; Economic Research Department, *Mississippi Statistical Summary of the Population, 1800–1980* (N.p., 1983), 1; Winans Autobiography, 56, 67–68, 163–64; Jones, *Concise History*, 27–30, 103, 108–9, 123–24, 148, 163; Blackman Journal, 6; Larry M. James, "Biracial Fellowship in Antebellum Baptist Churches," in Boles, ed., *Masters and Slaves*, 47–48; Mathews, *Religion in the Old South*, 197–200; Butler, *Awash in a Sea of Faith*, 250.

5. Winans Journal, February 11, April 1, July 22, August 12, 1821, July 22, 1823; Robert B. Alexander Diary, March 12, 1854, MDAH.

6. Church records in Casey, comp., *Amite County*, 2:413, 56, 251, 315, 59, 212, 173, 251–53, 315–20.

7. Casey, comp., *Amite County*, 2:413, 316; Salem Baptist Church Records, September 1830, August 1823, April 1826. For similar examples see James, "Biracial Fellowship," 42–44. David Bailey erred when he wrote, "Diverging from the tendency in Virginia and the Carolinas, few Baptist churches [in the Old Southwest] required evidence of conversion experiences from their communicants" (*Shadow on the Church*, 36).

8. Casey, comp., *Amite County*, 2:215, 315–16; Clear Creek Baptist Church, Adams County, Records, April 24, 1836, SBHC; Boles, *Great Revival*, 131. For other examples of biracial baptisms in the state see James, "Biracial Fellowship," 41–42.

9. Montrose Presbyterian Church, Jasper County, Records, October 12, 1844, MDAH; Concord Baptist Church Records, May 1843.

10. Bethlehem Baptist Church, Rules of Decorum, 1835; Boles, *Black Southerners*, 160; New Hope Baptist Church, Rules of Decorum, 1819.

11. Susan Dabney Smedes, *Memorials of a Southern Planter*, ed. Fletcher M. Green (Jackson, Miss., 1981), 71. See also Rachel N. Klein, *Unification of a Slave State: The Rise of the Planter Class in the South Carolina Backcountry, 1760–1808* (Chapel Hill, 1990), 289.

12. First Baptist Church Records, Louisville, Miss., August 1836, SBHC; Liberty Baptist Church Records, Jackson, Miss., August 1851, SBHC; Mars Hill Baptist Church Records, Summit, Miss., October 15, 1864, SBHC; East Fork Baptist Church Records in Casey, comp., *Amite County*, 2:21; James, "Biracial Fellowship," 41–42.

13. Winans Journal, February 22, June 1, July 10, 1821, June 14, 1823.

14. Mathews, *Religion in the Old South*, 202; Raboteau, *Slave Religion*, 134; William Summer Jenkins, ed., *Records of the States of the United States*, microfilm (Washington, D.C., 1949), "The Revised Laws of Mississippi . . ." (1824), 390, "Laws of the State of Mississippi . . ." (1822), 184; Charles S. Sydnor, *Slavery in*

Mississippi (New York, 1933), 55; Mississippi Baptist Association, *Abstract History of the Mississippi Baptist Association for One Hundred Years . . .* (New Orleans, 1906), 23, 30; Casey, comp., *Amite County,* 2:315, 321, 323, 324, 330. See also Sobel, *World They Made Together,* 206–12. In his discussion of black preachers, Eugene Genovese noted that "even in the deepest South—Alabama, Mississippi, Louisiana—black preachers had large numbers of whites among their communicants right down until the war; in fact, they seem to have worked more easily and in greater numbers in Texas and the western Cotton Belt than they did further east" (*Roll, Jordan, Roll: The World the Slaves Made* [New York, 1976], 257).

15. Jones, *Complete History,* 2:294. For other examples of blacks receiving licenses to preach during this period see Bogue Chitto Baptist Church Records, September 1827; Hopewell Baptist Church Records, Franklin County, Miss., November 1825, MBHC; Zion Hill Baptist Church, in Casey, comp., *Amite County,* 2:315, 321; Winans Journal, May 19, 1821; Raboteau, *Slave Religion,* 134.

16. Foster, *Mississippi Baptist Preachers,* 19.

17. Winans Autobiography, 10; Winbourne M. Drake, ed., "The Road to Freedom," *JMH* 3 (January 1941): 44.

18. Jones Autobiography, 75; Will of John W. Hundley, October 16, 1829, in Mary G. Barker, Mavis Olivin Feltus, and Diane A. Stockfelt, comps., *Early Will Records of Adams County, Mississippi* (N.p., 1975), 77; Jones, *Concise History,* 240, 116; Talley to William Winans, March 28, 1826, Winans Papers; Diary of Jacob Young, in Casey, comp., *Amite County,* 2:540; Lewis Hobbs to Winans, December 29, 1813, in Drake and Family Papers, MDAH; Jones, *Complete History,* 2:488. On antislavery sentiments among early evangelicals see Donald G. Mathews, *Slavery and Methodism: A Chapter in American Morality, 1780–1845* (Princeton, 1965); John Lee Eihghmy, *Churches in Cultural Captivity: A History of the Social Attitudes of Southern Baptists* (Knoxville, Tenn., 1972); H. Shelton Smith, *In His Image, But . . . : Racism in Southern Religion, 1780–1910* (Durham, N.C., 1972); James D. Essig, *The Bonds of Wickedness: American Evangelicals Against Slavery, 1770–1808* (Philadelphia, 1982).

19. Diary of Jacob Young in Casey, comp., *Amite County,* 2:540.

20. Pisgah Church Records in Casey, comp., *Amite County,* 2:94, see also 102, 106; Bailey, *Shadow on the Church,* 100; Sarepta Baptist Church Records, 1810.

21. Casey, comp., *Amite County,* 2:123–25; Bailey, *Shadow on the Church,* 140–41.

22. Pearse, *Narrative,* 53; Winans Journal, December 24, 26, 1820, February 16, May 20, June 27, 1821, July 21, 1823; Winans Autobiography, 164–65.

23. Winans Journal, June 27, 1821.

24. Winans Journal, June 27, 1821; Jones, *Complete History,* 1:36, 165–66, 417, 420, 451–60, 2:315–16.

25. McLemore, *History of Mississippi,* 1:238, 252, 254, 276; Claiborne, *Mississippi,* 391.

26. McLemore, *History of Mississippi,* 1:234; Winans Autobiography, 166; Jenkins, ed., *Records of the States,* Miss. B1, Reel 1, 1807–1823, "Statutes of the

Mississippi Territory . . ." (1816), 382; "The Revised Code of the Laws of Mississippi . . ." (1824), 390; B2 Reel 2, 1805–22, "Laws of the State of Mississippi . . ." (1822), 184.

27. Winans Autobiography, 166–67, 172; Mississippi Baptist Association, *Republication of the Minutes*, 87; Leavell and Bailey, *Complete History*, 1:129; Claiborne, *Mississippi*, 391. Allan Nevins is one of the few historians to describe this important event, though he incorrectly identifies Winans as a Jacksonian Democrat. He was, in fact, a Whig and a strong supporter of Henry Clay. See Nevins, *Ordeal of the Union*, 2 vols. (New York, 1947), 1:540–41. Jenkins, ed., *Records of the States*, "Laws of the State of Mississippi" (1822), 184. A similar political struggle over slaves' religious meetings occurred in South Carolina, and there, too, evangelicals were successful. See Klein, *Unification*, 290–91.

28. Winans Autobiography, 167; Sydnor, *Slavery in Mississippi*, 53–55, 95, 228, 237; Mathews, *Religion in the Old South*, 231–36; Raboteau, *Slave Religion*, 163–64.

29. Mississippi Baptist Association, *Republication of the Minutes*, 167–68.

30. Leavell and Bailey, *Complete History*, 1:77; Boyd, *Popular History*, 70; Bethany Baptist Church Records, May 1829.

31. Jones, *Complete History*, 2:117, 140; Sydnor, *Slavery in Mississippi*, 204–6.

32. Sydnor, *Slavery in Mississippi*, 203–8; Norwood Allen Kerr, "The Mississippi Colonization Society (1831–1860)," *JMH* 43 (February 1981): 1–30; American Colonization Society, *Annual Reports* (New York, 1969), 1832, p. 11. For broader studies of colonization see Floyd J. Miller, *The Search for a Black Nationality: Black Emigration and Colonization, 1787–1863* (Urbana, Ill., 1975), and Philip J. Staudenraus, *The African Colonization Movement, 1816–1865* (New York, 1961).

33. Sydnor, *Slavery in Mississippi*, 208–9; Jones, *Complete History*, 2:29, 31–33, 79, 148, 389, 535; American Colonization Society, *Annual Reports*, 1840, p. 7, 1842, p. 20, 1857, Appendix.

34. Sydnor, *Slavery in Mississippi*, 210–14, 218; *South-Western Religious Luminary*, January 1838; Birney to Ralph R. Gurley, April 8, 13, 1833, in Dwight L. Dumond, ed., *Letters of James Gillespie Birney, 1831–1857*, 2 vols. (Gloucester, Mass., 1966), 1:65–66, 70.

35. Sydnor, *Slavery in Mississippi*, 214, 223, 237; "The Religious Life of Capt. E. B. Randolph, a Methodist Church Leader"; "Families of Randolph and Sherman"; "Capt. Edward B. Randolph"; Will of May 9, 1846; Randolph to "Dear Brother," July 6, 1844; Randolph to "the Preacher in charge and members of the M.E. Church in Columbus," undated [1845], all in Randolph-Sherman Papers, MSU; William Winans to Benjamin M. Drake, October 4, 1834, Drake Papers, Cain Archives.

36. Elisa [Elisha?] Thilman to Randolph, May 11, 1848, Randolph-Sherman Papers; see also Hector Belton to Dr. John Ker quoted in Sydnor, *Slavery in Mississippi*, 235; see also 218.

37. Jones, *Complete History*, 2:240; Sydnor, *Slavery in Mississippi*, 215–217n.

38. Robert L. Finley to Winans, February 25, 1837; J. Gales to Winans, Febru-

ary 15, 1839; Untitled speech (1840s) in Political Addresses and Writings, all in Winans Papers; Winans to Benjamin Drake, August 28, 1835, February 25, 1850, Drake Papers, Cain Archives; *New Orleans Christian Advocate,* January 12, 1859; Smith to Winans and Winans to Smith, *Liberty* (Miss.) *Advocate,* March 31, 1838; R. S. Finley to John Ker, August 5, 1847, in Franklin L. Riley, ed., "A Contribution to the History of the Colonization Movement in Mississippi," *PMHS* 9 (1906): 396–99; Sydnor, *Slavery in Mississippi,* 215–17. Technically, the society functioned for several years after 1840; its officers carried out its business, but it lacked widespread support.

39. Genovese quoted in Drew Gilpin Faust, ed., *The Ideology of Slavery: Proslavery Thought in the Antebellum South, 1830–1860* (Baton Rouge, 1981), 9.

Chapter 5.   *No Tameness, No Satiety: Flush Times, 1830–1860*

1. Reuben Davis, *Recollections of Mississippi and Mississippians* (New York, 1890), 19; Joseph G. Baldwin, *The Flush Times of Alabama and Mississippi: A Series of Sketches* (New York, 1854); Moore, *Emergence of the Cotton Kingdom,* 16, 28; Sellers, *Market Revolution,* 353–54.

2. The removal of the Native Americans from the South has generated an extensive literature. For works specific to Mississippi see Daniel H. Usner, Jr., "American Indians on the Cotton Frontier: Changing Economic Relations with Citizens and Slaves in the Mississippi Territory," *Journal of American History* 72 (September 1985): 297–317; and Carolyn Keller Reeves, ed., *The Choctaw Before Removal* (Jackson, Miss., 1985).

3. Miles, *Jacksonian Democracy,* 117–19; Moore, *Emergence of the Cotton Kingdom,* 116–45.

4. *Baptist* (Nashville, Tenn.), May 1835; *Proceedings of a Meeting to Consider the Propriety of Forming a Baptist State Convention Held . . . December, 1836,* 10; Willie D. Halsell, ed., "A Stranger in a Strange Land," *Alabama Historical Quarterly* 30 (Summer 1968): 74–75.

5. Baldwin quoted in Sellers, *Market Revolution,* 353. Churches not only expelled members who proved unwilling or unable to conform to their teachings, they also recalled letters of dismission granted to members who were later deemed unworthy. See, for example, Bethlehem Baptist Church Records February 1852. For an example of a preacher who lost his standing see the case against the Reverend Samuel L. L. Scott, Crystal Springs Circuit Records, Methodist Episcopal Church, July 1851, MDAH; "Imposters Out!," *New Orleans Christian Advocate,* April 14, 1855.

6. Newton Haskin James, "Josiah Hinds: Versatile Pioneer of the Old Southwest," *JMH* 2 (January 1940): 25; Moore, *Emergence of the Cotton Kingdom,* 18–19; Miller, *History of North Mississippi Methodism,* 19, 28.

7. Miller, *History of North Mississippi Methodism,* 35–36.

8. E. T. Baird, *Historical Sketch of the Bethel Presbyterian Church, Lowndes County, Miss. . . .* (Columbus, Miss., 1885), 6.

9. Miller, *History of North Mississippi Methodism,* 42–44.

10. *South-Western Religious Luminary,* May 1837; Aberdeen Baptist Association, *Minutes of the Second Anniversary . . .* (Aberdeen, Miss., 1845), 8.

11. Miles, *Jacksonian Democracy,* 18–32.

12. Miles, *Jacksonian Democracy,* 32–44; Winbourne M. Drake, "The Mississippi Constitutional Convention of 1832," *JSH* 23 (August 1957): 354–70.

13. Claiborne, *Mississippi,* 423–27.

14. Miles, *Jacksonian Democracy,* 29–32; Claiborne, *Mississippi,* 425–26.

15. Miles, *Jacksonian Democracy,* 57–59, 62, 64–65, 79–81, 96, 99, 101, 104–12, 114–16, 117, 125; Claiborne, *Mississippi,* 426–27; Edwin A. Miles, "Franklin E. Plummer: Piney Woods Spokesman of the Jackson Era," *JMH* 14 (January 1952): 1–34.

16. Davis, *Recollections,* 68–71.

17. Davis, *Recollections,* 110–11, 136, 198, 271; First Methodist Church Records, Columbus, Miss., 1838 (MSU); Sydnor, *American Revolutionaries,* 44–59. For an example of Mississippi slaves singing campaign songs see Andrew Jackson Jaragin Interview, in George P. Rawick, ed., *The American Slave: A Composite Biography* (Westport, Conn., 1977), Supp., ser. 1, vol. 8, pt. 3, p. 1129.

18. H. S. Fulkerson, *Random Recollections of Early Days in Mississippi* (Baton Rouge, 1937), 108; Henry S. Foote, *Casket of Reminiscences* (1874; rpt. New York, 1968), 194–95, 428–37.

19. George Lewis Prentiss, ed., *Memoir of S. S. Prentiss,* 2 vols. (New York, 1855), 2:302. Prentiss also found that a perception of religiosity could win votes; see p. 338. *Tennessee Baptist,* December 14, 1848.

20. Wyatt-Brown, *Southern Honor,* 102–14; Davis, *Recollections,* 112.

21. Smedes, *Memorials of a Southern Planter,* 152–53.

22. Wyatt-Brown, *Southern Honor,* 339–50; Patricia C. Click, *The Spirit of the Times: Amusements in Nineteenth-Century Baltimore, Norfolk, and Richmond* (Charlottesville, Va., 1989), 60–71; Randy J. Sparks, "Gentleman's Sport: Horse Racing in Antebellum Charleston," *South Carolina Historical Magazine* (January 1992): 15–30. The Methodist Quarterly Conference in Columbus resolved in 1836 that it disapproved of members patronizing coffee houses, theaters, race tracks, billiard rooms, and circuses. See First Methodist Church, Columbus, Miss., Records, 1836, 1838. For other examples of men disciplined for gambling and horse racing see Bethlehem Baptist Church Records, September 1853, First Baptist Church, Louisville, Miss., Records, December 1845, Galilee Baptist Church Records, 1849, Ebenezer Baptist Church Records, 1807, 1813, East Fork Baptist Church Records, 1850, Jerusalem Baptist Church Records, 1816, in Casey, comp., *Amite County,* 2:19–20, 56–57, 225–26, 252, 257–58.

23. Sellers Diary, May 16, 1815; Wyatt-Brown, *Southern Honor,* 350–61; Anne C. Loveland, *Southern Evangelicals and the Social Order, 1800–1860* (Baton Rouge, 1980), 180–85; Jones, *Concise History,* 252; *New Orleans Christian Advocate,* April 9, September 17, 1853; Copy of Blackman sermon in Winans Manuscript Sermons, Winans Papers; Lyon Journal May, August 1857, James H. Lyon Papers, MSU; *South-Western Religious Luminary,* July 1837; *Liberty Advocate,* May 2, 1846.

24. C. A. Hyland to "My Dear Son," July 3, 1851, Chamberlain-Hyland-Gould Papers, Barker Center; Bazil G. to Carrie Kiger, October 29, 1852, Kiger Family Papers, Natchez Trace Collection, Barker Center.

Chapter 6.   *Apples of Gold in Pictures of Silver: From Sects to Denominations, 1830–1860*

1. *Sacred Harp* (1869), 89.

2. Douglas, *Natural Symbols,* 40–41; M. Richard Niebuhr, *The Kingdom of God in America* (1937; rpt. Middletown, Conn., 1988), 164–84; Zuckerman, "Holy Wars, Civil Wars," 209.

3. Butler, *Awash in a Sea of Faith,* 268–70.

4. Membership figures for Methodists and Baptists cited in Samuel S. Hill, ed., *Encyclopedia of Religion in the South* (Macon, Ga., 1984), 486–87. Figures for Presbyterians in Thompson, *Presbyterians in the South,* 1:175, 433. These figures may be imprecise. As one contemporary wrote, "We place no confidence . . . in conference statistics. They are so irregularly and uncertainly gathered and reported" (*New Orleans Christian Advocate,* November 30, 1859). Butler, *Awash in a Sea of Faith,* 268–76; Boles, *Great Revival,* 143–64.

5. Posey, *Baptist Church,* 34–36, 73; John B. Boles, *Religion in Antebellum Kentucky* (Lexington, Ky., 1976), 42–46; Cotton, *Of Primitive Faith,* 18–27; Benjamin Griffin, *A History of the Primitive Baptists of Mississippi* . . . (Jackson, Miss., 1853), 95–97; Boyd, *Popular History,* 54; Mississippi Baptist Association, *Abstract History,* 32; Women's Missionary Union of Mississippi, *Hearts the Lord Opened,* 13, 16–17; Bertram Wyatt-Brown, "The Antimission Movement in the Jacksonian South: A Study in Regional Folk Culture," *JSH* 36 (November 1970): 510, 514.

6. New Bethel minutes quoted in Cotton, *Of Primitive Faith,* 26; Griffin, *History of Primitive Baptists,* 172–78; Mathews, *Religion in the Old South,* 125–28; Boles, *Religion in Antebellum Kentucky,* 135–37; Wyatt-Brown, "Antimission Movement," 502–3, 515; David Edwin Harrell, Jr., "The Evolution of Plain-Folk Religion in the South, 1835–1920," in Samuel S. Hill, ed., *Varieties of Southern Religious Experience* (Baton Rouge, 1988), 24–30.

7. Griffin, *History of Primitive Baptists,* 177–78. By 1844 at least 900 antimissionary preachers, 1,622 churches, and 68,000 members had left the Baptist church in the South (Wyatt-Brown, "Antimission Movement," 527).

8. James E. Tull, *A History of Southern Baptist Landmarkism in the Light of Historical Baptist Ecclesiology* (New York, 1980), 154–231, 413–15 (quotations on pp. 155, 156, and 200).

9. Tull, *Southern Baptist Landmarkism,* 247–55 (quotation on p. 248).

10. Tull, *Southern Baptist Landmarkism,* 134, 138–43; Mississippi Baptist Association, *Abstract History,* 76, 81, 95, 111; *Tennessee Baptist,* February 17, March 2, 9, 1848.

11. *Biographical and Historical Sketches,* 1:364–65.

12. Ancel Henry Bassett, *A Concise History of the Methodist Protestant Church* . . . (Baltimore, 1887), 38, 148–50; Mathews, *Religion in the Old South,* 128–29.

13. Harris Autobiography, 24–27; William Lee Hamrick, *The Mississippi Conference of the Methodist Protestant Church* (Jackson, Miss., 1957), 22–30.

14. The Methodist Protestant church had several circuits in the state, but in 1871 these disbanded and rejoined the Methodists (*Biographical and Historical Sketches*, 364).

15. *Biographical and Historical Sketches*, 356–58; Percy L. Rainwater, "Conquistadors, Missionaries, and Missions," *JMH* 27 (April 1965): 140–41; Sparks, "Mississippi's Apostle of Slavery," 89–106; Boles, *Great Revival*, 159–63; Mathews, *Religion in the Old South*, 163–64.

16. *Biographical and Historical Sketches*, 358–59. There were about sixty Cumberland Presbyterian churches in the state by 1860 (Hill, ed., *Encyclopedia of Religion*, 486–87).

17. Smylie to Moderator of the Synod of Mississippi, October 24, 1836, Claiborne Papers, MDAH; Butler, *Awash in a Sea of Faith*, 275.

18. Amite and Florida Auxiliary Bible Society Minutes December 7, 1815, June 1835, MDAH; Winans Autobiography, 71, 91, 127; Casey, comp., *Amite County*, 2:193; Jones, *Complete History*, 2:28–31; James Smylie to James Lattimore, September 2, 1837, Claiborne Papers; Synod of Mississippi and South Alabama, *Extract from the Records of the Synod of Mississippi and South Alabama, from 1829 to 1835* (Jackson, Miss., 1880), 129 (quotation), 16, 22, 29, 70, 119; Butler, *Awash in a Sea of Faith*, 277–79; Hatch, *Democratization*, 125–27, 141–46, 202–4.

19. Winchester, *Religion of the Bible*, 6, 7, 17, 23, 40–41; *South-Western Religious Luminary*, September 1836; *Nashville Western Methodist*, November 15, 1833, February 28, 1834; *New Orleans South-Western Baptist Chronicle*, May 13, 1848.

20. Synod of Mississippi and South Alabama, *Extracts from the Records of the Synod*, 16, 22, 118; J. L. Power, "Church History," manuscript in First Presbyterian Church Records, Jackson, Miss., MDAH; First Methodist Church Records, Columbus, Miss., 1837, 1851, 1859; *New Orleans Christian Advocate*, June 28, 1856; *Mississippi Baptist*, May 12, 1859; Harris Gaylord Warren, "Vignettes of Culture in Old Claiborne," *JMH* 20 (July 1958): 128; Panola Baptist Association, *Minutes of the Fourth Anniversary of the Panola Baptist Association* (Panola, Miss., 1847), 6. For a comprehensive study of the Sunday school movement see Anne Boylan, *Sunday School: The Formation of an American Institution, 1790–1880* (New Haven, 1988).

21. *Mississippi Baptist*, September 16, 1858; First Methodist Church Records, Columbus, Miss., Second Conference, 1846; Thompson, *Presbyterians in the South*, 1:206, 210; Janet Duitsman Cornelius, *"When I Can Read My Title Clear": Literacy, Slavery, and Religion in the Antebellum South* (Columbia, S.C., 1991), 110–12, 126–28.

22. Eugene D. Genovese and Elizabeth Fox-Genovese, "The Religious Ideals of Southern Slave Society," *Georgia Historical Quarterly* 70 (Spring 1986): 13.

23. Moore, "Religion, Secularization, and the Shaping of the Culture Industry," 227, 236–37; Benjamin M. Drake to the American Tract Society, Natchez, n.d., Drake and Family Papers, MDAH; "The Life of the Reverend Benjamin Chase, as

Recorded in His Own Hand, in a Two Volume Diary," manuscript in Rev. J. Whitner Kennedy Papers, MDAH; Butler, *Awash in a Sea of Faith*, 277–79; Hatch, *Democratization*, 125–27, 141–46, 202–4.

24. Robert Rogers, "From Alienation to Integration: A Social History of Baptists in Antebellum Natchez" (Ph.D. dissertation, New Orleans Baptist Theological Seminary, 1990), 43–48 (*Luminary* quoted on p. 47).

25. Rogers, "From Alienation to Integration," 43–48. In New England new seminaries established in the nineteenth century were also a part of the professionalization of the clergy. See Donald M. Scott, *From Office to Profession: The New England Ministry, 1750–1850* (Philadelphia, 1978), 61–64. On the clergy's desire for professionalization as part of a broader pattern see Samuel Haber, *The Quest for Authority and Honor in the American Professions, 1750–1900* (Chicago, 1991).

26. Samuel Andrew Agnew Diary, September 6, 1865, microfilm, MSU; Hatch, *Democratization*, 125.

27. John Buford Cain, *Methodism in the Mississippi Conference, 1846–1870* (Jackson, Miss., 1939), 216–18. For a story with a similar message see *New Orleans Christian Advocate*, February 24, 1854.

28. Elijah Steele to Henry H. Bridges, August 10, 1837, Steele Letters; Robinson Diary, July 1832; Winans Journal, February 3, 1855; *Mississippi Baptist*, July 23, 1856; Winans to Drake, June 25, 1851, Drake Papers, Cain Archives; *New Orleans Christian Advocate*, April 17, 1851, May 15, 22, 1852; *Biographical and Historical Sketches*, 476; John Johnson, *Recollections of the Rev. John Johnson and His Home . . .* (Nashville, Tenn., 1869), 75; Rogers, "From Alienation to Integration," 94; Academy Baptist Church Records, Tippah County, June, September 1844, MSU. The Concord Baptist Church erected in 1843 and the Baptist church in Rehoboth were of roughly the same dimensions (forty by fifty feet). Log churches were probably smaller; one Methodist log church erected in the 1820s measured twenty by twenty feet. Lorenzo Dow Langford Autobiography, 14, Cain Archives; *New Orleans South-Western Baptist Chronicle*, January 22, July 8, 1848. The same debate plagued other southern evangelicals. See Christopher H. Owen, "By Design: The Social Meaning of Methodist Church Architecture in Nineteenth-Century Georgia," *Georgia Historical Quarterly* 71 (Summer 1991): 221–53.

29. Augusta H. Rice to "My dear Lute," December 14, 1852; Rice to Maria Hopkins Walker, July 19, 1853 (quotations), Rice Collection, MSU.

30. Augusta H. Rice to "My dear Lute," December 14, 1852, Rice Collection; *New Orleans Christian Advocate*, September 22, 1855; Jones, *Complete History*, 2:274–76, 286; Boyd, *Popular History*, 121, 104; *Mississippi Baptist*, September 17, 1857, July 22, 1858; *South-Western Religious Luminary*, September, October 1836.

31. E. Brooks Holifield, *The Gentlemen Theologians: American Theology in Southern Culture, 1795–1860* (Durham, N.C., 1978), 17–31, 39–49; Hatch, *Democratization*, 193–209; Scott, *From Office to Profession*, 64–65; Jones Autobiography, 60; Bridges to Steele, December 29, 1836, Steele Letters; *New Orleans Christian Advocate*, March 2, 1859; E. G. Cook to B. M. Drake, February 26, 1857, Drake and Family Papers, MDAH. Cook, a Methodist minister in Vicksburg, was concerned that ministers in towns might become "the object of laughter & may be of contempt."

32. Winans quoted in Holifield, *Gentlemen Theologians*, 17, 27; *New Orleans South-Western Baptist Chronicle*, December 4, 1847; Methodist Episcopal Church, South, *Minutes of the Annual Conferences, 1847–48* (Nashville, Tenn., 1848), 139, 140, 206.

33. E. Brooks Holifield, "The Penurious Preacher? Nineteenth-Century Clerical Wealth, North and South," *Journal of the American Academy of Religion* 58 (Spring 1990): 17; Cain, *Methodism in the Mississippi Conference*, 29; Holifield, *Gentlemen Theologians*, 29. Holifield found that in 1860 the average wealth of southern urban ministers was $10,177 compared to $4,376 for the same group in the North. *Liberty Advocate*, March 28, 1839; T. L. Miller, ed., *In Memoriam: Life and Labors of the Rev. William Hamilton Watkins, D.D. . . .* (Nashville, Tenn., 1886), 24, 38–48; James, *Antebellum Natchez*, 245, 247; Harris Autobiography, 20–24, 32; Jones Autobiography, 8; Moore, *Emergence of the Cotton Kingdom*, 248. For similar examples see Lacy K. Ford, Jr., *Origins of Southern Radicalism: The South Carolina Upcountry, 1800–1860* (New York, 1988), 13–14.

34. R. H. Rivers, *The Life of Robert Paine, D.D., Bishop of the Methodist Episcopal Church, South* (Nashville, Tenn., 1884), 102; Jones, *Concise History*, 135–37, 139; Winans to Drake, August 15, 1834, February 10, 1857, Drake Papers, Cain Archives; Cain, *Methodism in the Mississippi Conference*, 187–88; undated clipping from the *Nashville Christian Advocate*, Winans Scrapbook, Winans Papers; *New Orleans Christian Advocate*, July 10, 1850; Winans Journal, February 10, 1855; Drake Autobiography, Drake Papers, Cain Archives; Hawkins, *Methodism in Natchez*, 42.

35. *Nashville Western Methodist*, November 8, 1833.

36. Cotton, *Of Primitive Faith*, 53–54; Casey, comp., *Amite County*, 2:337–39; *Mississippi Baptist*, September 17, 1857; Boyd, *Popular History*, 121; Fellowship Baptist Church Records, Lauderdale County, September 1849, SBHC; Amite Primitive Baptist Association, *Minutes of the Amite Primitive Baptist Association . . . 1885* (Middletown, N.Y., 1885), 5–15.

37. *South-Western Religious Luminary*, October 1836; Jones, *Concise History*, 63; Robinson Diary, June 7, 1854; Alexander Diary, March 19, 1854, June 13, 1861; *New Orleans Christian Advocate*, March 10, 1855.

38. *South-Western Religious Luminary*, February 1838; *Mississippi Baptist*, March 18, 1858; Jones, *Complete History*, 1:61, 447, 448, 2:220, 320–21; Agnew Diary, December 9, 1865; *New Orleans Christian Advocate*, July 10, 1850, April 12, 1851, July 17, 1852, February 5, June 11, July 9, 30, 1853, March 10, 1855; Winans to Drake, May 12, 1859, Drake Papers, Cain Archives; Tynes Diary, 10.

39. Jones, *Complete History*, 1:334, 459.

40. Jones, *Complete History*, 2:408; *New Orleans Christian Advocate*, April 12, 1851, February 5, 1853; Winans Journal, February 10, 1855; "Church Music," *Western Messenger* 1 (June 1835): 134–37. See also Owens, "By Design," 247–48.

41. Alexander Diary, August 11, 1865; *New Orleans Christian Advocate*, June 18, 1853; Jones Autobiography, 91; *Mississippi Baptist*, March 18, 1858.

42. First Presbyterian Church Records, Port Gibson, Miss., 18–19, MDAH; Sophia Boyd Hays Diary, March 7, April 8, 1858, Hays-Ray-Webb Collection, MDAH; Alexander Diary, October 16, 1861.

43. *New Orleans Christian Advocate*, August 9, 1851, May 20, August 19, 1854, July 5, 1856, May 5, 1866; Jones Autobiography, 106–8; T. Walker to Benjamin M. Drake, 1858, Drake Papers, Cain Archives; Alexander Diary, August 22, 1856, March 6, 1859; Robert Gordon Diary, June 26, 1853, MDAH; B. M. Drake to Susan Drake, August 19, 1857, Drake and Family Papers, MDAH; W. L. Lipscomb to "Dear Mother," January 1, 1850, W. L. Lipscomb and Family Letters, MDAH; Jones Journal, p. 77, March 20, 1835; W. B. Jones, *Methodism in the Mississippi Conference, 1870–1894* (Nashville, Tenn., 1951), 99, 114, 366, 462; ? to Elijah Steele, June 14, 1838, Steele Letters; Carthage Circuit Record Book, Methodist Episcopal Church, June 27, September 5, 1857, Cain Archives; *Mississippi Baptist*, May 12, 1859; *Nashville Western Methodist*, January 31, 1834; Schmidt, *Holy Fairs*, 205–12; Power, "Centennial Celebration of Old Bethany Church," 29.

44. *New Orleans Christian Advocate*, August 9, 1851, October 23, 1852, November 6, 1852, August 6, November 5, December 10, 1853, July 29, August 4, September 9, October 7, 14, 1854, May 26, August 20, September 22, 1855, August 30, September 13, October 4, 1856, August 17, September 14, November 3, 1859, November 7, 1860; *Mississippi Baptist*, April 22, May 6, 27, June 10, 24, August 5, 19, 26, September 2, 9, 16, October 14, 1858, September 22, October 20, 1859; Winans Journal, August 1, October 1–7, 1842; Harris Autobiography, 60; Ann to Elijah Steele, July 5, 1859, Steele Letters.

45. *New Orleans Christian Advocate*, July 10, 1850.

46. Jones Autobiography, 86; Howze Journal, August 21, 26, September 3, 1854, Isham Robertson Howze Papers, MDAH; Harris Autobiography, 32–33; Undated Biographical Sketch in Charles Kimball Marshall Papers, MDAH; *New Orleans Christian Advocate*, February 17, 1855.

47. James, "Josiah Hinds," 25.

48. The literature on Jacksonian politics is extensive, but my characterization of Whigs and Democrats and the interaction of religion and politics is drawn largely from Lawrence Frederick Kohl, *The Politics of Individualism: Parties and the American Character in the Jacksonian Era* (New York, 1989); Ronald P. Formisano, *The Birth of Mass Political Parties, Michigan, 1827–1861* (Princeton, 1971); Watson, *Liberty and Power*, and Daniel Walker Howe, "The Evangelical Movement and Political Culture in the North During the Second Party System," *Journal of American History* 77 (March 1991): 1216–39. On the broader connections between religion and the market see Zuckerman, "Holy Wars, Civil Wars," 205–40. Quotation from Formisano, *Birth of Mass Political Parties*, 102. See also Oakes, *Slavery and Freedom*, 121–36. Some scholars who have searched for links between southern religious affiliation and political behavior have noted that Primitive Baptists supported the Democratic party, but because members of the larger denominations such as the Methodists and Missionary Baptists were more divided in their political loyalties, these scholars have concluded that no clear relationship existed between politics and religion. The split between modernists and traditionalists within these larger denominations may explain the division in party loyalty. See Harry L. Watson, *Jacksonian Politics and Community Conflict: The Emergence of the Second Party System in Cumberland County, North Carolina* (Baton Rouge,

1981), 241–42, and Marc W. Kruman, *Parties and Politics in North Carolina, 1836–1865* (Baton Rouge, 1983), 15. The distinction between modernists and traditionalists may also explain Daniel Walker Howe's observation that "the Methodist clergy seem to have moved into the Whig party more readily than their laity" ("Evangelical Movement," 1231). Some Mississippians noted an affinity between Baptists and Methodists and the Democratic party. See J. H. Sleeper to John Chamberlain, March 7, 1853, Chamberlain-Hyland-Gould Papers; and Fulkerson, *Random Recollections*, 108.·

49. Cotton, *Of Primitive Faith*, 29; Tombigbee Baptist Association of the Primitive Order, "Minutes of the Annual Sessions, 1846–1884," Circular Letters of 1848 and 1852, microfilm, MSU; *New Orleans Christian Advocate*, March 13, 1852, August 13, 1853; Zuckerman, "Holy Wars, Civil Wars," 212–13.

50. T. H. Breen, " 'Baubles of Britain': The American and Consumer Revolutions of the Eighteenth Century," *Past and Present* 119 (May 1988): 73–104.

51. McLemore, *History of Mississippi Baptists*, 128, 159; Miles, *Jacksonian Democracy*, 146–47, 164–65; Formisano, *Birth of Mass Political Parties*, 116; Kohl, *Politics of Individualism*, 74; Watson, *Liberty and Power*, 176.

52. James, "Josiah Hinds," 25; Kohl, *Politics of Individualism*, 152–57; Formisano, *Birth of Mass Political Parties*, 107–8.

53. Formisano, *Birth of Mass Political Parties*, 137; Howe, "Evangelical Movement," 1225–27.

54. Cotton,· *Of Primitive Faith*, 50–51; Claiborne, *Mississippi*, 356, 426; Mathews, *Religion in the Old South*, 135; Wyatt-Brown, "Antimission Movement," 502–3; Zuckerman, "Holy Wars, Civil Wars," 212–13, 218–19.

Chapter 7.   *The Lashes of a Guilty Conscience: Evangelical Proslavery and Slave Missions*

1. James Smylie, *Review of a Letter from the Presbytery of Chillicothe, to the Presbytery of Mississippi, on the Subject of Slavery . . .* (Woodville, Miss., 1836), 3.

2. Fox-Genovese, *Within the Plantation Household*, 53–70; Elizabeth Fox-Genovese, "Family and Female Identity in the Antebellum South: Sarah Gayle and Her Family," in Carol Bleser, ed., *In Joy and in Sorrow: Women, Family, and Marriage in the Victorian South, 1830–1900* (New York, 1991), 18–20; Kulikoff, *Agrarian Origins*, 7, 18–24, 212, 265. Jack P. Maddex, Jr., noted the connection between proslavery ideology and a hierarchical social ideology in " 'The Southern Apostasy' Revisited: The Significance of Proslavery Christianity," *Marxist Perspectives* 2 (Fall 1979): 132–41. Donald G. Mathews explored some aspects of evangelical individualism in *Religion in the Old South*, 13, 19, 39–40, 43–44, 60–65, 77–78.

3. Jones, *Concise History*, 240; Flint, *Recollections*, 342–43; Larry E. Tise, *Proslavery: A History of the Defense of Slavery in America, 1701–1840* (Athens, Ga., 1987), 33–36; Jordan, *White Over Black*, 292–94, 342, 486; James Oakes, *The Ruling Race: A History of American Slaveholders* (New York, 1982), 96–122; Drew R. McCoy, *The Elusive Republic: Political Economy in Jeffersonian America* (Chapel

Hill, 1980), 251–52; Sydnor, *Slavery in Mississippi*, 239; Maddex, "Southern Apostasy," 133; Clarence L. Mohr, "Slaves and White Churches in Confederate Georgia," in Boles, ed., *Masters and Slaves*, 158–59; Abraham Lincoln, *Abraham Lincoln: Speeches and Writings, 1832–1858*, ed. Don E. Fehrenbacher (New York, 1989), 447. For a review of the historiography of southern attitudes toward slavery see Gaines M. Foster, "Guilt Over Slavery: A Historiographical Analysis," *JSH* 56 (November 1990): 665–94. Foster concludes that southerners did not suffer feelings of guilt over slavery, though like many southern historians his focus on the Civil War distorts his view of the earlier history of the region. For a view more sensitive to the complexities proslavery ministers faced see William W. Freehling, "James Henley Thornwell's Mysterious Antislavery Moment," *JSH* 57 (August 1991): 383–406.

4. Sydnor, *Slavery in Mississippi*, 239.

5. On the importance of clergymen in the proslavery debate see Tise, *Proslavery*, 124–79.

6. Faust, *Ideology of Slavery*, 5; Jones Journal, April 7, 12, May 8, June 6, 21, 1835, December 5, 1836; Jones, *Complete History*, 2:488; Winans to Daniel de Vinne, August 31, 1841, Winans Papers. Winans's letters clearly show that he, too, moved from anti- to proslavery.

7. Sparks, "Mississippi's Apostle of Slavery," 89–91.

8. Sparks, "Mississippi's Apostle of Slavery," 91–92.

9. Tise, *Proslavery*, 124–79 (quotation on p. 177). Jack P. Maddex referred to this group as "proslavery social activists" ("From Theocracy to Spirituality: The Southern Presbyterian Reversal on Church and State," *Journal of Presbyterian History* 54 [Winter 1976]: 438).

10. Casey, comp., *Amite County*, 2:171–72; Jones, *Concise History*, 239–42; Benjamin Chase to Smylie, February 1, 1828, Claiborne Papers; Faust, *Ideology of Slavery*, 7–8; Hamer, "Beginnings of Presbyterianism in Mississippi," 213–14; David Donald, "The Proslavery Argument Reconsidered," *JSH* 37 (February 1971): 3–31.

11. Jones, *Concise History*, 240–41; Sparks, "Mississippi's Apostle of Slavery," 97–98.

12. Sparks, "Mississippi's Apostle of Slavery," 98.

13. Sparks, "Mississippi's Apostle of Slavery," 98–99; *Christian Herald*, October 1, 1836; Jones, *Concise History*, 240–41; Smylie to J. Chamberlain, March 28, 1837, Chamberlain to Smylie, December 7, 1836, Smylie to the Senate and House of Representatives of the State of Louisiana, 1837, Claiborne Papers; Walter Brownlow Posey, *Frontier Mission: A History of Religion West of the Southern Appalachians to 1861* (Lexington, Ky., 1966), 342; Cabiness and Cabiness, "Religion in Ante-Bellum Mississippi," 222; E. N. Elliott, ed., *Cotton Is King, and Pro-Slavery Arguments . . .* (Augusta, Ga., 1860), p. x; Smylie, *Review of a Letter*; Gerrit Smith, *Letter of Gerrit Smith to Rev. James Smylie, of the State of Mississippi* (New York, 1837); Synod of Mississippi and South Alabama, *Extracts from the Records*, 278–83.

14. Tise, *Proslavery*, 122–23, 328–30; Sparks, "Mississippi's Apostle of Slavery," 104–5.

15. Lawrence Stone, *The Family, Sex and Marriage in England, 1500–1800* (New York, 1977), 653, 666–80; Michael Walzer, *The Revolution of the Saints: A Study in the Origins of Radical Politics* (Cambridge, Mass., 1965), 49; Isaac, *Transformation*, 308–11; Daniel Blake Smith, *Inside the Great House: Planter Family Life in Eighteenth-Century Chesapeake Society* (Ithaca, N.Y., 1980), 21, 284–97; Michael Zuckerman, "William Byrd's Family," *Perspectives in American History* 12 (1979): 255–311; Mary Beth Norton, *Liberty's Daughters: The Revolutionary Experience of American Women, 1750–1800* (Boston, 1980), 228–94; Stephanie McCurry, "The Two Faces of Republicanism: Gender and Proslavery Politics in Antebellum South Carolina," *Journal of American History* 78 (March 1992): 1245–64.

16. Thomas C. Thornton, *An Inquiry into the History of Slavery . . .* (Washington, D.C., 1841), 92; Eugene D. Genovese, " 'Our Family White and Black': Family and Household in the Southern Slaveholders' World View," in Bleser, ed., *In Joy and in Sorrow*, 69–87; Mitchell Snay, "American Thought and Southern Distinctiveness: The Southern Clergy and the Sanctification of Slavery," *Civil War History* 35 (December 1989): 322.

17. Sparks, "Mississippi's Apostle of Slavery," 103; Winchester, *Religion of the Bible*, 17–23; Fox-Genovese, *Within the Plantation Household*, 64; McCurry, "Two Faces," 1245–46, 1249–51. On the importance of the family in southern proslavery ideology see Eugene D. Genovese, *The World the Slaveholders Made: Two Essays in Interpretation* (New York, 1969), 195–202.

18. *Mississippi Baptist*, July 14, 1859; Daniel Baker, *A Series of Revival Sermons* (Pennfield, Ga., 1847), 28; *Tennessee Baptist*, November 16, 1848.

19. Thornton, *Inquiry into the History of Slavery*, 65–67; Winans to Daniel de Vinne, August 31, 1841, Winans Papers.

20. Lincoln, *Abraham Lincoln*, 363, 395–400, 456–58 (quotation on p. 396). On Lincoln's devotion to the Declaration and his understanding of the Revolution's legacy see Garry Wills, *Lincoln at Gettysburg: The Words That Remade America* (New York, 1992), 38, 85, 100–111, 124, 145–47.

21. *New Orleans Christian Advocate*, October 5, 1859; Smylie, *Review of a Letter*, 74.

22. Crystal Springs Circuit, Methodist Quarterly Conference Records, August 1844; *Proceedings of a Meeting to Consider the Propriety of Forming a Baptist State Convention*, 17; Winans to Daniel de Vinne, August 31, 1841, Winans Papers; Sydnor, *Slavery in Mississippi*, 242; McLemore, *History of Mississippi Baptists*, 146; Jones, *Complete History*, 2:346–47. For examples see *New Orleans Christian Advocate*, June 26, 1852, January 24, 31, 1857, January 12, 1859; *Mississippi Baptist*, July 23, 1857, September 1858, February 16, March 1, 1860; Jack P. Maddex, Jr., "Proslavery Millennialism: Social Eschatology in Antebellum Southern Calvinism," *American Quarterly* 31 (Spring 1979): 46–62; Maddex, "From Theocracy to Spirituality," 440; *Mississippi Baptist*, June 3, September 16, 1858, October 13, 1859, March 22, 1860.

23. Hawkins, *Methodism in Natchez*, 67; Dumond, ed., *Letters of James Gillespie Birney*, 1:58; *Liberty Advocate*, March 31, 1838. The *Advocate* was published in Amite County, and a member of Smylie's family was an editor.

24. Jones, *Concise History*, 186–87; Jones, *Complete History*, 2:501, 524, 543, 545.

25. John Buford Cain, *The Cradle of Mississippi Methodism* (N.p., n.d.), 41; Winans Journal, December 16–20, 1844; Randolph to "the Preacher in Charge," undated [1844?], "The Religious Life of Capt. E. B. Randolph, a Methodist Church Leader," Randolph to the Rev. G. P. Sparks, June 28, July 16, 1845, Randolph-Sherman Papers; Mathews, *Religion in the Old South*, 160–64; First Methodist Church, Columbus, Miss., Quarterly Conference Records, 1833–59, August 1, 1844; Harris Autobiography, 60; Thomas O. Summers, ed., *Autobiography of the Rev. Joseph Travis, A.M. . . .* (Nashville, Tenn., 1855), 185; William Warren Sweet, *The Story of Religion in America* (New York, 1939), 433–39; Posey, *Frontier Mission*, 352–63.

26. *Proceedings of the Ninth Annual Meeting of the Convention of the Baptist Denomination of the State of Mississippi . . . 1845* (Jackson, Miss., 1845), 24; Sweet, *Story of Religion in America*, 428–33; Posey, *Frontier Mission*, 363–72; William Wright Barnes, *The Southern Baptist Convention, 1845–1953* (Nashville, Tenn., 1954), 12–32.

27. Synod of Mississippi and South Alabama, *Extracts from the Records*, 117; George M. Marsden, *The Evangelical Mind and the New School Presbyterian Experience: A Case Study of Thought and Theology in Nineteenth-Century America* (New Haven, 1970); Elwyn A. Smith, "The Role of the South in the Presbyterian Schism of 1837–1838," *Church History* 29 (March 1960): 44–63; Bailey, *Shadow on the Church*, 230–36; Smylie, *Review of a Letter*; Sweet, *Story of Religion in America*, 375–79; Posey, *Frontier Mission*, 372–73; Thompson, *Presbyterians in the South*, 1:362–412.

28. *New Orleans Christian Advocate*, July 10, 1850, October 5, 1859; Jones, *Complete History*, 2:346–47; Allen Cabiness, *Life and Thought of a Country Preacher* (Richmond, Va., 1941), 147; Milton C. Sernett, *Black Religion and American Evangelicalism: White Protestants, Plantation Missions, and the Flowering of Negro Christianity, 1787–1865* (Metuchen, N.J., 1975), 41–58.

29. Jones, *Complete History*, 2:241, 376, 443; Mathews, *Religion in the Old South*, 138.

30. Jones, *Methodism in the Mississippi Conference*, 474–78; Bailey, *Shadow on the Church*, 227; Jones, *Complete History*, 271, 283; Methodist Episcopal Church, South, *Minutes of the Annual Conferences*, 31, 402, 412, 415. Mississippi was divided among the Mississippi, Alabama, and Memphis conferences. Crawfordville Methodist Church Records, Crawford, Miss., Prairie Hill and Crawfordville Circuit Records, 1843–60, May 1, 1845, July 2, 1850, March 1, 1861; First Methodist Church, Columbus, Miss., Quarterly Conference Records, 1849, 1854, 1855, 1856, 1857; *New Orleans Christian Advocate*, November 25, 1854.

31. *New Orleans Christian Advocate*, November 17, 1855, August 20, October 8, 1853, May 5, 1855; *Mississippi Baptist*, July 23, 1857, September 16, 1858;

John Hebron Moore, ed., "Two Documents Relating to Plantation Overseers of the Vicksburg Region, 1831–1832," *JMH* 16 (January 1954): 31–32.

32. Moore, ed., "Two Documents," 35; *New Orleans Christian Advocate*, July 10, 1850, May 26, 1855, March 7, 1860; Walter Wade Plantation Diary, June 11, July 9, 1854, MDAH; Gordon Diary, May 22, 1853.

33. *New Orleans Christian Advocate*, September 23, 1854, November 17, 1855.

34. *Mississippi Baptist*, October 20, 1859; Jones, *Complete History*, 2:346, 430, 488, 347, 317, 226, 554–55; *New Orleans Christian Advocate*, November 25, 1854, March 7, 1860; Sydnor, *Slavery in Mississippi*, 56–59. Thomas Thornton's pamphlet, *Inquiry into the History of Slavery*, is a good example of a proslavery tract emphasizing racial differences in blatantly racist terms.

35. *New Orleans Christian Advocate*, January 3, 1857.

36. Methodist Episcopal Church, South, *Minutes of the Annual Conference*, 1845, 1846, pp. 32, 82; Jones Journal, 77; Jones Autobiography, 177, 119, 71; Mathews, *Religion in the Old South*, 138–39.

37. Freehling, "Thornwell's Mysterious Antislavery Moment," 395; Methodist Episcopal Church, South, *Minutes of the Annual Conference*, 1845, 1846, pp. 31, 81; Jones to B. M. Drake, May 6, 1840, Drake Papers, Cain Archives; *New Orleans Christian Advocate*, November 6, 1852; Raboteau, *Slave Religion*, 57–58. A Baptist minister in Virginia observed that the slaves' religious beliefs resulted from "instructions received from leading men amongst themselves" (reprinted in *New Orleans Christian Advocate*, August 25, 1855).

38. Jones Journal, 78; *New Orleans Christian Advocate*, November 29, 1851, May 5, 26, 1855, October 11, 1856.

39. Mathews, *Religion in the Old South*, 140.

Chapter 8.   *The Outside Row: The Biracial Evangelical Experience, 1830–1860*

1. Boles, *Black Southerners*, 158.

2. Kenneth M. Stampp, *The Peculiar Institution: Slavery in the Ante-Bellum South* (New York, 1956), 158–61; John W. Blassingame, *The Slave Community: Plantation Life in the Antebellum South* (New York, 1979), 84–87; Genovese, *Roll, Jordan, Roll*, 202–9; Du Bois, *Souls of Black Folk*, 141.

3. Sydnor, *Slavery in Mississippi*, 219–20, 223–24, 234; Jones, *Complete History*, 2:300; Beulah Baptist Church Records, Tippah County, May 1859, SBHC; Winans Journal, August 3, 24, 1845; Rawick, ed., *American Slave*, Supp., ser. 1, vol. 6, pt. 1, 58; *Mississippi Baptist*, August 26, 1858; Robinson Diary, January 1, 1859; Robert L. Hall, "Black and White Christians in Florida, 1822–1861," in Boles, ed., *Masters and Slaves*, 87–88.

4. *New Orleans Christian Advocate*, February 6, 1860. On black preachers and the "invisible church," see Genovese, *Roll, Jordan, Roll*, 255–79; Raboteau, *Slave Religion*, 231–39; Mathews, *Religion in the Old South*, 207.

5. Hopewell Baptist Church Records, November 1825, July, November 1827, October 1829; Bogue Chitto Baptist Church Records, September, December 1827,

February 1828; New Hope Baptist Church Records, December 1830, March, June 1832, June, November 1834, September 1839; Magnolia Baptist Church, Claiborne County, Records, April 1853, SBHC; First Baptist Church, Louisville, Records, August 1851; Bethany Baptist Church Records, June 1858.

6. Patrick H. Thompson, *The History of the Negro Baptists in Mississippi* (Jackson, Miss., 1898), 25–36; Bethany Baptist Church Records, May 1829; Jesse Laney Boyd, Sr., "History of the Baptists in Rankin County," *JMH* 12 (July 1950): 165; Leavell and Bailey, *Complete History of Mississippi Baptists*, 1:77; Boyd, *Popular History of the Baptists in Mississippi*, 70; Mount Moriah Baptist Church, Choctaw County, Records, April 1848, MSU; Bethesda Baptist Church Records, November 1848.

7. Aberdeen Baptist Association, *Minutes of the Second Anniversary*, 8. See also the detailed suggestions from a similar committee appointed by the Columbus Baptist Association in the same year in Columbus Baptist Association, *Minutes of the Columbus Baptist Association . . . 1845* (N.p., n.d. [1845]), 2–3. Not surprisingly, associations in the Piney Woods or hills of northeastern Mississippi, where slavery was limited, showed fewer black members.

8. *Proceedings of the Third Annual Meeting of the Convention of the Baptist Denomination of the State of Mississippi . . . 1839* (Natchez, Miss., 1839), p. 10.

9. Rawick, ed., *American Slave*, Supp., ser. 1, vol. 10, pt. 5, p. 2237.

10. Clear Creek Baptist Church Records, January 20, 1845, May 1846; Concord Baptist Church Records, January 1846, February 1854; Academy Baptist Church Records, July 1848, April 1850; Dr. John Hunter Diary, p. 2, in First Presbyterian Church, Jackson, Miss., Papers; Bethesda Baptist Church Records, January 1855; Liberty Baptist Church Records, June 1860.

11. Liberty Baptist Church Records, June 1860; Concord Baptist Church Records, February 1854; Sydnor, *Slavery in Mississippi*, 55; W. A. Evans, *A History of First Baptist Church, Aberdeen, Mississippi, 1837 to 1945 . . .* (Aberdeen, Miss., 1945), 25; Reminiscences and Stories: No. 11, Dr. J. M. Heard, Evans Memorial Library; Thompson, *History of the Negro Baptists in Mississippi*, 32; Larry M. James, "Biracial Fellowship in Antebellum Baptist Churches," in Boles, ed., *Masters and Slaves*, 54–57.

12. Bethesda Baptist Church Records, 1846, August 1851; Concord Baptist Church Records, September 1851; Bethlehem Baptist Church Records, February 1848; Beulah Baptist Church Records, 1857; Rawick, ed., *American Slave*, Supp., ser. 1, vol. 6, pt. 1, p. 311; vol. 10, pt. 5, pp. 2087, 2006; vol. 9, pt. 4, p. 1472; vol. 8, pt. 3, pp. 1230, 1128; Jones Journal, p. 42; Jones, *Complete History*, 2:408; *New Orleans Christian Advocate*, October 25, 1851; Gene Ramsay Miller, "A History of North Mississippi Methodism, 1820–1890" (Ph.D. dissertation, Mississippi State University, 1964), 106.

13. Thompson, *History of the Negro Baptists in Mississippi*, 24–29; James, *Antebellum Natchez*, 251; Port of Aberdeen Clippings File, 52, Evans Memorial Library; Mathews, *Religion in the Old South*, 199–207; Sobel, *Trabelin' On*, 314–31, 355–56; Raboteau, *Slave Religion*, 188–207; Union Baptist Association, *Min-*

utes of the Thirty-fifth Anniversary of the Union Baptist Association . . . 1856 (New Orleans, 1856), 12.

14. Port of Aberdeen Clippings File, 52. The Aberdeen church employed white ministers. Jonathan Beasley, "Blacks—Slave and Free—Vicksburg, 1850–1860," *JMH* 38 (February 1976): 12; Nash K. Burger, ed., "An Overlooked Source for Mississippi Local History: The Spirit of Missions, 1836–1854," *JMH* 7 (July 1945): 173.

15. Winans Journal, January 22, 1853, January 9, 1842; Jones Journal, June 7, 1835; Agnew Diary, March 16, 1857.

16. *Mississippi Baptist,* April 8, 1858.

17. *Mississippi Baptist,* January 7, 1858; Casey, comp., *Amite County,* 2:294, 230, 307, 24, 29, 309.

18. Magnolia Baptist Church Records, August 1853; Bethesda Baptist Church Records, August 1849.

19. Winans Journal, August 12, 1821; First Presbyterian Church, Holly Springs, Miss., Records, November 7, 1842, MDAH; First Baptist Church, Louisville, Records, June 1849; Academy Baptist Church Records, December 1859.

20. Academy Baptist Church Records, July 1854; Casey, comp., *Amite County,* 2:300; Bethany Baptist Church Records, August, October 1833; Bethesda Baptist Church Records, August 1849, January 1856; Magnolia Baptist Church Records, August 1853; Liberty Baptist Church Records, August 1853, March 1858, January 1860. Frank Hughes, a former slave in Clay County, remembered "patarollers" policing separate black services at biracial churches. See Rawick, ed., *American Slave,* Supp., ser. 1, vol. 8, pt. 3, p. 1062; James, "Antebellum Black Churches," 54–55.

21. Concord Baptist Church Records, January 1845; Liberty Baptist Church Records, May 1854; Sernett, *Black Religion,* 96–97.

22. *New Orleans Christian Advocate,* August 23, 1856.

23. Rawick, ed., *American Slave,* Supp., ser. 1, vol. 7, pt. 2, p. 615; vol. 6, pt. 1, p. 157; vol. 7, pt. 2, pp. 757, 744, 784, 623, 537, 345, 749, 594–95; vol. 8, pt. 3, pp. 1212, 1325, 1197, 1171, 1128–29, 1062, 845; vol. 9, pt. 4, pp. 1588–89, 1567, 1411, 1381; vol. 10, pt. 5, pp. 2410–11, 2370–71, 2337, 2315, 2251, 2237, 2233, 2107–8, 1984.

24. Most of these former slaves would have been children in the antebellum period so perhaps they were expected to serve their masters at church while adult slaves were allowed to worship more freely. See Rawick, ed., *American Slave,* Supp., ser. 1, vol. 6, pt. 1, p. 310; vol. 10, pt. 5, p. 2358; vol. 7, pt. 2, p. 764; vol. 9, pt. 4, p. 1390; vol. 10, pt. 5, p. 2370; Alexander Diary, January 9, April 17, 1859.

25. Concord Baptist Church Records, May 1842; First Baptist Church, Louisville, Records, February 1851; Rawick, ed., *American Slave,* Supp., ser. 1, vol. 9, pt. 4, p. 1472.

26. Rawick, ed., *American Slave,* Supp., ser. 1, vol. 7, pt. 2, p. 797; vol. 8, pt. 3, p. 1321; vol. 9, pt. 4, p. 1779; vol. 10, pt. 5, p. 2087.

27. Rawick, ed., *American Slave,* Supp., ser. 1, vol. 6, pt. 1, pp. 58–59, 285; vol. 9, pt. 4, pp. 1772, 1488, 1489, 1779; vol. 8, pt. 3, pp. 1171, 823, 1321; vol. 10, pt. 5, pp. 2058–59, 2048, 2087.

28. T. M. Bond and Family, Biography File, MBHC; Howze Journal, January 24, 1854.

29. George C. Osborn, "Plantation Life in Central Mississippi as Revealed in the Clay Sharkey Papers," *JMH* 3 (October 1941): 279; "Biographical Sketch of Rev. Jeremiah Davis Mann" in Bertie Shaw Rollins Papers, MSU; Rawick, ed., *American Slave*, Supp., ser. 1, vol. 8, pt. 3, p. 818; Jonathan C. Burney to B. M. Drake, April 10, 1833, Drake Papers, Cain Archives; Will of John W. Hundley, October 16, 1829, in Barker, Feltus, and Stockfelt, comps., *Early Will Records*, 77.

30. Donald, "Proslavery Argument Reconsidered," 8; Alexander Diary, April 30, July 20, 1854, August 20, 21, 22, September 3, 1856, October 27, November 30, 1854, January 9, April 17, July 23, 1859, July 12, 1861, February 28, 1862. See also William W. Freehling, *Prelude to Civil War: The Nullification Controversy in South Carolina, 1816–1836* (New York, 1968); Genovese, *World the Slaveholders Made*; Genovese, *Roll, Jordan, Roll*, 84–85, 120–21; Charles G. Sellers, "The Travails of Slavery," in Sellers, ed., *The Southerner as American* (Chapel Hill, 1960), 40–71.

31. Rawick, ed., *American Slave*, Supp., ser. 1, vol. 9, pt. 4, pp. 1597, 1571; vol. 10, pt. 5, p. 2337.

32. Clear Creek Baptist Church Records, April 24, 1836.

33. Boles, *Black Southerners*, 158.

Chapter 9. *A Wholesome Godly Discipline: Churches as Moral Courts, 1806–1870*

1. East Fork Baptist Church Records in Casey, comp., *Amite County*, 2:53–55; Bruce Lenam, "The Limits of Godly Discipline in the Early Modern Period with Particular Reference to England and Scotland," in Kasper von Greyerz, ed., *Religion and Society in Early Modern Europe, 1500–1800* (London, 1984), 125. For other studies of the history of the process see Kenneth R. Davis, "No Discipline, No Church: An Anabaptist Contribution to the Reformed Tradition," *Sixteenth Century Journal* 13 (Winter 1982): 43–58; Frits G. N. Broeyer, "A Pure City: Calvin's Geneva," in Walter E. A. van Beek, ed., *The Quest for Purity: Dynamics of Puritan Movements* (Berlin, 1988), 37–61; Walzer, *Revolution of the Saints*; Butler, *Awash in a Sea of Faith*, 173–74.

2. Mississippi Baptist Association, *Republication of the Minutes*, 1810 and 1814, pp. 17–20; Zion Baptist Association, *Minutes of the Twenty-third Annual Meeting . . . 1854* (N.p., n.d.), 20.

3. Winans sermon, "The Devil," in Charles F. Deems, ed., *The Southern Methodist Pulpit*, 3 vols. (Richmond, Va., n.d.), 3:208, 211; Zion Baptist Association, *Minutes* (1854), 21; Broeyer, "A Pure City," 5.

4. Griffin, *History of the Primitive Baptists*, 11, 82; A. S. Worrell, *Review of Corrective Church Discipline* (Nashville, Tenn., 1860), xiii; W. Hamilton Watkins sermon in Deems, ed., *Southern Methodist Pulpit*, 3:223–24, 227; Mathews, *Religion in the Old South*, 42. Rhys Isaac notes the ambivalence of individual-

ism and communality in evangelicalism in *Transformation,* 170–72, and Michael Zuckerman observed that "not even the emergent religious movements of the 19th Century ever really relinquished the moral ideals that the industrial economy made archaic. Methodism, Baptism, and a multitude of smaller sects of antebellum evangelicalism elevated the individual will at the crisis of conversion but then subjected it to collective criticism and control ever after" ("Holy Wars, Civil Wars," 223).

5. Mathews, *Religion in the Old South,* 43; Miller, *Life of the Mind,* 67.

6. Timothy L. Smith, "Righteousness and Hope: Christian Holiness and the Millennial Vision in America, 1800–1900," *American Quarterly* 31 (Spring 1979): 21, 23, 29–30; Fox-Genovese and Genovese, "Divine Sanction," 212–13, 215, 220–22; Genovese and Fox-Genovese, "Religious Ideals of Southern Slave Society," 4–5, 7–8, 10–11; Klein, *Unification,* 296.

7. Wyatt-Brown, *Southern Honor,* xviii.

8. Charles Clifton Bolton, "The Failure of Yeoman Democracy: Poor Whites in the Antebellum South" (Ph.D. dissertation, Duke University, 1989), 207–10; Robert M. Calhoun, *Evangelicals and Conservatives in the Early South, 1740–1861* (Columbia, S.C., 1988), 111; Frederick A. Bode, "The Making of Southern Evangelical Communities: Twiggs County, Georgia, 1820–1861," paper presented at the Southern Humanities Council Annual Conference, University of North Carolina at Chapel Hill, February 14, 1992; Ted Ownby, *Subduing Satan: Religion, Recreation, and Manhood in the Rural South, 1865–1920* (Chapel Hill, 1990), 12–18. Wyatt-Brown noted that "by the 1830s . . . religious precept, somewhat democratic in character, transformed the ideal of gentility" (*Southern Honor,* 102).

9. William Willis Boddie, *History of Williamsburg* (Columbia, S.C., 1923), 71.

10. Durward Dunn, *Cades Cove: The Life and Death of a Southern Appalachian Community, 1818–1937* (Knoxville, Tenn., 1988), 99–121.

11. Bode, "Making of Southern Evangelical Communities"; Calhoun, *Evangelicals and Conservatives,* 111; *New Orleans Christian Advocate,* March 1, 1851; *Western Methodist,* January 31, May 2, 1834; Salem Baptist Association, *Minutes of the Fifth Anniversary . . . 1866* (Jackson, Miss., 1866), 11; Mount Olive Baptist Association, *Proceedings . . .* (Meridian, Miss., 1877), 3.

12. Clarence L. Mohr, "Slaves and White Churches in Confederate Georgia," in Boles, ed., *Masters and Slaves,* 156.

13. Edmund S. Morgan, *Visible Saints: The History of a Puritan Idea* (Ithaca, N.Y., 1963), 143; Rowland Berthoff, *An Unsettled People: Social Order and Disorder in American History* (New York, 1971), 241; Ownby, *Subduing Satan,* 204–8. For examples of the debate over discipline see *Western Methodist,* November 29, December 13, 27, 1833, January 17, 31, April 25, May 2, 1834; *New Orleans Christian Advocate,* March 1, 1851; Salem Baptist Association, *Minutes of the Fifth Anniversary,* 11.

14. Salem Baptist Church Records, June 1821, August, November 1822, January, February, March 1823.

15. Mathews, *Religion in the Old South,* 47–48, 102; Bailey, *Shadow on the*

Church, 52; Agnew Diary, January 24, 1864, June 4, 1865; *New Orleans Christian Advocate*, September 22, 1865. Ted Ownby found that men were disciplined for moral offenses five times more often than women (*Subduing Satan*, 134–36).

16. Winans Autobiography, 167; *New Orleans Christian Advocate*, November 5, 1863; Winans Journal, May 6, 23, 1821; Rev. Joseph B. Stratton, *A Pastor's Valedictory: A Selection of Early Sermons . . .* (Natchez, Miss., 1899), 256–57. Conferences in this sample charged eight white men with selling liquor. On alcohol consumption see W. J. Rorabaugh, "Estimated U.S. Alcoholic Beverage Consumption, 1790–1860," *Journal of Studies on Alcohol* 27 (March 1976): 357–63.

17. Jones, *Concise History*, 182; Liberty Baptist Church Records, February 1850; Bethlehem Baptist Church Records, April 1842; First Presbyterian Church Records, Vicksburg, Miss., 1850, MDAH; *New Orleans Christian Advocate*, February 22, 1851. For examples of articles praising the family see *South-Western Religious Luminary*, September, November, December 1836; Galilee Church Records, 1853, in Casey, comp., *Amite County*, 2:211–50; Norman H. Clark, *Deliver Us from Evil: An Interpretation of American Prohibition* (New York, 1971), 12–13, 33–34, 43, 60, 53; Ian R. Tyrrell, "Drink and Temperance in the Antebellum South: An Overview and Interpretation," *JSH* 48 (November 1982): 485–510; Posey, *Frontier Mission*, 303–17. Methodist women and ministers worked together to persuade the Mississippi legislature to pass a temperance bill in the 1840s. The Reverend Charles K. Marshall was called the "Apostle of Temperance." See Cain, *Methodism in the Mississippi Conference*, 122. Wyatt-Brown also discusses the link between alcohol and violence, including wife abuse, in *Southern Honor*, 280–84.

18. David Levinson, "Social Setting, Cultural Factors and Alcohol-Related Aggression," in Edward Gottheil, Keith A. Druley, Thomas E. Skoloda, and Howard M. Waxman, eds., *Alcohol, Drug Abuse and Aggression* (Springfield, Ill., 1983), 41–58; New Zion Baptist Church Records, Choctaw County, June and July 1858, MSU. For examples of intoxication linked with fighting and profanity see Bethesda Baptist Church Records, January 1854; Bethany Baptist Church Records, December 1857; and Spring Hill Baptist Church Records, Choctaw County, December 1858, MSU. For examples of alcohol and profanity see Bethlehem Baptist Church Records, February 1851, April 1856; Mount Moriah Baptist Church Records, March 1857; Bethesda Baptist Church Records, January 1857, May 1858, October 1860; Beulah Baptist Church Records, June 1855; and Academy Baptist Church Records, August 1848.

19. Jones, *Methodism in the Mississippi Conference*, 283; Frederick Law Olmsted, *The Cotton Kingdom* (1861; rpt. New York, 1984), 350; First Presbyterian Church Records, Holly Springs, April 12, 1844, November 21, 1846, MDAH; Bethlehem Baptist Church Records, March 1866.

20. Bethlehem Baptist Church Records, January 1845, May 1862 (the man, L. Sutherland, was excluded in March 1865); Concord Baptist Church Records, January 1848; Bethesda Baptist Church Records, April, May, June, July, August, November 1850, January, May, August 1857.

21. Salem Baptist Church Records, November 1816; Winans Autobiography, 77–78; Bethlehem Baptist Church Records, June 1850; Mississippi Baptist Association,

Republication of the Minutes, 164; *South-Western Religious Luminary*, September 1836.

22. Wyatt-Brown, *Southern Honor*, 250, 281–82; Lewis, "Republican Wife," 689, 693–99, 707–16; *New Orleans Christian Advocate*, September 7, 1859; T. L. Mellen, ed., *In Memoriam: Life and Labors of the Rev. William Hamilton Watkins, D.D. . . . .* (Nashville, Tenn., 1886), 24.

23. Bethesda Baptist Church Records, December 1858, April, August, September, October, November 1859, May, November 1860.

24. Casey, comp., *Amite County*, 2:280, 281; Winans Journal, May 23, 1842, December 20, 1852. In 1864 slaves belonging to J. F. Thankersley's family became rebellious. Thankersley attempted to "correct" them and shot a slave girl, who died from her wounds. The College Hill Presbyterian Church conference ruled that he acted properly. See College Hill Records in Maude Morrow Brown, "What Desolations! At Home in Lafayette County, Mississippi, 1860–1865," 221–23, manuscript in Brown Papers, MDAH.

25. Bethany Baptist Church Records, July 1832; Galilee Church Records in Casey, comp., *Amite County*, 1:232; Winans Journal, December 26, 1820; Rawick, ed., *American Slave*, Supp., ser. 1, vol. 8, pt. 3, pp. 845, 899; vol. 9, pt. 4, pp. 1644, 1864; vol. 6, pt. 1, p. 202. There were three additional cases involving white men and slaves: one in which a man sold liquor to slaves, another in which a man purchased a slave without a clear title, and a third in which a man was charged for holding a "negro party" after the war.

26. Friedman, *Enclosed Garden*, 11–18.

27. Synod of Mississippi and South Alabama, *Extracts from the Records*, 423. Ownby's statistics from ninety-seven churches across the South closely resemble my sample (*Subduing Satan*, 119, 134–35).

28. *Mississippi Baptist*, September 1836.

29. Spring Hill Baptist Church Records, June 1858; Bethany Baptist Church Records, September 1831; Dwight B. Heath, "Alcohol and Aggression: A 'Missing Link' in a Worldwide Perspective," in Gottheil et al., eds., *Alcohol*, 92; W. J. Rorabaugh, *The Alcoholic Republic: An American Tradition* (New York, 1979), 12–13. On the Old South as patriarchal see, for example, Oakes, *Ruling Race*, 201–4, 217–18, and Johnson, "Planters and Patriarchy," 45–72. See also Joseph R. Gusfield, *Symbolic Crusade: Status Politics and the American Temperance Movement* (Urbana, Ill., 1963), 28.

30. Friedman, *Enclosed Garden*, 14, 131.

31. Galilee and Ebenezer Church Records in Casey, comp., *Amite County*, 2:250, 280.

32. Elizabeth Fox-Genovese, "Religion in the Lives of Slaveholding Women of the Antebellum South," in Lynda L. Coon, Katherine J. Haldane, and Elisabeth W. Sommers, eds., *That Gentle Strength: Historical Perspectives on Women in Christianity* (Charlottesville, Va., 1990), 208; Clinton, *Plantation Mistress*, 95–97, 160–63; Stratton, *Pastor's Valedictory*, 227–41.

33. First Baptist Church, Louisville, Records, May, June, September 1849.

34. Lawrence W. Levine, *Black Culture and Black Consciousness: Afro-*

American Folk Thought from Slavery to Freedom (New York, 1977), 123–24. Rawick, ed., *American Slave*, Supp., ser. 1, vol. 9, pt. 4, p. 1571; Frederick Douglass, *The Narrative and Selected Writings*, ed. Michael Meyer (New York, 1984), 122; Genovese, *Roll, Jordan, Roll*, 603–8.

35. Bailey, *Shadow on the Church*, 191–92.

36. Casey, comp., *Amite County*, 2:39, 247; Bethesda Baptist Church Records, August, September 1863; Beulah Baptist Church Records, August 1865.

37. James J. Collins, "Alcohol Use and Expressive Inter-personal Violence: A Proposed Explanatory Model," in Gottheil et al., eds., *Alcohol*, 11.

38. Bethesda Baptist Church Records, February 1851, May 1852; Bethany Baptist Church Records, July 1846, July 1853; Genovese, *Roll, Jordan, Roll*, 643–45; Boles, *Black Southerners*, 89; First Methodist Church, Columbus, Conference, 1845.

39. Howze Journal, December 30, 1853. On the separation of slave spouses see Herbert G. Gutman, *The Black Family in Slavery and Freedom, 1750–1925* (New York, 1976), 151–55.

40. Jones Journal, April 7, 1835. Winans paid $725 for the husband of one of his slaves. He "was moved to this purchase by a desire to keep a husband and wife together" (Winans Journal, January 26–31, 1854).

41. *Mississippi Baptist*, October 13, 1859; Agnew Diary, May 28, 1864, December 30, 1869, January 27, 1870; Robinson Diary, March 1, May 26, 1866; Alexander A. Lomax Notebook, December 30, 1865, January 6, 1866, MDAH. John G. Jones performed ceremonies for slaves. See Jones Journal, 78. Genovese, *Roll, Jordan, Roll*, 476–77; Gutman, *Black Family*, 270–75.

42. Lyon Journal, 112–14.

43. Bethany Baptist Church Records, May 1858.

44. Boles, *Black Southerners*, 42.

45. Bethany Presbyterian and Zion Hill Baptist Church records in Casey, comp., *Amite County*, 2:315–52.

46. Charges made in support of the slave code include running away, theft, disobedience, hiding runaways, rebellion, threatening mistress, and possession of a weapon.

47. Bethany Church Records in Casey, comp., *Amite County*, 2:189–90.

48. Bethany Church Records in Casey, comp., *Amite County*, 2:189–90. Many slaves of both sexes expressed their hatred of drivers and threatened to kill them; some actually accomplished the deed. See Genovese, *Roll, Jordan, Roll*, 371–73.

49. Gutman, *Black Family*, 61–71.

50. Genovese, *Roll, Jordan, Roll*, 465–68; Sobel, *Trabelin' On*, 229–31; Bethany Baptist Church Records, April 1824; Gutman, *Black Family*, 61–71, 18, 20–21, 35–36, 151–55, 158–59.

51. Bethlehem Baptist Church Records, November 1849; Gutman, *Black Family*, 18–23.

52. Genovese, *Roll, Jordan, Roll*, 648; Gutman, *Black Family*, 265. See also Clarence L. Mohr, "Before Sherman: Georgia Blacks and the War Effort, 1861–1865," *JSH* 45 (August 1979): 331–52.

53. Zion Hill Baptist Church Records in Casey, comp., *Amite County*, 2:325–52.

54. Zion Hill records in Casey, *Amite County*, 2:317.

55. Fellowship Baptist Church Records, January, February 1857; Concord Baptist Church Records, March 1858; Spring Hill Baptist Church Records, October 1866; Salem Baptist Church Records, November 1819.

56. Concord Baptist Church Records, December 1841, May 1842, January, February 1844, October, November 1846, September 1847; Academy Baptist Church Records, July, September 1849.

57. Concord Baptist Church Records, May 1845, August 1848; First Baptist Church, Louisville, Records, May 1848, May, June 1849, September 1849. See also Clear Creek Baptist Church Records, January 20, 1845; Bethesda Baptist Church Records, August 1849, March 1850, April 1854.

58. Cabiness and Cabiness, "Religion in Ante-Bellum Mississippi," 215; New Hope Baptist Church Records, June 1832, June 1834, March 1832.

59. Fox-Genovese and Genovese, "Divine Sanction," 229.

60. Ownby, *Subduing Satan*, 204–7; Christopher Waldrep, " 'So Much Sin': The Decline of Religious Discipline and the 'Tidal Wave of Crime,' " *Journal of Social History* 23 (Spring 1990): 535–52.

61. Rivers, *Life of Robert Paine*, 191–93.

Chapter 10.   *The Desolations of Zion: Evangelicals in the Civil War and Reconstruction, 1861–1876*

1. Willie Morris, *Terrains of the Heart and Other Essays on Home* (Oxford, Miss., 1981), 33. See Katherine L. Dvorak, "After Apocalypse, Moses," in Boles, ed., *Masters and Slaves*, 173–91.

2. *New Orleans Christian Advocate*, January 12, October 5, 1859; *Mississippi Baptist*, October 13, March 24, 1859, November 25, 1858, February 16, March 1, 22, 1860; Ray Holder, ed., "On Slavery: Selected Letters of Parson Winans, 1820–1844," *JMH* 36 (November 1984): 341; Tynes Diary, 11. On the evangelical contribution to secession see C. C. Goen, *Broken Churches, Broken Nation: Denominational Schisms and the Coming of the American Civil War* (Macon, Ga., 1985).

3. Clement Eaton, *A History of the Old South: The Emergence of a Reluctant Nation* (New York, 1966), 499. For further information on secession in Mississippi see Percy L. Rainwater, *Mississippi: Storm Center of Secession, 1856–1861* (Baton Rouge, 1938), and William L. Barney, *The Secessionist Impulse: Alabama and Mississippi in 1860* (Princeton, 1974).

4. Teasdale quoted in *Mississippi Baptist*, October 13, 1859; James A. Lyon, *A Lecture on Christianity and the Civil Laws* (Columbus, Miss., 1859), passim; Lyon Journal, March 23, 1859, 1861; Charles A. Rich, "The History of French Camp Presbyterian Church" (M.A. thesis, Mississippi State University, 1967), 13–14; John H. Aughey, *The Fighting Preacher* (Chicago, 1899); Aughey, *The Iron Furnace: or, Slavery and Secession* (Philadelphia, 1863). Several other Unionist ministers are identified in W. Harrison Daniel, *Southern Protestantism in the Confederacy* (Bedford, Va., 1989), 46.

5. Jones Autobiography, 118. For other examples of Unionist ministers see Miller, "History of North Mississippi Methodism," 148.

6. Rivers, *Life of Robert Paine*, 145, 158, 147, 157.

7. Casey, comp., *Amite County*, 2:59.

8. Casey, comp., *Amite County*, 2:118; O. D. Bowen, *Gospel Ministry of Forty Years* (Handsboro, Miss., 1911), 10; Agnew Diary, December 20, 1860, January 12, 1861, April 18, 1864; Lyon Journal, June 1861, pp. 39–41; Academy Baptist Church Records, May 1861.

9. Alexander Diary, June 13, 1861, February 28, 1862, August 21, 1863; James W. Silver, *Confederate Morale and Church Propaganda* (New York, 1957), 64–66, 95; Drew Gilpin Faust, *The Creation of Confederate Nationalism: Ideology and Identity in the Civil War South* (Baton Rouge, 1988), 24–30; Richard Beringer, Herman Hattaway, Archer Jones, and William N. Still, Jr., *The Elements of Confederate Defeat: Nationalism, War Aims, and Religion* (Athens, Ga., 1988), 32–43.

10. Mecklin Diary, February 14–15, 17, 1862; Lyon Journal, 33; Lucy Irion Journal, April 1862, Irion-Nelson Family Papers, MDAH; Cordelia Scales to "Dearest Darling Loulie," May 15, 1862, Cordelia Lewis Scales Letters, MDAH; Anne Firor Scott, *Natural Allies: Women's Associations in American History* (Urbana, Ill., 1991), 68–72.

11. Beulah Baptist Church Records, January 1862; Bethlehem Baptist Church Records, August 1861, June 1862. Academy Baptist Church had no regular preaching or conferences from 1862 to 1864 (Academy Baptist Church Records, November 8, 1864). Prairie Hill and Crawfordsville Circuit Records, September 3, 1861, January 24, 1862; Liberty Baptist Church Records, May 1861; Agnew Diary, June 1, 6, August 31, October 26, December 21, 1862, February 1, August 12, 16, 1863; Cain, *Methodism in the Mississippi Conference*, 297.

12. Rawick, ed., *American Slave*, Supp., ser. 1, vol. 6, pt. 1, p. 202; vol. 7, pt. 2, p. 785; vol. 8, pt. 3, p. 899; Agnew Diary, July 30, August 18, October 29, 30, November 1, 1862; Anonymous Diary, Natchez, July 30, 1863, MDAH; Alexander Diary, 1863, 1864; W. Maury Darst, ed., "The Vicksburg Diary of Mrs. Alfred Ingraham (May 2–June 13, 1863)," *JMH* 64 (May 1982): 168 and passim; James L. Roark, *Masters Without Slaves: Southern Planters in the Civil War and Reconstruction* (New York, 1977), 81–85.

13. Tynes Diary, 11. See Roark, *Masters Without Slaves*, 55–58.

14. Agnew Diary, 30; Isaac A. Duncan to W. E. Duncan, June 10 [1862 or 1863?] in Maude Morrow Brown, "What Desolations! At Home in Lafayette County, Mississippi, 1860–1865," 61, typescript, MDAH; Anonymous Diary, Natchez, July 14, 16, 28, September 20, November 25, 1863; Allan Hargrove to Mary Hargrove, April 16, 1864, Allan Hargrove Papers, MDAH; Myra Smith Diary in Eunice J. Stockwell Papers, December 1, 1861, April 13, November 16, 1862, December 23, 1863, MDAH; Clarence L. Mohr, "Slaves and White Churches in Confederate Georgia," in Boles, ed., *Masters and Slaves*, 160–62; Faust, *Confederate Nationalism*, 30–32, 82–84; Beringer et al., *Elements of Confederate Defeat*, 121, 159–67.

15. Lyon Diary, 62–67, 73, 101; John K. Bettersworth, ed., "Mississippi Unionism: The Case of the Reverend James A. Lyon," *JMH* 1 (January 1939): 37–52; Silver, *Confederate Morale*, 20.

16. College Hill Church Records reproduced in Brown, "What Desolations!," 105–8. See also Smith Diary, April 13, 1862, December 23, 1863; Anonymous Diary,

Natchez, July 14, 16, 28, 30, 1863; Mellen, ed., *In Memoriam*, 48; Allan Hargrove to Mary, April 16, 1864, and undated [1864?], Hargrove Papers; Mary Vaughn to Louisa Clark Boddie, February 22, 1863, Boddie Family Papers, MDAH.

17. Anonymous Diary, Natchez, July 16, 28, 1863.

18. Strong River Baptist Association, *Minutes of the Eleventh Annual Meeting . . . 1863* (Brandon, Miss., 1863), Appendix C; Strong River Baptist Association, *Minutes of the Ninth Anniversary of the Strong River Baptist Association . . . 1861* (Jackson, Miss., 1861), 14; Cain, *Methodism in the Mississippi Conference*, 339; Aberdeen Baptist Association, *Minutes of the Twenty-first Anniversary of the Aberdeen Baptist Association . . . 1864* (N.p., 1864), Appendix B; Spring Hill Baptist Church Records, October 1864; Sophie Hays to "Sister Lit," October 28, 1863, Hays-Ray-Webb Collection; Drew Gilpin Faust, "Christian Soldiers: The Meaning of Revivalism in the Confederate Army," *JSH* 53 (February 1987): 63–90; Shaeffer quoted in Miller, *History of North Mississippi Methodism*, 157; John K. Bettersworth, *Confederate Mississippi: The People and Policies of a Cotton State in Wartime* (Baton Rouge, 1943), 293; Lyon Journal, October 9, 1863. Bethesda Baptist Church membership rose from 87 whites and 82 blacks in 1861 to 103 whites and 113 blacks in 1865 (Bethesda Baptist Church Records, 1861 list and 1865 list). Lucy Irion Journal, January 20, 1861; *New Orleans Christian Advocate*, January 27, 1866.

19. Silver, *Confederate Morale*, p. 64; Faust, *Confederate Nationalism*, 41–57. For examples of hardships at home see John K. Bettersworth, ed., *Mississippi in the Confederacy: As They Saw It* (Baton Rouge, 1961), 286–316. Strong River Baptist Church, *Minutes, 1863*, Appendix D.

20. Casey, comp., *Amite County*, 2:307–10, 348–50, 91, 92, 245–46, 249–50, 48, 75; Aberdeen Baptist Association, *Minutes of the Eighteenth Anniversary of the Aberdeen Baptist Association . . . 1861* (Greensboro, Miss., 1862); Aberdeen Baptist Association, *Minutes, 1864*. Some churches in the association showed impressive gains in white membership, suggesting that the revival was not universal and that some churches suffered greater disruptions than others. Agnew Diary, September 8, 9, 10, October 9, 1863, August 14, September 28–October 2, 24, 1864. At Port Gibson in 1863, "the white congregation does not promise very favorably: promise of good among the Blacks" (Port Gibson Station, Minutes of the Quarterly Conference of the Methodist Episcopal Church, South, February 28, 1863, Cain Archives); Bettersworth, *Confederate Mississippi*, 300–302.

21. Cain, *Methodism in the Mississippi Conference*, 296, 339; Jones Autobiography, 117.

22. Tynes Diary, 11; *New Orleans Christian Advocate*, January 27, 1866; Casey, comp., *Amite County*, 2:40; Thomas L. Connelly and Barbara L. Bellows, *God and General Longstreet: The Lost Cause and the Southern Mind* (Baton Rouge, 1982), 14–29; Berringer et al., *Elements of Confederate Defeat*, 154–67; Charles Reagan Wilson, *Baptized in Blood: The Religion of the Lost Cause, 1865–1880* (Athens, Ga., 1980), 58–78.

23. Lyon Journal, 102, 107; *Proceedings of the Twenty-seventh Session of the Baptist State Convention . . . 1866* (Jackson, Miss., 1866), 22; Cain, *Methodism in the Mississippi Conference*, 386. Georgia evangelicals expressed the same senti-

ments. See Mohr, "Slaves and White Churches in Confederate Georgia," 153–72; Beringer et al., *Elements of Confederate Defeat*, 162–67.

24. "The Cause and Design of the War of Southern Independence," Edward Fontaine Sermons, MSU.

25. Salem Baptist Association, *Minutes of the Fifth Anniversary . . . 1866*, 10; Smith Diary, December 23, 1863, May 28, 1865, excerpts in Stockwell Papers; Tynes Diary, 11.

26. Smith Diary, December 23, 1863, May 28, 1865, excerpts in Stockwell Papers; Tynes Diary, 11; Wilson, *Baptized in Blood*, 66–69, 71–78.

27. See Eric Foner, *Reconstruction: America's Unfinished Revolution, 1863–1877* (New York, 1988), 78.

28. "Free Grace Baptist Church, Colored Organized 1869," in Rollins Papers; *New Orleans Christian Advocate*, January 27, 1866; Port Gibson Station, Minutes of the Quarterly Conference, June 18, 1864, October, December 1865; Liberty Baptist Church Records, August 1865; Cain, *Methodism in the Mississippi Conference*, 358–59, 390–91, 409–10; Jones Journal, 1866; Agnew Diary, July 20, 23, 1864; Tynes Diary, 13; Agnew Diary, November 24, August 18, 1866; W. H. C. Shaw to B. B. Butler, December 27, 1867, Rollins Papers.

29. Lyon Journal, 140–43, 210–11; Agnew Journal, August 27, 1870.

30. A. T. Morgan, *Yazoo; or on the Picket Line of Freedom in the South* (Washington, D.C., 1884), 103–9; Michael Wayne, *The Reshaping of Plantation Society: The Natchez District, 1860–1880* (Baton Rouge, 1983), 137–39; Thompson, *History of the Negro Baptists in Mississippi*, 32, 36; James T. Currie, *Enclave: Vicksburg and Her Plantations, 1863–1870* (Jackson, Miss., 1980), 172–73.

31. Thompson, *History of the Negro Baptists in Mississippi*, 79, 44; Morgan, *Yazoo*, 271.

32. Michael William Fitzgerald, "The Union League Movement in Alabama and Mississippi: Politics and Agricultural Change in the Deep South During Reconstruction" (Ph.D. dissertation, University of California, Los Angeles, 1986), 39–40, 78, 140; Mount Olivet Baptist Association, *Minutes of the Third Annual Session . . . 1871* (Columbus, Miss., 1871), 10; Maria Waterbury, *Seven Years Among the Freedmen* (1891; rpt. Freeport, N.Y., 1971), 90–91; Foner, *Reconstruction*, 428; Buford Stacher, *Blacks in Mississippi Politics, 1865–1900* (Washington, D.C., 1978), 25, 76–78; Currie, *Enclave*, 197–98; Revels A. Adams, *Cyclopedia of African Methodism in Mississippi* (N.p., 1902), 86–87.

33. Randy J. Sparks, " 'The White People's Arms Are Longer Than Ours': Blacks, Education, and the American Missionary Association in Reconstruction Mississippi," *JMH* 54 (February 1992): 16, 5.

34. Sparks, " 'White People's Arms,' " 16–20; Central Baptist Association, *Minutes of the Twenty-first Annual Session of the Central Baptist Association . . . 1866* (Jackson, Miss., 1866), Appendix D; Central Baptist Association, *Minutes of the Twenty-third Annual Session of the Central Baptist Association . . . 1868* (Jackson, Miss., 1868), Appendix G; Clarence G. Walker, *A Rock in a Weary Land: The African Methodist Episcopal Church During the Civil War and Reconstruction* (Baton Rouge, 1982), 75–76, 83–107.

35. Sparks, "'White People's Arms,'" 19. See also Noralee Frankel, "Workers, Wives and Mothers: Black Women in Mississippi, 1860–1870" (Ph.D. dissertation, George Washington University, 1983), 213–14.

36. Waterbury, *Seven Years*, 118–20, see also 41, 154–55. Another northerner recorded a similar examination meeting at which visionary experiences were related. See George C. Benham, *A Year of Wreck: A True Story by a Victim* (New York, 1880), 303–4. On these aspects of African-American religion see Raboteau, *Slave Religion*, 4–86, 266–71; Genovese, *Roll, Jordan, Roll*, 232–55; Olli Alho, *The Religion of the Slaves: A Study of the Religious Tradition and Behavior of the Plantation Slaves in the United States, 1830–1865* (Helsinki, Finland, 1976); Levine, *Black Culture and Black Consciousness*, 35–39, 61; Sobel, *World They Made Together*, 200–203.

37. Waterbury, *Seven Years*, 195–96. This service also bears strong resemblance to the modern foot-washing ceremony among black Mississippi Baptists described in Chapter 2. For a discussion of the ring shout see Raboteau, *Slave Religion*, 66–73.

38. Bethany Baptist Church Records, May, July 1871; Tishomingo Baptist Association, *Proceedings of the Ninth Annual Session of the Tishomingo Baptist Association . . . 1869* (Memphis, Tenn., 1869), 8; Mississippi Baptist Association, *Minutes of the Sixty-first Anniversary of the Mississippi Baptist Association . . . 1867* (Memphis, Tenn., 1868), 9; Jones Autobiography, 125–27.

39. Thompson, *History of the Negro Baptists in Mississippi*, 41, 519–20.

40. Mount Olivet Baptist Association, *Minutes of the First Annual Session of the Mount Olivet Baptist Association . . . 1869* (N.p., 1869); Mount Olivet Baptist Association, *Minutes of the Third Annual Session . . . 1871*, 5–6; Mount Olivet Baptist Association, *Minutes of the Fourth Annual Session of the Mt. Olivet Baptist Association . . . 1872* (Columbus, Miss., 1872), 14–15; Mount Olive Baptist Association, *Proceedings of the Mt. Olive Baptist Association . . . 1877* (Meridian, Miss., 1877); Thompson, *History of the Negro Baptists of Mississippi*, 49, 62, 81, 84, 109, 127–28, 135–36, 371. See also Sardis Missionary Baptist Association, *Minutes of the First Session of the Sardis Missionary Baptist Association . . . 1870* (Memphis, Tenn., 1870).

41. Waterbury, *Seven Years*, 20; Joe M. Richardson, *Christian Reconstruction: The American Missionary Association and Southern Blacks, 1861–1890* (Athens, Ga., 1986), 46.

42. Thompson, *History of the Negro Baptists of Mississippi*, 92, 108.

43. Thompson, *History of the Negro Baptists of Mississippi*, 62–65, 327, 360–61.

44. *New Orleans Christian Advocate*, September 8, November 24, 1866; Spring Hill Baptist Church Records, October 1865; Bethlehem Baptist Church Records, July 1868, August 1869; Philadelphia Missionary Baptist Church, Choctaw County, Records, October 1867, September 1870, MSU; Tynes Diary, 14; Salem Baptist Association, *Minutes of the Fourth Annual Meeting . . . 1865* (Mobile, Ala., 1865), 11; Salem Baptist Association, *Minutes of the Eleventh Annual Session . . . 1872* (Enterprise, Miss., 1872), 11; Aberdeen Baptist Association, *Minutes of the Twenty-second Session . . . 1865* (Jackson, Tenn., 1865), and *Minutes of the Twenty-fifth*

Annual Session . . . 1868 (N.p., 1868); Cain, *Methodism in the Mississippi Conference,* 420, 435, 462–63; Jones, *Methodism in the Mississippi Conference,* 47; H. P. Lewis, *An Autobiography of Rev. H. P. Lewis* (N.p., 1913), 34–35; Janet Sharp Hermann, *The Pursuit of a Dream* (New York, 1981), 187–89.

45. Agnew Diary, May 14, 18, June 4, August 19, 24, 28, 29, September 6, 8, 9, 10, 16, 24, October 3, 30, 1865, April 1, 1866.

46. Agnew Diary, August 18, 19, 24, 28, 31, September 1, 2, 6, 30, 1866, June 30, 1867; Line Creek Baptist Church ordained a former slave in 1866. See Casey, comp., *Amite County,* 2:82.

47. Agnew Diary, July 21–24, August 3, 19, September 8, 24, 29, 1867, April 19, August 9, 23, 1868, April 18, June 6, July 4, August 8, 16, 29, October 30, 31, 1869, April 10, July 20, 30, 31, August 21, 27, September 20, 23, 1870, April 2, 17, July 29, 30, October 28, 29, 1871, February 15, December 14, 1872; Leon F. Litwack, *Been in the Storm So Long: The Aftermath of Slavery* (New York, 1979), 252–61.

48. Agnew Diary, January 14, March 2, 1873, August 2, 1874, April 18, August 1, 1875.

49. Elizabeth Irion Journal, Irion-Neilson Papers, 29. The unidentified female Natchez diarist recorded a similar event in 1863. See Anonymous Diary, July 28, 1863; Litwack, *Been in the Storm So Long,* 176, 198, 222, 226, 244, 252–61; Rawick, ed., *American Slave,* Supp., ser. 1, vol. 7, pt. 2, p. 567.

50. Cain, *Methodism in the Mississippi Conference,* 433; Boles, *Black Southerners,* 201; *New Orleans Christian Advocate,* August 11, December 15, 1866; Academy Baptist Church Records, September 1865; Philadelphia Missionary Baptist Church Records, June 1866, MSU. Dvorak, "After Apocalypse, Moses," in Boles, ed., *Masters and Slaves, 173–91.*

51. Jones, *Complete History,* 2:68–69, 67.

52. Jones Autobiography, 125–27; Genovese, *Roll, Jordan, Roll,* 97–112.

53. Agnew Diary, August 18, 1866, April 18, June 6, July 4, August 8, October 30, 31, 1869; Rawick, ed., *American Slave,* Supp., ser. 1, vol. 9, pt. 4, pp. 1151, 1601; vol. 7, pt. 2, pp. 671, 615, 345, vol. 8, pt. 3, p. 868.

54. Sparks, "'White Peoples' Arms,'" 2–3, 6, 16; Thompson, *History of the Negro Baptists in Mississippi,* 32, 52, 58, 99–100, 157.

55. *New Orleans Christian Advocate,* August 11, December 15, 1866; Cain, *Methodism in the Mississippi Conference,* 441, 457.

56. Casey, comp., *Amite County,* 2:310, 56–76; Rawick, ed., *American Slave,* Supp., ser. 1, vol. 9, pt. 4, p. 1601; Bethany Baptist Church Records, July 1871.

57. Academy Baptist Church Records, November 1865, August 1869, August 1870; Magnolia Baptist Church Records, July 1867, December 23, 1871; Liberty Baptist Church Records, May 1866, July, August 1867, May 1872; Hopewell Baptist Church Records, August 1871.

58. Bethesda Baptist Church Records, March, November 1866, April, May, August, November, December 1867, January, October 1868, December 1869; Boles, *Black Southerners,* 202.

59. Salem Baptist Association, *Minutes of the Ninth Annual Session of the Salem Baptist Association . . . Jasper County, Mississippi . . . 1870* (Lauderdale

Station, Miss., 1870), 6, 11; *Minutes of the Fourth Annual Meeting . . . 1865*, 11; *Minutes of the Fifth Anniversary . . . 1872*, 7, 11. See also statistical tables in Aberdeen Baptist Association, *Minutes of the Twenty-second Session . . . 1865; Minutes of the Twenty-fifth Annual Session . . . 1868;* Fellowship Baptist Church Records, May 1874, January 1876.

BIBLIOGRAPHY

ABBREVIATIONS

Barker Center	Eugene C. Barker Texas History Center, University of Texas, Austin, Texas
Cain Archives	J. B. Cain Archives, Millsaps College, Jackson, Mississippi
Evans Memorial Library	Evans Memorial Library, Aberdeen, Mississippi
JMH	*Journal of Mississippi History*
JSH	*Journal of Southern History*
MBHC	Mississippi Baptist Historical Commission, Mississippi College, Clinton, Mississippi
MDAH	Mississippi Department of Archives and History, Jackson, Mississippi
MSU	Special Collections, Mississippi State University, Starkville, Mississippi
PMHS	*Publications of the Mississippi Historical Society*
SBHC	Southern Baptist Historical Commission, Nashville, Tennessee

UNPUBLISHED SOURCES

Church Records

Academy Baptist Church. Tippah County. MDAH.
Bethany Baptist Church. Jefferson Davis County. SBHC.
Bethesda Baptist Church. Hinds County. SBHC.
Bethlehem Baptist Church. Choctaw County. MSU.
Beulah Baptist Church. Tippah County. SBHC.
Bogue Chitto Baptist Church. Pike County. MBHC.
Carolina Presbyterian Church. Session Book. MDAH.
Carthage Circuit Record Book. Methodist Episcopal Church. Cain Archives.
Clear Creek Baptist Church. Adams County. SBHC.
Concord Baptist Church. Winston-Choctaw Counties. MSU.
Crawfordville Methodist Church. Crawford, Mississippi. MSU.

Crystal Springs Circuit. Methodist Episcopal Church. MDAH.

Enon Baptist Church. Itawamba County. MSU.

Fellowship Baptist Church. Lauderdale County. SBHC.

First Baptist Church. Louisville, Mississippi. SBHC.

First Methodist Church. Columbus, Mississippi. MSU.

First Methodist Church. Jackson, Mississippi. "Recording Steward's Book," 1847–49, 1865–74. Cain Archives.

First Presbyterian Church. Holly Springs, Mississippi. MDAH.

First Presbyterian Church. Jackson, Mississippi. MDAH.

First Presbyterian Church. Natchez, Mississippi. MDAH.

First Presbyterian Church. Port Gibson, Mississippi. MDAH.

First Presbyterian Church. Vicksburg, Mississippi. MDAH.

Hopewell Baptist Church. Franklin County. MBHC.

Liberty Baptist Church. Jackson, Mississippi. SBHC.

Magnolia Baptist Church. Claiborne County. SBHC.

Mars Hill Baptist Church. Summit, Mississippi. SBHC.

Montrose Presbyterian Church. Jasper County. MDAH.

Mount Moriah Baptist Church. Choctaw County. MSU.

Mount Pisgah Baptist Church. Choctaw County. MSU.

New Hope Baptist Church. Monroe County. Evans Memorial Library.

New Zion Baptist Church. Choctaw County. MSU.

Old Lebanon Presbyterian Church. Choctaw County. MSU.

Philadelphia Missionary Baptist Church. Choctaw County. MSU.

Port Gibson Station. Quarterly Conference Minutes. Methodist Episcopal Church. Cain Archives.

Prairie Hill and Crawfordville Circuit. Methodist Episcopal Church. MSU.

Salem Baptist Church. Jefferson County. SBHC.

Sarepta Baptist Church. Franklin County. MSU.

Spring Hill Baptist Church. Choctaw County. MSU.

Tombigbee Baptist Association of the Primitive Order. Minutes of the Annual Sessions, 1846–84. MDAH.

Woodville Methodist Church. Woodville, Mississippi. MDAH.

Manuscript Collections

Agnew, Samuel Andrew. Diary. Microfilm. MSU.

Alexander, Robert B. Diary and Account Ledger. MDAH.

Amite and Florida Auxiliary Bible Society. Minutes. MDAH.

Anonymous Diary. Natchez. MDAH.

Bachman, G. W. "Sketches and Incidents of Life, 1839–1914." MSU.

Blackman, Learner [Launer]. Journal. Cain Archives.

Boddie Family. Papers. MDAH.

Bond, T. M. and Family. Biography File. MBHC.

Brown, Maude Morrow. Papers. MDAH.

Chamberlain-Hyland-Gould Papers. Barker Center.

Chapman Family Papers. MDAH.

Claiborne, J. F. H. Papers. MDAH.

Cook, Mrs. Jared Reese. Diary. MDAH.

Dana, Charles B. Papers. MDAH.

DeHay, Elizabeth Norton. Papers. MDAH.

Downs, Lettie Vick. Journal. MDAH.

Drake, Benjamin M. Papers. Cain Archives.

Drake, Benjamin M. and Family Papers. MDAH.

Elizabeth Female Academy. Subject File. MDAH.

Evans, Dr. Holder Garthur. Diary. MDAH.

Fontaine, Charles D. and Family. Papers. MDAH.

Fontaine, Edward. Sermons. MSU.

Gordon, Robert. Diary. MDAH.

Grafton, Cornelius W. Papers. MDAH.

Hargrove, Allan. Papers. MDAH.

Harris, Rev. Henry J. Autobiography. Cain Archives.

Hays, Sophia Boyd. Diary and Letters. Hays-Ray-Webb Collection. MSU.

Howze, Isham Robertson. Papers. MDAH.

Hughes, Henry. Papers. MDAH.

Irion-Neilson Family. Papers. MDAH.

Jones, John G. Autobiography and Journal. MDAH.

Kennedy, Rev. J. Whitmer. Papers. "The Life of Reverend Benjamin Chase." MDAH.

Kiger Family Papers. Natchez Trace Collection. Barker Center.

Langford, Lorenzo Dow. Autobiography. Cain Archives.

Lipscomb, W. L. and Family. Letters. MDAH.

Lomax, Alexander A. Notebook. MDAH.

Lowry, Rev. Thomas Jefferson. Memoranda. MDAH.

Lyon, James H. Papers. MSU.

McNabb, Eliza R. Letters. MDAH.

Marshall, Charles Kimball. Papers. MDAH.

Mecklin, Augustus Harvey. Papers. MDAH.

Montgomery, Joseph A. and Family. Papers. MDAH.

Natchez Orphan Asylum Records. Natchez Trace Collection. Barker Center.

Nicholson, Flavellus G. Diary-Journal. MDAH.

Nicholson, James M. Diary. MDAH.

Official Archives of the State of Mississippi. Legislature. MDAH.

Port of Aberdeen Clippings File. Evans Memorial Library.

Rabb, Matilda C. Letters. MDAH.

Randolph-Sherman Papers. MSU.

Reminiscences and Stories. Evans Memorial Library.

Rice, Augusta H. Letters. Rice Collection. MSU.

Robertson, Norvelle, Sr. Autobiography. MDAH.

Robinson, Nancy M. Diary. MDAH.

Rollins, Bertie Shaw. Papers. MSU.

Sager, Sarah Knox Harris. Recollections. Sager Collection. MDAH.

Scales, Cordelia Lewis. Letters. MDAH.

Scofield, Lorenzo. Diary. MBHC.

Sellers, Samuel. Diary. Cain Archives.

Steele, Elijah. Letters. MDAH.
Stockwell, Eunice J. Papers. MDAH.
Strickland, Belle. Diary. MDAH.
Tynes, Walter Edwin. Diary. MDAH.
Wade, Walter. Plantation Diary. MDAH.
Weeks, Levi. Letters. MDAH.
Winans, William. Papers. Cain Archives.
Winston, E. T. and Family. Papers. MDAH.

THESES, DISSERTATIONS, AND UNPUBLISHED PAPERS

Archer, Kate. "History of the Methodist Ladies Co-operative Association, Methodist
   Church, Port Gibson, Mississippi." Microfilm. MSU.
Bode, Frederick A. "The Making of Southern Evangelical Communities: Twiggs
   County, Georgia, 1820–1861." Paper presented at the Southern Humanities
   Council Annual Conference, University of North Carolina at Chapel Hill,
   February 14, 1992.
Bolton, Charles Clifton. "The Failure of Yeoman Democracy: Poor Whites in the
   Antebellum South." Ph.D. dissertation, Duke University, 1989.
Cashin, Joan Ellen. "Family, Kinship, and Migration in the Antebellum South." Ph.D.
   dissertation, Harvard University, 1985.
Downey, J. C. "The Music of American Revivalism, 1740–1800." Ph.D. dissertation,
   Tulane University, 1968.
Ellington, C. L. "The Sacred Harp Tradition of the South: Its Origin and Evolution."
   Ph.D. dissertation, Florida State University, 1969.
Fitzgerald, Michael William. "The Union League Movement in Alabama and
   Mississippi: Politics and Agricultural Change in the Deep South During Recon-
   struction." Ph.D. dissertation, University of California, Los Angeles, 1986.
Frankel, Noralee. "Workers, Wives and Mothers: Black Women in Mississippi,
   1860–1870." Ph.D. dissertation, George Washington University, 1983.
Grant, Minnie Spencer. "The American Colonization Society in North Carolina."
   M.A. thesis, Duke University, 1930.
Harper, Louis Keith. "The Historical Context for the Rise of Old Landmarkism." M.A.
   thesis, Murray State University, 1986.
Hickin, Patricia P. "Antislavery in Virginia, 1831–1861." Ph.D. dissertation, University
   of Virginia, 1968.
Kennedy, Larry Wells. "The Fighting Preacher of the Army of Tennessee: General
   Mark Perrin Lowrey." Ph.D. dissertation, Mississippi State University, 1976.
Miller, Gene Ramsey. "A History of South Mississippi Methodism, 1820–1900." Ph.D.
   dissertation, Mississippi State University, 1964.
Rich, Charles A. "The History of the French Camp Presbyterian Church." M.A. thesis,
   Mississippi State University, 1967.
Rogers, Robert. "From Alienation to Integration: A Social History of Baptists in Ante-
   bellum Natchez." Ph.D. dissertation, New Orleans Theological Seminary, 1990.
Sims, J. N. "The Hymnody of the Camp Meeting Tradition." Ph.D. dissertation, Union
   Theological Seminary, 1960.

PUBLISHED SOURCES

Newspapers and Periodicals

Mississippi Baptist.
Natchez Messenger.
New Orleans Christian Advocate.
New Orleans South-Western Baptist Chronicle.
New Orleans Western Methodist.
South-Western Religious Luminary.
Tennessee Baptist.
Virginia Evangelical and Literary Magazine.
Western Messenger.
Western Methodist (Nashville).

Aberdeen Baptist Association. *Minutes of the Second Anniversary . . . 1845.* Aberdeen, Miss., 1845.
———. *Minutes of the Fifth Annual Meeting . . . 1848.* Houston, Miss., 1848.
———. *Minutes of the Sixth Annual Meeting . . . 1849.* Pontotoc, Miss., 1849.
———. *Minutes of the Seventh Annual Meeting . . . 1850.* Aberdeen, Miss., 1850.
———. *Minutes of the Ninth Annual Session . . . 1852.* Aberdeen, Miss., 1852.
———. *Minutes of the Tenth Annual Session . . . 1853.* Philadelphia, Miss., 1853.
———. *Minutes of the Eleventh Annual Session . . . 1854.* Aberdeen, Miss., 1854.
———. *Minutes of the Twelfth Session . . . 1855.* Aberdeen, Miss., 1856.
———. *Minutes of the Eighteenth Anniversary . . . 1861.* Greensboro, Miss., 1862.
———. *Minutes of the Nineteenth Session . . . 1862.* Greensboro, Miss., 1862.
———. *Minutes of the Twenty-first Anniversary . . . 1864.* N.p., 1864.
———. *Minutes of the Twenty-second Session . . . 1865.* Jackson, Tenn., 1865.
———. *Minutes of the Twenty-fourth Annual Session . . . 1867.* Atlanta, Ga., 1868.
———. *Minutes of the Twenty-fifth Annual Session . . . 1868.* N.p., 1868.
———. *Minutes of the Thirty-seventh Annual Session . . . 1880.* Jackson, Miss., 1880.
Adams, Revels A. *Cyclopedia of African Methodism in Mississippi.* N.p., 1902.
Alford, Terry. *Prince Among Slaves.* New York, 1977.
Alho, Olli. *The Religion of the Slaves: A Study of the Religious Tradition and Behavior of the Plantation Slaves in the United States, 1830–1865.* Helsinki, Finland, 1976.
American Colonization Society. *Annual Reports.* 1818–61. New York, 1969.
Amite Primitive Baptist Association. *Minutes of the Amite Primitive Baptist Association . . . 1885.* Middletown, N.Y., 1885.
Appleby, Joyce. *Capitalism and a New Social Order: The Republican Vision of the 1790s.* New York, 1984.
Aughey, John H. *The Fighting Preacher.* Chicago, 1899.
———. *The Iron Furnace: or, Slavery and Secession.* Philadelphia, 1863.
Bachelard, Gaston. *The Poetics of Space.* Boston, 1969.
Bailey, David T. *Shadow on the Church: Southwestern Evangelical Religion and the Issue of Slavery, 1783–1860.* Ithaca, N.Y., 1985.

Bailyn, Bernard. *The Ideological Origins of the American Revolution.* Cambridge, Mass., 1967.

Baird, E. T. *Historical Sketch of the Bethel Presbyterian Church, Lowndes County, Miss. . . .* Columbus, Miss., 1885.

Baker, Daniel. *A Series of Revival Sermons.* Pennfield, Ga., 1847.

Baker, Osmon C. *Guide-Book in the Administration of the Discipline of the Methodist Episcopal Church.* New York, 1855.

Baklanoff, Joy Driskell. "The Celebration of a Feast: Music, Dance, and Possession Trance in the Black Primitive Baptist Footwashing Ritual." *Ethnomusicology* 31 (Fall 1987): 381–94.

Baldwin, Joseph G. *The Flush Times of Alabama and Mississippi: A Series of Sketches.* New York, 1854.

Baptist State Convention. *Second Annual Report . . . 1824.* Natchez, Miss., 1825.

Barker, Mary G., Mavis Olivin Feltus, and Diane A. Stockfelt, comps. *Early Will Records of Adams County, Mississippi.* N.p., 1975.

Barnes, William Wright. *The Southern Baptist Convention, 1845–1953.* Nashville, Tenn., 1954.

Barney, William L. *The Secessionist Impulse: Alabama and Mississippi in 1860.* Princeton, 1974.

Bartley, Numan V. *The Evolution of Southern Culture.* Athens, Ga., 1988.

Bassett, Ancel Henry. *A Concise History of the Methodist Protestant Church. . . .* Baltimore, 1887.

Beasley, Jonathan. "Blacks—Slave and Free—Vicksburg, 1850–1860." *JMH* 38 (February 1976): 1–32.

Benham, George C. *A Year of Wreck: A True Story by a Victim.* New York, 1880.

Beringer, Richard, Herman Hattaway, Archer Jones, and William N. Still, Jr. *The Elements of Confederate Defeat: Nationalism, War Aims, and Religion.* Athens, Ga., 1988.

Berthoff, Rowland. *An Unsettled People: Social Order and Disorder in American History.* New York, 1971.

Bettersworth, John K. *Confederate Mississippi: The People and Policies of a Cotton State in Wartime.* Baton Rouge, 1943.

———. *Mississippi in the Confederacy: As They Saw It.* Baton Rouge, 1961.

———, ed. "Mississippi Unionism: The Case of the Reverend James A. Lyon." *JMH* 1 (January 1939): 37–52.

Biographical and Historical Sketches of Mississippi. 2 vols. Spartanburg, S.C., 1978.

Blassingame, John W. *The Slave Community: Plantation Life in the Antebellum South.* New York, 1979.

Bleser, Carol, ed. *In Joy and in Sorrow: Women, Family, and Marriage in the Victorian South, 1830–1900.* New York, 1991.

Bloch, Ruth H. "The Gendered Meanings of Virtue in Revolutionary America." *Signs: Journal of Women in Culture and Society* 13 (Autumn 1987): 37–58.

Boddie, William Willis. *History of Williamsburg.* Columbia, S.C., 1923.

Boles, John B. *Black Southerners, 1619–1869.* Lexington, Ky., 1984.

———. *The Great Revival, 1787–1805: The Origins of the Southern Evangelical Mind.* Lexington, Ky., 1972.

———. *Religion in Antebellum Kentucky.* Lexington, Ky., 1976.

———, ed. *Masters and Slaves in the House of the Lord: Race and Religion in the American South, 1740–1870.* Lexington, Ky., 1988.

Bowen, O. D. *Gospel Ministry of Forty Years.* Handsboro, Miss., 1911.

Boyd, J. L., Sr. "History of the Baptists in Rankin County." *JMH* 12 (July 1950): 162–68.

Boyd, Jesse Laney. *A Popular History of the Baptists in Mississippi.* Jackson, Miss., 1930.

Boylan, Anne. *Sunday School: The Formation of an American Institution, 1790–1880.* New Haven, 1988.

Breen, T. H. "'Baubles of Britain': The American and Consumer Revolutions of the Eighteenth Century." *Past and Present* 119 (May 1988): 73–104.

Bruce, Dickson D. *And They All Sang Hallelujah: Plain-Folk Camp-Meeting Religion, 1800–1845.* Knoxville, Tenn., 1974.

Burger, Nash K., ed. "An Overlooked Source for Mississippi Local History: The Spirit of Missions, 1836–1854." *JMH* 7 (July 1945): 171–78.

Butler, Jon. *Awash in a Sea of Faith: Christianizing the American People.* Cambridge, Mass., 1990.

Cabiness, Allen. *Life and Thought of a Country Preacher.* Richmond, Va., 1941.

Cabiness, Frances Allen, and James Allen Cabiness. "Religion in Ante-Bellum Mississippi." *JMH* 6 (October 1944): 191–224.

Cain, John Buford. *The Cradle of Mississippi Methodism.* N.p., n.d.

———. *Methodism in the Mississippi Conference, 1846–1870.* Jackson, Miss., 1939.

Calhoun, Robert M. *Evangelicals and Conservatives in the Early South, 1740–1861.* Columbia, S.C., 1988.

Campbell, Joseph. *The Masks of God.* Vol. 4: *Creative Mythology.* New York, 1968.

Carr, Anne E. *Transforming Grace: Christian Tradition and Women's Experience.* San Francisco, 1988.

Casey, Albert E., comp. *Amite County, Mississippi, 1699–1865.* 2 vols. Birmingham, Ala., 1948.

Cashin, Joan E. *A Family Venture: Men and Women on the Southern Frontier.* New York, 1991.

Censer, Jane Turner. "Southwestern Migration Among North Carolina Planter Families: 'The Disposition to Emigrate.'" *JSH* 57 (August 1991): 407–26.

Central Baptist Association. *Minutes of the Eighth Annual Session . . . 1853.* Jackson, Miss., 1853.

———. *Minutes of the Fifteenth Annual Session . . . 1860.* Jackson, Miss., 1860.

———. *Minutes of the Sixteenth Annual Session . . . 1861.* Jackson, Miss., 1861.

———. *Minutes of the Twenty-first Annual Session . . . 1866.* Jackson, Miss., 1866.

———. *Minutes of the Twenty-third Annual Session . . . 1868.* Jackson, Miss., 1868.

———. *Minutes of the Twenty-fourth Annual Session . . . 1869.* Jackson, Miss., 1869.

———. *Minutes of the Twenty-ninth Annual Session . . . 1874.* Vicksburg, Miss., 1875.

Claiborne, J. F. H. *Mississippi, as a Province, Territory and State. . . . 1880.* Reprint. Baton Rouge, 1964.

Clark, Norman H. *Deliver Us from Evil: An Interpretation of American Prohibition.* New York, 1971.

Clark, Thomas D., and John D. W. Guice. *Frontiers in Conflict: The Old Southwest, 1795–1830.* Albuquerque, N.M., 1989.

Click, Patricia C. *The Spirit of the Times: Amusements in Nineteenth-Century Baltimore, Norfolk, and Richmond.* Charlottesville, Va., 1989.

Clinton, Catherine. *The Plantation Mistress: Women's World in the Old South.* New York, 1982.

Cmiel, Kenneth. *Democratic Eloquence: The Fight for Popular Speech in Nineteenth-Century America.* New York, 1990.

Cobb, E. B., Jr. *The Sacred Harp: A Tradition and Its Music.* Athens, Ga., 1978.

Cold Water Baptist Association. *Minutes of the Twentieth Annual Session . . . 1861.* Memphis, Tenn., 1861.

Columbus Baptist Association. *Minutes of the Columbus Baptist Association . . . 1845.* N.p.: N.d. [1845].

——— . *Minutes of the Eleventh Anniversary . . . 1848.* Houston, Miss., 1848.

Connelly, Thomas L., and Barbara L. Bellows. *God and General Longstreet: The Lost Cause and the Southern Mind.* Baton Rouge, 1982.

Coon, Lynda L., Katherine J. Haldane, and Elisabeth W. Sommers, eds. *That Gentle Strength: Historical Perspectives on Women in Christianity.* Charlottesville, Va., 1990.

Cornelius, Janet Duitsman. *"When I Can Read My Title Clear": Literacy, Slavery, and Religion in the Antebellum South.* Columbia, S.C., 1991.

Cott, Nancy F. *The Bonds of Womanhood: "Women's Sphere" in New England, 1780–1835.* New Haven, 1977.

Cott, Nancy F., and Elizabeth H. Pleck, eds. *A Heritage of Her Own: Toward a New Social History of American Women.* New York, 1979.

Cotton, Gordon A. *Of Primitive Faith and Order: A History of the Mississippi Primitive Baptist Church, 1780–1974.* Raymond, Miss., 1974.

Currie, James T. *Enclave: Vicksburg and Her Plantations, 1863–1870.* Jackson, Miss., 1980.

Daniel, W. Harrison. *Southern Prostestantism in the Confederacy.* Bedford, Va., 1989.

Darst, W. Maury, ed. "The Vicksburg Diary of Mrs. Alfred Ingraham (May 2–June 13, 1863)." *JMH* 64 (May 1982): 148–79.

Davis, Gerald L. *I got the Word in me and I can sing it, you know: A Study of the Performed African-American Sermon.* Philadelphia, 1985.

Davis, James E. *Frontier America, 1800–1840: A Comparative Demographic Analysis of the Settlement Process.* Glendale, Calif., 1977.

Davis, Kenneth R. "No Discipline, No Church: An Anabaptist Contribution to the Reformed Tradition." *Sixteenth Century Journal* 13 (Winter 1982): 43–58.

Davis, Natalie Zemon. *Society and Culture in Early Modern France.* Stanford, 1975.

Davis, Reuben. *Recollections of Mississippi and Mississippians.* New York, 1890.

Deems, Charles F. *Annals of Southern Methodism.* New York, 1856.

——— , ed. *The Southern Methodist Pulpit.* 3 vols. Richmond, Va., n.d.

Degler, Carl N. *The Other South: Southern Dissenters in the Nineteenth Century.* New York, 1974.

De Vinne, Daniel. *The Methodist Episcopal Church and Slavery. . . .* New York, 1857.

Donald, David. "The Proslavery Argument Reconsidered." *JSH* 37 (February 1971): 3–31.

Dorgan, Howard. *Giving Glory to God in Appalachia: Worship Practices of Six Baptist Subdenominations.* Knoxville, Tenn., 1987.

Douglas, Mary. *Natural Symbols: Explorations in Cosmology.* New York, 1973.

Douglass, Frederick. *The Narrative and Selected Writings.* Edited by Michael Meyer. New York, 1984.

Dow, Lorenzo. *History of the Cosmopolite, or the Writings of Rev. Lorenzo Dow. . . .* Cincinnati, 1857.

Drake, Benjamin M. *A Funeral Sermon Preached . . . on the Death of Mrs. A. F. W. Speer. . . .* Vidalia, La., [1849].

――――. *A Sketch of the Life of Rev. Elijah Steele.* Cincinnati, 1843.

Drake, Winbourne. "The Mississippi Constitutional Convention of 1832." *JSH* 23 (August 1957): 354–70.

――――, ed. "The Road to Freedom." *JMH* 3 (January 1941): 44–45.

Du Bois, W. E. B. *The Souls of Black Folk: Essays and Sketches.* Greenwich, Conn., 1961.

Dumond, Dwight L., ed. *Letters of James Gillespie Birney, 1831–1857.* 2 vols. Gloucester, Mass., 1966.

Dunn, Durwood. *Cades Cove: The Life and Death of a Southern Appalachian Community, 1818–1937.* Knoxville, Tenn., 1988.

Eaton, Clement. *Freedom of Thought in the Old South.* Durham, N.C., 1940.

――――. *A History of the Old South: The Emergence of a Reluctant Nation.* New York, 1966.

Economic Research Department. *Mississippi Statistical Summary of the Population, 1800–1980.* N.p., 1983.

Eihghmy, John Lee. *Churches in Cultural Captivity: A History of the Social Attitudes of Southern Baptists.* Knoxville, Tenn., 1972.

Elliott, E. N., ed. *Cotton Is King, and Pro-Slavery Arguments. . . .* Augusta, Ga., 1860.

Epstein, Barbara L. *The Politics of Domesticity: Women, Evangelicalism, and Temperance in Nineteenth-Century America.* Middletown, Conn., 1981.

Essig, James D. *The Bonds of Wickedness: American Evangelicals Against Slavery, 1770–1808.* Philadelphia, 1982.

Evans, W. A. *A History of First Baptist Church, Aberdeen, Mississippi, 1837 to 1945. . . .* Aberdeen, Miss., 1945.

Farrar, Daniel S., ed. "Alexander K. Farrar's Deed to Kingston Church, 1874." *JMH* 17 (January–October 1955): 135–41.

Faust, Drew Gilpin. "Christian Soldiers: The Meaning of Revivalism in the Confederate Army." *Journal of Southern History* 53 (February 1987): 63–90.

――――. *The Creation of Confederate Nationalism: Ideology and Identity in the Civil War South.* Baton Rouge, 1988.

――――. *The Ideology of Slavery: Proslavery Thought in the Antebellum South, 1830–1860.* Baton Rouge, 1981.

Finley, James Bradley. *Sketches of Western Methodism. . . .* Cincinnati, 1854.

Flint, Timothy. *Recollections of the Last Ten Years. . . .* Boston, 1826.

Foner, Eric. *Reconstruction: America's Unfinished Revolution, 1863–1877.* New York, 1988.

Foote, Henry S. *Casket of Reminiscences.* 1874. Reprint. New York, 1968.

Ford, Lacy K., Jr. *Origins of Southern Radicalism: The South Carolina Upcountry, 1800–1860.* New York, 1988.

Formisano, Ronald P. *The Birth of Mass Political Parties, Michigan, 1827–1861.* Princeton, 1971.

Foster, Gaines M. "Guilt Over Slavery: A Historiographical Analysis." *JSH* 56 (November 1990): 665–94.

Foster, L. S. *Mississippi Baptist Preachers.* St. Louis, 1895.

Fox-Genovese, Elizabeth. *Within the Plantation Household: Black and White Women of the Old South.* Chapel Hill, 1988.

Fox-Genovese, Elizabeth, and Eugene Genovese. "The Divine Sanction of Social Order: Religious Foundations of the Southern Slaveholders' World View." *Journal of the American Academy of Religion* 55 (Summer 1987): 226–27.

Freehling, William W. "James Henry Thornwell's Mysterious Antislavery Moment." *JSH* 57 (August 1991): 383–406.

———. *Prelude to Civil War: The Nullification Controversy in South Carolina, 1816–1836.* New York, 1968.

Friedman, Jean E. *The Enclosed Garden: Women and Community in the Evangelical South, 1830–1900.* Chapel Hill, 1985.

Fulkerson, H. S. *Random Recollections of Early Days in Mississippi.* Baton Rouge, 1937.

Galloway, Charles B. "Elizabeth Female Academy: The Mother of Female Colleges." *PMHS* 3 (1899): 169–78.

Genovese, Eugene D. *Roll, Jordan, Roll: The World the Slaves Made.* New York, 1976.

———. *The World the Slaveholders Made: Two Essays in Interpretation.* New York, 1969.

Genovese, Eugene D., and Elizabeth Fox-Genovese. "The Religious Ideals of Southern Slave Society." *Georgia Historical Quarterly* 70 (Spring 1986): 1–16.

Gewehr, Wesley M. *The Great Awakening in Virginia, 1740–1790.* Durham, N.C., 1930.

Goen, C. C. *Broken Churches, Broken Nation: Denominational Schisms and the Coming of the American Civil War.* Macon, Ga., 1985.

Gordon, Michael, ed. *The American Family in Social-Historical Perspective.* New York, 1978.

Gottheil, Edward, Keith A. Druley, Thomas E. Skoloda, and Howard M. Waxman, eds. *Alcohol, Drug Abuse and Aggression.* Springfield, Ill., 1983.

Graves, Fred R., comp. and ed. *The Presbyterian Work in Mississippi.* Jackson, Miss., 1927.

Greyerz, Kaspar von, ed. *Religion and Society in Early Modern Europe, 1500–1800.* London, 1984.

Griffin, Benjamin. *A History of the Primitive Baptists of Mississippi. . . .* Jackson, Miss., 1853.

Gusfield, Joseph R. *Symbolic Crusade: Status Politics and the American Temperance Movement.* Urbana, Ill., 1963.

Gutman, Herbert G. *The Black Family in Slavery and Freedom, 1750–1925.* New York, 1976.

Haber, Samuel. *The Quest for Authority and Honor in the American Professions, 1750–1900.* Chicago, 1991.

Halsell, Willie D., ed. "A Stranger in a Strange Land." *Alabama Historical Quarterly* 30 (Summer 1968): 61–75.

Hamer, T. L. "Beginnings of Presbyterianism in Mississippi." *PMHS* 10 (1909): 203–21.

Hamrick, William Lee. *The Mississippi Conference of the Methodist Protestant Church.* Jackson, Miss., 1957.

Harris, William C. *The Day of the Carpetbagger: Republican Reconstruction in Mississippi.* Baton Rouge, 1979.

Hatch, Nathan O. *The Democratization of American Christianity.* New Haven, 1989.

Hawkins, Henry G. *Methodism in Natchez.* Jackson, Miss., 1937.

Hawks, Joanne V., and Shelia L. Skemp. *Sex, Race, and the Role of Women in the South.* Jackson, Miss., 1983.

Hermann, Janet Sharp. *The Pursuit of a Dream.* New York, 1981.

Hill, Samuel S. *Religion in the Southern States: A Historical Study.* Macon, Ga., 1983.

———. *Varieties of Southern Religious Experience.* Baton Rouge, 1988.

———, ed. *Encyclopedia of Religion in the South.* Macon, Ga., 1984.

Holder, Ray, ed. "On Slavery: Selected Letters of Parson Winans, 1820–1844." *JMH* 46 (November 1984): 323–54.

Holifield, E. Brooks. *The Gentlemen Theologians: American Theology in Southern Culture, 1795–1860.* Durham, N.C., 1978.

———. "The Penurious Preacher? Nineteenth-Century Clerical Wealth, North and South." *Journal of the American Academy of Religion* 58 (Spring 1990): 17–36.

Holmes, Jack D. L. "Barton Hannon in the Old Southwest." *JMH* 44 (February 1982): 69–79.

———. *Gayoso: The Life of a Spanish Governor in the Mississippi Valley, 1789–1799.* Baton Rouge, 1965.

———. "Spanish Religious Policy in West Florida: Enlightened or Expedient?" *Journal of Church and State* 15 (Spring 1973): 259–69.

Howe, Daniel Walker. "The Evangelical Movement and Political Culture in the North During the Second Party System." *Journal of American History* 77 (March 1991): 1216–39.

Ingraham, Joseph H. *The South-West, by a Yankee.* 2 vols. New York, 1968.

Irwin, Joyce, ed. *Sacred Sound: Music in Religious Thought and Practice.* Chico, Calif., 1983.

Isaac, Rhys. "Evangelical Revolt: The Nature of the Baptists' Challenge to the Traditional Order of Virginia, 1765 to 1775." *William and Mary Quarterly* 3d ser., 31 (July 1974): 345–68.

———. *The Transformation of Virginia: Community, Religion, and Authority, 1740–1790.* Chapel Hill, 1982.

Jackson, George Pullen. *Spiritual Folk-Songs of Early America.* New York, 1937.

———. *White Spirituals in the Southern Uplands.* 1933. Reprint. Chapel Hill, 1965.

James, D. Clayton. *Antebellum Natchez.* Baton Rouge, 1968.

James, Janet Wilson, ed. *Women in American Religion.* Philadelphia, 1980.

James, Newton Haskin. "Josiah Hinds: Versatile Pioneer of the Old Southwest." *JMH* 2 (January 1940): 22–33.

Jenkins, William Summer, ed. *Records of the States of the United States.* Washington, D.C., 1949.

Jensen, Joan M. *Loosening the Bonds: Mid-Atlantic Farm Women, 1750–1850.* New Haven, 1986.

Johnson, John. *Recollections of the Rev. John Johnson and His Home. . . .* Nashville, Tenn., 1869.

Johnson, Michael P. "Planters and Patriarchy: Charleston, 1800–1860." *JSH* 46 (February 1980): 45–72.

Jones, John G. *A Complete History of Methodism in the Mississippi Conference.* 2 vols. Nashville, Tenn., 1908.

———. *A Concise History of the Introduction of Protestantism into Mississippi and the Southwest.* St. Louis, 1866.

Jones, R. W. "Some Facts Concerning the Settlement and Early History of Mississippi." *PMHS* 1 (1898): 86–89.

Jones, W. B. *Methodism in the Mississippi Conference, 1870–1894.* Nashville, Tenn., 1951.

Jordan, Winthrop D. *White Over Black: American Attitudes Toward the Negro, 1550–1812.* Chapel Hill, 1968.

Judson Baptist Association. *Minutes of the Seventeenth Annual Session . . . 1869.* Tuscumbia, Ala., 1869.

Juster, Susan. "In a Different Voice: Male and Female Narratives of Religious Conversion in Post-Revolutionary America." *American Quarterly* 41 (March 1989): 34–62.

Kerr, Norwood Allen. "The Mississippi Colonization Society (1831–1860)." *JMH* 43 (February 1981): 1–30.

Klein, Rachel N. *Unification of a Slave State: The Rise of the Planter Class in the South Carolina Backcountry, 1760–1808.* Chapel Hill, 1990.

Kohl, Lawrence Frederick. *The Politics of Individualism: Parties and the American Character in the Jacksonian Era.* New York, 1989.

Kruman, Marc W. *Parties and Politics in North Carolina, 1836–1865.* Baton Rouge, 1983.

Kulikoff, Allan. *The Agrarian Origins of American Capitalism.* Charlottesville, Va., 1992.

———. *Tobacco and Slaves: The Development of Southern Cultures in the Chesapeake, 1680–1800.* Chapel Hill, 1986.

Lambert, Frank. "Pedlar in Divinity: George Whitefield and the Great Awakening, 1737–1745." *Journal of American History* 77 (December 1990): 812–37.

Leavell, Z. T., and T. J. Bailey. *A Complete History of Mississippi Baptists: From the Earliest Times.* 2 vols. Jackson, Miss., 1904.

Lebsock, Suzanne. "Complicity and Contention: Women in the Plantation South." *Georgia Historical Quarterly* 74 (Spring 1990): 59–83.

———. *The Free Women of Petersburg: Status and Culture in a Southern Town, 1784–1860.* New York, 1984.

Levine, Lawrence W. *Black Culture and Black Consciousness: Afro-American Folk Thought from Slavery to Freedom.* New York, 1977.

———. *Highbrow/Lowbrow: The Emergence of Cultural Hierarchy in America.* Cambridge, Mass., 1988.

Lewis, H. P. *An Autobiography of Rev. H. P. Lewis.* N.p., 1913.

Lewis, Jan. "The Republican Wife: Virtue and Seduction in the Early Republic." *William and Mary Quarterly* 3d ser., 44 (October 1987): 689–721.

Lincoln, Abraham. *Abraham Lincoln: Speeches and Writings, 1832–1858.* Edited by Don E. Fehrenbacher. New York, 1989.

Litwack, Leon F. *Been in the Storm So Long: The Aftermath of Slavery.* New York, 1979.

Loveland, Anne C. *Southern Evangelicals and the Social Order, 1800–1860.* Baton Rouge, 1980.

Lumpkin, William L. *Baptist Foundations in the South: Tracing Through the Separates the Influence of the Great Awakening, 1754–1787.* Nashville, 1961.

Lynch, John Roy. *Reminiscences of an Active Life: The Autobiography of John Roy Lynch.* Edited by John Hope Franklin. Chicago, 1970.

Lyon, James A. *A Lecture on Christianity and the Civil Laws.* Columbus, Miss., 1859.

McCoy, Drew R. *The Elusive Republic: Political Economy in Jeffersonian America.* Chapel Hill, 1980.

McCurry, John D., comp. *The Social Harp.* 1855. Reprint. Athens, Ga., 1973.

McCurry, Stephanie. "The Two Faces of Republicanism: Gender and Proslavery Politics in Antebellum South Carolina." *Journal of American History* 78 (March 1992): 1245–64.

McLemore, Richard A. *A History of Mississippi.* 2 vols. Hattiesburg, Miss., 1973.

———. *A History of Mississippi Baptists, 1780–1970.* Jackson, Miss., 1971.

Maddex, Jack P., Jr. "From Theocracy to Spirituality: The Southern Presbyterian Reversal on Church and State." *Journal of Presbyterian History* 54 (Winter 1976): 438–57.

———. "Proslavery Millennialism: Social Eschatology in Antebellum Southern Calvinism." *American Quarterly* 31 (Spring 1979): 46–62.

———. "The Southern Apostasy Revisited: The Significance of Proslavery Christianity." *Marxist Perspectives* 2 (Fall 1979): 132–41.

Marsden, George M. *The Evangelical Mind and the New School Presbyterian Experience: A Case Study of Thought and Theology in Nineteenth-Century America.* New Haven, 1970.

Mathews, Donald G. *Religion in the Old South.* Chicago, 1977.

———. "The Second Great Awakening as an Organizing Process, 1780–1830: An Hypothesis." *American Quarterly* 21 (Spring 1969): 23–43.

———. *Slavery and Methodism: A Chapter in American Morality, 1780–1845.* Princeton, 1965.

Mellen, T. L., ed. *In Memoriam: Life and Labors of the Rev. William Hamilton Watkins, D.D. . . .* Nashville, Tenn., 1886.

Methodist Episcopal Church, South. *The Doctrines and Discipline of the Methodist Episcopal Church, South.* Charleston, S.C., 1851.

———. *Minutes of the Annual Conferences . . . 1845–1851.* Richmond, Va., 1846–53.

Miles, Edwin A. "Franklin E. Plummer: Piney Woods Spokesman of the Jackson Era." *JMH* 14 (January 1952): 1–34.

———. *Jacksonian Democracy in Mississippi.* New York, 1970.

Miller, Floyd J. *The Search for a Black Nationality: Black Emigration and Colonization, 1787–1863.* Urbana, Ill., 1975.

Miller, Gene Ramsey. *A History of North Mississippi Methodism, 1820–1900.* Nashville, Tenn., 1966.

Miller, Perry. *The Life of the Mind in America from the Revolution to the Civil War.* New York, 1965.

Miller, T. L., ed. *In Memoriam: Life and Labors of the Rev. William Hamilton Watkins, D.D. . . .* Nashville, Tenn., 1886.

Mills, Samuel J., and Daniel Smith. *Report of a Missionary Tour. . . .* Andover, Mass., 1815.

"Minutes of Zion Baptist Church of Bucatunna, Wayne County, Mississippi." *Mississippi Genealogical Exchange* 19 (Winter 1973): 123–25.

Mississippi Baptist Association. *Abstract History of the Mississippi Baptist Association for One Hundred Years. . . .* New Orleans, 1906.

——. *Minutes of the Forty-third Anniversary . . . 1849.* Natchez, Miss., 1849.

——. *Minutes of the Forty-fourth Anniversary . . . 1850.* Natchez, Miss., 1850.

——. *Minutes of the Forty-fifth Anniversary . . . 1851.* Natchez, Miss., 1851.

——. *Minutes of the Forty-sixth Anniversary . . . 1852.* Natchez, Miss., 1852.

——. *Minutes of the Forty-seventh Anniversary . . . 1853.* Natchez, Miss., 1853.

——. *Minutes of the Forty-ninth Anniversary . . . 1855.* Natchez, Miss., 1855.

——. *Proceedings of the Fiftieth Anniversary . . . 1856.* Nashville, Tenn., 1856.

——. *Minutes of the Fifty-second Anniversary . . . 1858.* New Orleans, 1858.

——. *Minutes of the Fifty-third Anniversary . . . 1859.* Jackson, Miss., 1859.

——. *Minutes of the Fifty-fourth Anniversary . . . 1860.* Jackson, Miss., 1860.

——. *Minutes of the Fifty-fifth Anniversary . . . 1861.* Jackson, Miss., 1861.

——. *Minutes of the Fifty-sixth Annual Session . . . 1862.* Jackson, Miss., 1862.

——. *Minutes of the Sixtieth Anniversary . . . 1866.* Liberty, Miss., 1866.

——. *Minutes of the Sixty-first Anniversary . . . 1867.* Memphis, Tenn., 1868.

——. *Minutes of the Sixty-second Anniversary . . . 1868.* Memphis, Tenn., 1869.

——. *Minutes of the Sixty-third Anniversary . . . 1869.* Natchez, Miss., 1869.

——. *Minutes of the Sixty-fourth Anniversary . . . 1870.* Summit, Miss., 1870.

——. *Minutes of the Sixty-seventh Anniversary . . . 1873.* Natchez, Miss., 1873.

——. *Minutes of the Sixty-eighth Anniversary . . . 1874.* Memphis, Tenn., 1874.

——. *Minutes of the Sixty-ninth Anniversary . . . 1875.* Memphis, Tenn., 1875.

——. *A Republication of the Minutes of the Mississippi Baptist Association, from Its Organization in 1806 to the Present Time.* New Orleans, 1849.

Mississippi River Baptist Association. *Minutes of the Ninth Anniversary . . . 1852.* Clinton, La., 1852.

——. *Minutes of the Twelfth Anniversary . . . 1854.* New Orleans, 1854.

——. *Minutes of the Fourteenth Anniversary . . . 1856.* Clinton, La., 1856.

——. *Minutes of the Fifteenth Anniversary . . . 1857.* New Orleans, 1857.

——. *Minutes of the Seventeenth Anniversary . . . 1859.* New Orleans, 1859.

Miyakawa, T. Scott. *Protestants and Pioneers: Individualism and Conformity on the American Frontier.* Chicago, 1964.

Mohr, Clarence L. "Before Sherman: Georgia Blacks and the War Effort, 1861–1865." *JSH* 45 (August 1979): 331–52.

Moody, Anne. *Coming of Age in Mississippi.* New York, 1968.

Moore, John Hebron. *The Emergence of the Cotton Kingdom in the Old Southwest: Mississippi, 1770–1860.* Baton Rouge, 1988.

——. "Local and State Governments of Antebellum Mississippi." *JMH* 44 (May 1982): 105–16.

——, ed. "Two Documents Relating to Plantation Overseers of the Vicksburg Region, 1831–1832." *JMH* 16 (January 1954): 31–32.

Moore, Margaret DesChamps. "Religion in Mississippi in 1860." *JMH* 22 (October 1960): 223–38.

Moore, R. Laurence. "Religion, Secularization, and the Shaping of the Culture Industry in Antebellum America." *American Quarterly* 41 (June 1989): 216–42.

Morgan, A. T. *Yazoo, or on the Picket Line of Freedom in the South.* Washington, D.C., 1884.

Morgan, Edmund S. *Visible Saints: The History of a Puritan Idea.* Ithaca, N.Y., 1963.

Morris, Willie. *North Toward Home.* Boston, 1967.

———. *Terrains of the Heart and Other Essays on Home.* Oxford, Miss., 1981.

Mount Olive Baptist Association. *Proceedings of the Mt. Olive Baptist Association . . . 1877.* Meridian, Miss., 1877.

Mount Olivet Baptist Association. *Minutes of the First Annual Session . . . 1869.* N.p., 1869.

———. *Minutes of the Third Annual Session . . . 1871.* Columbus, Miss., 1871.

———. *Minutes of the Fourth Annual Session . . . 1872.* Columbus, Miss., 1872.

Mount Pisgah Baptist Association. *Minutes of the Seventh Annual Meeting . . . 1843.* Brandon, Miss., 1843.

Natchez Orphan Asylum. *Annual Report of the Managers and Officers of the Natchez Orphan Asylum. . . .* Natchez, Miss., 1855.

Nevins, Allan. *Ordeal of the Union.* 2 vols. New York, 1947.

New Hope Primitive Baptist Association. *New Hope Primitive Baptist Association Minutes . . . 1877.* Corinth, Miss., 1877.

Niebuhr, H. Richard. *The Kingdom of God in America.* 1937. Reprint. Middletown, Conn., 1988.

Norton, Mary Beth. *Liberty's Daughters: The Revolutionary Experience of American Women, 1750–1800.* Boston, 1980.

Oakes, James. *The Ruling Race: A History of American Slaveholders.* New York, 1982.

———. *Slavery and Freedom: An Interpretation of the Old South.* New York, 1990.

Olmsted, Frederick Law. *The Cotton Kingdom.* 1861. Reprint. New York, 1984.

Osborn, George C. "Plantation Life in Central Mississippi as Revealed in the Clay Sharkey Papers." *JMH* 3 (October 1941): 277–88.

Otken, Charles H. "Richard Curtis in the Country of the Natchez." *PMHS* 3 (1900): 147–53.

Owen, Christopher H. "By Design: The Social Meaning of Methodist Church Architecture in Nineteenth-Century Georgia." *Georgia Historical Quarterly* 75 (Summer 1991): 221–53.

Ownby, Ted. *Subduing Satan: Religion, Recreation, and Manhood in the Rural South, 1865–1920.* Chapel Hill, 1990.

Panola Baptist Association. *Minutes of the Fourth Anniversary of the Panola Baptist Association.* Panola, Miss., 1847.

———. *Minutes of the Fifth Annual Meeting . . . 1848.* Panola, Miss., 1848.

Pearl River Baptist Association. *Minutes of the Twenty-fifth Annual Meeting . . . 1844.* Monticello, Miss., 1844.

———. *Minutes of the Forty-first Anniversary . . . 1860.* Monticello, Miss., 1860.

Pearse, James. *A Narrative of the Life of James Pearse.* Rutland, Vt., 1825.

Pitts, Walter. "Keep the Fire Burnin': Language and Ritual in the Afro-Baptist Church." *Journal of the American Academy of Religion* 56 (Spring 1988): 377–97.

Polk, Noel, ed. *Natchez Before 1830.* Jackson, Miss., 1989.

Posey, Walter Brownlow. *The Baptist Church in the Lower Mississippi Valley, 1776–1845.* Lexington, Ky., 1957.

———. *The Development of Methodism in the Old Southwest, 1783–1824.* 1933. Reprint. Philadelphia, 1974.

———. *Frontier Mission: A History of Religion West of the Southern Appalachians to 1861.* Lexington, Ky., 1966.

Power, Kate M. "Centennial Celebration of Old Bethany Church." In *Minutes of the Presbyterian Historical Society of the Synod of Mississippi.* N.p., 1908.

Prentiss, George Lewis, ed. *Memoir of S. S. Prentiss.* 2 vols. New York, 1855.

Proceedings of a Meeting to Consider the Propriety of Forming a Baptist State Convention Held . . . December, 1836. Natchez, Miss., 1837.

Proceedings of the Ninth Annual Meeting of the Convention of the Baptist Denomination of the State of Mississippi . . . 1845. Jackson, Miss., 1845.

Proceedings of the Third Annual Meeting of the Convention of the Baptist Denomination of the State of Mississippi . . . 1839. Natchez, Miss., 1839.

Proceedings of the Twenty-seventh Session of the Baptist State Convention . . . 1866. Jackson, Miss., 1866.

Rable, George C. *But There Was No Peace: The Role of Violence in the Politics of Reconstruction.* Athens, Ga., 1984.

Raboteau, Albert J. *Slave Religion: The "Invisible Institution" in the Antebellum South.* New York, 1978.

Rainwater, Percy L. "Conquistadors, Missionaries, and Missions." *JMH* 27 (April 1965): 123–47.

———. *Mississippi: Storm Center of Secession, 1856–1861.* Baton Rouge, 1938.

Ramsey, A. C. *The Autobiography of A. C. Ramsey.* Edited by Jean Strickland. N.p., n.d.

Rawick, George P., ed. *The American Slave: A Composite Biography.* Westport, Conn., 1977.

Reeves, Carolyn Keller, ed. *The Choctaw Before Removal.* Jackson, Miss., 1985.

Richardson, Joe M. *Christian Reconstruction: The American Missionary Association and Southern Blacks, 1861–1890.* Athens, Ga., 1986.

Riley, Franklin L., ed. "A Contribution to the History of the Colonization Movement in Mississippi." *PMHS* 9 (1906): 396–99.

Rivers, R. H. *The Life of Robert Paine, D.D., Bishop of the Methodist Episcopal Church, South.* Nashville, Tenn., 1884.

Roark, James L. *Masters Without Slaves: Southern Planters in the Civil War and Reconstruction.* New York, 1977.

Rogers, Tommy W. "T. C. Thornton: A Methodist Educator of Antebellum Mississippi." *JMH* 44 (May 1982): 136–47.

Rorabaugh, W. J. *The Alcoholic Republic: An American Tradition.* New York, 1979.

———. "Estimated U.S. Alcoholic Beverage Consumption, 1790–1860." *Journal of Studies on Alcohol* 27 (March 1976): 357–63.

Rosenberg, Bruce. *The Art of the American Folk Preacher.* New York, 1970.

Rutman, Darrett B., and Anita H. Rutman. *A Place in Time: Middlesex County, Virginia, 1650–1750.* New York, 1984.

Ryan, Mary P. "The Power of Women's Networks: A Case Study of Female Moral Reform in Antebellum America." *Feminist Studies* 5 (Spring 1979): 66–85.

———. *Womanhood in America: From Colonial Times to the Present.* New York, 1979.

Salem Baptist Association. *Minutes of the Fourth Annual Meeting . . . 1865.* Mobile, Ala., 1865.

———. *Minutes of the Fifth Anniversary . . . 1866.* Jackson, Miss., 1866.

———. *Minutes of the Eighth Annual Meeting . . . 1869.* Lauderdale Springs, Miss., 1869.

———. *Minutes of the Ninth Annual Session . . . 1870.* Lauderdale Station, Miss., 1870.

———. *Minutes of the Eleventh Annual Session . . . 1872.* Enterprise, Miss., 1872.

Sardis Missionary Baptist Association. *Minutes of the First Session of the Sardis Missionary Baptist Association . . . 1870.* Memphis, Tenn., 1870.

Schermerhorn, John F., and Samuel J. Mills. *A Correct View of That Part of the United States Which Lies West of the Allegheny Mountains, with Regard to Religion and Morals.* Hartford, Conn., 1814.

Schlissell, Lillian. *Women's Diaries of the Westward Journey.* New York, 1982.

Schmidt, Leigh Eric. "A Church-Going People Are a Dress-Loving People: Clothes, Communication, and Religious Culture in Early America." *Church History* 58 (March 1989): 36–51.

———. *Holy Fairs: Scottish Communions and American Revivals in the Early Modern Period.* Princeton, 1989.

Scott, Anne Firor. "The Ever Widening Circle: The Diffusion of Feminist Values from the Troy Female Seminary, 1822–1872." *History of Education Quarterly* 19 (Spring 1979): 3–25.

———. *Natural Allies: Women's Associations in American History.* Urbana, Ill., 1991.

Scott, Donald M. *From Office to Profession: The New England Ministry, 1750–1850.* Philadelphia, 1978.

Sellers, Charles G. *The Market Revolution: Jacksonian America, 1815–1846.* New York, 1991.

———, ed. *The Southerner as American.* Chapel Hill, 1960.

Sernett, Milton C. *Black Religion and American Evangelicalism: White Protestants, Plantation Missions, and the Flowering of Negro Christianity, 1787–1865.* Metuchen, N.J., 1975.

Silver, James W. *Confederate Morale and Church Propaganda.* New York, 1957.

Smedes, Susan Dabney. *Memorials of a Southern Planter.* Edited by Fletcher M. Green. Jackson, Miss., 1981.

Smith, Daniel Blake. *Inside the Great House: Planter Family Life in Eighteenth-Century Chesapeake Society.* Ithaca, N.Y., 1980.

Smith, Elwyn A. "The Role of the South in the Presbyterian Schism of 1837–1838." *Church History* 29 (March 1960): 44–63.

Smith, Gerrit. *Letter of Gerrit Smith to Rev. James Smylie, of the State of Mississippi.* New York, 1837.

Smith, H. Shelton. *In His Image, But . . .: Racism in Southern Religion, 1780–1910.* Durham, N.C., 1972.

Smith, Timothy L. "Righteousness and Hope: Christian Holiness and the Millennial Vision in America, 1800–1900." *American Quarterly* 31 (Spring 1979): 21–45.

Smith-Rosenberg, Carroll. *Disorderly Conduct: Visions of Gender in America.* New York, 1985.

Smylie, James. *A Review of a Letter from the Presbytery of Chillicothe, to the Presbytery of Mississippi, on the Subject of Slavery. . . .* Woodville, Miss., 1836.

Snay, Mitchell. "American Thought and Southern Distinctiveness: The Southern Clergy and the Sanctification of Slavery." *Civil War History* 35 (December 1989): 311–28.

Sobel, Mechal. *Trabelin' On: The Slave Journey to an Afro-Baptist Faith.* Westport, Conn., 1979.

———. *The World They Made Together: Black and White Values in Eighteenth-Century Virginia.* Princeton, 1987.

Sparks, Randy J. "Gentleman's Sport: Horse Racing in Antebellum Charleston." *South Carolina Historical Magazine* 93 (January 1992): 15–30.

———. "Mississippi's Apostle of Slavery: James Smylie and the Biblical Defense of Slavery." *JMH* 51 (May 1989): 89–106.

———. " 'The White People's Arms Are Longer Than Ours': Blacks, Education, and the American Missionary Association in Reconstruction Mississippi." *JMH* 54 (February 1992): 1–27.

Springfield Baptist Association. *Minutes of the Second Annual Session . . . 1875.* Meridian, Miss., 1875.

———. *Minutes of the Third Annual Session . . . 1876.* Morton, Miss., 1876.

———. *Minutes of the Fourth Annual Meeting . . . 1877.* Memphis, Tenn., 1877.

Spring Hill Baptist Association. *Minutes of the Fourth Annual Session . . . 1873.* Jackson, Miss., 1874.

Stacher, Buford. *Blacks in Mississippi Politics, 1865–1900.* Washington, D.C., 1978.

Stampp, Kenneth M. *The Peculiar Institution: Slavery in the Ante-Bellum South.* New York, 1956.

Staudenraus, Philip J. *The African Colonization Movement, 1816–1865.* New York, 1961.

Stone, Lawrence. *The Family, Sex and Marriage in England, 1500–1800.* New York, 1977.

Stratton, Joseph B. *Memorial of a Quarter-Century's Pastorate.* Philadelphia, 1869.

———. *A Pastor's Valedictory: A Selection of Early Sermons . . .* Natchez, Miss., 1899.

Striefford, David M. "The American Colonization Society: An Application of Republican Ideology to Early American Reform." *JSH* 45 (May 1979): 201–20.

Strong River Baptist Association. *Minutes of the Seventh Anniversary . . . 1859.* Jackson, Miss., 1859.

———. *Minutes of the Ninth Anniversary . . . 1861.* Jackson, Miss., 1861.

———. *Minutes of the Eleventh Annual Meeting . . . 1863.* Brandon, Miss., 1863.

———. *Minutes of the Twelfth Annual Meeting . . . 1864.* Brandon, Miss., 1864.

———. *Minutes of the Sixteenth Annual Meeting . . . 1868.* Jackson, Miss., 1868.

———. *Minutes of the Eighteenth Annual Meeting . . . 1870.* Jackson, Miss., 1870.

———. *Minutes of the Nineteenth Annual Meeting . . . 1871.* Jackson, Miss., 1871.

Stroupe, Henry S. " 'Cite Them Both to Attend the Next Church Conference': Social

Control by North Carolina Baptist Churches, 1772–1908." *North Carolina Historical Review* 52 (April 1975): 156–70.

Summers, Thomas O., ed. *Autobiography of the Rev. Joseph Travis, A.M. . . .* Nashville, Tenn., 1855.

Swearingen, Mark. "Luxury at Natchez: A Ship's Manifest from the McDonough Papers." *JSH* 3 (May 1937): 188–90.

Sweet, Leonard I., ed. *The Evangelical Tradition in America.* Macon, Ga., 1984.

Sweet, William Warren. "The Churches as Moral Courts of the Frontier." *Church History* 2 (March 1933): 3–21.

———. *Men of Zeal: The Romance of American Methodist Beginnings.* New York, 1935.

———. *Revivalism in America.* New York, 1944.

———. *The Story of Religion in America.* New York, 1939.

Sydnor, Charles S. *American Revolutionaries in the Making: Political Practices in Washington's Virginia.* Chapel Hill, 1952.

———. *Slavery in Mississippi.* New York, 1933.

Synod of Mississippi and South Alabama. *Extracts from the Records of the Synod of Mississippi and South Alabama, from 1829 to 1835.* Jackson, Miss., 1880.

Thompson, Ernest Trice. *Presbyterians in the South, 1607–1861.* 3 vols. Richmond, Va., 1963.

Thompson, John B. *Studies in the Theory of Ideology.* Berkeley, 1984.

Thompson, Patrick H. *The History of the Negro Baptists in Mississippi.* Jackson, Miss., 1898.

Thornton, Thomas C. *An Inquiry into the History of Slavery. . . .* Washington, D.C., 1841.

Tise, Larry E. *Proslavery: A History of the Defense of Slavery in America, 1701–1840.* Athens, Ga., 1987.

Tishomingo Baptist Association. *Proceedings of the Ninth Annual Session of the Tishomingo Baptist Association . . . 1869.* Memphis, Tenn., 1869.

Tull, James E. *A History of Southern Baptist Landmarkism in the Light of Historical Baptist Ecclesiology.* New York, 1980.

———. "The Landmark Movement: An Historical and Theological Appraisal." *Baptist History and Heritage* 10 (January 1975): 3–18.

Tyrrell, Ian R. "Drink and Temperance in the Antebellum South: An Overview and Interpretation." *JSH* 48 (November 1982): 485–510.

Union Baptist Association. *Minutes of the Thirty-third Anniversary . . . 1853.* New Orleans, 1854.

———. *Minutes of the Thirty-fourth Anniversary . . . 1854.* New Orleans, 1854.

———. *Minutes of the Thirty-fifth Anniversary . . . 1856.* New Orleans, 1856.

———. *Minutes of the Thirty-seventh Anniversary . . . 1857.* Jackson, Miss., 1857.

———. *Minutes of the Thirty-eighth Anniversary . . . 1858.* Jackson, Miss., 1858.

———. *Minutes of the Thirty-ninth Anniversary . . . 1859.* Jackson, Miss., 1859.

———. *Minutes of the Fortieth Annual Session . . . 1860.* Jackson, Miss., 1860.

———. *Minutes of the Forty-first Annual Session . . . 1861.* Jackson, Miss., 1861.

———. *Minutes of the Fiftieth Annual Meeting . . . 1870.* Crystal Springs, Miss., 1870.

———. *Minutes of the Fifty-first Annual Session . . . 1871.* Crystal Springs, Miss., 1871.

──────. *Minutes of the Fifty-second Annual Session . . . 1872.* Crystal Springs, 1872.

Usner, Daniel H., Jr. "American Indians on the Cotton Frontier: Changing Economic Relations with Citizens and Slaves in the Mississippi Territory." *Journal of American History* 72 (September 1985): 297–317.

──────. *Indians, Settlers, and Slaves in a Frontier Exchange Economy: The Lower Mississippi Valley Before 1783.* Chapel Hill, 1992.

Van Beek, E. A., ed. *The Quest for Purity: Dynamics of Puritan Movements.* Berlin, 1988.

Van Der Merwe, Peter. *Origins of the Popular Style: The Antecedents of Twentieth-Century Popular Music.* Oxford, 1989.

Wailes, B. L. C. *Memoir of Leonard Covington by B. L. C. Wailes Also Some of General Covington's Letters.* Edited by Nellie Wailes Brandon and W. M. Drake. N.p., 1928.

Waldrep, Christopher. "'So Much Sin': The Decline of Religious Discipline and the 'Tidal Wave of Crime.'" *Journal of Social History* 23 (Spring 1990): 535–52.

Walker, Clarence G. *A Rock in a Weary Land: The African Methodist Episcopal Church During the Civil War and Reconstruction.* Baton Rouge, 1982.

Wallace, Anthony F. C. *Religion: An Anthropological View.* New York, 1966.

Walzer, Michael. *The Revolution of the Saints: A Study in the Origins of Radical Politics.* Cambridge, Mass., 1965.

Warren, Harris Gaylord. "Vignettes of Culture in Old Claiborne." *JMH* 20 (July 1958): 125–46.

Waterbury, Maria. *Seven Years Among the Freedmen.* 1891. Reprint. Freeport, N.Y., 1971.

Watson, Harry L. *Jacksonian Politics and Community Conflict: The Emergence of the Second Party System in Cumberland County, North Carolina.* Baton Rouge, 1981.

──────. *Liberty and Power: The Politics of Jacksonian America.* New York, 1990.

Wayne, Michael. *The Reshaping of Plantation Society: The Natchez District, 1860–1880.* Baton Rouge, 1983.

Weidman, Judith L., ed. *Women Ministers.* San Francisco, 1981.

Welter, Barbara. *Dimity Convictions: The American Woman in the Nineteenth Century.* Athens, Ohio, 1976.

Whittington, G. P., ed. "Dr. John Sibley of Natchitoches, 1757–1837." *Louisiana Historical Quarterly* 10 (October 1927): 474–97.

Wills, Garry. *Lincoln at Gettysburg: The Words That Remade America.* New York, 1992.

Wilson, Charles Reagan. *Baptized in Blood: The Religion of the Lost Cause, 1865–1920.* Athens, Ga., 1980.

Winchester, S. G. *The Religion of the Bible, the Only Preservation of Our Civil Institutions. . . .* Natchez, Miss., 1838.

Women's Missionary Union of Mississippi. *Hearts the Lord Opened: The History of Mississippi Women's Missionary Union.* Jackson, Miss., 1954.

Wood, Forrest G. *The Arrogance of Faith: Christianity and Race in America from the Colonial Era to the Twentieth Century.* New York, 1990.

Wood, Gordon S. *The Creation of the American Republic, 1776–1787.* Chapel Hill, 1969.

──────. *The Radicalism of the American Revolution.* New York, 1992.

Worrell, A. S. *Review of Corrective Church Discipline.* Nashville, Tenn., 1860.

Wright, David F. *The Bible in Scottish Life and Literature*. Edinburgh, 1988.

Wyatt-Brown, Bertram. "The Antimission Movement in the Jacksonian South: A Study in Regional Folk Culture." *JSH* 36 (November 1970): 501–29.

———. "God and Honor in the Old South." *Southern Review* 25 (April 1989): 283–96.

———. *Southern Honor: Ethics and Behavior in the Old South*. New York, 1982.

Yazoo Baptist Association. *Proceedings of the Sixteenth Annual Session . . . 1867*. Memphis, Tenn., 1867.

Young, Jacob. *Autobiography of a Pioneer. . . .* Cincinnati, 1857.

Zion Baptist Association. *Minutes of the Nineteenth Annual Meeting . . . 1854*. N.p., n.d.

———. *Minutes of the Twentieth Annual Meeting . . . 1855*. N.p., n.d.

———. *Minutes of the Twenty-third Annual Meeting . . . 1858*. Aberdeen, Miss., 1859.

———. *Minutes of the Twenty-fifth Annual Meeting . . . 1860*. N.p., n.d.

———. *Minutes of the Twenty-sixth Annual Meeting . . . 1861*. N.p., n.d.

———. *Minutes of the Twenty-seventh Annual Meeting . . . 1862*. Greensboro, Miss., 1862.

———. *Minutes of the Thirty-second Annual Meeting . . . 1867*. N.p., n.d.

———. *Minutes of the Thirty-third Annual Meeting . . . 1868*. N.p., n.d.

———. *Minutes of the Thirty-fourth Annual Meeting . . . 1869*. Winona, Miss., 1869.

———. *Minutes of the Thirty-fifth Annual Meeting . . . 1870*. Memphis, 1870.

———. *Minutes of the Thirty-sixth Annual Meeting . . . 1871*. Coffeeville, Miss., 1871.

———. *Minutes of the Thirty-eighth Annual Meeting . . . 1873*. Memphis, 1873.

Zuckerman, Michael. "Holy Wars, Civil Wars: Religion and Economics in Nineteenth-Century America." *Prospects* 16 (1992): 205–40.

———. "William Byrd's Family." *Perspectives in American History* 12 (1979): 255–311.

INDEX